The International Strindberg

The International Strindberg

New Critical Essays

Edited by
Anna Westerståhl Stenport

Northwestern University Press
Evanston, Illinois

Northwestern University Press
www.nupress.northwestern.edu

Printed in the United States of America

10 9 8 7 6 5 4 3 2 1

Library of Congress Cataloging-in-Publication Data

The international Strindberg : new critical essays / edited by Anna Westerståhl Stenport.
p. cm.
Includes bibliographical references.
ISBN 978-0-8101-2850-7 (pbk. : alk. paper)
1. Strindberg, August, 1849–1912—Criticism and interpretation. 2. Modernism (Literature) I. Stenport, Anna Westerståhl.
PT9816.I56 2012
839.726—dc23
2012020391

∞ The paper used in this publication meets the minimum requirements of the American National Standard for Information Sciences—Permanence of Paper for Printed Library Materials, ANSI Z39.48-1992.

CONTENTS

ACKNOWLEDGMENTS

Envisioning and creating this edited volume has been a pleasure from start to finish. Linda Haverty Rugg has been deeply involved from the very beginning, and I am grateful to her for invaluable insights and incisive feedback throughout the process. The book has benefited from the intellectual commitment and editorial skills of two University of Illinois research assistants, Kurt Hollender and Lawrence Smith. Faculty, scholars, and students at the universities of Illinois, Urbana-Champaign; California, at Berkeley; and Copenhagen, Gothenburg, Lund, and Uppsala have shared their interest and provided valuable comments. Northwestern University Press acquisitions editor Henry L. Carrigan championed the proposal from its inception; Peter Raccuglia and other members of the Press staff have been equally supportive. Contributing authors have been remarkable collaborators: engaged, creative, responsive, and prompt.

No project of this scope can be completed without funding. I am grateful to the following agencies and institutions for awarding critical resources: the University of Illinois Center for Advanced Study, the Campus Research Board, and the College of Liberal Arts and Sciences' Helen Corley Petit Fund; the Barbro Osher Pro Suecia Foundation; and the Anna Lindh Fellowship in the Europe Center at Stanford University.

As I write these acknowledgments, a centenary commemorative year marking the death of August Strindberg in 1912 is in full swing. My final words of gratitude are to August himself for showing me, and so many others around the world, alternate and fascinating aspects of the complexity and wonder involved in living in and through international modernity.

The International Strindberg

Introduction: The International Strindberg

Anna Westerståhl Stenport

Outside of his native country, August Strindberg (1849–1912) is best known as a playwright. His early naturalist plays are identified with a relentless interest in making the conflicts of the psychological and the domestic "private" shamelessly public. His later dramatic output seems to render a different onstage experience of subjectivity, including that of a subconscious or dreaming mind. Subjectivity questions have nevertheless guided interpretations of Strindberg works, whether early or late, whether in the form of prose, dramatic text, poetry, or painting, for more than a century. A plenitude of biographical interpretations that link the author's creative output to events in his life is only one aspect of a dominant subjectivity paradigm. Though multiple other scholars complicate Strindbergian self-presentation and challenge any identification of an imagined I with a presumed autobiographical voice, the subjectivity-analysis paradigm has remained strong. This book argues that it is time to firmly establish an alternate trajectory for Strindberg studies, one specifically manifesting that an international constitution and subsequent disbursement is critical to the formation of a lasting legacy of Strindberg's multifaceted output.

Strindberg made a name for himself as a playwright in Europe—especially in French- and German-speaking countries—exactly at a time when theatrical practices were undergoing radical changes, transitioning from the spectacular and entertainment-oriented diversions of the nineteenth century into a serious art form in which bourgeois norms were challenged. Theater, for Strindberg and many of his European contemporaries, became a new didactic practice in the service of an internationally constituted avant-garde and for the purposes of critical examination. Strindberg's large and comprehensive prose production is equally significant in its international and comparative contexts (his poetry and pictorial art—photography and oil paintings—share these characteristics).

Written in two languages (Swedish and French), Strindberg's prose spans all the major literary genres of the European late nineteenth century, including novelistic and short story fiction, autobiography, scientific treatises, historical and ethnographic prose, political pamphlets, essays on arts and aesthetics, and religious and philosophical writing. In strikingly individualistic ways, his works address all major cultural and intellectual questions of late-nineteenth-century modernity. These also challenge the dominant discourses of modernity: the nation-state, capitalism, urbanization, secularization, democracy, gender and racial equality, scientific investigation, and emergent aesthetic forms of representation. Strindberg's writing almost never conforms to dominant ideologies. As this book shows, what Strindberg's oeuvre offers us today are under-explored and provocative venues for investigating both the formation and persistence of modernity as a mode of existence constituted by encounters with, experiences of, and challenges to the international. It also illustrates the ways in which past and current ideas of modernity are internationally constituted.

Strindberg's work embodies and helped accelerate a sense of emergent internationalism at the end of the nineteenth century. His life was similarly international. Born and raised in Stockholm, he spent nearly half of his life as a professional writer outside Sweden, traveling around the European continent, often with his family in tow. He may be canonized in Sweden as the Father of Modern Swedish Literature and one of the foremost innovators of the Swedish language, yet he is more than "just" a Swedish writer. His influence continues to extend beyond the borders of Sweden in multiple ways, as it did during his lifetime. Strindberg was invested in the idea of intellectual internationalism, of idea transfer across borders. His writing engages directly with other central aspects of international modernity. For example, a prominent topos is movement between regions and countries, or, in the later plays, between symbolic "stations" of a mind that nevertheless remained rendered as concrete and material. Strindberg's voluminous correspondence of more than 10,000 letters testifies to the international context in which he was active: his missives and telegrams crisscrossed the European continent as part of a communication revolution, whose accelerated nature has become constitutive of modernity.

Strindberg clearly imagined and understood his own writing as internationally constituted and oriented. Drawing on a nascent European interest in his writing, and capitalizing on the international appeal of provocative topics of sexuality and class in plays such as *The Father* (*Fadren,* 1887) or *Miss Julie* (*Fröken Julie,* 1888), Strindberg's breakthrough in

Paris in 1894 reflects more than the efforts of "just another" would-be Parisian. His writing in French, his auto-translation into French, and his topical interest in France (including an 1886 ethnographic study of French peasantry critical of Paris) illustrate both an understanding of the centrality of French culture at the end of the nineteenth century and the need to challenge precisely its international allure. The work *Among French Peasants* (*Bland franska bönder,* 1886) is deeply critical of both Paris and French official culture, while productions in Paris of *The Father, Miss Julie,* and *Creditors* (*Fordringsägare,* 1888) in the early 1890s catered explicitly to avant-garde and radical groups whose international cachet and reach had already been established.

Despite their clear ambition toward international recognition, Strindberg's works and fictional worlds (including those of his autobiographies) are products of a nationally oriented European nineteenth-century paradigm, and thus were also influenced by nationalism's constant Other: colonialism. Strindberg wrote and lived both in tandem with and in revolt against nationalist master-narratives. He was deeply conflicted with respect to his own country, yet he was never unequivocally enthusiastic about another. The tension between national and international in Strindberg's oeuvre was enhanced by his experience of the exclusivity of national literary canons.

In fact, most of Strindberg's better-known works and protagonists transcend national contexts; it does not matter, really, if Miss Julie is a Swedish nobleman's daughter, or whether the dynamic set of *A Dream Play* (*Ett Drömspel,* 1902) reflects changes specific to Stockholm as Sweden's capital during a transformative urbanization process taking place at the end of the nineteenth century. Julie is the product of an aristocracy caught in a modern crisis, and the city that is radically transmogrified is the modern European capital. Similarly, Strindberg's later historical plays, such as *Erik XIV* (1899), are less investigations of Swedish history than explorations of modern challenges not only to the historical legacy of monarchies, but to the individual's existence within an encompassing govermentality. Well-known oil paintings by Strindberg, such as *Night of Jealousy* (*Svartsjukans natt,* 1893) and *Snowstorm at Sea* (*Snöstorm på havet,* 1894), collapse any borders between interiority and Swedish nineteenth-century landscape painting's participation in a nation-building project. *Night of Jealousy,* for example, expresses deep familiarity with a quintessential Swedish landscape—the rocky archipelago of the Baltic Sea—although the canvas was conceived and painted in an apartment in Berlin and offers far from an idyllic image of seascape. The abstraction of *Snowstorm* came through in a borrowed apartment at

Avenue de Neuilly in the Parisian suburb of Clichy. One of Strindberg's last prose narratives, *The Roofing Ceremony* (*Taklagsöl*, 1907), may be set in a Stockholm apartment bedroom, but it tells a story of colonialism and brutal exploration in Belgian Congo, including bringing to light Sweden's participation in that colonial paradigm.

To transcend a national context does not, of course, imply a facile renunciation of one's subjectivity. Strindberg's oeuvre consistently presents and refashions the modern subject, frequently in the mask of an autobiographical "I." Yet, what has been overlooked for a century is the ways in which this figural I participates in and configures a new drama of international modernity. Yes, Strindberg the author and a majority of his dramatic protagonists and narrative speakers may be experts in "self-dramatization," as a recent critical introduction to the author argues (Rugg, "The Art and Science of Self-Dramatization"). Indeed, Strindberg's "vital contribution," another critic emphasizes, may be "his role in dramatizing the experience of modernity by turning a life he knew best—his own—into theatre" (Szalczer, *August Strindberg,* 3). What the current book seeks to do, however, is to formulate how the author and his fictions may be construed as encapsulating the quintessentially modern—and modernist—subject as internationally constituted: expansive, dynamic, contingent, fragmentary, and self-reflexive. Strindberg exposed and manipulated both his own private sphere and that of his contemporaries to the world-as-audience, and allowed this kind of openness to become the new normal constitutive of modernity.

We should thereby not underestimate the influence of international contexts on Strindberg's "self-dramatization." As an émigré writer, he had firsthand experience of the struggle and hardship involved with trying to eke out a living as a professional writer committed to challenging both discourses of simplistic nationalism and facile internationalism. His lived experience also encompasses that of the nineteenth-century emigrant in search of a better life outside his home country. His intellectual proclivities, moreover, are closely aligned with later European modernist writers, whose lives and writing are marked by exile, displacement, and a sense of homelessness. Strindberg's own self-dramatization as well as his messy, fragmented, inconclusive, and tormented protagonists are products of a European and international modernity experience. As such, they also shape our understanding of modernity. Overlooking this context, we both misunderstand and, perhaps, underappreciate Strindberg's writing.

As this book argues, Strindberg did not just dramatize, narrate, and visually represent his own life—or that of any modern individual—merely as a psychological entity. He also envisions and formulates, like few of his contemporaries, another profound aspect of European nineteenth-century existence: its consistent challenge to any firm national affiliation and its uneasy relationship to international modernity. This tension between ideas of the national and the international is implicit and explicit in and throughout Strindberg's various works. In fact, the conception, distribution, reception, and legacy of his works in many ways destabilizes any orthodox understanding of national literary and dramatic art forms, especially within a late-nineteenth-century European context that prioritized literature and art as vehicles for nation-building. Strindberg's oeuvre is thereby international even in the most basic sense of the term, commonly defined, as "concerning or belonging to all or at least two or more nations," while also being "external" to and "outside (from or between other countries)." The reception and legacy of his works beyond the borders of Sweden, as well as the playwright's own interest in and consistent efforts in transcending national and linguistic boundaries, also mark Strindberg's oeuvre as transnational in scope and practice, as I have argued elsewhere (Stenport, *Locating August Strindberg's Prose*).

For most of his working life, Strindberg was a professional writer and only very rarely held other, more stable forms of employment. He had to live off his pen in an international literary marketplace that was predominantly based on a close association between the national project and literature—and drama—written in, for, and by participants who reinforced such contexts. Strindberg operated within this context—sometimes quite successfully—yet many of his works rebel against it: topically, thematically, formally, or linguistically. In addition, the workings of (repressive) state apparatuses in the service of nineteenth-century nationalism were a de facto obstacle to Strindberg in his career both at home and abroad. Few national theaters, like the Comédie Française in Paris or the Royal Dramatic Theater in Stockholm, were open to his plays. Yet, rather than seeking to appease such institutions, Strindberg consistently challenged such cultural gatekeepers. His writing (narrative, dramatic, epistolary, and essayistic) testifies again and again to his frustration with narrow conceptions of the national.

None of Strindberg's dramas (and only a few of his prose works) were ever uniformly well received in Sweden during his lifetime; nor were they lastingly or unproblematically integrated within another national framework. Even today, Strindberg continues to challenge the idea of what it means to be Swedish—especially when Swedishness is based in notions of egalitarian, gender-equal, consensus-based, secular, and moderate sociocultural practices. Yet, he helped shape the Swedish Social Democratic Party; turned to social radicalism at critical junctures of his life; and maintained a profound interest in religious inquiry, spanning atheism, Catholicism, and mysticism. This oscillation and this tension illustrate how Strindberg is a significant voice of European modernity. His works thereby reflect a received understanding of nation. At the same time, however, their content and form rebel against any straightforward affiliation. And it is also clear that Strindberg's writing takes a skeptical stance with respect to a vague rhetoric of internationalization—or, in twenty-first-century parlance, globalization.

For a large number of readers, students, and scholars, Strindberg the writer and artist represents a continuously challenging and profound source through which to analyze and contextualize Western, and particularly European, modernity in its international ramifications. This book exhibits the breadth and depth of intellectual inquiry raised by Strindberg's oeuvre a century after his death. As such, the collection builds on and reflects a move away from two dominant strands of critical inquiry: the first being a nation-based approach to criticism (i.e., Strindberg as the "Father of Modern Swedish Literature"), and the second being biographically invested criticism. In the latter approach especially, the political radicalism of the author's youth, his apparent misogyny, his reported medical insanity, and his interest in occultism have resulted in a critical tradition that has psychopathologized the author. This move has hampered serious intellectual engagement with the ideas manifest in Strindberg's works and the innovative formal strategies that make them worthy of consideration.

The International Strindberg represents and solidifies a significant and productive transition in Strindberg scholarship. Strindberg studies today, as evidenced by this volume and other recent works, are broadly comparative, both within Strindberg's varied oeuvre and in connection to others.[1] The present book also demonstrates the international nature of contemporary Strindberg inquiry through its contributors, a majority of whom straddle multiple national affiliations and linguistic contexts. The chapters included in this book reflect the range and scope of Strindberg's own production in multiple genres and media, as well as its international reach and impact. This collection identifies international influences upon Strindberg and considers those whom his works have influenced. All of the chapters are comparative across national contexts. All compare more than two literary, aesthetic, cultural, or philosophical traditions.

This introduction, and the chapters that follow, are organized in ways that reflect the eclectic nature of Strindberg's writing and intellectual project. Though this introduction includes an overview of Strindberg's international reach and reception in different national-language contexts, such an organizational approach is not suitable for the book as a whole.

Attempting to squeeze the wide-ranging arguments about Strindberg's heterogeneous renditions of and formulations for international modernity into simplistic categories based on chronological or geographical parameters of the nation-state (including its linguistic aspects) would counteract the motivation for this book. Such an organization risks contributing further to a whitewashing or streamlining of Strindberg's contribution to our understanding of international modernity. The contribution made by a volume such as *The International Strindberg* may well be inconclusive and unruly, or even inconsistent, and most certainly heterogeneous; if so, it fits its subject and demands our consideration.

Strindberg's International Reach

Despite the strong international interest in Strindberg, his drama is not and has never been globally performed on a large scale (in comparison with Henrik Ibsen's worldwide influence, Strindberg comes up short). The range of works performed outside Sweden is rather narrow, encapsulating, with some variation, *The Father* (*Fadren,* 1887), *Miss Julie* (*Fröken Julie,* 1888), *Dance of Death* (*Dödsdansen,* 1900), *A Dream Play* (*Ett Drömspel,* 1902), and *Ghost Sonata* (*Spöksonaten,* 1907). Nevertheless, successful adaptations of Strindberg plays beyond the borders of Sweden help make Strindberg's international legacy more complex. Alan Rickman's 2008 London production of *Creditors* (*Fordringsägare,* 1888), with guest performances at the Brooklyn Academy of Music in New York City, moved Strindberg's idea drama into a fierce and powerful performance of attraction and jealousy, far removed from a trite naturalistic interpretation. Similarly, *Miss Julie* has proved remarkably resilient to international production and adaptation, including across media. Alf Sjöberg's 1951 film, which won the Cannes Palme d'Or, experimented with theatrical cinematic space and arguably set the stage for worldwide recognition of Ingmar Bergman's subsequent auteur films; Mike Figgis's film *Miss Julie* (1999) successfully transplants the central conflict to an Irish late-nineteenth-century context; Birgit Cullberg's modern dance adaptation (1950) helped define her choreography to the world; and a 1985 South African production staged the central conflict as informed by apartheid race relations (Szalczer, *August Strindberg,* 134–36). Danish director Lars von Trier reworked the central relationship in his film *Manderlay* (2005), an appropriation that Mads Bunch's chapter in this volume identifies for the first time.

While Strindberg's international legacy as a playwright may be most closely associated with a handful of plays, this does not mean that

Strindberg's writing or the legacy brought forth from it is parochial or provincial; far from it. In fact, when compared with Ibsen and other major late-nineteenth-century European playwrights and novelists (from Chekhov to Zola), Strindberg's writing reflects more clearly a transition to international modernity and the turmoil it entails. Strindberg belongs squarely among other twentieth-century modernists such as Samuel Beckett, Franz Kafka, Rainer Maria Rilke, Joseph Conrad, and James Joyce, whose lives, marked by exile, migration, and multilingualism, resulted in works that engage questions similar to those taken up by Strindberg. Recent translations into English of some of Strindberg's lesser known and challenging prose works, including the violently expressive *Black Banners* (trans. Donald K. Weaver; *Svarta Fanor,* 1904); the interior monologue of *The Roofing Ceremony* (trans. David Mel Paul and Margareta Paul; *Taklagsöl,* 1907), or the postcolonial subtext of *Tschandala* (trans. Peter Graves; 1889); and the *Selected Essays* and *Letters I and II* (trans. and ed. Michael Robinson) indicate a continued interest in works that go beyond the top five, or perhaps top ten, of his dramatic works.

Similarly, Strindberg's status as a modernist visual artist has become increasingly foregrounded in an international context during the last decades, particularly through significant traveling exhibits of his photography and painting in the United States, England, Germany, and France since the mid-1990s. The Tate Modern's 2005 exhibit in London—with accompanying cultural events and productions of his plays—is one of the most significant examples of this revival. Through this exhibit and its accompanying catalog, Strindberg is clearly positioned first and foremost as an international modernist, rather than as one bound to a particular national context. In this book, Linda Rugg's and Maxime Abolgassemi's chapters explore different aspects of Strindberg as an international artist, with Rugg focusing on Strindberg's engagement with aspects of ecocritical localizing, and Abolgassemi developing some of Strindberg's affinities with French surrealism.

The International Strindberg and Swedish, French, German, and Anglo-American Contexts

The reception of Strindberg's works in different national and linguistic contexts is illustrative in a number of ways. As argued above, such characterization imposes an artificial order on a heterogeneous oeuvre. At the same time, by contrasting reception in different contexts, we get a clear sense of the range of reactions and interest Strindberg's works have evoked. Outside of Sweden, the availability of good translations and comprehensive editions have been determining factors for success, explaining in part why there were over 1,000 productions of 24 Strindberg plays in 62 German cities during the period from 1913 to 1915 (Kuhns 96) but hardly any in England during the same period. Similarly, Strindberg's own translations into French of the plays *Father* and *Creditors* helped usher them to production in Paris in 1894 and create a name for Strindberg as part of the French theatrical avant-garde. Yet, different national and linguistic contexts have clearly formed very different images of Strindberg and his works, the four major of these being the Swedish, French, German, and Anglo-American contexts.

Swedish

Very few of Strindberg's plays, narratives, or prose works were warmly received at the moment of inception or publication in the author's home country; exceptions include his breakthrough novel *The Red Room* (*Röda rummet,* 1879), early ethnographic-historical works such as *The Swedish People* (*Svenska folket i helg och söcken,* 1881–82), the naturalist novel *The People of Hemsö* (*Hemsöborna,* 1887), and some of the later historical plays. In contrast, *Miss Julie* could not be produced in Sweden until 1906 (it was first staged in 1889 at Strindberg's experimental theater in Copenhagen on a subscription basis to avoid censorship), while a stumbling, realistically set production of *A Dream Play* played to negative reviews no sooner than six years after completion. Strindberg thus became canonized as the "Father of Modern Swedish Literature" only after his death (he never received the Nobel Prize in Literature, for example, though several of his Swedish contemporaries did) and particularly through the first comprehensive edition of his collected writings, John Landquist's edition of the *Collected Writings* (*Samlade skrifter,* 1912–20).

Recent productions of Strindberg's plays in Sweden by non-Swedish directors and theater companies help illustrate the dynamic nature of Strindberg's drama, as seen from international perspectives, and as incorporated into a Swedish dramatic tradition. Robert LePage's production of *A Dream Play* at the Royal Dramatic Theater in Stockholm in 1994; Robert Wilson's characteristically stylized, truncated, and symbolic version of the same play at the Stockholm City Theater in 1998 and at the Brooklyn Academy of Music in 2000; internationally recognized choreographer Mats Ek's movement- and dance-oriented production at Dramaten (2007); and a recent adaptation by Jonas Hassen Khemiri entitled *Five Times God* (*Fem gånger gud,* 2008) are illustrative examples that challenge the national affiliation of Strindberg *through* the context of contemporary Swedish theater. Khemiri's reworking of Strindberg's text is particularly interesting, given that author's status as a prominent "new Swede," whose other fiction has integrated the voices of recent immigrants and represents Sweden as the multiethnic, multilingual nation it has effectively become at the turn of the twenty-first century.

Recent Strindberg productions in Sweden must be seen in contrast with the productions of the mid-twentieth century, which had clear and undisputed national and biographical affiliations, to lasting effect. These were exemplified by Gustaf Molander's epic productions at the Royal Dramatic Theater, conceived in close continuity with Martin Lamm's largely biographical scholarly interpretations of Strindberg's dramatic works. Such productions cemented the view of Strindberg's drama as straightforward reflections of the author's psyche and personal experiences—including those that seemed mad, misogynistic, or mystical—and projected this image successfully to Sweden and the world.[2] This legacy became further entrenched through Ingmar Bergman's many productions of Strindberg at the Royal Dramatic Theater from the 1960s through the 1990s. Perceived biographical links between Bergman and Strindberg were based not least on Bergman's own accounts and, in a Swedish context, can be seen as having narrowed the range of Strindberg enactments even further into an extension of the psyche of *auteur*-Bergman.

The international influences upon Strindberg are significant, of course, and he incorporated both contemporary and past international literary and cultural references into his writing. He received a fairly typical (male) middle-class Swedish education of the mid-nineteenth century, which included a thorough familiarization with Greek, Roman, and Judeo-Christian mythology and narratives; his schooling and early voracious reading also reflect the presence of French and German culture in Sweden at the time, including exposure to German idealist philosophy and poetry, neoclassicist French drama, Rousseau's philosophy, and contemporary realist French novels. Freddie Rokem's and Leonardo Lisi's chapters in this volume address Strindberg's European intellectual background and the author's creative reworking of these contexts. Thoroughly familiar with classic Swedish literature, Strindberg also discovered Shakespeare in Carl Hagberg's modern translations into Swedish, which portrayed the English playwright's language as dynamic, irreverent, and politically engaged. This influence can be discerned in Strindberg's first success as a dramatist in 1881 with a production of *Mäster Olof* (*Master Olof:* 1878, verse version; 1881, prose version).

Any consideration of a topic such as *The International Strindberg* must take into consideration particulars of Strindberg's language—both Swedish and French—and the critical importance translation practices play in the process. But his language, with its characteristic and idiosyncratic use of neologisms—including those that emphasize modernity's speed and industrial practices in juxtaposition with expressions taken from alchemy, botany, and the organic sphere—and its abbreviated expressions and unorthodox syntax, its incorporation of dialect and sociolects, its emphasis on sound, rhythm, cadence, and vocal expression, all amounted to a de facto reinvention of the Swedish language. Thus, Strindberg challenged the linguistic national affiliations that governed his time, including those of a stilted academic jargon, impenetrable bureaucratic officiousness, long-winded newspaper prose, and received idealist and romantic imagery. This varied linguistic range and depth, as Anne-Charlotte Hanes Harvey shows in her contribution to this volume, poses both challenges and opportunities for a translator, and especially for the purposes of stage production.

French

Strindberg's extended periods of self-induced exile outside Sweden offer another point of entry into *The International Strindberg,* particularly with respect to the French- and German-speaking literary and dramatic traditions. Strindberg may have left Sweden in 1883 to explore the possibilities of an émigré Scandinavian avant-garde in Paris or because of his disillusionment with Swedish politics and the academic and cultural establishment. His satirical prose work *The New Kingdom* (*Det nya riket,* 1882) leveled an assault at the provincialism and double standards that he saw as distinctive of the conservative Swedish elite and its emerging middle class, and a short story in *Getting Married* (*Giftas I,* 1884) was subsequently tried for blasphemy in a Swedish court. At the same time, his departure coincided with the large-scale working-class emigration from Sweden to North America, which accelerated exactly in the mid-1880s. During subsequent travels and extended stays throughout Europe, Strindberg and his writing evince a consistent challenge to national affiliation, including the monolingual paradigm such a position typically requires. Indeed, Strindberg used French, his adopted language, to compose what he labeled an autobiographical work, *A Madman's Defense* (*Le Plaidoyer d'un Fou,* written in 1888; first official publication in 1895 in France). This confession was made in a second language ostensibly to spare his wife's reputation in Sweden. Arguably, it was also because the story of psychological torment, sexual conflict, and unraveling of reason that Strindberg wanted to tell was international in terms of its appeal and, indeed, more closely aligned with taste in contemporary French and German writing than with those in Swedish. As Massimo Ciaravolo shows in an essay for this book, Strindberg, in ways clearly reminiscent of Baudelaire's prose poem strategies, juxtaposes his experiences of Paris and Stockholm in the long-poem cycle *Sleepwalking Nights on Awake Days* (*Sömngångarnätter på vakna dagar,* 1884). This text also prefigures some of Walter Benjamin's strategies to convey the fragmentation of modern urbanity in *The Arcades Project* (*Das Passsagen-Werk,* written 1927–40).

In the 1890s, much of Strindberg's writing in French was aimed explicitly for publication in Paris—both in scientific and occult publications and in literary reviews—and, as Sylvain Briens outlines in his chapter here, Paris functioned as a fruitful laboratory for Strindberg's aesthetic and scientific experimentation during this period. Strindberg's own strategies for internationalizing his work included wrangling for a Paris production of *Miss Julie* at André Antoine's naturalist Théâtre Libre in 1893 and providing translations of his plays *The Father* and *Creditors* for production at Lugné-Poë's symbolist Le Théâtre de l'Oeuvre in 1894. An often-overlooked part of this international legacy is that the Danish author and critic Herman Bang later directed two plays in a naturalist manner for Lugné-Poë. Despite these efforts, Strindberg "made a sensation" in France, "more as a woman-hater and alchemist, than as a playwright, and never, during his lifetime, did he succeed in gaining the favors of Parisian audiences" (Gravier 45–46). Unlike Ibsen's broad success in Paris (the two playwrights, along with the Norwegian Bjørnstjerne Bjørnsen, were part of a Scandinavian wave of new avant-garde drama in Paris in the early 1890s), Strindberg's celebrity was brief. His plays were produced only intermittently in France until after the Second World War, including a 1921 production of *Dance of Death,* and a short-lived but infamous production of *A Dream Play* by Antonin Artaud in 1928. Still, his influence on Artaud's conception of the Theater of Cruelty is evidence of his legacy in the French context, and both Cocteau and Sartre, it has been argued, were intimately inspired by Strindberg for several of their plays in the 1940s and 1950s (Gravier 49–51).

German

Strindberg may not have been as integrally involved in trying to shape his legacy in a German context as he was in the French, although he lived for significant periods of time in German-speaking regions in Switzerland and Austria, as well as in Berlin, and kept in close (albeit at times contentious) contact with his different German translators and publishers through the years. Strindberg's correspondence with Nietzsche and his interest in Nietzsche's philosophy is well known and constitutes a rich venue of comparison (Rokem 87–113; and Stern). But a less often acknowledged affinity between these two, as Tobias Dahlkvist shows in his contribution to this volume, stems from their respective interest in European fin-de-siècle decadence, inspired by French writers such as J.-K. Huysmans and Paul Bourget. Yet, it is indisputably the German-speaking context in which Strindberg's writing—particularly his drama—has been most fully integrated outside Sweden. His significance for the Berlin *Durch* circle of naturalist playwrights in the early 1890s, Arno Holz and Gerhardt Hauptmann among them, was influential, and was effected at least in part by Otto Brahm's productions of *The Father* in 1887 and *Miss Julie* in 1892, both at the Freie Bühne in Berlin. There is close affinity, particularly in matters of sexual frankness, between Strindberg's naturalist plays and Frank Wedekind's *Spring Awakening* (*Frühlings Erwachen,* 1891) and *Earth Spirit* (*Erdgeist,* 1895; later incorporated into the play known as *Lulu*). Part of Strindberg's successful integration into a German context stems from the early, proficient, and quite comprehensive translation of his works by Emil Schering, published in several editions as *Strindberg's Works* (*Strindbergs Werke,* 1909–20).

Strindberg may be associated in the German-speaking context with Nietzsche, naturalism, and Wedekind's early drama, but it is Max Reinhardt's expressionist Berlin productions—which took advantage of new technologies, including sophisticated lighting enhanced by electricity—that have most fully shaped his legacy. Indeed, Péter Szondi's discussion of Strindberg as one of the foremost examples of the subjective I-drama in the influential *Theory of the Modern Drama* (1956) shows that Strindberg, for Szondi, fully belongs to a German-European dramatic canon, rather than one associated with a Swedish national context. Part of Reinhardt's intriguing incorporation of Strindberg in a German context indicates that it was recognized, in the words of Austrian dramaturg Otto Zoff, as making such "a great impression on us [avant-garde directors] that it would be impossible to describe it" (cited and paraphrased from Kuhns 96). Some of these productions, as Szalczer shows in her chapter for this volume, underwent a transculturation process as they traveled back to Stockholm and introduced Strindberg as a modernist, and modern, playwright to his own national context. Further implications of Reinhardt's aesthetics are their integration into German silent cinema. Robert Wiene's *The Cabinet of Dr. Caligari* (1920), for example, echoes Strindberg's station drama *To Damascus I–III* (*Till Damaskus I–III,* 1898–1901) in its cinematic depiction of a circuitous and allegorical introspective journey, and in the asymmetrical, imbalanced, and askew cinematic set easily imaginable to be portraying a tormented interiority. Connections thus ran deep between Strindberg and Reinhardt. When Strindberg christened his own theater company, cofounded in 1907 with August Falck and located in the basement of a recently constructed apartment building in central Stockholm, he named it The Intimate Theater after Reinhardt's two stages in Berlin, the Kleines Theater and the Kammerspiele annex to the Deutsches Theater. Reinhardt had been greatly inspired by Strindberg's earlier plays and had staged *The Stronger* (*Den starkare,* 1889) and *Crimes and Crimes* (*Brott och brott,* 1899) at the Kleines Theater in 1902; some years later, Strindberg appears to have derived part of his inspiration for his own theater from him. Strindberg continued to exert influence in the German context well into the twentieth century, and particularly on the stage. Friedrich Dürrenmatt's *Play Strindberg* (1969) is a postmodernist and self-reflexive reworking of *Dance of Death,* while R. W. Fassbinder and Ingmar Bergman both attempted innovative Strindberg productions in West Germany in the 1970s. Strindberg is an essential part of German-language theater.

Anglo-American

Accounting for Strindberg's inclusion in an Anglo-American context is much more complicated, because it is elusive. Strindberg himself visited England only once, and then only for a few days. Though several translations into English had been published in the United States before the First World War, these are problematic: they expurgate, modify, and streamline Strindberg's original text.[3] Furthermore, these American editions were not easily obtainable in Britain. It was not until the 1920s and 1930s that reliable translations were beginning to be published in England. In addition to the issues of translation and publication, Strindberg's reception was also problematic. Strindberg and Ibsen have, as is well known, been received very differently in the British context. Ibsen had strong champions and proficient, influential translators (Eleanor Marx and Jeffrey Archer among them) in England early on. He was embraced by the women's rights movement following the famous 1889 production of *A Doll's House* (*Et Dukke-hjem,* 1879) at London's Novelty Theatre as well as by G. B. Shaw, whose formulation of Ibsen—and his major characters—as consummate actors against social hypocrisy and sexual double standards has shaped the Anglo-American Ibsen reception for over a century (*The Quintessence of Ibsenism,* 1891).

Strindberg's idiosyncratic output, including his open attitude toward sexuality in *Miss Julie* and subsequent misogynistic writing in pamphlets from the late 1880s, acted as a strong barrier to acceptance in England. As one critic writes in the early 1960s, "For most people in Britain, Strindberg is known only in one style: that of intense sexual conflict, in a mainly naturalist mode" (Williams, "Strindberg and the New Drama" 61). Nevertheless, clear affinities with Strindberg are seen in British playwrights such as John Osborne, Harold Pinter, and the plays of the Irish expatriate Samuel Beckett. Written both in English and French, Beckett's plays are full of echoes from Strindberg, notably between *Waiting for Godot* (*En Attendant Godot,* 1953) and *To Damascus;* and between *Endgame* (1957) and *Ghost Sonata.* Among contemporary British playwrights, Sarah Kane stands out as a direct descendant of Strindberg's tormented speakers of *Inferno* and *To Damascus.* Kane was a part of the "new British nihilists," a group of young writers emerging in the late 1980s. Her writing and unreserved "self-dramatization," to recall Rugg's previous description, shares a lot with Strindberg's. Her play *Blasted* (1995) shocked audiences with its sexual violence; like Strindberg's it oscillates between naturalism and expressionism.[4] Similarly, critics' attempts to psychopathologize her drama are eerily reminiscent of the hostile analysis Strindberg was subjected to by his contemporaries. This legacy is particularly striking in light of Kane's suicide, which seemed prefigured and rehearsed in the stark depiction of a tormented mind in *4.48 Psychosis* (2000). Sarah Kane's condensed language, brief stage directions, and uncanny self-reflexivity indicate the international reach of Strindbergian drama into the twentieth century.

Yet, an often-overlooked aspect of Strindberg's connection to English literature is discernible in the emergent modernist prose writing of the early twentieth century, composed by émigré and exile writers whose national affiliation, like Strindberg's own, was ever problematic. Strindberg's first-person narrative *The Roofing Ceremony* offers a case in point. With what appears to be a nod to Joseph Conrad's Marlow–Kurtz constellation, Strindberg's morphine-drugged and hallucinatory speaker suppresses his actions as a hunter of human trophies in the Belgian Congo, while the narrative's frame is based on the conceit of oral storytelling—much like that in *Heart of Darkness* (1903)—which helps destabilize first-person narrator reliability. At the same time, *The Roofing Ceremony,* as several scholars have explored, prefigures a stream-of-consciousness technique similar to that found in James Joyce's *Ulysses* (1922), by which

Strindberg experiments with the idea of narrative emulating the random and self-reflexive processes of human thought.

In U.S. theater history, two traditions have been dominant. The first is that of melodrama and spectacle, including a Broadway production history that includes an overwhelming interest in musicals. The second is an emphasis on method acting and naturalist production practices, assumed to serve as vehicles for psychological identification or social verisimilitude. In this context, Strindberg's idiosyncratic dramatic characters, disjointed narratives without clear development arcs or tidy resolutions, and sometimes tableau-oriented and abstract expositions have met resistance from the theater production establishment. By the mid-twentieth century, however, North American scholars Eric Bentley (*The Playwright as Thinker,* 1946), Martin Esslin (*Theatre of the Absurd,* 1961), and Robert Brustein (*The Theatre of Revolt,* 1964) had effectively integrated Strindberg into a minor canon of quintessentially modern and avant-garde playwrights, whose plays were significant to the modernist tradition in a comprehensive sense. When it comes to Strindberg and American playwrights, clear points of connection are to Edward Albee, who acknowledged his debt to Strindberg's *Dance of Death* in the creation of *Who's Afraid of Virginia Woolf* (1962); Sam Shepard; and Eugene O'Neill. Shepard's approach to subjectivity in his early works "bore marked resemblances to that which August Strindberg had employed in *A Dream Play,*" one critic remarks (Bottoms 38). The same critic notes that "if the goal for Shepard, as for Strindberg, was to depict something of the depth and complexity of the author's consciousness—thereby suggesting the expression of an authentic inner self, a center around which the fragments of experience can be assembled—these early pieces also display a contradictory tendency toward a *decenteredness*" (Bottoms 38). Shepard's "spontaneous" writing method can be compared with Strindberg's ideas for an "automatic art" (an idea which Maxime Abolgassemi also discusses in his chapter in this volume). The road between Strindberg and Shepard branches out to include Jack Kerouac, Alan Ginsberg, and William S. Burroughs.

That said, in the American context, the playwright who is most closely associated with Strindberg is O'Neill. The latter's unreserved acknowledgment of "the inspiration" by and "the debt" to Strindberg was made in his 1936 Nobel Prize acceptance speech. As O'Neill emphasizes, it "was reading his plays when I first started to write back in the winter of 1913–14 that, above all else, first gave me the vision of what modern drama could be, and first inspired me with the urge to write for the theatre myself." This legacy is addressed by the grandsire of cultural criticism, Raymond Williams, who argues that Strindberg's and O'Neill's development of modern tragedy—*Miss Julie* included—is instrumental for understanding tragedy less as a literary genre and more as a condition of the modern world. Williams situates particularly *Miss Julie, The Father,* and *Dance of Death* as social artifacts that account for "the tragedy of destructive relationships" but also explore "the joy of life in its tense and cruel struggles"—including those of the everyday (Williams, *Modern Tragedy,* 134). Williams's close linkage of O'Neill and Strindberg is significant because it illustrates in yet another way Strindberg's centrality for conceptions of international modernity. Strindberg's oeuvre, as this book shows, offers remarkably varied, comprehensive, and heterogeneous ways for exploring precisely issues like these.

Collection Trajectory

This book shows Strindberg's contributions to our understanding of international modernity. It also indicates that Strindberg was actively involved in shaping his own international legacy. As numerous chapters argue, his influence can be seen across national and linguistic contexts. Similarly, his writing reflects the fact that he lived a life shaped by emergent international modernity. The chapters in this book foreground multiple aspects of these intellectual, cultural, philosophical, and aesthetic contexts. Similarly, the chapters represent almost all of the major genres in which Strindberg worked: drama, prose fiction, poetry, art, and nonfiction writing. The chapters of this book are organized not according to chronology, national context, or genre, however, but are presented in ways that show the diversity of Strindberg's writing and the diversity of the topics of inquiry this writing's international reverberations raise.

Eszter Szalczer's essay "Stockholm—Berlin—Moscow: Strindberg and Avant-Garde Performance in the 1920s" juxtaposes two remarkable instances from the production history of Strindberg's drama, both from 1921, and both responding to world-historical events. Austrian-born director Max Reinhardt's staging of *A Dream Play* in Stockholm and subsequently in Berlin in the aftermath of World War I is compared with Russian director Evgeny Vakhtangov's production of *Erik XIV* (1899) in postrevolutionary Moscow. As Szalczer argues, these productions illustrate appropriations of play elements that in the dramatist's native environment had been perceived as distinctly Swedish: Swedish landscapes and character types in *A Dream Play,* and Swedish historical figures and events in *Erik XIV.* Yet, in their respective stagings of these Strindberg plays, both of these directors broke new ground for the theater arts in the context of their local cultural environment as well as across national contexts. In her comparison, Szalczer draws on studies of intercultural exchange, especially those involving the "transculturation" of dramatic texts, to help illustrate how these productions offset the assumptions of Swedish theatergoers as well as German and Soviet audiences.

If Max Reinhardt was one of Europe's most experimental theater directors of the early twentieth century, Danish Lars von Trier may be remembered as one of Europe's most innovative film directors of the first part of the subsequent century. Mads Bunch's "Castration Anxiety and Traumatic Encounters with the Real in the Works of August Strindberg and Lars von Trier" traces affinities between von Trier and Strindberg—suggesting that the two artists share a similar interest in unraveling and denuding any pretension of access to a Real, beyond the master-narratives induced by castration anxiety and sexual impotency. In this first sustained comparative analysis between Strindberg, von Trier, and cultural theorist Slavoj Žižek, Bunch identifies a number of recurring threads in von Trier's filmography that link him to Strindberg.

Maxime Abolgassemi's chapter "Reconsidering the Place of Strindberg in Surrealism: André Breton and the Light of the Objective Chance Encounter" investigates the connections between Strindberg's French-language writing of the 1890s and surrealist investigations of chance encounters. Abolgassemi connects Strindberg's aesthetic criticism in "The New Arts" ("Des Arts Nouveaux," 1894) and André Breton's and Strindberg's use of the Parisian cityscape to explore the revelatory potential of what they both describe as *magnifique* correlations between seemingly unrelated objects.

Linda Rugg's "Standing at the Bourne of the Modern: Strindberg's Ecological Subject in *By the Open Sea* and His Archipelago Paintings" explores the rise of international interest from the 1960s onward in Strindberg's evocative and occasionally nearly abstract landscape paintings. Reviewers and scholars have noted that Strindberg's paintings, products of an untrained amateur working with unorthodox materials and methods, stand at the threshold of international modernist art in much the same way his literature does. Rugg's chapter explores a striking motif within these paintings: the portal or the horizon beyond the edge of the archipelago, the place where land gives in to sea, and sea to sky. In these "[topoi] of liminality," Rugg argues, the representation of a particular archipelago landscape comes to stand as an icon for the idea of transition in scientific (evolutionary), historical, aesthetic, psychological, and theological terms.

In his chapter "Paris, Laboratory of Modernity: Modernist Experimentation and August Strindberg's Search for 'the Equation' in Paris," Sylvain Briens argues that the physical location of the French capital awarded Strindberg an unprecedented possibility for experimentation in both scientific and aesthetic registers. Briens investigates the correlation often posed between Strindberg and Zola by asking whether Strindberg, who positioned himself as a scientist rather than as a novelist or playwright during his stay in Paris in the mid-1890s, actually could follow Zola's recommendation in his 1890 essay on "The Experimental Novel," wherein he asks, "Why does not literature itself become a science, thanks to the experimental method?" (Zola, 81). Briens's chapter thus explores the multiple ways in which Paris becomes to Strindberg a double laboratory of modernity, one that is both aesthetic and scientific.

Strindberg's intellectual and artistic appetites for the new seem to have been nearly insatiable, yet his writing also reflects an interest in revising the received myths of a classical European education. Freddie Rokem's chapter "Voices and Visions in Fingal's Cave: Plato and Strindberg" focuses on how *A Dream Play*'s figuration of the Fingal's Cave in the last act reconfigures central aspects of Plato's philosophical parable of the cave in *The Republic*. As Indra's Daughter returns from the cave to the heavens, a structure of birth and death in Strindberg's play becomes a dramatic re-presentation of the Platonic transmigration of souls. But whereas Plato's cave is primarily a site of visual impressions, Strindberg's is primarily governed by sounds; thereby, Rokem argues, Strindberg has created a poetic alternative to Plato's philosophical cave experience.

In Anna Westerståhl Stenport's "Money Metaphors and Rhetoric of Resource Depletion: *Creditors* and Late-Nineteenth-Century European Economics" a materialist conception of European culture takes precedence. Though *Creditors* has generally been interpreted as drawing its main operative metaphors from science, medicine, and art, Stenport argues that a different model is at play as well. This model appears to negotiate between abstract and concrete economic registers. Drawing on late-nineteenth-century international developments in political economy, Stenport shows how Strindberg's economic discourse in the play actually reflects the pan-European interest in emergent modern economic theory.

Strindberg may be best known internationally as a playwright, yet a significant component of his production is made up of poetry. Massimo Ciaravolo's chapter "A Nineteenth-Century Long Poem Meets Modernity: *Sleepwalking Nights*" shows how Strindberg conceives of Stockholm and Paris in continued juxtaposition to one another, just as this juxtaposition allows the poet to investigate ramifications of displacement and disjuncture. More specifically, Ciaravolo investigates the hybrid effects created by imagining Stockholm through Paris, in the form of a long poem that also draws on the medieval Germanic *knittel* verse form.

Though counterintuitive given a critical context that emphasized the significance of the *Übermensch* concept, Strindberg's interest in the writings of Nietzsche also included a shared interest in the ramifications of late-nineteenth-century European decadence. Tobias Dahlkvist's chapter, "*By the Open Sea*—A Decadent Novel? Reconsidering Relationships Between Nietzsche, Strindberg, and Fin-de-Siècle Culture," foregrounds these under-explored connections through an inquiry of Strindberg's 1899 novel *By the Open Sea,* set in the Baltic archipelago. The protagonist of this novel, Dahlkvist shows, shares characteristics with J.-K. Husyman's quintessential decadent novelistic character Des Esseintes—including nervousness, interest in aesthetic ornamentation, and a disinterest in actualized productivity. These and other characteristics, Dahlkvist argues, reflect Nietzsche's critique of modern culture.

Part of Strindberg's international reach is closely tied to the effectiveness and availability of translation. Yet, as Anne-Charlotte Hanes Harvey argues in "'The Spoken Word Is All'—'Ordet det talade är allt': Translating Strindberg for the International Stage," critical aspects of translation for theater production have been overlooked. Based on the concept of platform translation, she argues that a translator serves more as a dramaturg—contextualizing and opening as many doors as possible for staging choices—than as a director; and that translators are the primary preserver of a playwright's "voice" in the target language. Harvey's article explores in detail, and with multiple examples, some of the concrete strategies for achieving this effect while translating Strindberg, and particularly into English for North American audiences.

Leonardo Lisi's chapter "The Art of Doubt: Form, Genre, History in *Miss Julie*" further explores a central paradox in Strindberg's formulation in the subtitle of the tragedy *Miss Julie,* namely the seeming opposition between "naturalist" and "tragedy [*sorgespel*]." Lisi investigates the interplay between determinism and free will in the play and resolves this juxtaposition with recourse to a dialectical interrelation of these two opposed representational logics. Lisi suggests that only Kierkegaard holds a view of tragedy compatible with Strindberg's play, thereby suggesting that the combination of ancient and modern characteristics into a single form provides a particularly fruitful model for Scandinavian drama during its period of transition into European modernity.

Notes

1. This collection thus contributes to an expansive and multidisciplinary body of scholarship by a number of thinkers in Sweden, Europe, and North America. The most significant of recent scholarship in this vein includes book-length studies by Olsson, *Levande död* and *Jag blir galen;* Szalczer, *August Strindberg* and *Writing Daughters;* Briens, *Paris Laboratoire;* Törnqvist, *Strindbergian Drama;* Marker and Marker, *Strindberg and Post-Inferno Drama;* Stern, *Nietzsche's Ocean, Strindberg's Open Sea;* Malekin, *Strindberg and Sacred Theater;* Stenport, *Locating August Strindberg's Prose;* Hockenjos, "Picturing Dissolving Views"; Lönngren, "Att röra en värld"; and Stounbjerg, "Uro og urenhed." Other significant work includes the edited collections *The Cambridge Companion to August Strindberg* (ed. Robinson) and *Det gäckande könet* (ed. Cavallin and Stenport) and chapters or sections in works by Rugg, *Picturing Ourselves;* Casanova, *The World Republic of Letters;* Chaudhuri, *The Geography of Modern Drama;* Case, *Performing Science and the Virtual;* Shideler, *Questioning the Father;* and Rokem, *Philosophers and Thespians.* Michael Robinson's formidable three-volume *International Annotated Bibliography of Strindberg Studies 1870–2005* is a veritable treasure trove—indeed it is indispensable—for the study of Strindberg's international reach, and the significance of this work cannot be underestimated for future Strindberg scholarship.

2. Hoogland's prescriptive 1962 essay "How to Produce Strindberg?" on Swedish Strindberg productions written for the fiftieth-anniversary commemoration of Strindberg's death makes this close relationship very clear; see also Szalczer's discussion of Molander's treatment of Strindberg's plays as "covert autobiography . . . set in hyper-realistic turn-of-the-century Stockholm milieu" in *August Strindberg* (186).

3. The Scribner Edition contained 24 plays in five volumes, translated by Edwin Björkman; a number of Strindberg works were also translated by Ellie Schleussner around the same time.

4. Featuring scenes of cannibalism and sodomy, *Blasted* was made infamous by the *Daily Mail*'s Jack Tinker, who called it "a disgusting piece of filth." The play quickly became a media event, and in the debacle the play's investigation of violence and gender was largely lost in a debate centering on the Royal Court's right to stage a play that, according to Tinker and others, "knows no bounds of decency" (Urban, "CRAVE," 496).

Works Cited

Ahlström, Stellan. *Strindbergs erövring av Paris: Strindberg och Frankrike 1884–1895*. Stockholm: Almqvist and Wiksell, 1956.

Austin, Paul. "August Strindberg, Sam Shepard, and the Expressionist Impulse." In *Expressionism and Modernism: New Approaches to August Strindberg*, ed. Michael Robinson and Sven Rossel. The proceedings of the 13th International Strindberg Conference, held in Linz, 1997. Vienna: Editions Praesens, 1999.

Bentley, Eric. *The Playwright as Thinker.* Minneapolis: University of Minnesota Press, 1946.

Bottoms, Stephen James. *The Theatre of Sam Shepard: States of Crisis.* Cambridge, Eng.: Cambridge University Press, 1998.

Briens, Sylvain. *Paris laboratoire de la littérature scandinave modern (1880–1905).* Paris: L'Harmattan, 2010.

Brustein, Robert. *The Theatre of Revolt.* Boston: Atlantic-Little Brown, 1964.

Casanova, Pascale. *The World Republic of Letters.* Trans. M. B. DeBevoise. Cambridge, Mass.: Harvard University Press, 2004.

Case, Sue-Ellen. *Performing Science and the Virtual.* New York: Routledge, 2007.

Cavallin, Anna, and Anna Westerståhl Stenport, eds. *Det gäckande könet: Strindberg och genusteori.* Stockholm: Symposion, 2006.

Chaudhuri, Una. *Staging Place: The Geography of Modern Drama.* Ann Arbor: University of Michigan Press. 1997.

Esslin, Martin. *Theatre of the Absurd.* New York: Knopf, 1961.

Gravier, Maurice. "Strindberg and French Drama." *World Theatre* 11, no. 1 (1962): 45–60.

Hockenjos, Vreni. "Picturing Dissolving Views: August Strindberg and the Visual Media of His Age." Ph.D. diss., Stockholm University, 2007. Stockholm: Acta Universitatis Stockholmiensis, 2007.

Hoogland, Claes. "How to Produce Strindberg?" *World Theatre* 11, no. 1 (1962): 67–79.

Kuhns, David F. *German Expressionist Theatre: The Actor and the Stage.* Cambridge, Eng.: Cambridge University Press, 1997. Print.

Lönngren, Ann-Sofie. "Att röra en värld: En queerteoretisk analys av erotiska trianglar i sex verk av August Strindberg." Ph.D. diss., Uppsala University, 2008. Lund: Föreningen för utgivande av Tidskrift för Litteraturvetenskap, 2009.

Malekin, Theo. *Strindberg and the Quest for Sacred Theatre.* Consciousness, Literature and the Arts 26. Amsterdam: Rodopi, 2010.

Marker, Frederick J., and Lise-Lone Marker. *Strindberg and Modernist Theatre: Post-Inferno Drama on the Stage.* Cambridge, Eng.: Cambridge University Press, 2002.

Olsson, Ulf. *Jag blir galen: Strindberg, vansinnet och vetenskapen.* Eslöv: B. Östlings bokförlag. Symposion, 2002.

———. *Levande död: Studier i Strindbergs prosa.* Stockholm: Symposion, 1996.

O'Neill, Eugene. "Nobel Prize Banquet Acceptance Speech." City Hall, Stockholm, Dec. 10, 1936. www.nobelprize.org.

Robinson, Michael, ed. *The Cambridge Companion to August Strindberg.* Cambridge, Eng.: Cambridge University Press, 2009.

———. *An International Annotated Bibliography of Strindberg Studies, 1870–2005.* 3 vols. London: Modern Humanities Research Association, 2008.

Rokem, Freddie. *Philosophers & Thespians: Thinking Performance.* Stanford, Calif.: Stanford University Press, 2009.

Rugg, Linda. "The Art and Science of Self-Dramatization." In *The Cambridge Companion to August Strindberg*, ed. Michael Robinson. Cambridge, Eng.: Cambridge University Press, 2009. 3–19.

———. *Picturing Ourselves: Photography and Autobiography.* Chicago: University of Chicago Press, 1997.

Shideler, Ross. *Questioning the Father: From Darwin to Zola, Ibsen, Strindberg and Hardy.* Stanford, Calif.: Stanford University Press, 1999.

Stenport, Anna Westerståhl. *Locating August Strindberg's Prose: Modernism, Transnationalism, and Setting.* Toronto: University of Toronto Press, 2010.

Stern, Michael. *Nietzsche's Ocean, Strindberg's Open Sea.* Berlin: Nordeuropa-Institut, 2008. Print.

Stounbjerg, Per. "Uro og Urenhed: Studier i Strindbergs selvbiografiske prosa." Ph.D. diss., Aarhus universitet. Århus: Aarhus Universitetsforlag, 2005.

Strindberg, August. *August Strindberg: Selected Essays.* Ed. and trans. Michael Robinson. Cambridge, Eng.: Cambridge University Press, 1996.

———. *Strindberg's Letters.* 2 vols. Ed. and trans. Michael Robinson. Chicago: University of Chicago Press, 1992.

Szalczer, Eszter. *August Strindberg.* New York: Routledge, 2010.

———. *Writing Daughters: August Strindberg's Other Voices.* London: Norvik, 2008.

Szondi, Peter. *Theory of the Modern Drama, Parts I–II.* Trans. Michael Hays. Durham, N.C.: Duke University Press, 1983.

Törnqvist, Egil. *Strindbergian Drama: Themes and Structure.* Stockholm: Almqvist and Wiksell, 1982.

Urban, Ken. "CRAVE. By Sarah Kane. Axis Company, Axis Theatre, New York. 8 November 2000." Performance review. *Theatre Journal* 53 (2001): 496–98.

Zola, Émile. *Le roman expérimental.* Paris: Garnier-Flammarion, 1971. Print.

Williams, Raymond. *Modern Tragedy.* Ed. Pamela McCallum. Peterborough, Ont.: Broadview, 2006.

———. "Strindberg and the New Drama of Great Britain." *World Theatre* 11, no. 1 (1962).

Stockholm—Berlin—Moscow: Strindberg and Avant-Garde Performance in the 1920s

Eszter Szalczer

> Performance is not something ancillary, accidental, or superfluous that can be distinguished from the play proper. The play proper exists first and only when it is played. Performance brings the play into existence, and the playing of the play is the play itself. . . . It comes to be in representation and in all the contingency and particularity of the occasions of its appearance. (Weinsheimer 109–10)

Strindberg, the playwright, would doubtless reject the theoretical stance that denies the priority of the script relative to its performance and reverses the conventional hierarchy between play-text and performance-text. But Strindberg, the ever-innovative theater artist, came quite close to such a view of his own work when in 1908 he warned August Falck, the young actor-manager of his Intimate Theater in Stockholm, not to stick to the letter of *Miss Julie* (*Fröken Julie,* 1888)—a play written twenty years earlier in a quite different cultural era—but to adjust it to the demands of the contemporary stage (Strindberg 296/235).[1] It is precisely this "contingency and particularity of the occasions" which appropriate the "play proper" even as bringing it into representation that I propose to explore in this chapter. I chose to spotlight two remarkable instances from the production history of Strindberg's drama, both from 1921, and both responding to world-historical events. Austrian-born director Max Reinhardt's staging of *A Dream Play* (*Ett drömspel,* 1901) in Stockholm and subsequently in Berlin in the aftermath of World War I serves as my first example; the Russian director Evgeny Vakhtangov's production of *Erik XIV* (1899) in postrevolutionary Moscow as the second. These productions illustrate appropriations of play elements that in the dramatist's native environment had been perceived as distinctly Swedish: Swedish landscapes and character types in *A Dream Play,* and Swedish historical figures and events in *Erik XIV.* Yet, with the staging of their respective Strindberg play, both of these directors broke new ground for the theater arts in the context of their local cultural environment as well as transnationally.

The field of performance studies has helped to shift the focus of theater scholarship from often reductive queries into "what" plays mean to considerations of "how" plays mean. For the purposes of this analysis I draw on those areas of performance theory that explore performative events (both theatrical and other forms of social interaction) as means of constructing and deconstructing identities and power structures. Studies of intercultural exchange, especially those involving the "transculturation" of dramatic texts, have also proved helpful in understanding the international currency of Strindberg's work as evidenced by the productions of Reinhardt and Vakhtangov. The term "intercultural" signifies "transactions between separate indigenous cultural systems, when, either unilaterally or mutually, elements of one culture are accepted or adopted in the other culture." Transculturation is a special case of intercultural exchange, "which brings forth artworks that combine elements from separate cultures and their indigenous artistic traditions" (Weber 27–28). Reinhardt's *A Dream Play* and Vakhtangov's *Erik XIV* serve as case studies of transculturation by means of performance.

Semiotics-based performance theory provides additional tools that help to trace the significance of temporal-historical changes within culture on the one hand, and the role of shifting spatial-geographical-political milieus on the other. Marvin Carlson's important study in theater semiotics reveals not only that a work of art may be considered "the manifestation of cultural experience, a way of being in the world," but also that interpretive codes are culturally determined as much as the codes built into the work at the time of its creation. "Like any cultural artifact removed either temporally or spatially from an originating context," argues Carlson, "the work of art becomes . . . open to new interpretations" as the result of "entering a new local semiosis." As it "moves through time and through different cultural surroundings, it accumulates interpretations" including traditions of critical commentary, which often "become associated with the work, affecting subsequent interpretations perhaps as much as the work itself." Carlson points out the specificity of the theater, among other art forms, as "a *performed* art," which, as opposed to painting, for example, "creates no total artifact available for subsequent experience and interpretation. Every performance is unique and unrepeatable, understood by whatever codes are available to that audience at that specific moment" (Carlson, *Theatre Semiotics* 111–13).

On the Margins: Exile and Transculturation

That Strindberg today is regarded as one of the most innovative dramatists of the modern stage, who produced a distinctly transnational oeuvre, depends upon a complex set of circumstances, many aspects of which have been explored by generations of scholars. One contributing factor, especially important to the subject of this essay, was his periods of voluntary exile abroad beginning in the early 1880s, resulting in significant exposures to the rapidly changing life and cultural ferment of such modern metropolitan centers as Berlin and Paris. Just as important, the radicalism of his plays positioned Strindberg for almost his entire career outside the domain of the theatrical establishment. His work was inspired by and, in its turn, informed the so-called independent theater movement, which consisted of the numerous experimental companies that sprang up throughout Europe in the late nineteenth century and offered alternatives to institutionalized theaters. Usually operating on a subscription basis, independent companies such as the Théâtre-Libre in Paris or the Freie Bühne in Berlin could navigate around the pitfalls of censorship to which public theaters were subjected. Due to the conservatism of the Swedish cultural establishment, Strindberg's most pioneering plays were produced abroad by independent theater companies long before they achieved a breakthrough, or sometimes even before they were performed in Sweden. While *The Father* (*Fadren,* 1887), for example, received its Swedish premiere at Nya Teatern in Stockholm in 1888, it was not until 1908 that it achieved a successful run with 77 performances at Strindberg's Intimate Theater venture in Stockholm. Meanwhile, in 1890, eighteen years before its triumph in Sweden, *The Father* had premiered in Berlin at the Freie Bühne, an influential independent company founded by the critic Otto Brahm in 1889 (Szalczer 48). This production was Strindberg's debut outside Scandinavia and his introduction to the German-speaking theater in which his work came to affect major modern developments.

Miss Julie (1888) was not only banned from public performance in Denmark, but it was also barred from the professional stage in Sweden for eighteen years after its completion. Its world premiere took place at a private performance on the makeshift stage of the Student Union at the University of Copenhagen on March 14, 1889, where it was performed only for two nights. Next it was produced in 1893 by André Antoine, the founder of the independent theater movement and exponent of naturalist staging practices, at his Théâtre-Libre in Paris. This production was seminal in establishing Strindberg as a key influence on the European modern stage. "*Miss Julie* made an enormous sensation," Antoine recorded in his diary on January 15, 1893. "Everything stimulated the audience—the subject, the setting, the packing into a single act an hour and a half in length enough action to sustain a full-length French play. Of course, there were sneers and protests, but it was, after all, something quite new" (Antoine 216). Strindberg's conquest of Paris continued when in 1894 the Théâtre de l'Oeuvre, the independent company that experimented with a symbolist mode of performance, produced *Creditors* (*Fordringsägare,* 1888) as part of its first season, followed by *The Father* in the second season.

The German premiere of *The Father* at the Freie Bühne was soon followed by several significant productions of Strindberg's other naturalistic plays. *Miss Julie* was performed there on a single night in 1892, but because of heated protests from the audience, it was taken off the program. *Creditors* was staged at the Residenzteater in Berlin in 1893 with some of the most prominent German actors of the time, and in 1899 the play saw a new production at the Theater in der Josefstadt in Vienna, succeeded by many other Strindberg premieres throughout Austria (Ollén 120, 139, 166). By the time the young Max Reinhardt opened Schall und Rauch, the avant-garde cabaret in Berlin, in 1901, there was a strong Strindberg tradition established in the German-speaking independent theater. In his Kleines Theater (the successor of Schall und Rauch) Reinhardt produced a series of Strindberg plays, including *The Bond* (*Bandet,* 1892) and *Crimes and Crimes* (*Brott och brott,* 1899) in 1902, and the still scandalous *Miss Julie* in 1904. These productions by independent companies during Strindberg's lifetime made the Swedish dramatist so popular in Germany that in the three years following his death—from 1913 to 1915—"there were more than 1,000 performances of twenty-four of his plays in sixty-two cities" (Innes 39).

In imperial Russia Strindberg met a more uneven reception. From the 1890s to 1917, translations of Nordic literature, highly popular in Russia during this period, swept the country in large quantities. Many versions of Strindberg's works, mostly via German translations rather than from the original Swedish, circulated, including five published versions of *The*

Father and six versions of *Miss Julie*. Between 1908 and 1912 two different publishers brought out Strindberg's collected works; one edition included twelve, the other fifteen volumes (Nikolajeva 113–14). The first Strindberg play on the Russian stage was *Crimes and Crimes,* produced in 1901 at the New Theater of St. Petersburg, where it was criticized for its pessimism. Then in 1905 the pioneering avant-garde director Vsevolod Meyerhold directed *The Father* in Tiflis, Georgia. By this time a new generation of Russian symbolist artists and poets seem to have embraced Strindberg; and even *The Father,* which he had declared his first naturalist work for the stage, was seen by them as an essentially symbolist piece (Nikolajeva 118). In 1912 Meyerhold became artistic director of the Fellowship of Actors, Writers, Musicians, and Artists, living communally at the seaside resort of Terijoki near the Finnish border. The company, which was interested mainly in symbolism, experimenting with techniques of commedia dell'arte and pantomime, put on *Crimes and Crimes* as a tribute to Strindberg who had passed away two months earlier. It was a stylized performance with symbolist use of color, light, shadow, and movement set within a black frame. Meyerhold's direction was seen as a protest against naturalism, represented by Konstantin Stanislavsky's Moscow Art Theater (Braun 122–24).

Miss Julie premiered at the New Theater of St. Petersburg in 1906. Because of the authorities' disapproval of the vast social difference between the lovers, Jean in these performances was promoted from lackey to estate manager (Ollén 114). Other Strindberg plays were censored as well. *Erik XIV,* for example, was banned in pre-revolutionary Russia because it presented a king disrespectfully and as a victim of revolt. So it seems that before 1917 Strindberg gained a position in progressive and experimental theatrical circles, while his work was ignored or rejected by the mainstream culture. Following the 1917 October Revolution, Strindberg productions became even scarcer. The 1921 *Erik XIV* at the First Studio of the Moscow Art Theater became the most famous staging of a Strindberg play ever seen on the Russian stage and remained in the repertoire even after Vakhtangov died in 1922 (Ollén 296). The year Lenin died, 1924, marked the beginning of Stalin's era, during which the avant-garde theatrical experiments that had an affinity with Strindberg's legacy were gradually stifled. Following a 1927 production of *The Father,* Russian audiences did not see a Strindberg play for virtually fifty years. In 1934 the First All-Union Congress of Soviet Writers announced that socialist realism was henceforth to be the exclusive style of Soviet writers and artists. This new style was defined as a combination of artistic representation "with the task of ideological transformation and education of the working man in the spirit of Socialism" (Baer, "Design" 57). Strindberg's perceived pessimism and subjectivism, and his bourgeois background, made his work impossible to conform to either Stalinist ideology or the doctrine of socialist realism.

Back in Sweden, *Miss Julie* was presented on the professional stage for the first time as late as 1906 in Lund, by August Falck's traveling company, which brought the production to Stockholm the next year. *A Dream Play* was performed in 1907, six years after its completion, at Svenska Teatern in Stockholm—the first and only production of the play during Strindberg's lifetime. The production was a failure, according to both Strindberg's and critics' accounts. The experience left Strindberg frustrated with the producers for neglecting his advice for a simplified, non-realistic set, and critics deemed the play a formless closet drama, unfit for the stage. Beyond the technical difficulties presented by the many scene changes if handled realistically, contemporary Swedish audiences were not ready to assimilate this radically unconventional piece. *A Dream Play* was not produced again until 1916, when German director Rudolf Bernauer staged it at the Theater im der Königgrätzerstrasse in Berlin, with Danish-German scenographer Svend Gade's decorative designs, cloaked in a fairy-tale-like atmosphere. Interestingly, it was Gade's design for Bernauer which was used in a stage version of the play later the same year in Gothenburg, Sweden (Bark 103).

These early productions illustrate both Strindberg's marginalized position within mainstream culture during his lifetime and the intercultural exchange his work prompted early on after his death. Intercultural performance studies help us understand the marginalization of the exile by hegemonic culture on the one hand, and the polyphonic encoding of the exile's text on the other. Reflecting upon the notion of the exile, cultural critic Edward Said feels that "you always bear within yourself a recollection of what you've left behind and what you can remember, and you play it against the current experience," which results in a "sense of counterpoint." By counterpoint Said means "things that can't be reduced to homophony." The very core of the exile's experience is "multiple identity, the polyphony of many voices playing off against each other, without . . . the need to reconcile them" (Marranca, Robinson, and Chaudhuri 43). The performances discussed in this chapter testify to such polyphonic encoding of Strindberg's work. Because he was an exile, both at home and abroad, his plays were embraced by the transnational independent theater movement, equally located outside the margins of mainstream culture. A closer look at these productions reveals Strindberg's dramatic texts as sites of sustained difference.

Mapping the Mind or Mapping a Life?

It is due to the perceived subjective quality of the later plays—where the action, the set, the dialogue, and the characters seem to chart a mental landscape—that Strindberg is credited with creating the modern ego-drama and is hailed as the forerunner of theatrical expressionism. But this perception of such works as the *To Damascus* trilogy (*Till Damaskus,* parts I–II, 1898; part III, 1901), *A Dream Play,* and the so-called Chamber Plays (1907–8) did not emerge from the texts at the time of their first appearance in print or in performance in Sweden. There and then they often prompted confusion and even ridicule (Szalczer 140, 178). The image of the proto-expressionist Strindberg was created retrospectively, following performances of these texts in Germany and Austria, and the simultaneous emergence of a generation of German expressionist dramatists in the late 1910s and 1920s. By 1921 Max Reinhardt (1873–1943) had inscribed his name in the pages of European theater history with his celebrated productions of Strindberg's late plays in Germany, including *The Dance of Death* (*Dödsdansen,* 1900), *Storm Weather* (*Oväder,* 1907), *The Pelican* (*Pelikanen,* 1907), and *The Ghost Sonata* (*Spöksonaten,* 1907) in the 1910s. In fact, Reinhardt's 1916 production of *The Ghost Sonata* at his Kammerspiele in Berlin, which toured in Sweden in 1917, opened the eyes of the Swedish public for the first time to the extent of their countryman's contributions to modernizing the stage. Swedish reviewers found it ironic that it would take a director from Germany to enlighten the Swedes about the immense theatrical potential of Strindberg's late drama (Ollén 472). Following *The Ghost Sonata,* Reinhardt went on to produce *The Burned House* (*Brända tomten,* 1907) in 1920 and finally *A Dream Play* in 1921. These productions increasingly turned Strindberg into a household name in Germany while, in turn, they helped Reinhardt develop his own expressionist staging style, which became the hallmark of his productions between the late 1910s and 1920s and which helped him establish himself as a quintessentially modernist director (Bark 103). In these productions Reinhardt gradually developed an expressionistic stage vocabulary—through sets, costumes, acting style, and sound and lighting effects—to evoke a terrifying, macabre world as the physicalization of a nightmarish inner reality.

A Dream Play presents the story of the daughter of the Indic god Indra, who, driven by her desire to learn about the human condition, incarnates as the earthly woman Agnes. Over the course of her journey on earth, where she is guided by the Officer, the Lawyer, and the Poet, she experiences all the contradictions of life that seem to perpetuate human suffering. At the conclusion of her journey she decides to leave the earth and return to heaven by entering a burning castle, atop which a chrysanthemum bud bursts into flower at the moment of her departure. The play's production history presents a quite different, but no less fascinating, journey.

Thanks to his international reputation achieved with his Strindberg cycle, Reinhardt was invited to Stockholm to direct *A Dream Play* at the Royal Dramatic Theater in 1921. One of the central elements in Reinhardt's staging was the expressionistic use of light to create a spooky, hostile, and stifling stage universe. Combined with the intricate lighting patterns, Reinhardt introduced a choral strategy that underpinned the theme of inescapable suffering. The actors were isolated from one another and from their surroundings by spotlights as they emerged from darkness, and the action of the main characters was watched by groups of spectral figures. At climactic moments only the anguished or menacing faces of these apparitions were illuminated. In the second half of the performance Reinhardt created haunting effects as he brought together individual groups of extras into a threatening crowd whose rhythmic movements were accompanied by angst-filled cries orchestrated to many voices, like a grand oratorio (Kvam 108–11).

The set, designed by Alfred Roller, consisted of pieces of furniture combined with a succession of painted backdrops in dark colors. Some constant visual elements—a door with the cloverleaf hole, for example—amidst the shifting stage images would enhance a sense of dreaming, or rather, of nightmare. Interestingly, while other aspects of the production received mixed reviews, Roller's designs were squarely rebuffed by critics in Stockholm as un-Swedish. Spectators were appalled to behold what many felt were dark horror scenarios where they had expected to see familiar landscapes—a beautiful Swedish bathing resort in the Stockholm archipelago as the setting for "Fairhaven," for example. Roller's "foreign, dry and colorless constructions" were condemned and contrasted with the brilliant work of such young Swedish artists as Isaac Grünewald, which critics and audience would have preferred to see instead (Ollén 408, my translation).

The music of Pantscho Wladigeroff, the young Bulgarian composer from Reinhardt's Deutsches Theater in Berlin, fared no better than the set. It was criticized for the lack of dreamlike qualities and was unfavorably compared with the music of Swedish composer Wilhelm Stenhammar, whose score for *A Dream Play* had been used in the Gothenburg performance in 1916 (Kvam 120). Overall, Swedish reviewers noted the "foreignness" of the production, the "transposition into German of the whole atmosphere of *A Dream Play,*" and they unanimously rejected Reinhardt's pessimistic vision (Marker and Marker 75). The concluding scene of the performance was vehemently condemned by Swedish critics. There was no redemption suggested: Indra's Daughter (Jessie Wessel) would not return to heaven, and there was no chrysanthemum bud opening atop the burning castle. Rather than offering the hope of liberation from earthly misery, Reinhardt's ending seemed to suggest that the heroine descended into hell. During her final speech she stepped into a pile of burning logs and disappeared through a trapdoor in the stage floor while, according to a sarcastic account, "the castle shone in a Bengal light like the closing ballet in a music-hall show" (qtd. in Marker and Marker 79).

The negative reception of Reinhardt's Stockholm production demonstrates how the meanings of plays are shaped by the specific historical moment and the political and cultural climate surrounding the performance. Swedish critics had apparently expected to see their own national *Dream Play,* which was closer to the lighthearted fantasy of the 1916 Bernauer production, even if that vision of the play also originated with a "foreign" director. In addition, they expected to see their own national artists, Grünewald and Stenhammar, create a Swedish milieu. Reinhardt's production was an interesting case of how local semiosis prevented the acceptance of what was perceived as encoded "foreignness" in the performance of a Swedish play. It became apparent that Bernauer's fairy-tale-like interpretation had been domesticated and made part of the Swedish tradition of understanding Strindberg's text. Critics in 1921 still pitted the new production against the one they remembered from 1916.

Reinhardt's approach was indeed radically different from Bernauer's. The latter's playful interpretation, combining spectacle and humor, emphasized the theme of redemption, while Reinhardt's dark vision of *A Dream Play* presented an allegory of suffering humanity in an infernal shadow world. In the unfavorable reception of Reinhardt's production in Stockholm one can discern a clash between several sets of local semiosis. Sweden, a country that maintained neutrality in World War I, responded with enthusiasm to what appears to have offered an escapist fantasy by a German director in the early years of the war. Reinhardt's production was rejected because it read the devastating effects of a lost war into the play and presented it as the embodiment of existential dread and spiritual angst in the face of an overpowering, nightmarish reality.

In late 1921, following the Stockholm premiere, Reinhardt took his production "home" to Berlin, to be performed in German at the Deutsches Theater. Within the confines of this essay it is impossible to discuss the details of the semiotically charged role of translation in the signifying processes of performance. Textual translation is therefore treated here only as one element among many of cultural translation. Reinhardt's overall vision and concept for the performance in Berlin did not change. But here he worked with his own permanent company whose strengths he was familiar with. The Deutsches Theater was renowned for its superb ensemble acting developed during Reinhardt's leadership. Against the suggestive background images of Franz Dworsky, choreographed mass scenes evolved to the accompaniment of Wladigeroff's music. Rather than a goddess and an outsider visiting earth, Helene Thimig portrayed Agnes as a martyr, a frail and suffering human being. Dressed in black, she stepped out of the darkness into a blaze of light in the opening scene. Eugen Klopfer's remarkable performance was noted for his presentation of the Lawyer as a Christ figure from the slums, "a mixture of a man from the lower depths and a ghost" (qtd. in Marker and Marker 81). These performances resonated with the experiences of Berliners emerging from the desolation of the war. Contributing to the operations of local semiosis, the use of performers well known to spectators from previous productions usually enhances receptivity, as it did in Berlin. Interestingly, while Stockholm spectators experienced their own performers speaking their own language on the stage, the foreignness of the directorial vision and that of the visual and musical elements seem to have cannibalized the performance in the perceptions of the Swedish audience. The production of the same play text, translated into the language of the local audience, produced different perceptions in Berlin than it did in its original language in Stockholm.

The afterlife of Reinhardt's version of *A Dream Play* in Stockholm demonstrates how local semiosis continues to evolve over time, sometimes for decades after the closing of the performance. This process is aided by the phenomenon of "ghosting," central to the theatrical experience historically. The recycling of texts, spaces, bodies, and other elements of theatrical performance prompts in spectators an awareness not of similarity, but of identity, of what had been experienced before. The memory of previous performances or previously experienced elements of a performance haunts and affects the meanings construed by the current experience. By way of ghosting, dramatic texts, as staged again and again in the theater, become sites for "storage and mechanism for the continued recirculation of cultural memory" (Carlson, *Haunted Stage* 8).

The reception of *A Dream Play*'s next staging in Sweden fourteen years later sheds light on the process of ghosting and the continued workings of local semiosis around the play-text. *A Dream Play* was staged again at the Royal Dramatic Theater in Stockholm in 1935 directed by Olof

Molander (1892–1966). In this epoch-making production, Molander's approach was inspired by the work of one of the early and most influential Strindberg scholars, Martin Lamm. In his two-volume book on Strindberg's drama, Lamm explored the autobiographical background of each play in great detail (Lamm, *Strindbergs dramer*). In a pre-production interview published in *Dagens Nyheter,* Molander explained his directorial concept. He argued, after Lamm, that *A Dream Play* was the most autobiographical among Strindberg's plays and claimed that he discovered "a line—Strindberg's own lifeline" encoded in the text. According to this view, Strindberg represented life exactly as he experienced it, and therefore his dream images on the stage must have "an incredible reality." For Molander this translated into a realistic—or rather, as he called it in the interview, "hyper-realistic"—presentation of the dream sequences (Bark 118–19, my translation). While Molander's emphasis on realism was a reaction to what he thought was Reinhardt's exaggerated and subjectively distorted foregrounding of the negative aspects of life, he also rejected Strindberg's demand for a stylized visual presentation. Thus Lamm's commentary and the perceived need to reaffirm the distinct Swedishness of *A Dream Play* prompted an encoding which suppressed both the foreignness of the previous production still haunting the play's performance tradition and Strindberg's expressed call for the "dematerialization" of the dream (Strindberg 293/234).

One of the innovations of Molander's production—directly related to his biographical reading of the play—was his identification of the three male lead characters with Strindberg (Lamm, *August Strindberg* 324–26). Lars Hanson in the role of the Officer presented the author's youthful and passionate alter ego, and he was praised by critics for creating one of the most memorable and—as opposed to Reinhardt's actor fourteen years earlier—most "Swedish" characters in the performance:

> His . . . face radiated childish goodness and unsuspecting openness, which, with all his silly absentmindedness, made him quite irresistible. His chivalric, blond, Swedish lieutenant-appearance revealed a boyishness, which made it entirely natural for us to discover him again at the school-bench. (Beijer 209, my translation)

Gabriel Alw, as the Lawyer with a tormented Christ-like face, played the mature Strindberg persona, and Ivar Kåge, as the wise elderly Poet, even wore a Strindberg mask. Contrary to Reinhardt's production, where the Poet was simply one of the anguished and struggling people, Molander gave the Poet the superior role of "the omniscient consciousness, the artist dreamer" (Marker and Marker 84). Elements of local color and hints at Strindberg's life could be found in each scene, and in Molander's staging the Strindberg of *A Dream Play* became

> a Swedish Strindberg who dreamed of the Swedish archipelago and of the turn-of-the-century Stockholm milieu. All the fantastical elements of the play had such a powerful effect, not because, as in the German production [of Reinhardt] they were stressed and made profound, but because they appeared a natural part of reality. (Ollén 410, my translation)

Thus, while Reinhardt's staging of the play had been noted in Sweden for its "foreignness," Molander capitalized on audiences' familiarity with the dramatist's life and the Swedish milieus, and his production became a great audience and critical success.

It is interesting to note how unstable the system of signifieds appears across the different performances, and how meanings of the same play are constructed by the changing cultural context of its performance. What in Reinhardt's direction stood for soul-landscapes and the torment and anguish of a collective consciousness turned into heart-warming memories of childhood and youth charted onto the hyper-realistic landscape shared by the long-dead playwright and the audience. A new, distinctly Swedish tradition of Strindberg performance was initiated by Martin Lamm's authoritative mapping of the playwright's life onto his texts—a critical interpretation, which in turn was built into the semiotic coding of subsequent Swedish productions for a long time to come. But as the perceived "foreignness" of Reinhardt's earlier production shows, Lamm's scholarly analysis and Molander's artistic interpretation responded to the already culturally defined expectations of the Swedish public. Reinhardt's *A Dream Play* in Stockholm, at the Swedish national theater, geographically located at the center of high culture in the heart of the Swedish capital, failed to change these expectations, and therefore it can be seen as an example of "acculturation," or the "inscription of a . . . foreign code in a native structure" which resists its assimilation (Weber 35). Even though the Stockholm production was staged in the original language shared by the playwright and the audience, a sense of otherness dominated the theatrical experience because of the directorial encoding. This otherness of the stage director's vision challenged the processes of local semiosis that were to shape the theatrical experience as a whole. Reinhardt's version of the same production in Berlin, however, seems to have accomplished a genuine transculturation of Strindberg's piece, its integration into the local cultural context, the deconstruction of the codes of "Swedishness," and "its wrenching displacement to a 'historically and socially different situation' " (Weber 35). Discussing cases of theatrical transculturation, Carl Weber here cites the Polish critic Jan Kott, whose famous book *Shakespeare, Our Contemporary* (published in English in 1964) influenced several Shakespeare productions, including Peter Brook's *A Midsummer Night's Dream* and *King Lear* at the Royal Shakespeare Company in the early 1970s. Kott's scholarly assessment of Shakespeare, which grew out of the cultural ferment of the era, thus contributed to local semiosis in a way similar to the role of Lamm in inspiring Swedish Strindberg productions in the 1930s. Yet, while Kott's approach opened up classic dramatic texts to resonate with the experience of contemporary audiences across the European cultural landscape, Lamm's biographical mapping of Strindberg's plays worked to delimit the range of valid interpretations to the experience of a Swedish audience.

Erik XIV and the Russian Revolution

In 1899 Strindberg wrote a play about the dethroning of the Swedish king Erik XIV (1533–77). Eighteen years later, the last ruler of the Russian Empire, Tsar Nicholas II, was swept away in a series of cataclysmic events known as the Russian Revolution. The 1921 production of *Erik XIV* in Moscow was a remarkable instance of a Strindberg play mingling with the drama that unfolded at the time and place of its performance. *Erik XIV* was the first of Evgeny Vakhtangov's (1883–1922) last three productions before his untimely death from cancer. This work also came to mark a turning point in his artistic outlook at which the formerly avid disciple of Konstantin Stanislavsky (cofounder and leader of the Moscow Art Theater) departed from the latter's naturalism and started developing an avant-garde and anti-realistic stage technique.

In *Erik XIV* Strindberg created a fascinating character study of a weak ruler whose mind breaks down as he becomes a victim of circumstances. In the Moscow production the tragic predicament of the Swedish king was adapted to the postrevolutionary Russian context, where all performance aspects were calibrated to echo the tumultuous sociopolitical moment. At this time Moscow was the seat of the Bolshevik government, which had fought a bloody civil war since 1917. As revolutionary Russia moved the power center from imperial Petrograd to Moscow, the city became the site of a complex political, strategic, and cultural activity of extraordinary intensity. The headquarters of the government and those of the Soviet State Committee of Defense and the General Staff of the

Red Army were in Moscow at this time. The streets of Moscow were brimming with parades and marches celebrating holidays of the labor movement and meetings of the Third International, and open-air mass spectacles with thousands of participants and tens of thousands of spectators reenacted the triumphant battles of the Revolution and the Civil War. A whole young generation of avant-garde artists (including the creators of the *Erik XIV* production) rejected the "bourgeois materialism" of the realistic tradition and threw themselves into constructivist, cubist, and futurist experiments under the slogan "Art into Life." They presented "living newspapers" and organized agitprop brigades that performed revolutionary poems and propaganda skits in a circus- and poster-like fashion at improvised spaces in the streets, at factories, department stores, and construction sites (Baer, "Manifestos"). In 1919 a newspaper columnist wrote, "It is hardly possible to point to any other epoch when the theatre would have occupied such an exceptionally great place in people's lives. . . . Everywhere, throughout the . . . Republic, there is an insatiable thirst for the theatre." Another contemporary testimony stated, "All Russia is acting, some kind of elemental process is taking place where the living fabric of life is being transformed into the theatrical" (Rudnitsky 41).

While in imperial Russia the theater had been the privilege of the educated upper classes, following the October Revolution factory workers, peasants, and soldiers filled the auditoriums. Anatoly Lunacharsky, the first people's commissar for education, called upon the theater both to educate the people (large portions of the population were illiterate at the time) and to serve as a platform for political agitation (see Rudnitsky 41). In this ferment of social change, the role of the theater was also redefined. Artists who had experimented with avant-garde techniques before the revolution, including Vladimir Tatlin, Alexandra Exter, Liubov Popova, and many others, found a testing ground for new ideas in the collective medium of the theater. Even Kazimir Malevich seems to have moved into abstraction via the theater, with his set and costume designs for the "futurist spectacle" *Victory over the Sun* (*Pobeda nad soltsem*) at the Luna Park Theater in St. Petersburg in 1913. In the wake of the October Revolution, Vsevolod Meyerhold, the director who had staged *Crimes and Crimes* in 1912, invented the term "Theatrical October" to indicate that social revolution goes hand-in-hand with a theatrical revolution (Baer, "Design").

The production of *Erik XIV* was part of the theatrical flurry in Moscow. It was an avant-garde performance at the Moscow Art Theater's First Studio—a training ground for young actors—directed by Vakhtangov. Michael Chekhov, one of the greatest actors of the era, played the title role, and renowned artist/architect/designer Ignaty Nivinsky created the scenery and costumes. The collaboration of these three figures—the director, performer, and designer—resulted in a unique topical interpretation of Strindberg's play. The performance, though non-realistic, still reflected the deepest felt reality of contemporary Moscow audiences.

In April 1919, bound to his hospital bed, Vakhtangov wrote several notes and articles on "the theater of the people," including "The Responsibility of the Artist," which reads as an artistic manifesto for the postrevolutionary period and clearly corresponds with his directorial approach and interpretation of *Erik XIV:*

> The red line of the Revolution divided the world into "the old" and "the new." Not a single area of human life is left unaffected. . . . The material, spiritual, psychological, and intellectual realms of our existence have all been stirred up by a powerful thunderstorm the like of which is unknown in history. . . . There are still some . . . who believe that the fire brigades will step in and extinguish the fire that had been smoldering in the souls of the people for centuries. They should . . . read the books that tell the stories, not of Granddad Tsar, but of the life of that thousand-faced creature called the People! . . . If the artist wants to create "the new" after the arrival of the Revolution, then s/he must create together "with" the people. . . . In order to triumph in creating "the new" the artist . . . needs the touch of the motherland. This motherland is the people. . . . What "people" do I mean? Since we are all people. I mean the people who created the Revolution. (Neumark 263, 265–67, my translation)

On March 26, 1921, preparing for a series of projected, though unrealized, lectures at the First Studio in conjunction with the rehearsals of *Erik XIV,* Vakhtangov jotted down some notes in regard to the theater of the times. "Death to naturalism," declares the former Stanislavsky disciple. He now condemns the detailed representation of reality on the stage and rejects the character actor in favor of the performer who is able to grasp the typical and the grotesque in the character (Neumark 273–75). In his directorial notes Vakhtangov analyzes Erik's character as a type representing the self-destructive despot:

> Erik is destined to misfortune.
> He creates only to destroy.
> He is caught up in the struggle between the dying world of the ghostly, bloodless courtiers and the lively world of simple people. . . . Heaven and hell, fire and water, master and slave—he is forged of contrasts

> [and therefore] he must inevitably destroy himself. And he is destroyed. His successor mounts the throne to the tact of the funeral march. . . . And the executioner already stands behind the throne. Autocracy, self-contradictory in its very being, will be destroyed sooner or later. The new king will follow the same fate. (Neumark 282–83, my translation)

Vakhtangov then goes on to articulate the new artistic direction that the studio was to take with the production of *Erik XIV.* He describes a programmatic transculturation of the Swedish history play, where the formal production elements would provide the new signifying system that connects the piece with the contemporary audience:

> When the MAT's Studio decided to put on a play by Strindberg (for whom, according to *Kultura Tyeatra,* enthusiasm in Germany has amounted to a veritable cult), it aimed at creating a performance where the interior content would give meaning to the . . . form. The interpretation of each . . . element of the play stems from our own time. . . . [Thus] the performance style (the decaying world of the court—a heavy, static, and rigid world—contrasted with the vivacious world [of the common people]—a dynamic and colorful world), and the solutions for the sets and costumes . . . were all dictated by a sense of contemporaneity. . . . Until now, true to the teachings of Stanislavsky, the Studio strove to learn the art of empathy. . . . Now the Studio enters a new phase of exploring theatrical forms. This is our first experiment for which our era of the Revolution showed the way. (Neumark 284, my translation)

Vakhtangov's statement is confirmed by the recollections of Serafima Birman, the actress in the role of the Dowager Queen, written in 1962. According to Birman, the production focused on the main theme of the play: the relationship between the people and the ruler. At this time, the actors were as keenly aware as the director that the tasks of the studio had become more complex than before. The goal to accomplish "the closest possible imitation of life" was replaced by the endeavor to present "a summary of the essential factors of life." When judging the performance, Birman reminds us, "one must not forget the time of its creation. The opinions of spectators and critics . . . of the time differed from those of later generations." Later critics denounced the production as a deviation from leftist theater, a formalist and abstract performance. Birman feels that the audience and critics in 1921 understood that Vakhtangov's purpose was to express the tragedy of the people and of Erik by new, innovative means:

> This performance was about . . . how the common people . . . were turned into a faceless mob by a nobility doomed to death, and how they were humiliated by their insane ruler. In a country where autocracy had been abolished only recently; where the foundations of a new order that would secure freedom for all working people had been laid down only recently, the message of the play was clearly understood both by us actors and by the spectators. . . . Instead of plays dealing with personal problems in stuffy, confined rooms, we longed for the expansion of space, for wider perspectives. This striving was splendidly expressed by the directorial interpretation. (Neumark 285, my translation)

For the mise-en-scène Vakhtangov envisioned "arrows on the crown, arrows on the sword, arrows on the clothes, on the faces, and on the walls," which provided the central visual motif for the production (Neumark 283, my translation). Flashes of lightning, often suggested simply by abstract zigzag lines, were repeated in every aspect of Nivinsky's designs, including the sets, the costumes, and the makeup. Michael Chekhov's Erik, for example, had blood-red arrows on his costume that "symbolized the blood which was on his conscience," while the exaggerated zigzag shape of his eyebrows lent his character "the mark of insanity." Even his first entrance was like "a dart of lightning" in an effort to immediately "shoot the audience inwardly" (Worrall 118). Serafima Birman also describes how the Queen's state of mind was physicalized in her outward appearance. The actress created a mask-like facial expression by fastening one of her eyelids so that she could not close her eye, thus fixing even internally the sensation that half of the Queen's face, as well as her spirit, was paralyzed (Neumark 285). One critic wrote, "Birman, as the widow, skeletonic and sinister, brings on to the stage the chill of the grave. The acting of the dead is peculiarly queer and rigid, . . . the voices flat and savourless, the eyes unseeing. Even in scenes of violent action the dead forms move with bloated, purplish weight of decay" (qtd. in Worrall 115).

In his "cumbersome silver attire" Michael Chekhov played Erik as seemingly apathetic and indifferent, "then suddenly driven into furious activity by terror, the impotence of rage. . . . Abnormally dilating eyes, dropping intonation and the nervous movement of his thin hands betrayed suffering and anguish. At the moment when Erik threw the magnificent royal mantle from his shoulders with one short, quick movement, his boyish thinness, his frailty immediately became apparent. Erik personified weakness itself, impotence itself" (Rudnitsky 53).

This comment suggests that Moscow audiences identified Erik with Nicholas II, the last Russian tsar who was forced to abdicate in response to the 1917 February Revolution. Nicholas is historically regarded as an incompetent monarch, unfit for the daunting task of ruling the immense Russian Empire (Ferro 2). Similarly to Erik XIV, who in historical records is unfavorably compared to his great father, Gustav Vasa, Nicholas has often been described as a mockery of his father, Alexander III. Of Michael Chekhov's presentation reviewers reported that he

> found an accentuated and articulate form for the rendition of the tragic quality of Erik—in every gesture, movement, posture in space: the hand that darted out and remained suspended in the air; the hopeless melancholic gaze of the sick, wide-opened eyes on the elongated, wondering face; the thin hands and feet slipping out from the silver raiments; the sudden upflights and plungings of the now timid and now bold movements. (qtd. in Gordon 9)

Nivinsky's cubist-expressionistic scenery provided a frame of reference that linked the Swedish history play to the contemporary Russian circumstances. The set designs echoed Nivinsky's 1919 painting, *Red Lightning,* which is a modernist allegory of the October Revolution. In the painting the modern rectangular shapes of working people's houses and factory chimneys, and a marching Red Army regiment, are juxtaposed with the classically shaped palaces of the aristocracy who flee from the relentless thunderbolts commanded by the revolution: the forceful figure of a proletarian-soldier towering above the rooftops. The dark red of the new clashes with the faded gold of the old world. Similar visual techniques—the juxtaposition of the old and new, the breaking up of the picture plane and of linear perspective, and the angular shapes of shafts of lightning that pierce the surface of the image—are characteristic of Nivinsky's sets for *Erik XIV.* In his design for act 1 the old world still dominates: the terrace of the royal palace with its heavy columns and classical ornamentation creates a dark, cave-like interior with a vista of church spires blocking the horizon. The view thus provided follows Strindberg's stage directions, but the churches show strikingly Russian features, and the geometrical forms combined with an expressionistic use of chiaroscuro evoke a sense of uneasy stillness and impending volcanic eruption. The asymmetrical composition and a clash of curves and sharp angles eliminate visual harmony and lend a sense of unrest and foreboding to the image.

The design for act 2, which is set at Göran Persson's (the King's Chancellor, played by Boris Sushkevich) home, is more realistic than those for the first and the last act, in the sense that it truly represents the interior of a house. There are variations of stylistic elements from act 1; for example, the grid pattern of the tiled floor and coffered ceiling is now repeated in the window bars, recapitulating the arrow motif, which suggests the constant threat of the revolution as well as a sense of imprisonment. The design for the final act shows the royal palace again, but by now the churches have disappeared; the central supporting column leans as if toppled; and a whirlwind of zigzagging lines create a structure that seems to collapse upon itself. The grids and arrows have become more chaotic, showing the palace as a prison-like and deathly place at the edge of an abyss (Rudnitsky 53).

Even the lighting effects contributed to the correspondence between the stage-world and the contemporary reality outside the theater, suggesting both Erik's disturbed mental state and the extraordinary, tense life of the city. Accounts recall angular streaks of lightning flickering against a black backdrop, and claim that

> it was impossible to separate [this production] from [the] Moscow of the period, from destroyed buildings, red flags, street posters, Red Army detachments on the march, search lights stabbing the night sky above the Kremlin, solitary automobiles cutting through the streets and rumors flying from flat to flat. (qtd. in Rudnitsky 53)

Vakhtangov's staging set the courtiers' ghostlike figures against the "sullen, threatening crowd of common people" who, in act 4, invaded "the inner sanctum of the palace" (Rudnitsky 53). In keeping with the logic of his analysis of Erik's self-destructive nature, Vakhtangov took the liberty of changing the ending. Critic Victor Gromov describes the concluding scene thus:

> Göran Persson bursts out in despair: "We are done for!" . . . And Erik, along with Göran, takes his own life. Strindberg's text does not suggest their suicide. This was interpolated by Vakhtangov, following a clear artistic logic. Erik drinks poison . . . and Göran asks for his share. . . . The poison acts instantaneously: sagging strangely, Erik-Chekhov extends his hand toward Göran and says quietly, "Take me to Karin." And Göran utters his last sentence just as quietly, "I take you . . . as always . . . wherever you want!" They exit together—into death.
>
> Meanwhile the wedding banquet has ended. The people, led by Måns [Karin's father], prepare to hail the king; the castle, however, has been invaded by the rebellious princes, and the people are ordered to cheer the new king, John, instead of Erik. John enters with solemn, heavy gait,

> like a stone statue. . . . When Prince Carl reminds him of his promise of sharing the throne, John spits out his words sharply: "I don't know—what—you mean!" Amidst the confused cries of the frightened people, "Hail our King John III," the curtain descends. (Neumark 287, my translation)

For audiences and critics in 1921 the performance of *Erik XIV* revealed the disintegration of a power structure that had been recycled for centuries. But as Serafima Birman points out in her memoirs, the production was judged by later critics quite differently. In his study of leading figures of the Soviet stage, Nick Worrall cites the view of Vakhtangov's biographer N. G. Zograf that "the production did not focus on the struggle against feudalism, or on the situation of the people, but on the psychological drama" of Erik, which led to an interpretation of the play as an expressionistic monodrama, where everything and everyone was shown through Erik's distorted perspective (Worrall 93). Zograf's comments, however, must be taken with caution, as they clearly contradict testimonies by contemporary critics, the performers, and the director himself. Zograf's book was published in 1939, when socialist realism prevailed as the official aesthetic, which implied that previous avant-garde experiments had to be devalued as decadent bourgeois art. While according to pictorial evidence and contemporary accounts each element of the production was indeed distinctly expressionistic, the style did not serve to focus on the psychology of the central character, but on the contrary, to visualize the underlying social and political themes. As he wrote and published in the late 1930s and 1940s, it is no wonder that Zograf denounces Vakhtangov's first successful attempt to depart from Stanislavsky's naturalism at a time when Stalin's purges of the intelligentsia—including Meyerhold's arrest, torture, and execution—affected all areas of culture, not the least literary and theatrical criticism. It is ironic that Stanislavsky's realism, the only tolerated, and even encouraged, theatrical style that survived the Stalinist era, has its origins in pre-revolutionary bourgeois culture (Baer, "Design" 59). Zograf's interpretation of the production is interesting not because of its factuality, but because it reveals how the processes of local semiosis keep reconfiguring the meanings of performances long after their fleeting existence. As Worral's 1989 citation indicates, Zograf's ideological framing of a performance from eighteen years before contributes to how the production is received even half a century later.

For audiences in 1921 the dramatic-visual universe of the performance suggested clear parallels with the doomed last days of the Russian autocracy on the one hand and reflected the present-day reality of Moscow residents on the other. This was an era of soaring hopes and optimism at the dawn of a new world order and of exultation over bringing an end to age-old subjugation. But it was also an era of chaos and fear; of clashes between the Red Army and the White Guards; of deportations and persecutions; of Bolshevik squads crushing down on deserters; of famine and devastation both in the rural and urban areas; of millions of deaths suffered in a prolonged civil war. *Erik XIV* partook in the performance of world-historical change as it mirrored the riveting drama going on in the streets outside the theater, where the Russian people struggled to rewrite their own history. Strindberg's play about the Swedish king thus achieved "the crossing of cultural borders between nations/societies" in the performance event. Performance scholars have observed many such crossings in the history of the avant-garde and theorized that whenever "a society's stage was ripe for a change because its traditional performance codes had become obsolete," artists turned to ideas, forms, and structures from other—often geographically or temporally distant—cultures (Weber 36). Both Reinhardt's production of *A Dream Play* in Berlin and Vakhtangov's *Erik XIV* in Moscow were instances where the integration of the "foreign" into the "own" fostered new modes of performance directly responding to local and contemporary social realities.

Notes

1. The first page number in this citation indicates a published English translation of Strindberg's text, and the second refers to the Swedish original, as found in *Samlade Verk*.

Works Cited

Antoine, André. *Memories of the Théâtre-Libre*. Trans. Marvin Carlson. Ed. H. D. Albright. Coral Gables, Fla.: University of Miami Press, 1964.

Baer, Nancy van Norman. "Design and Movement in the Theatre of the Russian Avant-Garde." In *Theatre in Revolution: Russian Avant-Garde Stage Design 1913–1935*, ed. Nancy van Norman Baer, 35–59. New York: Thames and Hudson, 1992.

———. "Manifestos of the Russian Avant-Garde." In *Theatre in Revolution: Russian Avant-Garde Stage Design 1913–1935*, ed. Nancy van Norman Baer, 176–84. New York: Thames and Hudson, 1992.

Bark, Richard. *Strindbergs drömspelteknik i drama och teater.* Lund: Studentlitteratur, 1981.

Beijer, Agne. *Teaterrecensioner 1925–1949*. Stockholm: Föreningen Drottningholmsteaterns Vänner, 1954.

Braun, Edward. *Meyerhold: A Revolution in Theatre*. Iowa City: University of Iowa Press, 1995.

Carlson, Marvin. *The Haunted Stage: The Theatre as Memory Machine*. Ann Arbor: University of Michigan Press, 2001.

———. *Theatre Semiotics: Signs of Life.* Bloomington: Indiana University Press, 1990.

Ferro, Marc. *Nicholas II: Last of the Tsars.* Trans. Brian Pearce. Oxford: Oxford University Press, 1995.

Gordon, Mel. "Michael Chekhov's Life and Work: A Descriptive Chronology." *TDR* 27, no. 3 (Autumn 1983): 3–21.

Innes, Christopher. *Avant-Garde Theatre, 1892–1992.* London: Routledge, 1993.

Kott, Jan. *Shakespeare, Our Contemporary.* Garden City, N.Y.: Doubleday, 1964.

Kvam, Kela. *Max Reinhardt og Strindbergs visionære dramatik.* Copenhagen: Akademisk forlag, 1974.

Lamm, Martin. *August Strindberg.* Stockholm: Bonniers, 1948.

———. *Strindbergs dramer.* Vols. 1, 2. Stockholm: Bonniers, 1924, 1926.

Marker, Frederick J., and Lise-Lone Marker. *Strindberg and Modernist Theatre: Post-Inferno Drama on the Stage.* Cambridge, Eng.: Cambridge University Press, 2002.

Marranca, Bonnie, Marc Robinson, and Una Chaudhuri. "Criticism, Culture, and Performance: An Interview with Edward Said." In *Interculturalism and Performance,* ed. Bonnie Marranca and Gautam Dasgupta. New York: PAJ Publications, 1991. 38–59.

Neumark, Anna, ed. *Vakhtangov műhelye.* Budapest: Gondolat, 1979.

Nikolajeva, Maria. "Strindberg Through the Eyes of the Russian Critics." In *The Moscow Papers,* ed. Michael Robinson. Stockholm: Strindbergssällskapet, 1998.

Ollén, Gunnar. *Strindbergs dramatik.* Stockholm: Sveriges Radio, 1961.

Rudnitsky, Konstantin. *Russian and Soviet Theater 1905–1932.* Trans. R. Permar. New York: Harry N. Abrams, 1988.

Strindberg, August. *Open Letters to the Intimate Theater.* Trans. W. Johnson. Seattle: University of Washington Press, 1966.

———. *Teater och Intima Teatern.* In *Samlade Verk* vol. 64. Ed. Per Stam. Stockholm: Norstedt, 1999.

Szalczer, Eszter. *August Strindberg.* London: Routledge, 2011.

Weber, Carl. "AC/TC: Currents of Theatrical Exchange." In *Interculturalism and Performance,* ed. Bonnie Marranca and Gautam Dasgupta. New York: PAJ Publications, 1991. 27–37.

Weinsheimer, Joel C. *Gadamer's Hermeneutics: A Reading of "Truth and Method."* New Haven, Conn.: Yale University Press, 1985.

Worrall, Nick. *Modernism to Realism on the Soviet Stage: Tairov—Vakhtangov—Okhlopkov.* Cambridge, Eng.: Cambridge University Press, 1989.

Castration Anxiety and Traumatic Encounters with the Real in the Works of August Strindberg and Lars von Trier

MADS BUNCH

It is commonly acknowledged by scholars that August Strindberg has been a source of inspiration for Danish director Lars von Trier, not least due to the many interviews following the release of *Antichrist* (2009), in which von Trier himself has pointed out the connections to Strindberg.[1] It seems, however, that this pertinent influence runs much deeper than what has so far been uncovered. In fact, the influence from Strindberg seems to permeate the works of von Trier on so many levels that he could arguably be regarded as one of the director's *most* important influences. Both have been understood as radical visionaries within their aesthetic form of expression, and specifically as purveyors of a distinct Nordic radicalism. Von Trier's varied cinematic expression includes the technically brilliant montage and back projection strategies of the meta-noir early masterpiece *Zentropa* (1991), the spearheading of the Dogme 95 movement, and the experimental films of *Dogville* (2003) and *Manderlay* (2005). Von Trier has called the two latter "fusion films"—"a fusion between, film, theatre and literature" (Björkman 241)—and coined the "fusion film" as a whole new genre.

Like Strindberg's heterogeneous dramatic production, spanning the naturalist reimagination of stage space, décor, and costume in *Miss Julie* (*Fröken Julie,* 1888) to the fluid spatio-temporality of *A Dream Play* (*Ett drömspel,* 1901) with an experimental set design, von Trier's films continue to challenge commonly acknowledged artistic genres and forms and, like Strindberg's did, export a particular branch of radical Scandinavian modernism abroad. Von Trier's "Dogme 95 Manifesto" and "Vow of Chastity" (both 1995; *Dogme 95,* uncredited) can even be regarded as a meta-connection to Strindberg's naturalist manifesto in the "Preface" to *Miss Julie,* where Strindberg is propagating a new naturalistic theater form. Von Trier's manifestos also propagate a new radical naturalism in cinema (handheld camera, no artificial sets, no music, etc.). His arguments and criticism of 1995 filmmaking praxis have many similarities to the ones Strindberg uses with regard to the theater tradition in 1888. Von Trier's fusion films can also be seen as another way to follow in Strindberg's footsteps by trying to invent a whole new form, just as Strindberg did in his later experimental and expressionistic plays.

Von Trier's interest in Strindberg started years before he began making films. He grew up only a few miles away from Skovlyst (now Geelsgaard), where Strindberg wrote *Miss Julie* during the turbulent summer of 1888. At the age of twenty, von Trier wrote a long article about Strindberg's stay at Skovlyst and published it in a local newspaper: "På vanviddets rand i Holte. En beretning om August Strindberg i Holte—en frugtbar krisetid" ("On the Brink of Madness in Holte. An Account of August Strindberg in Holte—A Productive Time of Crisis," my trans.) One of the most interesting elements of the article is that Trier signed it Lars *von* Trier. Scholars have mentioned that Trier added the "von" to his name when he was attending the Danish Film School (1979–83) and as a tribute to Joseph von Sternberg or even as a provocation toward his teachers (Stevenson 20–21). But the "von" signature in the newspaper appears three years before von Trier started at the Danish Film School. Von Trier himself points to Strindberg as the main source of inspiration behind this radical decision:

> In the middle of the 1970s I read an awful lot of Strindberg, and Nietzsche, of course. During Strindberg's crisis in Paris—which is always called his "inferno crisis"—he signed his letters "Rex," the royal signature. I thought it was pretty funny. I liked that . . . both the craziness and the arrogance of it. So I started adding a "von" to my name. (Björkman 2)

Aside from adding the "von" to his name, elements from August Strindberg's dramas and personal life have found their way into the films and self-presentation of Lars von Trier (many have indeed associated von Trier with both lunacy and arrogance).

The careers of von Trier and Strindberg also share further characteristics: their works have often been better received abroad than in their home countries. In addition, both continue to challenge norms of social decorum, particularly in their depiction of gender roles and sexuality. Specifically, both deal with gender-based conflicts and psychoanalytical traumas, which appear to challenge persistent Scandinavian and Western identification with rationality, moderation, and social and gender equality. This study will focus on the male protagonists of Strindberg and von Trier in order to show how the psychological complex of castration anxiety permeates the characters and determines their behavior toward the female protagonists.

Slavoj Žižek's Theoretical Framework and Links to Strindberg and von Trier

In order to penetrate and understand the psychoanalytical subject matter in Strindberg's and von Trier's works, the theories of Slovenian philosopher and psychoanalyst Slavoj Žižek will be used because they offer a beneficial theoretical framework for this analysis. Žižek himself mentions both Strindberg's and—especially—von Trier's works more than once in his writings (on Strindberg, see for example *Gaze and Voice as Love Objects* 2, 215, and *Interrogating the Real* 65; on von Trier, see among others "Femininity Between Goodness and Act," *Revolution at the Gates* 219–22, and *Interrogating the Real* 307). No extensive discussion relating Žižek to Strindberg and von Trier has yet been undertaken, which is what I aim to pursue in the following. But before entering into the analysis, I will briefly explain some of the core ideas of Žižek's theoretical framework of relevance to the ensuing discussion.

We find the Real, the Symbolic, and the Imaginary to be the three core elements in what Lacan and Žižek believe to be the triadic (Borromean) structure of all being. What we normally refer to as "reality" is articulated through signification (the symbolic) and the characteristic patterning of images and archetypal fantasies (the imaginary). The Real by contrast does not belong to the (symbolic-imaginary) order of signification but is precisely what cannot be incorporated into such an order. It is a negative ground from which the two others derive. The order of the Symbolic can thus be regarded as an ordered structure (civilization, language) deriving from an ongoing attempt to escape the chaos and disintegrative effects of the Real (death, destruction, disaster, chaos). The structure of the Symbolic is in principle open-ended with its infinite combinations of *signification* and organization, but the Imaginary seeks to domesticate this open-endedness through the imposition of a *fantasmatic* (illusory fantasies that narrate the Symbolic). In other words, the Imaginary arrests the Symbolic around certain fundamental fantasies (Žižek and Daly 6–7), and this way of forming imaginary narratives (fantasies) is a way for us to orient ourselves in the open-endedness of the Symbolic. Most of these fantasies are particular to the individual and function as fundamental narratives upon which we understand and explain ourselves. Žižek uses a brilliant example from the film *The Silence of the Lambs* concerning the female protagonist Clarice Starling to illustrate how the Symbolic is arrested by the Imaginary:

> In a close approximation to a Lacanian psychoanalyst, what Lecter seeks to discover is the specific way in which the symbolic universe of Starling is structured (in tendential terms at least) around a fundamental fantasy—the crying of the lambs and the failed attempt to save them. The point is that Starling makes sense of the world (she is able to narrate symbolically "who she is" for the Other) precisely through a certain arresting fantasy at the level of the imaginary. (Žižek and Daly 6–7)

But some fantasies of death, horror, and trauma are connected to the realm of the Real and are commonly shared (for example, the fear of going blind, being paralyzed, losing one's children, and so on), and in some cases even gender-specific. For example, the male horror fantasy of castration. Aside from uncovering this archetypal male fantasy of castration in the works of Strindberg and von Trier, I will also show how Žižek's newly reworked and expanded theories about the Real (which he now divides into the real Real, the symbolic Real, and the imaginary Real) can be employed to explain the haunting anatomy of the works of Strindberg and von Trier.

Male Protagonists: Castration Anxiety and Impotent Violence

In both Strindberg's and von Trier's works we find male protagonists whose actions are determined and guided by an archetypal neurotic fear of castration as a fundamental fantasy that unconsciously structures their symbolic universe and guides their behavior. The theory of castration ultimately derives from Sigmund Freud but was later developed by Jacques Lacan into a more general theory about the sexes. Subsequently it has been promoted and further developed by Žižek:

> The most salient example of this is in *Totem and Taboo*, where Freud developed Darwin's myth of the primal father. According to Freud, men lived in relatively small groups within which the strongest male jealously prevented sexual promiscuity by keeping all the females for himself. Hence, while all men were subject to his phallic law, there existed one

> male who was not, yet nonetheless by which the law itself was grounded (SE, 13:125). On the basis of this example, one can also describe the masculine formula of sexuation in terms of castration: all men are castrated, but there is one exception that proves the rule. The exception has the function of the father who subsequently establishes the set of men, thereby allowing for a unitary trait: all men are castrated. . . . Lacan's point is that there is no objectifying trait that defines woman as a whole in the way that castration defines men as a whole. (Pound 106–7)

The male protagonists of Strindberg's naturalistic plays are for the most part sensitive yet ambitious men who find themselves trapped in the very rigid, masculine, and authoritarian structure of the late nineteenth century. None of Strindberg's male protagonists are depicted as being able to successfully fulfill the demands of nineteenth-century masculinity, or what Žižek calls "the symbolic 'big Other'—the 'substance' of our social existence, the impersonal set of rules that coordinate our existence" (*Interrogating,* 320), which in this case is the "impersonal set of rules that coordinate" masculinity and potency and define it as "successful provider and breadwinner."

The Captain in *The Father* (*Fadren,* 1887) is ill, sensitive, and his career plans within the military and the sciences are failing, and his relationship with his wife is deteriorating. In *Creditors* (*Fordringsägare,* 1888), the male protagonist Adolf (the same name as Adolf in *The Father* and in character quite similar) is bedridden and physically and mentally ill. He finally dies when he finds out that it is his wife's former husband who has turned up and started manipulating their marriage. Humiliating money problems constantly haunt the Captain from *The Dance of Death* (*Dödsdansen,* 1900), and Jean in *Miss Julie* has become a neurotic due to his low social status and intense feelings of fear and paranoia toward his omnipotent superior, the Count (87/168, 110/190).[2] This inability to live up to the late nineteenth-century demands of a successful macho man (note that both protagonists in *The Father* and *The Dance of Death* are military men) creates for the male protagonists a framework based on humiliation and intense feelings of impotence. In Žižekian terms, the imaginary fantasy of castration becomes the fundamental fantasy with which they arrest the Symbolic around and which guides their behavior toward the female protagonists. This behavior commonly plays out as accusations that the female protagonists look down upon them and only want to control them and spoil their prospects for recognition in the military, science, or business. Or it plays out as impotent accusations of adultery, most prominent in *The Father* and *Creditors,* which literally points out the male protagonist's fear of castration and emasculation. Some of the female protagonists in Strindberg's plays can thus be regarded as "scapegoats"—agents who are blamed for something that has nothing to do with them:

> As Beattie points out, Girard's scapegoat theory sheds further light on psychoanalysis that is applicable to Žižek. It is the nature of scapegoating that one masks the innocence of the victim, and hence the random nature of the sacrificial process. This is what Žižek would call the impotence of violence, violence that acts to mask castration rather than the violence incurred by a traumatic shift within the symbolic itself. (Pound 124)

It is exactly the traumatic shift within the symbolic itself, the impossible demands of patriarchal society for them to be real "macho men" in combination with a time in history when women are asserting their individuality in traditional male-dominated areas, that seems to be the real source of the violence that acts to mask their own castration and impotence. Many of Strindberg's plays deal with this archetypal male complex of castration anxiety, first and foremost simply because it is an integrated, archetypal part of male psychology, but also because Strindberg lived in a specific time in history when gender roles were radically changing for the first time in Western history, causing turbulence, resistance, and insecurity on the part of the male agent, who not only had to live up to the traditional role of the macho man implied by the big Other, but at the same time had to deal with a new, stronger, and more independent woman.

Miss Julie: The Impossible Revolt Against the Big Other

Strindberg also seems to have been very aware that the strict patriarchal hierarchies of the late nineteenth century produced anxiety and paranoia. In his semiautobiographical *Son of a Servant* (*Tjänstekvinnans son I–II,* 1886), Strindberg indicates how this strict power structure produces male anxiety:

> Above him loomed a hierarchy of authorities wielding various rights, from the right of seniority of his brothers to the supreme tribunal of his father. And yet above his father was the deputy-landlord, who always threatened him with the landlord. This last was generally invisible because he lived in the country, and perhaps, for that reason, was the most feared of all. (2/10)

Many of Strindberg's plays, for example, *Miss Julie, The Dance of Death,* and *A Dream Play,* operate with this notion of an invisible—seemingly omnipotent—agency of power which is haunting the male protagonists, creating paranoia and trauma. This agency is what Žižek calls the Other of the big Other, "who effectively 'pulls the strings' behind the visible, public Power. This other, obscene, invisible power structure acts the part of the 'Other of the Other' in the Lacanian sense, the part of the meta-guarantee of the consistency of the big Other (the symbolic order that regulates social life)" ("The Big Other Doesn't Exist"). In nineteenth-century society, God normally played the role of "the Other of the big Other," the meta-guarantee for the consistency of Christian-bourgeois norms (the big Other) and the notions of the sanctity of marriage and the submissive role of the woman. We can regard "the Count" in Strindberg's most frequently staged play, *Miss Julie,* as an equivalent to this anxiety-producing agency, "the Other of the big Other," who has immense influence over the behavior of the characters—especially Jean—even though he is not physically there (like God):

> What's that? I thought the bell moved!—No! Shall we stop it with paper ——To be so afraid of a bell!—Yes, but it's not just a bell—there's somebody behind it—a hand sets it in motion—and something else sets that hand in motion—but if you stop your ears—just stop your ears! Yes, but then he'll go on ringing even louder—and keep on ringing until someone answers. (110/190)

The Count is indeed an omnipotent authority, the "Other of the big Other," who guarantees the late feudal social norms of division (the big Other) still in play at the estate, and Jean is indeed the impotent subject of his whims and wills, as we see in the above quotation. But as the play unfolds, this structure is reversed, and we witness how a seemingly impotent man, symbolically castrated by the Count, for just one night is granted the power and potency of the agency oppressing and castrating him, when he gets a chance to have sex with the Count's daughter. Jean is aware of how his ambitions "to climb" (the social ladder) are impossible in the type of society he lives in, and he ultimately takes this frustration out on Miss Julie. His having sex with her becomes a violent act of impotence, since their relationship is not possible within the structure of late-nineteenth-century social reality, which he is perfectly aware of and even though she tries to fool herself into believing otherwise. The sexual encounter must then be understood as a way for him to get revenge on a society, the big Other, represented by Miss Julie in the absence of the Count—a patriarchal society that symbolically has castrated him by denying him the right to climb socially and choose his own sexual partners, even though he is intelligent, hardworking, and ambitious. A traumatic gridlock in the symbolic order prevents him from building a better life for himself, and when he cannot build, he chooses to destroy. Having sex with the daughter of the omnipotent Count (the Freudian "primal father") becomes his revenge, but he is also painfully aware that if the affair comes out, his life will be ruined. He will be facing charges of rape and adultery and probably life in prison and maybe even death. A real revolt is impossible, and if he wants to save himself from the omnipotent destructive powers of the Count, who has just returned to the estate, the only way out is Miss Julie's suicide.

Manderlay: Von Trier's *Miss Julie*

Manderlay (2003) stands out as von Trier's most prominent rewriting of Strindberg's *Miss Julie*. The connection has been widely overlooked by scholars, because attention so far has focused on *Breaking the Waves* (1996)[3] and *Antichrist* (Bunch 159). But in *Manderlay* we find a very obvious parallel to the Miss Julie/Jean relation in the protagonist-antagonist couple, Grace and Timothy. In *Manderlay*, Grace is also an upper-class woman (a "society woman," as Timothy calls her) like Miss Julie. In the absence of her father, she has become the new leader of a former slave colony, the estate of Manderlay. Grace is also repeating Miss Julie's fatal encounter with Jean, when she eventually has sex with the former black slave Timothy. A man socially inferior to her like Jean, who in von Trier's script is also described as a "proudy nigger." Timothy's characterization is eerily reminiscent of Jean's statements on working-class pride in *Miss Julie*. The mental battle between Grace and Timothy is further escalated by the clear sexual undertones and explicit erotic tensions, shifting back and forth between attraction and repulsion. Grace, like Miss Julie, also naively believes that everyone is equal, regardless of social class and gender (or race), and that her interaction with the former black slaves is uncomplicated, even though she is in a superior situation. Timothy's pattern of reaction toward his female superior Grace is similar to Jean's and has its roots in the same feelings of inferiority and of being stuck in a situation with no way out. Timothy's impotence is obvious in the bizarre sex scene, where he covers Grace's face with a white handkerchief and stages the intercourse as a kind of rape, where he is holding her down while aggressively penetrating her. In the words of Žižek this is "violence that acts to mask castration," and in this case Timothy literally masks the face of his scapegoat, the innocent object of his violence. He is symbolically raping the powerful agency he is subjugated to, as the only way of compensating for his lack of power in the social hierarchy at Manderlay, where he in fact belongs to the very bottom tier (though Grace believes the opposite to be the case). Grace thus becomes Timothy's scapegoat for problems caused by a traumatic shift within the symbolic order, the breakdown of the old set of regulations (slavery) and new ideas of democracy and free enterprise promoted by this young, self-confident woman in a male-dominated environment.

Another obvious parallel to the traumatic yet hidden agency as represented by "The Count" in *Miss Julie* is Grace's father, the gangster leader. Grace's gangster father shares many characteristics with the Count: he is the hidden, but big, omnipotent agency, "the Other of the big Other," whose persona, power, and money regulate the behavior of the characters without his being physically present. As the absent Count he acts as a guarantee for the consistency of the power of the big Other, in this case the norms and ideas of liberalism and democracy represented by his daughter Grace. This is also von Trier's way of showing how military force and capitalism have taken over as the postmodern version of the Other of the big Other guaranteeing the consistency of the big Other; the ideas of liberalism and democracy as "the impersonal set of rules that coordinate our existence." As Jean points out in *Miss Julie,* "Do you know who your earliest ancestor was? A miller who let the king spend the night with his wife during the Danish war" (96/166). The point is of course that there is no "Other of the big Other" in an ontological sense. These meta-agencies of power are not founded on solid ontological truths but are agencies that primarily function to consolidate and guarantee the consistency of "the visible, public power" (Žižek, "The Big Other Doesn't Exist"), even though the agents of public power claim otherwise.

When Grace's father returns in the last scene, in which he has given Grace one chance—and one chance only—to leave Manderlay with him, we hear the clock of Manderlay strike, which is again an echo of a scene in *Miss Julie,* where Jean thinks he hears the bell move also in the last scene (110/190). But as a result of an absurd decision to vote on what the time should be in Manderlay, the clock is off, and Grace is too late. Her father has left for good, and she is now entirely on her own, fleeing the revenge of the former slaves. As the last image before the closing credits, we find her, lonely and haunted, running across a map of the United

States to the soundtrack of David Bowie's "She Was a Young American." Grace is, in the film, indeed portrayed as a young and naive American (or Western) woman with all the right ideals but without any practical knowledge or experience with the workings of the world. As a sheltered, young upper-class woman, she subscribes to an idealistic fantasy of equality and of crossing the borders of social classes without consequences. This also means that on a deeper psychoanalytical level, Grace's approach to the slaves, while based on her ideals of equality, is just an attempt to avoid the traumatic fact that social groups and cultures are *very different* and that this gap cannot be mediated through an ideological fantasy about freedom and democracy. "What ideology offers is the symbolic construction of reality—the ultimate fantasy—as a way to escape the traumatic effects of the Real" (Žižek and Daly 10).

Von Trier appears to be arguing, along the lines of Žižek, that instead of trying to mediate this fundamental cultural discrepancy through an ideological fantasy of Western liberalism and democracy as the only solution, one should instead acknowledge the gap and try to find other and more complex solutions to a peaceful coexistence (Žižek and Daly 117). Miss Julie and her ideals about equality are also annihilated when reality returns in the guise of the Count and the catastrophic dimension, the Real of her sexual encounter with Jean, shatters her imaginary fantasy of overcoming the social barriers of the late nineteenth century. If Jean faces imprisonment, Miss Julie faces the horror of being pregnant with a bastard child of one of her father's male servants, which is a horrible nightmare fantasy turning frighteningly real. In a society with strict borders between the social classes, this is the worst imaginable scenario for a young upper-class woman (and for her father too), indeed, to such a degree that suicide could be regarded as the better option.

Grace is not destroyed physically like Miss Julie, but is broken down mentally and deeply alienated when she sees her idealistic fantasy disappear in the abyss of the cultural gap between her Western ideology and the ancient "real" mindset of the former slaves. And here von Trier also seems to suggest—along the lines of Strindberg in *Miss Julie*—that one of the worst traumas for a young woman is to lose her idealistic fantasy, the imaginary fantasy that we are all equal, that we as individuals can transgress the borders of culture, class, and race, without any traumatic consequences. In both *Miss Julie* and *Manderlay,* Strindberg and von Trier bluntly show us how the borders of social class, gender, race, and culture will always in some way exist, even though we would like to think differently, and *that* seems to be the real trauma in these two works.

The Echo of the Straitjacket

As we have seen, Strindberg's and von Trier's male protagonists share characteristics, including what appears to be a repetitive reworking of similar psychological issues that hinge on traumatic inferiority complexes, both sexual and social, along the lines of what Žižek outlines as symptomatic of masculinity. One critic suggests that Lars von Trier (not unlike Strindberg) is telling the same story in his films with regard to his male protagonists, depicting a "passive, paranoid man, a megalomaniac, who is bedridden (as in *Breaking the Waves*) or buried alive (as in *Antichrist*), while sexually abusing a sick or mentally ill woman to the point of death in order to produce images of sadomasochist desire and voyeuristically satisfy his sexuality" (Romer n. pag.). Even though Knud Romer's analysis only tells half of the story, he does point out an important common trait for von Trier's male protagonists (especially after the *Europe Trilogy,* 1984–91), which is that they all seem to be trapped or fixated in different ways, physically and mentally. This setup is very obvious in *Breaking the Waves,* where Jan lies in the hospital bed, paralyzed from the neck down and unable to move, but with his brain still functioning. He is in darkest despair and on the brink of a mental breakdown, which he is trying to overcome by asking his wife, Bess, to have sex with strangers in order to compensate for his own broken phallus, which is literally dysfunctional as part of his paralysis.

But the character of the sexually and socially paralyzed man is actually foreshadowed in von Trier's *The Kingdom* II (*Riget* II, 1997). In this television series, the haunting character of Lillebror (Little Brother) makes manifest the essence of male impotence. Little Brother's body grows way too fast, and he must be strung up in the hospital bed in order to prevent his limbs from breaking. The double horror is that Little Brother's mental development is that of a young man in his twenties (he has a grown man's head and full ability to think and speak), even though he is only a few months old. He is being taken care of by the doctors and his mother, to whose decisions he is totally subjected. He is fixated in a traumatizing role, where he is conscious but has no power or potency. There is a pertinent connection to Strindberg's plays in this character figuration in the films of Lars von Trier and there even seems to be a direct meta-narrative connection to *Creditors,* where Tekla consistently calls her ill and bedridden husband Adolf "lilla bror" (little brother) throughout the play (28/229, 29/230, 31/236, 52/272) in order to emasculate him during their venomous discussions: "My heart is so big, you see, little brother, that there's room in it for many more than you" (31/236) and later: "Adolf. 'You hate me then?' Tekla. 'No, I don't. And I don't believe I ever shall. But that of course is because you are a child' " (38/247); this achieves the same effect of castration and emasculation. Even in the final scene, when he dies and she is full of remorse, she calls him both "my darling child" and "little brother" (52/272).

Little Brother's situation in *The Kingdom* is also similar to the infant-like state in which the grown man the Captain finds himself in *The Father* after being lured into the straitjacket at the end of the play (49–53/94–98). By then, the Captain is portrayed as an impotent and powerless child with his arms strapped and trapped in the straitjacket and surrounded by women of three generations, to whose powers he is entirely subjected. Similarly, in von Trier's *Manderlay,* we find Timothy strapped to the whipping block, while Grace is savagely whipping him, and in *Antichrist* we are confronted with a male protagonist bound to a big grindstone by the female protagonist, who is attaching it to his leg while he is unconscious. These different scenes are all different versions of the "Ur-scene," the straitjacket scene from Strindberg's *The Father,* and are different ways for von Trier to symbolically stage the same traumatic condition: the male castration complex.

In many of von Trier's films, the male protagonists try to compensate for feelings of inferiority and impotence through violence exercised toward the female protagonists in order to reclaim the potency they feel is absent. This is a behavior we have seen in many of Strindberg's works too, but this type of impotent violence is taken further in von Trier's films. In *Breaking the Waves,* Jan forces Bess to have sex with strangers; in *Dogville,* Tom turns a blind eye to the sexual abuse of Grace; in *Manderlay,* Timothy performs sadistic intercourse with Grace. There seem to be a fifty–fifty ratio with regard to the outcome of this "battle of the sexes" in von Trier's films, and we actually find just as many of von Trier's male protagonists who eventually break down trying to exercise their power over the female protagonist through various forms of violence (Tom and Timothy), as we find male protagonists succeeding (Jan and "He" in *Antichrist*), just as the case is in regard to Strindberg. Von Trier himself is well aware of the redundancy of this—and other—motifs in his own films: "My story is practically the same every time. I'm well aware of that by now" (Romer n. pag.). But he is also perfectly aware that his male protagonists fail over and over again: "My male protagonists are basically idiots, who don't understand shit. In 'Antichrist,' too. So, of course things get fucked up!" (Romer n. pag.). The so-called misogynistic behavior of the male protagonists in Lars von Trier's films must be understood within this context, namely that von Trier is well aware of the reasons behind his male protagonists' behavior and that these actions are consistent with the psychology of the characters (which is also the case for Strindberg). Von Trier also sees these actions as part of a self-reflexive, indeed meta-narrative, framework for his films connecting him through Strindberg to the artistic tradition of late-nineteenth-century Scandinavian drama. He does not condone their actions but instead points his finger toward what he sees as a common and dominant trait in male psychology: castration anxiety and feelings of impotence compensated for through violence. Von Trier thus manages to say something true about male psychology and behavior, just like Strindberg does in his plays, whether we like it or not.

Traumatic Encounters with the Real

One of the reasons why both Strindberg's and von Trier's work have called forth such strong and opinionated views may be that both address and depict our deepest anxieties and fears with an honesty that is unusual even among avant-garde artists. Their most experimental and challenging works—from *Miss Julie* to *Antichrist*—can, in fact, be closely related to Slavoj Žižek's understanding of the terror and complexity of the Real (indeed, Žižek has been referred to as the "philosopher of the Real" [Myers 29]).

> I'm more and more convinced that there are at least three notions of the Real. I would say that the very triad of real, symbolic and imaginary is in a way mapped onto or projected into the Real itself. So we have to put it in brutal terms: real Real, imaginary Real and Symbolic Real. . . . The result of all this is that, for Lacan, the Real is not impossible in a sense that it can never happen—a traumatic kernel which forever eludes our grasp. No, the problem with the Real is that it happens and *that's* the trauma. *The point is not that the Real is impossible but rather that the impossible is Real.* A trauma, or an act, is simply the point when the Real happens, and this is difficult to accept. . . . One aspect of the Real is that it's impossible, but the other aspect is that it happens but it is impossible to sustain, impossible to integrate. And this second aspect, I think, is more and more crucial. (Žižek and Daly 68–71)

Žižek has developed his notion of the Real through Lacan, Hegel, and Freud. In Strindberg's and von Trier's works we see how the imaginary Real (the collective nightmare fantasies of castration) is turning real Real (is actually coming true for the characters), and that is the true horror of their works: the impossible fantasy is real. Žižek uses the example of the terrorist attacks of 9/11 as an example to describe this phenomenon of trauma caused by the Real as a realization of the imaginary Real:

> Yet it is not simply at the level of cinema and cyberspace that the imaginary Real is experienced. The tragedy of 11 September 2001 can also be looked at from this perspective (Žižek 2002). In a way we could say that, especially for Americans, the trauma was doubly inscribed. First there was the cataclysmic event itself but, second, there was this dimension of the imaginary Real in which popular fantasies regarding the orgiastic destruction of New York (viz. *Independence Day, Godzilla, Deep Impact,* to name but a few) seemed to erupt through to reality—and thereby to render meaningless any escape back to reality. In this way the trauma of 11 September was intensified precisely as a result of this transdimensional breach; this transgression of the subliminal injunction that fantasies should "stay there" and not pursue us. (Žižek and Daly 9–10)

Examples of these archetypal imaginary nightmare fantasies belonging to the imaginary Real that suddenly turn real Real in the case of Strindberg include: that we are not the father of our own children (The Captain in *The Father*), that we will never be able to rise socially even though we have the potential to do so (Jean in *Miss Julie*), that we have sex with a man below our class with the risk of giving birth to a bastard child and being ostracized by society (*Miss Julie*), that the former husband of our wife suddenly turns up and destroys our marriage (*Creditors*), or that we are stuck forever on a small island in a venomous and disastrous relationship (*The Dance of Death*). In the case of von Trier: that we are paralyzed and not able to have sex anymore (Jan in *Breaking the Waves*), that the woman we love turns out to be a Nazi terrorist (Kessler in *Zentropa*), that the woman we love has molested and killed our child and now wants to kill us ("She" in *Antichrist*), that we become pedophile killers without being aware of it (Fisher in *The Element of Crime*), or that we are bringing death and disease instead of the cure without being aware of it (Mesmer in *Epidemic*). Of the archetypal female imaginary fantasies of horror and trauma we can also mention a lineup of worst-case scenarios turning catastrophically real Real: that our child dies in the moment of the highest physical pleasure and that we go mad and self-mutilate ourselves ("She" in *Antichrist*), that our child is asking us to kill it, and we have no other option than to do it (Judith in *The Kingdom* II), that the love of our life turns into a paralyzed sadist asking us to have sex with strangers (Bess in *Breaking the Waves*), or that we are raped by people who promised to protect us (Grace in *Dogville*).

In Strindberg's and von Trier's works we see how these gender-based collective fantasies of horror and destruction belonging to the imaginary Real become real Real, like a nightmare coming true. That is the real trauma for both the protagonists and for us as readers/audience. Žižek further argues that horror movies are built around this dynamic of a nightmare coming true, but where the protagonist fights the demon or serial killer and manages to escape back into reality. But in the experimental, norm-pushing, and self-reflexive works by Strindberg and von Trier, there is no waking up for the protagonists. *The Father* provides a prominent example of how the imaginary Real becomes real Real and there is no waking up. The Captain's paranoid fantasy of the imaginary Real that he is not the "real" father of his child (which is an archetypal male nightmare) actually becomes real (at least in his own imagination), fed by Laura's manipulative suggestions. The Captain himself falls apart and eventually becomes the real Real himself: a representation of pure horror and madness, physically constrained in a straitjacket while he is having a stroke. The imaginary Real becoming real Real, and thus inescapable, is the ultimate kernel of Strindberg's and von Trier's works. It is the very core of their anatomy and what makes them so haunting, since we are all a part of the collective imaginary nightmare fantasies they stage, and that is what makes their works so impossible to escape. And that is also why their works remain so powerful and ultimately so challenging to social conventions, whether those of the late nineteenth century or the early twenty-first century.

Traumatic Struggles with the Idol Strindberg

Von Trier has obviously integrated many serious Strindbergian elements in his films, but Strindberg himself and many core themes from his works are also present as comedy in the works of von Trier. These works include the eight-episode television series *The Kingdom* I–II (1994, 1997) and the feature film *The Boss of It All* (*Chefen for det hele*, 2007). The television series *The Kingdom* is a very special mix of thriller and comedy with "spiritism" and "the occult" as dominant topics and Strindberg as an important part of the meta-narrative. We are introduced to the meta-narrative concerning Strindberg twenty-five minutes into the first episode through Rigmor, Dr. Helmer's partner and head nurse:

RIGMOR: Stig you can be a little brusque, you know. But do you know why I love you?
DR. HELMER: No.
RIGMOR: Would you like to know?
DR. HELMER: No.
RIGMOR: I love you because you are a great man. All the others are so tiny. . . . When are you going to move your things into my place?
DR. HELMER: I have to get settled first.
RIGMOR: My little August Strindberg. You do have his curls.
DR. HELMER: You know I don't like it when you touch my hair.
(*The Kingdom* I, episode 1. My translation.)

The dialogue above reads as if it could have been cut out of one of Strindberg's own plays, and Dr. Helmer (the only Swedish doctor at the hospital called The Kingdom) and his paranoia and dominating, impolite attitude toward the other employees is indeed very similar to the legacy of Strindberg's attitude and behavior in real life. *The Kingdom* also stages a parody of one of the core themes in Strindberg's and von Trier's works, "the battle of the sexes." The parody is illustrated by the relationship between Dr. Helmer and Rigmor that turns increasingly venomous as the TV series progresses and culminates in the bizarre and very funny scene where Rigmor blackmails Dr. Helmer into marrying her, using an anesthesia report that proves Dr. Helmer is guilty of severe medical malpractice. The Swedish actor Ernst Hugo Järegård, who plays Dr. Helmer, furthermore has a physical appearance that is strikingly similar to the older Strindberg. Järegård died in 1998, the year after *The Kingdom* II was released, but as von Trier points out in an early article from 1976, he was one of the all-time best Strindberg actors and even played the role of Strindberg himself in Per Olov Enquist's debut play *The Night of the Tribades* (*Tribadernas Natt,* 1975),[4] which makes the meta-connections to Strindberg in von Trier's *The Kingdom* even clearer.

On another level, *The Kingdom* also deals with Strindberg's changing approach to spiritism and the occult, as represented by the shifts from the naturalist works of the 1880s to those associated with the so-called Inferno Crisis of the mid-1890s. In the first episodes of *The Kingdom,* Dr. Helmer resents Fru Drusse and her spiritual séances, calling her a simulant, a hysteric person who just wants attention. This resentful notion of spiritism is in line with how Strindberg portrays the female protagonist Thekla in the short story "Shortcuts" ("Genvägar," 1888), where he takes a scientific and psychological approach to the phenomenon through his studies of Charcot, Blenheim, and Nordau. But Strindberg's understanding of spiritism and the occult turned away from the scientific approach during the Inferno Crisis and became much more emotional and mystic. At the time, he became interested in quasi-elements such as the teachings of Swedenborg, spiritism, and the occult, as represented in *Inferno* (*Inferno,* 1897), *Legends* (*Legender,* 1898), and the Swedenborgian drama *Crime and Crime* (*Brott och Brott,* 1899). Dr. Helmer undergoes the same transformation as Strindberg did in real life during the eight episodes of *The Kingdom* I. After initially behaving as a rigorous scientist, scorning Rigmor for her interest in the occult practices of Haiti and theories of natural healing, he becomes increasingly paranoid and interested in black magic and voodoo. He eventually flies to Haiti to buy a special zombie drink in order to make Dr. Hook psychotic, so that the latter will not be able to reveal the crucial anesthesia report that proves Helmer guilty of medical malpractice. We also find a reference to Swedenborg, when Fru Drusse is talking to one of the patients at The Kingdom, who has just entered into "The Swedenborgian Room," and toward the end we find Dr. Helmer running around in the empty halls of The Kingdom as if haunted and pursued by invisible spirits.

Von Trier's desire to poke fun at elements belonging to Strindberg's private life—his emotional demeanor and fascination by hypnosis and the occult—can be regarded as a way for him to deal with various sides of his own personality that he himself has difficulty accepting. Von Trier—like Strindberg—has always been divided between a strict Darwinist scientific view of the world, most strongly expressed in *Manderlay* and *Antichrist,* and less scientifically rigid notions of hypnosis and religion (von Trier was a Catholic for some time) as ways to escape the traumatic realities of the Darwinist anti-transcendent Real. The concept of hypnosis is especially prevalent in *The Europe Trilogy* but is turned into a parody in *The Kingdom,* where Strindberg's fascination with the occult in the guise of Dr. Helmer becomes the vehicle of the parody. Eventually this parody is a self-mockery, a way for von Trier to create distance from the side of himself that is fascinated with quasi-science and religion and the hypnosis theme of *The Europe Trilogy* that he retrospectively feels embarrassed about.

Aside from sharing the same interest as Strindberg in quasi-scientific areas, von Trier also has an extreme emotional side just like Strindberg. The extreme side of him surfaces when he is working with his actors and especially the female leads, where the dynamic often takes on dimensions similar to the Strindbergian "battle of the sexes." As a consequence of this dynamic, Icelandic singer and actress Björk has refused to ever work with von Trier again, and in Jesper Jargil's documentary *The Humiliated* (*De ydmygede*, 1998), about the shooting of *The Idiots* (*Idioterne*, 1998), we see how Anne Louise Hasager has a nervous breakdown on camera forced by von Trier, who later admitted that he had secretly been in love with her during the shooting. Von Trier's behavior during the shooting of *The Idiots* is truly erratic and Strindbergian. From von Trier's own diary *Idioterne: Manuskript og dagbog (Dogme 2: Idioterne)* [*The Idiots: Script and Diary (Dogma 2: The Idiots)*, my translation] published in connection with the film, we see how he is violently jealous of the male lead (Kristoffer) and how he has paranoiac visions that the whole cast hates him. One day he turns up naked and tells everyone on the set that today is "naked day," and if they want to work with him, they have to be naked too—a sort of bully tactic. But as the control freak he is, he has huge difficulties accepting this emotional and erratic side of himself.

Such inner antagonism appears to be a reason why von Trier is both repelled and deeply fascinated by Strindberg's uncontrollable side, where no feelings are bottled up, but are expressed violently and honestly without the normal filter of social decorum and without shame. Strindberg and his erratic behavior are also mentioned directly in von Trier's comedy *The Boss of It All*. Von Trier is poking fun at the cliché about the great artist who is an abusive and violent person but because he makes great art:

> KRISTOFFER: Strindberg was misunderstood too.
> RAVN: Oh.
> KRISTOFFER: People were always talking. They said he pushed his wife down the stairs.[5]
> RAVN: And he didn't?
> KRISTOFFER: Sure, but that doesn't make him less of a writer.
> RAVN: No.[6] (My translation.)

The Boss of It All is basically a parody of *The Idiots* but also a final, humorous blow to the idea that there *is* an Other of the big Other. The story line is that the owner and real boss Ravn has invented a nonexistent company boss in the United States to hide behind, since he is unable to take responsibility for his shady and cynical decisions, when facing his employees. When Ravn gets the opportunity to sell the company and take all the profits for himself, he is forced to bring the "Boss of It All" face-to-face with potential buyers. Since there is no "Boss of It All" in the United States (no "Other of the big Other"), Ravn hires a failed actor, Kristoffer, to play this part. The idea of the big Other is driven into absurdity when, toward the end of the film, Kristoffer claims that he is actually not the real boss but that there is another boss above him—an Other of the Other of the big Other. This is quite possibly a humorous self-reflexive meta-commentary on the invisible and absent omnipotent agencies in both *Miss Julie* and his own *Manderlay*, but also a way for von Trier to underline the fact that there is no Other of the big Other as Žižek claims. This agency is a phantom of our own imagination and only functions as a justification of the power and consistency of the big Other, in this case Ravn's egotistical, cynical, and unethical behavior toward his employees.

Danish actor Jens Albinus plays the role as the "Boss of It All." He also played the lead role in *The Idiots*, where the character was named Kristoffer. We also find many of the same actors from the group in *The Idiots* playing the characters in the employee group of the company. The cynical yet impotent manipulator Ravn thus appears to be von Trier's parody of himself and his behavior as the director of *The Idiots*. The meta-narrative connections to *The Idiots* are numerous, and it lies outside the purpose of this chapter to mention them all, but the point is that we see how von Trier uses Strindberg as a vehicle for self-mockery. In this case it is a mockery of his own abusive behavior during the shooting of *The Idiots* (and in many of his other films), and the ethically questionable practice that he, like the main characters Ravn and Kristoffer, is willing to do anything to push his own artistic projects, even if it involves pushing people down the stairs mentally (Bunch 155). This was indeed also the trademark of Strindberg's artistic career, and here we see how von Trier eerily repeats not only the themes of Strindberg's dramas, but also significant patterns in his personal life.

On a deeper psychoanalytical level the parody of Strindberg becomes von Trier's way to deal with sides of his own personality and violent behavior that the rational side of him has such difficulty accepting. But it is also a way to deal with his own castration anxiety with regard to the big icon Strindberg—this "primal father" figure and omnipotent purveyor of Nordic artistic tradition—and create independence and distance through irony and comedy.

Conclusion

In their works, Strindberg and von Trier repeatedly, indeed repetitiously, challenge social and gender norms. Their works stage and visualize a challenge to what people are normally able (and allowed to) verbalize and enact, and transgress the common idea that nightmares should stay where they belong: in the realm of the Imaginary. This is what makes their works so disturbing and provocative, and the main reason why they have been subject to such debate over the years. The ongoing debate "for" or "against" von Trier's films, starting with the heated debate about Jan's sadism and the masochistic sacrificial behavior of Bess in *Breaking the Waves,* is in many ways similar to the "for" or "against" Strindberg debate in the late nineteenth century, where the Christian-bourgeois establishment and its critic spokesmen deemed Strindberg's work to be immoral, perverse, misogynistic, lunatic, and blasphemous. Von Trier has also faced the same type of accusations by multiple scholars and film critics (Winters 1996; Scallan and Garin 1997; Romney 2004 according to Bainbridge 4; but also Nestingen 121), even though the behavior of his protagonists can be explained perfectly within the theoretical framework of psychoanalysis dealing with male castration anxiety. From a psychoanalytical perspective these violent and resentful reactions are very similar to the type of resistance a patient undergoing psychoanalysis initially meets the analyst with, when he starts to dig under the surface of what the patient and society commonly recognize as proper and acceptable behavior. In the world of Strindberg and von Trier we, the audience, are the resistant patients. It is time to stop resisting.[7]

Notes

1. http://www.list.co.uk/article/19091–antichrist-lars-von-trier-interview/; http://www.theblurb.com.au/Issue108/Antichrist.htm; http://www.citypaper.com/film/review.asp?rid=15461.

2. When referring to Strindberg works, I note page references to the published English translation first, followed by references to the Swedish original in *Samlade Verk.*

3. Bainbridge overlooks the *Manderlay* connection to *Miss Julie* and instead claims that the plot of the play is mainly reworked in *Breaking the Waves* (Bainbridge 4).

4. "For nogen tid siden kunne skuespilleren Ernst Hugo Järegård skue ud over 'Dramatens' fyldte sal, aften efter aften når han gav rollen som Strindberg i Per Olov Enquists skuespil 'Tribadernes Nat', til bedste" (von Trier n. pag.); ("Not that long ago the actor Ernst Hugo Järegård could gaze out over the packed hall of the 'Dramaten,' when evening after evening he played the role as Strindberg in Per Olov Enquist's play 'The Night of the Tribades' to the point of excellence"; my translation).

5. Lars von Trier is probably confusing the incident where Strindberg pushed Marie David, and not his wife Siri von Essen, down the steps at Strindberg's cottage in Runarö in June 1891 (Lagercrantz 224).

6. *The Boss of It All*, chapter 11, "Ravn's Dirty Laundry." The text is a direct transcription of the English subtitles.

7. Thanks to J. Robertson McIlwain for editing help and to Anna Stenport and Brin Friesen for valuable comments and discussions.

Works Cited

Bainbridge, Caroline. *The Cinema of Lars von Trier: Authenticity and Artifice.* London: Wallflower, 2007.

Björkman, Stig, ed. *Trier on von Trier.* Trans. Neil Smith. London: Faber and Faber, 2003.

Bunch, Mads. "Behind Idealism: The Discrepancy between Philosophy and Reality in the Cinema of Lars von Trier." *Scandinavian-Canadian Studies* 19 (2010): 144–63.

Dogme 95. "Manifesto"; "Vow of Chastity." Reprinted in *Purity and Provocation: Dogme 95*, ed. Mette Hjort and Scott MacKenzie, 199–200. London: British Film Institute, 2003.

Lagercrantz, Olof. *August Strindberg.* Trans. Anselm Hollo. New York: Farrar, Straus and Giroux, 1984.

Myers, Tony. *Slavoj Žižek.* 3rd ed. London: Routledge, 2007.

Nestingen, Andrew. *Crime and Fantasy in Scandinavia.* Seattle: University of Washington and Museum Tusculanum, 2008.

Pound, Marcus. *Žižek: A (Very) Critical Introduction.* Cambridge: Wm. B. Eerdmans, 2008.

Romer, Knud. Interview with Lars von Trier. "A Hearse Heading Home." *FILM#Magazine* 66 (2009): n. pag. Online.

Strindberg, August. *Creditors: Five Plays of Strindberg.* Trans. Elizabeth Sprigge. New York: Anchor Books, Doubleday, 1960.

———. *Fadren* (1887). In *August Strindberg: Samlade Verk* 27. Stockholm: Almqvist and Wiksell, 1984. 11–98.

———. *The Father.* In *Miss Julie and Other Plays.* 2nd ed. Trans. Michael Robinson. Oxford: Oxford University Press, 2008.

———. *Fordringsägere* (1888). In *August Strindberg: Samlade Verk* 27. Stockholm: Almqvist and Wiksell, 1984. 197–272.

———. *Frøken Julie* (1888). In *August Strindberg: Samlade Verk* 27. Stockholm: Almqvist and Wiksell, 1984.

———. *Miss Julie.* In *Miss Julie and Other Plays.* 2nd ed. Trans. Michael Robinson. Oxford: Oxford University Press, 2008. 71–110.

———. *The Son of a Servant.* Trans. Claud Field. New York: G. P. Putnam's Sons, Knickerbocker, 1913.

———. *Tjänstekvinnans son I–II* (1886). In *August Strindberg: Samlade Verk* 21. Stockholm: Norstedts, 1989.

Stevenson, Jack. *Lars von Trier.* London: British Film Institute, 2002.

von Trier, Lars. "På vanviddets rand i Holte. En beretning om August Strindberg i Holte—en frugtbar krisetid." *Det grønne område.* January 28, 1976: n. p. PDF.

Žižek, Slavoj. "The Big Other Doesn't Exist." *Lacan Dotcom* (1997): n. pag. Online.

———. "Femininity Between Goodness and Act." *Lacanian Ink* 14 (1999): 26–40. http://www.lacan.com/frameXIV3.htm.

———. *Interrogating the Real.* Writings by Slavoj Žižek (series). Ed. Rex Butler and Scott Stephens. New York: Continuum, 2008.

———. *Revolution at the Gates: Žižek on Lenin, the 1917 Writings.* London: Verso, 2004.

———. "'There Is No Sexual Relationship.'" In *Gaze and Voice as Love Objects,* ed. Reneta Saleci and Slavoj Žižek. Durham, N.C.: Duke University Press, 1996.

Žižek, Slavoj, and Glyn Daly. *Conversations with Žižek.* 2nd ed. Cambridge: Polity, 2005.

Films

Antichrist. Dir. Lars von Trier. Copenhagen: Zentropa, 2009. DVD.

The Boss of It All. Dir. Lars von Trier. Copenhagen: Zentropa, 2007. DVD.

Breaking the Waves. Dir. Lars von Trier. Copenhagen: Zentropa, 1996. DVD.

Dancer in the Dark. Dir. Lars von Trier. Copenhagen: Zentropa, 2000. DVD.

Dogville. Dir. Lars von Trier. Copenhagen: Zentropa, 2003. DVD.

The Element of Crime. Dir. Lars von Trier. Copenhagen: Per Holst Film, 1984. DVD.

Epidemic. Dir. Lars von Trier. Copenhagen: Element film in collaboration with the Danish Film Institute, 1987. DVD.

Europa. Dir. Lars von Trier. Copenhagen: Nordisk Film, 1991. DVD.

The Humiliated. Dir. Jesper Jargil. Copenhagen: Jesper Jargil Film, 1998. DVD.

The Idiots. Dir. Lars von Trier. Copenhagen: Zentropa, 1998. DVD.

The Kingdom. Dir. Lars von Trier. Copenhagen: Zentropa. Part one, 1994. Part two, 1997. DVD.

Manderlay. Dir. Lars von Trier. Copenhagen: Zentropa, 2005. DVD.

Reconsidering the Place of Strindberg in Surrealism: André Breton and the Light of the Objective Chance Encounter

Maxime Abolgassemi

André Breton mentions Strindberg's name in only two places in his oeuvre: one almost insignificant because of its purely anecdotal nature, and the other such an encomium that it is astonishing.[1] The first reference to Strindberg concerns the incidents provoked in June 1928 by a band of surrealists led by André Breton against Antonin Artaud's short-lived production of *A Dream Play* (*Ett drömspel,* 1901) at the Théâtre Alfred-Jarry in Paris. The sabotage stemmed from Breton's conviction that drama, because it is scripted and elaborately produced in a theater setting, lacked the spontaneity and immediacy associated with surrealism (Swerling 68–71). The second occurrence, however, expresses such admiration that it appears almost unbelievable: in the work *Arcane* 17, originally published in 1944, André Breton erected a personal pantheon of men having acceded to an "inexorable attitude of sedition and of defiance" in the face of social conventions, wherein he nominated "Pascal, Nietzsche, Strindberg and Rimbaud" (*Arcane 17* 44).[2]

One may venture to ask by just what measure Strindberg would merit such an eminent position in Breton's eyes, as the Scandinavian writer's name would never reappear so prominently again in his writing. More generally, the question posed here is why Strindberg's work could have sustained a rapport with surrealism, when the Swedish author died in 1912 and the first *Manifesto of Surrealism* (*Manifeste du surréalisme*) was published in 1924? Generally, Strindberg is best known as a playwright in France, and most of the plays for which he is known internationally—perhaps with the exception of *A Dream Play* (1901), *To Damascus* (*Till Damaskus,* 1899), and *Ghost Sonata* (*Spöksonaten,* 1907)—have not been interpreted in France as obviously correlated to the tenets of surrealism—though there are, in fact, multiple intriguing connections. To find a convergence between Strindberg's writing and that of Breton, who is particularly representative as the figurehead of French surrealism, we need to investigate two examples of Strindberg's prose writing from the late 1890s in particular: *Inferno* (1897) and *Legends* (*Légendes,* 1898).

Published in Paris in its original French in 1898 at Mercure de France, *Inferno* is one of few Strindberg prose narratives known to French readers, but it seems not to have been read by Breton or the surrealists, despite the work on the edition performed by Marcel Réja. The critic, poet, and psychiatrist Réja was known by Breton for his book *Art Among the Mad* (*Art chez les fous, le dessin, le prose, la poésie,* 1907) as well as for introducing Strindberg's colleague Edvard Munch to a broader audience, describing him as "a cultural symbolist who evokes universality by his unself-conscious non-allegorical allegories, [and] his ability to pierce the exterior" (cited in Prideaux 169). A connection between Breton and Strindberg could thus have been made via Réja, but it does not appear to have happened despite the fact that Réja's preface to the French edition clearly signals his understanding of *Inferno* as intriguingly innovative, indeed as offering in terminology prefiguring that of a later surrealist idiom a "theory of coincidences, a legislation of chance" (8; see Stenport 105–6).

Moreover, the second French edition of *Inferno* from 1947 remained unknown to the surrealists. Though there are several possible tangential connections between Strindberg and Breton, the radical praise in *Arcane 17* remains a mystery. Etienne-Alain Hubert, a leading expert on Breton and editor of his collected works in four large volumes in the *Collection de la Pléiade,* suggests that Breton could have read texts by Strindberg, including *Inferno,* during his stay in North America (1941–46), when he read widely and encountered many new writers (research interview). Others have seen the connections between Strindberg's later writing and the surrealist movement: Thomas Mann, for example, offers the following evaluation: "A Naturalist as well as a neo-Romantic, he [Strindberg] anticipates Expressionism, making the entire generation working under that name indebted to him. At the same time, he is the first Surrealist—the first in every sense" (*Altes und Neues* 1953; cited in Rugg 6).

In this chapter, I do not propose to identify direct traces of Strindberg in the writing of Breton and other surrealists. Instead, I want to take seriously the still understudied significance of the stylistic, topical, and thematic correlations and convergences between the two writers. These connections are apparent to anyone who has studied both authors. The links are manifest in the ways their texts demonstrate genre juxtaposition (often challenging boundaries between autobiography and fiction), stylistic amalgamation (including dialogue, reportage, and lyrical description), dedication to the idea of creative experimentation, and interest in the limitations of logical reasoning and the expansive power of dreaming, free association, and the unconscious. In this chapter, I will focus on pertinent connections that can be made between Breton's autobiographical and poetic trilogy set largely in Paris, *Nadja* (1928), *The Communicating Vessels* (*Les vases communicants,* 1932) and *Mad Love* (*L'amour fou,* 1937), and Strindberg's similarly autobiographical and poetic trilogy *Inferno, Legends,* and *Jacob Wrestles* (*La lutte avec l'ange,* 1898), also set largely in Paris. I am especially interested in the possibility of using the surrealist concept of *le hasard objectif* (the objective chance [encounter]) to begin investigating Breton's effusive 1947 reference to Strindberg in *Arcane 17.*

Before moving to a close reading of the intriguing correlations between Strindberg and Breton, particularly in terms of existential perspectives as envisioned in peripatetic ambulation in the cityscapes of *Nadja* and *Mad Love,* and in *Inferno* and *Legends,* we need to address Strindberg's prefiguration of key tenets of surrealism in one of his better-known essays on aesthetics, "The New Arts! Or the Role of Chance in Artistic Creation" ("Des arts nouveaux! Ou le hasard dans la production artistique," 1894), and in his subsequent discussions of artistic practice.

The New Arts!

Indeed, it seems that Breton and his fellow surrealists saw connections most fully with Strindberg the painter and aesthetic critic. An exhibit of Strindberg's arguably proto-surrealist painting from the late 1890s at the Musée d'Art Moderne in Paris in 1962 appears to have had a strong effect on them. Breton is reported by Fernando Arrabal to have exclaimed his enthusiasm: "He saw it all before us" (cited in Swerling 187). The essay "The New Arts," written in French, for a French audience, and published in 1894 in the Parisian *Revue des Revues,* was included in the exhibition catalog for the Strindberg exhibit in Paris. This critical essay, which prefigures tenets of surrealist aesthetics, was thus only discovered by the Surrealists in 1962. Their fascination is such that they decided immediately to reprint it in the Surrealist journal *La Brèche,* in September the same year, in which it was announced by Gérard Legrand, in brief introductory remarks, as an "unknown text of Strindberg [which] gives us in advance the common value that surrealism has been developing" (Legrand 1).

What is "The New Arts" about? Nothing less than the founding principle that puts chance at the center of artistic practices in modern art. There are multiple examples of how modern art has been developed either by seeking the intervention of nature (music that can be created by the wind in reeds with holes, for example) or by the unintentional human action, as in the "scrapings palette" that painters do not think about when rubbing the palette knife to clean or prepare shades "at random." To Strindberg, it is in these non-considered moments that the artist releases unimagined creative powers, and "all is revealed as a charming jumble of unconscious and conscious" ("Des arts nouveaux!"149). The Strindbergian term "unconscious" is not necessarily Freudian, but should rather be understood as the kind of unconscious introduced by Breton in *The Communicating Vessels*, after he passionately read Frederic William Henry Myers's psychoanalytic writings available in the 1920s.

The important point of Strindberg's essay is that art must take new paths by releasing itself from technical control, as in an intentional search of capabilities and directed aesthetic purposes, and instead move toward the mediation of random and accidental shocks. Strindberg describes one such experience in "The New Arts," which associates embodied practices with aesthetic innovation. Wanting to model a bust in clay, he was disappointed with the result, unable to obtain the pathos he sought. Suddenly he let fall his "hand upon the head of the unfortunate" bust ("Des arts nouveaux!" 151). The hand that falls inadvertently reconfigures all to perfection in the sculpture by which hair, head, arms, legs take the desired shape "and everything is transformed into a nine-year-old boy crying and hiding the tears in his hands"; with a bit of retouching, "the statue was perfect" (151). This approach to artistic creation differs markedly from Strindberg's interest in Émile Zola's tenets of naturalism only a few years prior.

Indeed, naturalism as a movement was in crisis in the mid-1890s, and Strindberg's formulation of a "new art" seemed to herald a different aesthetic mode, and also to be changing the very terms of the problem at the heart of the contemporary mimesis debate. Art should no longer prescribe the imitation of nature but should "imitate the way nature creates" (153). Chance would in Strindberg's conceptualization be the most significant vehicle, so that "this is the natural art because the artist works as a capricious nature, without specific purpose" (149). The artist who allows chance to form the accident of his hand is thus more realistic—more real—than the one who voluntarily applies the technique of mimesis. More important, such a conceptualization opens up the possibility of magical intervention in reality, as in a waking dream when acting goes "without specific purpose." This is exactly how the concept and method of the "surreal" was defined in 1924 by Breton in the first *Manifesto:* "I believe in the future resolution of these two states, apparently so contradictory, that are the dream and reality, into a kind of absolute reality, a *surreality,* if one may so say" (*Manifeste du surréalisme* 319).

The surrealists were furthermore particularly impressed when they discovered that this Swede writing awkward French was the inventor of a concept critical to their theory and practice. Questioning a "form of art to come," Strindberg plans to make "a theory for the automatic art" ("Des arts nouveaux" 151), forging a link to what will become a famous formulation of surreal creativity in 1920 when Breton and Philippe Soupault wrote *Magnetic Fields* (*Les champs magnétiques*), the first work of literary surrealism composed through the technique of "automatic writing." If the surrealists would have known about it earlier, Strindberg's little essay should have been a reference for them.

Surrealist Practices

Beyond applying himself to his method, Strindberg was undeniably a pioneer of surrealist practice. In reading the Paris sections of *Inferno* we find many explorations of what would later become tenets of surrealist practice, including a new role of assigning meaning at random and exploring fortuitous chance encounters. Strindberg is interested in everything that nature and chance produce as artwork already formed: faces in the folds of a pillow (*Inferno* 257), a landscape "perfectly designed" in the traces at the bottom of a zinc bowl after a chemical experiment (*Inferno* 277), "a block like a giant face" caused by drops of a storm on the paper (*Inferno* 278), "masterpieces of primitive sculpture" (*Inferno* 245) in coals in the stove (which Edvard Munch, his Norwegian friend visiting him in Paris, authenticates as really true works of art).[3] Roger Caillois, a companion of Breton in the early 1930s, later wrote extensively on the idea of beauty created by nature as an art form associated with surrealist aesthetics. Stones, Caillois writes, can be "objects who receive from nature their origin and appearance, but seem as obviously manufactured as that of monetary currency" (Caillois 41). The surrealist review *Minotaure* includes in the double issue 3 and 4 of December 1933 a section on "involuntary sculptures" such as a "bus ticket rolled" symmetrically, a "chance morphological toothpaste" ("le hasard morphologique du dentifrice"), a "piece of soap representing the automatic forms of modern style, found in a sink" (un "morceau de savon représentant des formes automatiques modern'style, trouvé dans un lavabo") (*Minotaure* vol. 3–4, 68). Similarly, Strindberg focuses on random shapes that can be deciphered from wood fibers, like the diabolical ones that unmask the malicious doctor he perceives to be haunting him in *Inferno* (316). In a similar way, Max Ernst developed a complete artistic project under the name of *frottages* (rubbings). In the sixth issue of the journal *Le Surréalisme au service de la Révolution* (1933), he explained the genesis of his idea. Obsessed by the floor's grooves enriched by much scrubbing at a hotel in which he was staying, he decided to put "on them at random pieces of paper" and to "rub them by graphite pen" (cited in Breton, "Situation de l'objet surréaliste" 493). Oscar Dominguez conducted in the same spirit what he called *décalcomanies du désir* ("decalcomania with no preconceived object," as reported by Breton in *Le Surréalisme et la peinture* 502–4). Many surrealistic works respond to Strindberg's "Clexographies": paper folding on paint producing symmetrical forms (like *Rorschach Test* by Paul Eluard).

The concept of *le merveilleux* (the wonderful) can be understood as another area in which the surrealists and Strindberg share sensibilities. The speaker of *Inferno* appears to succumb to it with fascination, as when he sees little hands, clasped in prayer, inside the shell of a sprouted nut, or when he undertakes to establish an evolutionary "unitary chemistry" (*Inferno* 178), by taking shortcuts on the equivalences of atomic weights (see Abolgassemi). *Le merveilleux* has always been promoted as a precious way of wonderment (see Mabille 13). André Breton stated firmly that "the marvelous is always beautiful, anything marvelous is beautiful, there is even only the marvelous that could be beautiful" (*Manifeste du surréalism* 319). Strindberg cultivated what appears to be a taste for the wonderfulness of scientific practice intermingled with aesthetic expression as well; Strindberg's experimental "célestrographies" of the late 1890s were inspired by photography and astronomy (as indicated in the catalog of the 2003 Parisian exhibition "Dream Trajectories" in the "Pavillon des Arts," which features Strindberg's experiments). Vincent Gille discusses several relevant comparisons between Strindberg's "célestrographies" and Max Ernst's book of lithographs *Maximiliana: The Illegal Practice of Astronomy* published in 1965 (Gille 129). By poetic analogy, Strindberg suggests in chapter 6 of *Inferno*, subtitled "Essay on Rational Mysticism," that there is such a thing as natural photography that prints on the backs of fish seascapes (the silver scales are impressed by the sun, the sea acting as developer and fixer). Surrealist Roger Caillois made many studies on what can be called "animal mimicry" (*mimétisme animal*), including aesthetic implications for natural symmetry (Caillois has one very Strindbergian study about the aesthetics of the wings of butterflies), in the review *Minotaure* during the early 1930s (like his famous study of the praying mantis in *Minotaure* 5 from 1934 [26]).

Strindberg's understanding of aesthetics and artistic and scientific practice opens a main tendency in modern and contemporary art: the decline of the artist and the rise of the process of creating, where processes of random creation are given a prominent place. Vincent Bounoure, responsible for the presentation of the reprint of Strindberg's essay "The New Arts" in *La Brèche,* analyzes it clearly: "the only human intervention is to choose the method that is sufficient to trigger the infinite variations authorized by chance" (Bounoure 32). Max Ernst expresses a similar understanding of the power of chance: "constantly restricting my own active participation . . . , I managed to attend *as a spectator* at the birth of the paintings" (cited in Breton, "Situation de l'objet surréaliste" 494). As a simple observer of a wonderful creation that operates under his eyes, it is possible to "create a masterpiece without an author, fruit of chance and the random encounter," as the philosopher of surrealism, Ferdinand Alquié, noted (136). Marcel Duchamp believed exactly in this process, as demonstrated by his systematized research into the possibility of "canning chance," attempted in the artwork *3 Standard Stoppages* (*3 stoppages étalon*), as well as by his "ready-mades," featuring a "common object promoted to the dignity of art through the choice of the artist" (Breton and Eluard 837) and emphasizing that the only possible action that still remains is the choice of those industrial objects. But it is not only the artistic approach and related statements that help show and acknowledge the deep affinity binding Strindberg to surrealism and Breton. Chance is indeed more than a mode of artistic discovery, *it is also a mode of testing life, seen as an ordeal,* which both men are experiencing intensely, and sometimes disturbingly.

Chance, the New Guide? Risks Involved

Received and historically contextualized as an autobiographical work, *Inferno* is powerfully shaped by Strindberg's tormented thought processes, relating the need to defend himself from attacks coming from all directions—the mysterious powers that seem to guide his life in a Swedenborgian fashion, malevolent humans around him, and disturbing environmental sensory impacts. Yet, *Inferno* is clearly also a literary work of great accomplishment. Strindberg incorporates selected fragments of his life and draws on startling juxtapositions, which make individual, and sometimes fragmented sections, transform into a complex narrative of estrangement and wonder. Recently arrived in Paris, Strindberg's speaker proclaims in the opening pages of *Inferno* to have relinquished literature in favor of ambitious scientific experiments in chemistry and alchemy, asserting that the apparent turn to the natural sciences will eventually award him recognition and success in the City of Light. Subsequent appearances of menacing signs of diverse concealed aggressions, manifestations "of the powers," and of accidental encounters challenge his purportedly rational and scientific interest. This juxtaposition between an interest in scientific method and the practice of magic interpretation gives a clear indication of *Inferno*'s affinity with later surrealist theory and practice (see also Stenport 103–7). The emphasis on chance and the creative process in *Inferno* and *Legends* arguably helped Strindberg move toward a new and audacious writing style—a precursor to expressionism and modernism—in the years to follow. This new style is characterized by the power of dreaming in *To Damascus* (1898) and *A Dream Play* (1901). These plays emphasize the unconscious mental processes of accidental meetings and inexplicable correlations between phenomena and people, which are key components of later French surrealism.

In *Inferno,* Strindberg's speaker enters combat tinted by Don Quixoticism against obtuse spirits and among dolorous interrogations on religion. During the progressive and ambivalent access to the elements of doctrine of his compatriot Swedenborg, the speaker also gets in touch with the "inexplicable coincidence" (399): diverse accidents, junctions, and encounters. These components would also intrigue the surrealists well before the appearance of the term *le hasard objectif* (the "objective chance") in *The Communicating Vessels* in 1932. Surrealism calls it "objective," because random facts cause meaningful coincidences that are *objectively* observable from the outside.

This process is significant in André Breton's novel *Nadja,* about a young woman's gradual descent into madness and hospitalization, and which emphasizes the random nature of encounters in the city environment as critical to the creative process and the narrative structure of the novel. In a passage similar to one in *Inferno,* Breton describes how Nadja, who the speaker unexpectedly meets on the street, mysteriously pronounces to him exactly the words he had just read in a rare book from 1750 (*Nadja* 698). It is clear that the speaker is not to be construed as crazy: a reader can verify the facts (her potential testimony, the book references, the picture and photos inserted in the text to prove her story). This episode functions like Munch's visit, which confirmed that neither Strindberg nor his first-person protagonist in *Inferno* were to be construed as crazy when seeing in ordinary lumps of black coal in a regular stove finished and indeed exquisite sculptures (*Inferno* 245).

Both Breton and Strindberg blame narrow conceptualizations of reason for preventing the creation of meaning sensitive to chance, though this process should be seen as a revelatory guide in life. Both writers have to confront the usual logics, which condemn them, and insinuate their bordering on madness. But it is a risk they both take and run with: they write in the same terms with respect to their readers, with the same defensive and revolutionary energy: "I am not mad" (*Inferno* 186 and *Les vases communicants* 166).

Yet neither is totally stripped of doubt in their process and in their projects: that is why *Inferno,* full of its protagonist's interest in scientific experimentation, makes a strong distinction between the practices advocated by the speaker and those of mainstream scientific practice: "this is not science that has gone bankrupt, but only science outdated, distorted" (205). This criticism is motivated through multiple relations of signs and inexplicable doings. Like Strindberg, Breton loves science as a possibility to deploy imagination, but he hates its assumption of sterilized rationality. He, for example, with an immovable constancy, spoke out against "absolute rationalism" and the poor strictly "realistic attitude" in the first *Manifesto* (*Manifeste du surréalisme* 313). This is a position he maintained, including in the later radical appeal to remittance in the cause of the "withered" logic in *Arcane 17* (54), twenty years after.

Likewise, Strindberg is attentive to events that reveal another coherence than those institutionalized by rational science: "the accident or the coincidence, in this event marked by an unshakable logic?" (*Inferno* 257). André Breton reports clearly that it is therefore necessary to attentively await "the irruption of a solution which, by reason of its own nature, we cannot attain by the ways of ordinary logic" (*L'amour fou* 682).

The Lost Steps

For both Breton and Strindberg, the city of Paris—including its scale, layout, and landmark buildings—is a privileged site for aesthetic experimentation. The authors share an interest in exploring the creative possibilities awarded by getting lost, physically, in the city. In fact, for Breton, one condition for letting chance play its occurrences is, paradoxically (but exactly corresponding to the instructions prescribed for the artist), to accord total autonomy to steps taken while walking through the urban landscape. One has to go forward or turn around "unaware," he emphasizes (*Nadja* 691). In *Mad Love,* chance made the expected woman—Jacqueline, the Naiad—finally visible by the mysterious power to which the walker delegates the responsibility to surprise him: "Who accompanies me in this hour in Paris without driving me and whom, besides, do I not myself guide?" (*L'amour fou* 715). Our "lost," accidental steps take us where we need to go and it is only if we pursue the "random from our steps" (*Nadja* 688) that new streets, new areas, can be revealed. Strindberg expresses a similar conception of the creative power of losing one's way in a large city. "Two steps led me to the grand boulevards," Strindberg writes in a well-known section of *Inferno,* which outlines his experiences getting lost in the area around Porte Saint-Martin and introduces his understanding of random juxtaposition of objects and stimuli as triggers for scientific and aesthetic experimentation (189). The Boulevard Bonne-Nouvelle similarly astonishes Breton's speaker in *Nadja:* "I do not know, in fact, why my steps carry me there; why I go there almost always without specific reason; without any specific cause but this obscure given, namely that it is there that *something* will happen (?)" (*Nadja* 661–63).

Breton and Strindberg both draw on the trope of deciding on a travel destination only at the very last moment, wherein an opportune decision is made from the accident of the instant: "we might not have chosen what we did there earlier, however; the first departure time was ours" (Breton, *L'amour fou* 769). The destination proved to be Fort-Bloqué and, once there, the speaker resorts to "marching without well-determined objective." Strindberg: "arriving without premeditation at the Montparnasse rail station, I took the train to Meudon. I get off the train at this village, which I visit for the very first time" (*Inferno* 245). Meudon was at that time far from a tourist destination, and the decision to travel and spend the day there appears to be a random act, yet, as is made clear in *Inferno,* Meudon becomes a privileged location. There the speaker, by interpreting random clues from material objects found on streets and in shop windows, begins to formulate answers about his tormented relationship to his wife as well as identifying clues to his alchemy experiments.

Both authors gravitate toward strategic, even magic, locations that make perfect sense within their narrative universes, and which seem to be haunted by past experiences, both private and public. Nadja, Place Dauphine, hallucinates about a prison experience taking place before her birth (*Nadja* 695) in the Conciergerie, while Strindberg's speaker suffers an impressive flood of trans-historical images in response to the single evocation of the name "Chauveau-Lagarde," perceived on a signboard in the Montparnasse cemetery (*Inferno* 227). These effects seem to be triggered not only by signs and locations in the urban landscape but also to be the puzzling results of semantic connotations of the verb "to haunt," chosen by Breton and Strindberg in all its diachronic density. Summoned by Breton in the first lines of *Nadja,* he uses the adage, "tell me the company you keep [literally, "whom you haunt"], I will tell you who you are." Breton's wordplay in *Nadja* illustrates how the expression transcends its nineteenth-century meaning of "general frequentation" to evoke the presence of spirits or phantoms, which constituted a fascinating and productive movement to Breton. To frequent a place, with an intensity conferred by the objective chance experienced there, means to haunt it as if we, starry-eyed witnesses of striking temporal interference, become able "to play in [our] life the role of a phantom," as proclaimed by the first lines of *Nadja.* For both Strindberg and Breton, Paris, through the chance encounters it allows, creates a complex web of interaction. Strindberg, for example, identifies the city walker as a prisoner of a necessity which exceeds him: in a topographical reactivation of the image, Strindberg speaks of a "vicious circle": "Finally, here's my vicious circle that I walk twice a day, my life has been framed in this orbit with such a fate, if I would take a new road, I find myself disoriented, as if I lost parcels of my ego, my memories, my thoughts, my affections" (*Légendes* 522). Both authors identify locations in the city that attract them in a fundamental though inexplicable way. The Quartier Saint-Denis, Breton writes, "has exerted attraction on me for years" (*Les vases communicants* 173), while Strindberg asserts that "this edifice [the church Saint-Germain-l'Auxerrois] has always exerted a powerful attraction on me" (*Légendes* 571). Walter Benjamin named similar expressions of attraction a "phenomenon of peddling in space," and the analysis of such chance encounters "the fundamental experience of the flaneur" (*Paris, capitale du XIXe siècle* 437). Benjamin's formulation, allowed by the large metropolis, illustrates critical affinities between Breton and Strindberg. Such a phenomenon, Benjamin explains, "allows for simultaneous perception of all that which is potentially entering in a single space. The space hurls in the twinkling of an eye to the flaneur" (437).

The Secrets of Les Halles at Night

We terminate this investigation of affinities between Breton and Strindberg by way of a nocturnal stop, leading to one of the most iconic locations of late-nineteenth-century Paris. The great market at Les Halles, and the area surrounding it, is etched in the minds of readers of French literature, not least through Émile Zola's representation in *The Bowels of Paris* (*Le ventre de Paris,* 1873). Breton and Strindberg award this location very different meanings than the voracious market forces at work in Zola's naturalist novel; they turn this location and the chance encounters it elicits into an exploration of myth as it is juxtaposed with a modern world. Readers of *Mad Love* will recall the grace of that night during which Jacqueline Lamba, figured as an Ondine Naiad, accompanies Breton's speaker for a stroll down to the bank of the river Seine, along the Quai des Fleurs, and heading toward Les Halles. A similar section can be found in *Legends,* which describes Strindberg's return to Paris at the end of the summer of 1897. Traversing again many of the sites of agonized vexations suffered the previous year, and described at length in *Inferno,* Strindberg's speaker appears lost and helpless in the Parisian capital. One day, an American painter, who in *Inferno* had been suspected of being a Francis Schlatter doppelgänger (Schlatter was an American faith healer, and *Revue des Revues* had published his photograph), knocks on his door. The two companions then pass an evening of rediscovered good humor and, as the cafés of the boulevards are about to close, they move toward Les Halles. The name Baratte, a celebrated place which Gérard de Nerval had immortalized in his *Nights of October* (*Les nuits d'Octobre,* 1852—see chapter 15), is tossed out in conversation, and provokes an expression of precisely the kind of surrealist chance encounter we have traced in this chapter.

> The Café Baratte, next to the Halles, has always elicited in me a marvelous attraction, without my knowing why. Possibly what draws me is that it is in such close proximity to the Halles. When it is night on the Boulevards, it is morning in the Halles, where it is in any case morning all through the night. The melancholic night does not exist with an enforced idleness and its somber dreams. The spirit which is inebriated in the immaterial worlds has a desire to return in base to the milieu of eating and filthiness, of sin and uproar. (*Légendes* 563)

Why does this passage seem to invite so many connections with Breton's writing about the necessity of venturing out, of becoming lost, and of surrendering to the chance encounters of the city? The first phrase in the quote above concurs with Breton's interests in the attraction exerted by particular Parisian places; in *Nadja,* for example, he seems to allow for the possibility of random chance encounters in *strategic places,* "provided obscurely in the landmarks" (748). Similarly, Strindberg's formulation of the experience being akin to one of dreaming, of finding his spirit freed by approximation to the material, filth, and consumption, offers up an image of surreal juxtaposition.

In *Mad Love,* Les Halles and surrounding areas provoke similarly strong expressions that oppose the world of sentiments to that of pure materiality. If the "lyrical comportment" of surrealism asserts itself on this late night walk in *Mad Love,* it is as part of the vision of the foods and provisions retrieved from the embankment: "My gaze on the magnificent [*magnifiques*] cubes, white, red, green of the first vegetables of the season, slipping unluckily onto the pavement sleek with horrible offal" (*L'amour fou* 716). Magnificent colorful images of fruits and vegetables are opposed to glistening animal offal: two universes, two destinies. In *Mad Love* the character of Jacqueline Lamba reveals to the speaker the meaning of his life; she is a central catalyst and a necessary outcome of chance possibilities, of the objective chance encounter Breton's figure has been led by. She is also associated with an elevated speech that opens up a final oratorical question, through which a confrontation between "good" and "evil" plays out. This female figure is thus a veritable Eurydice, who guides the man through a forest of indices and who permits him to traverse the exceptional with "great giddy exhaustion," which has befallen him at the end of a confounding labyrinth where "the sidewalks bifurcate inexplicably by turns, according to an itinerary as capricious as possible" (*L'amour fou* 714).

In *Legends,* we find a similar mythic connection to experiences associated with Les Halles. Strindberg's speaker (with companion) traverses the road as an Orpheus in search of a truth which is drawn as a contrast between two worlds, one of the sentiments and immateriality, the other of embodied experiences and materiality: "On me, this stench of fish, of meat and vegetables, and the detritus over which one steps, provokes the effect of a magnificent [*magnifique*] contrast with the elevated subjects which we happen to be discussing" (*Légendes* 563). Strindberg and Breton use the same word—*magnifique*—to indicate their fascination and the potential of the chance encounter. The passage from Strindberg, moreover, functions as a trigger for a particularly provocative expression of involuntary memory, elicited by a voyage of return to the maleficent places of the Parisian past, which lead to new chance encounters: "At that moment, I recall a night, two years past, with the same friend in this café. We had been discussing the hidden powers of the soul and, foolish me, for many reasons, the role of the brain as a thinking machine" (*Légendes* 564). Conjuring up the image of the human brain as a thinking machine, as an inanimate object possibly disassociated from what we may understand as the essence of humanness—emotions, creativity, contingency, and the capacity to recognize and experience the possibility of random chance encounters—lead the interlocutors to the idea of purchasing a brain. The presumably scientific, or at least rationally motivated decision to investigate the composition of an (animal) brain thus leads them to the kind of chance encounter the discussion of "brain-as-machine" would seem to preclude.

> We are descending to the Halles, requesting a brain. We have entered a cave where it is necessary to pass by the gangways and under the sewers. Finally, we find ourselves in a room strewn with bloody carcasses and organs. We splash through the blood and we are coming to the chamber reserved for brains. The blood-covered men there, with cudgels and chisels in the same state, striking the heads of beasts cut in fashion to facilitate the splitting of the skull to extract the brain. We have purchased one and we are ascending again to the light, but the frightening scene has pursued us even to the table at the café where the supposed machine to think was exhibited. (*Légendes* 564–65)

This descent into Les Halles is one of a descent into hell; among the chthonic sources of life and death there lies at the heart the quest of a secret: it is this flood of materiality that shocks an Orpheus, without his Eurydice, reascending to the light of the café. Once there, he hears a musical score of lyres, eerily reminiscent of that which is associated with the border of the worlds: "It is the filth of which we are created and re-created three times per day; and when one comes from the semi-darkness, from the filthiness, from the repulsive figures, and such a one enters into the friendly café, one is greeted by the light, the warmth, the song, the mandolins and the guitars" (*Légendes* 563).

Breton's description of his and Jacqueline's experiences at Les Halles may seem to lie at the opposite end of those described by Strindberg, yet a similarly mythic association is generated by the regenerative fertility suggested by the approach to the Quai des Fleurs, bathed in the grand immortal sun of the sunflower associated with the tower of Saint-Jacques:

> It is marvelous to see them a last time, assembled according to species on the tops of the wagons which transport them, as if they had been born similarly, the ones to the others from the sowing. . . . All the flowers, starting even with those least extravagant of this climate, with pleasure inflect their force to render me all the youthfulness of the sensation." (*L'amour fou* 720)

Jacqueline, the "beautiful vagabond" of *Mad Love,* can afterward cull the secret of this powerful rebirth:

> While, as in a dream, other flower beds sprawl out always in front of us, you bend alongside over these flowers enveloped in shadow, as if it were less to breathe them in than to ravish their secret; and such a gesture, in itself alone, is the most touching answer that we could make to this question that I do not ask you. This profusion of riches at our feet cannot fail to be interpreted as a luxury in advance; life makes me approach her, even more so necessarily through you. (*L'amour fou* 721)

Breton's descriptions of the marvelous opportunities awarded him through the chance meeting with Jacqueline is accompanied by descriptions of obscure interactions with shadows, which envelop what can best be described as the vegetal muses in the stalls around Les Halles; the vegetables and the woman, coalescing into an expression that "one can only be a part of this same radiance" (721). The poet can therefore exclaim, "That this curtain of shadow lift away and that I let myself be led without fear toward the light!" (720).

The two nights described by Strindberg and Breton, each experienced differently in the vicinity of Les Halles, are nevertheless full of resonant imagery and affinities. The descriptions join together completely as two circumambulations of the tension between evil and good, obscurity and light, spirit and material, and attraction and repulsion in the search for a secret that the moment and the objective chance encounter suddenly make possible. The two journeys are directionally opposed, however; ascending toward the Seine in the one, plunging under the earth in the other. Similarly, a vegetative world in Breton is juxtaposed with an animal world in Strindberg; the efflorescence of the vernal, awakened by the flowers in *Mad Love,* is opposed to the bloodiness and dismemberment of the degraded meat in *Légendes;* a sublime presence of the Ondine at last encountered is contrasted with descriptions of idle prostitutes that cross paths with Strindberg; Breton's night of the sunflower diverges from a Strindbergian night of blood and of butchered flesh. The night at Les Halles is not invested with the same importance in the economy of the two works (for Breton it is a climactic moment; for Strindberg it indicates one of several experiments), but each shines with that burst, haunted, of the places of mysterious attraction that indicate the objective chance encounter, and which we have shown in this chapter to be of such paramount importance for both writers. In these two cases it is a question of an exceptional insight into a truth disclosing, at the end of the night, a superior and unknown order—one accessible only by inviting the possibility of a chance encounter.

It therefore strikes us as certain, despite all other clear divergences between these writers (including that the oeuvres of both are so extremely varied), that Breton and Strindberg shared an interest in a common problematic and method. They were both searching for innovative ways to insert chance and the random encounter into the aesthetic and creative process, while also taking the chance encounter as an existential guide for discovering new parts, and paths, of life and art. Whatever de facto knowledge Breton had of Strindberg's work, a profound analogy can be drawn between the two writers—one that remains sorely underexplored. This analogy finally makes comprehensible the tribute in *Arcane 17*, and, more important, it gives us the occasion to reconsider the position that Strindberg should have in relation to surrealism.

Notes

1. Brief sections of an earlier version of this chapter were included in my article "August Strindberg/André Breton à la lumière du hasard objectif," published in *Mélusine* 27 (2007): 245–55. I wish to thank Lawrence Smith of the University of Illinois for assistance with translation and language editing of this article.

2. Translations into English from French are my own, unless otherwise noted.

3. Munch is not directly identified as a character in *Inferno*, but it is generally assumed that *Inferno*'s reference to an unnamed Danish painter in fact refers directly to him.

Works Cited

Abolgassemi, Maxime. "La 'chimie unitaire' d'un écrivain: August Strindberg en 1895." *Atala 10 La Science* 10 (2007): 159–73.

Alquié, Ferdinand. *Philosophie du Surréalisme*. Paris: Flammarion, 1956.

Benjamin, Walter. *Paris, capitale du XIXe siècle, le Livre des Passages*. Paris: Éditions du Cerf, 1989.

Bounoure, Vincent. "Des arts nouveaux ou le hasard dans la production artistique (Strindberg)." *La Brèche* 3 (1963): 32. Online.

Breton, André. *L'amour fou*. In *Oeuvres complètes II*. Paris: Gallimard, 1992. 673–785.

———. *Arcane 17*. In *Oeuvres complètes III*. Paris: Gallimard, 1999. 35–95.

———. *Le surréalisme et la peinture*. In *Oeuvres complètes IV*. Paris: Gallimard, 2008. 345–846.

———. *Les vases communicants*. In *Oeuvres complètes II*. Paris: Gallimard, 1992. 102–215.

———. *Manifeste du surréalisme*. In *Oeuvres complètes I*. Paris: Gallimard, 1988. 309–46. Print.

———. *Nadja*. In *Oeuvres complètes I*. Paris: Gallimard, 1988. 643–753.

———. "Situation de l'objet surréaliste." In *Position politique du surréalisme*. In *Oeuvres complètes II*. Paris: Gallimard, 1992. 411–500.

Breton, André, and Paul Eluard. *Dictionnaire abrégé du surréalisme*. In *Oeuvres complètes II*. Paris: Gallimard, 1992. 787–862.

Caillois, Roger. *Malversations*. Paris: Fata Morgana, 1993.

Gille, Vincent. "Le Ciel du rêve." In *Trajectoires du rêve*. Paris: Paris Musées, 2003. 127–39.

Hubert, Etienne-Alain. Research interview with Maxime Abolgassemi. Paris, June 2005.

Legrand, Gérard. "A l'heure d'été." *La Brèche* 3 (1963): 1. Online.

Mabille, Pierre. *Le merveilleux*. Paris: Fata Morgana, 1992.

Minotaure 3–4 (1933).

Minotaure 5 (1934).

Prideaux, Sue. *Edvard Munch: Behind the Scream*. New Haven, Conn.: Yale University Press, 2007.

Réja, Marcel. "Avant-Propos." In *Inferno*, by Auguste Strindberg. Paris: Société de Mercure de France, 1898. 5–11.

Rugg, Linda. "The Art and Science of Self-Dramatization." In *The Cambridge Companion to August Strindberg*, ed. Michael Robinson. Cambridge, Eng.: Cambridge University Press, 2009. 3–19.

Stenport, Anna Westerståhl. *Locating August Strindberg's Prose: Modernism, the Transnational, and Setting*. Toronto: University of Toronto Press, 2010.

Strindberg, August. "Des arts nouveaux! Ou le hasard dans la production artistique." In *Strindberg: Peintre et photographe*. Paris: Éditions de la Réunion des Musées Nationaux, 2001. 149–53.

———. *Inferno*. In *Oeuvre autobiographique II*. Paris: Mercure de France, 1990. 159–402.

———. *Légendes*. In *Oeuvre autobiographique II*. Paris: Mercure de France, 1990. 403–586.

Swerling, Anthony. *Strindberg's Impact in France*. Cambridge: Trinity Lane, 1971.

Standing at the Bourne of the Modern: Strindberg's Ecological Subject in *By the Open Sea* and His Archipelago Paintings

Linda Haverty Rugg

One hundred years after August Strindberg's death, the time may have come to consider his work through the prism of ecocriticism, an international theoretical approach that took shape in North America during the 1990s and has been gaining ground and momentum steadily since. To cite ecocritic Cheryll Glotfelty, one of the pioneers of the theoretical movement: "Simply defined, ecocriticism is the study of the relationship between literature and the physical environment. Just as feminist criticism examines language and literature from a gender-conscious perspective, and Marxist criticism brings an awareness of modes of production and economic class to its reading of texts, ecocriticism takes an earth-centered approach to literary studies."[1] Glotfelty has placed ecocriticism in the company of other politically engaged approaches to literature, and with this in mind, one might also add that tracing the historical dimension of human representations of the natural world is an essential element of ecocritical thought. Much of ecocriticism to date has focused on American nature writing, but Strindberg's observations on the environment, both essayistic and novelistic, offer an unusually rich field for ecocritical analysis on an international scope. His prescience and insights into ecology can shed light on a historical aspect of the rapidly evolving study of ecology and culture.

While Strindberg's earlier plays (such as *Miss Julie* [*Fröken Julie,* 1888] and *The Father* [*Fadren,* 1887]) are often described as "naturalist" in terms of their relationship to Darwinian thought and their realist aesthetic, it is important to note that Strindberg was much more of an actual naturalist than this categorization of his dramas implies.

He authored a collection of essays on flowers and animals during the 1880s; he was deeply involved in (al)chemical experimentation and scientific writing during the period he painted his archipelago paintings; he immersed himself in the study of scientific experiments and movements of his time; and he would go on to author an essay on Swedish nature in 1897, an extended work on mineral prototypes in 1898, and numerous occasional pieces on scientific topics. Strindberg's particular approach to science, however, exists in close relationship to his artistic vision. While he declares in the 1890s that he wants to give up literary writing for the higher calling of scientific experimentation, the way he looks at the world (and frames his scientific experiments) derives from the way he learned to see and express himself as an artist—both as a literary author deeply attached to images and precise description of the physical world, and as a painter. And conversely, his literary writing reflects a penetrating knowledge of science. The two optics of literature and science, usually opposed in present-day thinking, are, in Strindberg's case, one.

Much of Strindberg's scientific experimentation and writing took place in Paris, and a number of his most important scientific texts were written originally in French. He desired an international audience for his discoveries, and the alchemical experiments that preoccupied him during his time in Paris were oriented toward a universalism in nature: the discovery of the essential material that makes up all matter in the world. But his nature writings in Swedish tended to focus on very particular aspects of the Swedish natural environment, though he felt that the conclusions he drew through specific observation had universal implications. So the dual optic of literature and science has a correlative dual nature in its oscillation between the microscopic and macroscopic, the particular and the universal.

In order to demonstrate how Strindberg's environmental optic works, I would like to focus on his paintings of the 1890s and his novel *By the Open Sea* (*I havsbandet,* 1890), describing and discussing what I take to be the ecological subject of Strindberg's archipelago art. Peter Szondi wrote insightfully in the 1950s of Strindberg's "I-dramas," the dramas that express the perspective of an individual consciousness, one which in Strindberg's case looks much like what we would imagine to be Strindberg's own. Strindberg's prose fiction texts, often just as fascinating but less famous internationally than his plays, have often been interpreted similarly either as autobiographical or as expressions of the interior of a modernist psyche. This is not quite what I mean when I refer to Strindberg's ecological subject. While it is true that the novel I have chosen to discuss charts the breakdown of a modern psyche, I do not agree entirely with Eric O. Johannesson's point that the reality depicted in *By the Open Sea* emerges solely from the protagonist's consciousness, that "the world of external reality no longer appears in its quality of otherness, as an objective reality, but only as a mental image" (Johannesson 147). Nor do I agree with the interpretations of Strindberg's paintings that tend to interpret them as representations of his interior life (see Carlson, Kesting, and Söderström). Both the novel and the seascapes are situated in a real and specific environment, where Strindberg lived during the year he wrote *By the Open Sea:* the Stockholm archipelago.[2] And while it is admittedly the case that a particular and sometimes peculiar modernist optic filters our view of Strindberg's archipelago, the images emerge from an engagement with a specific geographic and cultural environment. Grischka Petri, in writing of Strindberg's theories on art, argues that some interpreters of his paintings take Strindberg's modernist and proto-surrealist theoretical pronouncements too much into consideration. In his writing on art, for instance, Strindberg advocates for images that leave interpretation entirely up to the viewer (something he calls *skogssnuvismus*), but it is not the case that his own images are non-mimetic or have no point of reference. As Petri writes, "it is obviously absurd to discover a desert landscape in [Strindberg's forest painting] *Underlandet*" ("es ist zum Beispiel evident unsinnig, auf *Wunderland* eine Wüstenlandschaft zu entdecken," Petri 93, my translation).

So setting is not immaterial, and it involves the establishment of a particular earthly setting that makes the ecological subject possible. At the same time, the ecological subject is per definition international, as the environment recognizes no national boundaries. In my analysis I would like to use the term "subject" in a couple of different ways. First we can take the term to signify "subject" as in "theme." Strindberg's archipelago paintings and novels (*By the Open Sea* is his second archipelago novel) explore the position of human beings in a literally liminal natural space, at the edge of the sea, where land, sea, and sky meet and where human civilization runs up against its natural boundary. Sven Delblanc and Ulf Olsson have both pointed out the significance of this setting in terms of the issues raised in *By the Open Sea;* the outer edges of the archipelago provide a geographical position and cultural landscape that allow Strindberg to meditate on conflict and transformation within culture. Strindberg depicts the archipelago culture in *By the Open Sea* and other prose texts as a repository of traditionalism, as a society resistant to the transformative power of modernism. And in all of his archipelago fiction, modern forces in the form of a protagonist, an innovator who means to work change, invade this last bastion of traditional culture. Thus the relationship of modern humanity to the natural world and traditional culture is Strindberg's ecological subject.

"Subject" can also be taken to refer to the governing consciousness of the work of art, but it would be a mistake to refer to the crusading modernist protagonist as the ecological subject of Strindberg's archipelago texts. True, it is the story of the protagonist's psyche that dominates *The People of Hem's Island* (*Hemsöborna,* 1887), "The Silver Marsh" ("Silverträsket," 1898), "The Quarantine Master's Second Tale" ("Karantänmästarens andra berättelse," 1902), and, in particular, *By the Open Sea.* But rather than identifying the novel's speaking subject with a particular figure within the novel, I would instead like to imagine the "ecological subject" as a particular discursive position.

Ecocritic Christopher Manes, in his essay "Nature and Silence," posits that an ecologically concerned literature attempts to give voice to an otherwise silent natural world, and similarly, in Norwegian philosopher Arne Naess's "ecosophy," the ecological subject is an evolved form, so to speak, of the human subject. Naess, in his philosophical writing, argues for a revised notion of the self that would not distinguish between the human subject and nature: "through the wider Self every living being is intimately connected, and from this intimacy follows the capacity of identification" (233). Essentially the two perspectives voiced by Manes and Naess revolve around the same idea: that it is fallacious to distinguish absolutely between the human subject and nature as subject, and concomitantly, it is fallacious to place the human subject at the apex of nature. *By the Open Sea* offers a vivid illustration of what can happen when a human insists on imagining himself as dominant within the natural world. At the same time, it is the human voice that "speaks a word for nature," to cite Manes. *By the Open Sea* offers an account of a human being who strives to overcome nature's voice and is ultimately silenced by nature. The fallacy of imagining human domination over nature proves to be the fatal error for a modern protagonist, something the text communicates through its ecological perspective.

In *By the Open Sea* and the archipelago paintings an ecological subject takes shape and is allowed to speak; as Douglas Feuk argues in his interpretation of Strindberg's images, the paintings "*embody meaning*" (24; emphasis in original). I would argue that the meaning has to do with the human encounter with nature, which is the liminal space where the ecological subject finds its voice. This is the place Strindberg returns to again and again in his paintings. And *By the Open Sea,* often read as an exploration of Nietzschean philosophy or as a portrait of an artist or as a reflection of Strindberg's own experience, might also be read with the following question in mind: what happens to humankind when modernity runs up against the natural world? This is the essential ecocritical question, and it is the problem I would like to explore through both Strindberg's paintings and the novel.

A Question of Optic

Imagine a suite of sun-bright seascapes: the perspective is out onto the open sea with the beach at our feet. In the foreground, a lone flower (*Purple Loosestrife*) or a toadstool (*Solitary Toadstool*) or a single track of human footprints marks the band of color as sand (see Hedström for reproductions of Strindberg's paintings, with English commentary). Just beyond, the meeting between sand and sea can barely be perceived. It runs along as an only occasionally discernable, wavy line, wavy to match the pattern of the surf as it comes in. The color of the water and the sand are distinct from one another, but not markedly so, and at times the difference becomes nearly imperceptible. The eye has to work hard to find where land ends and sea begins. In the middle distance we see a more distinct line: the horizon where sea meets sky. But even here it is difficult to be sure of the material difference between the two realms divided by the line of horizon. They are both light blue and diaphanous. Douglas Feuk writes of the seascapes: "Boundaries and differences are vague. Air seems to have the same density as stone, and rock seems mysteriously joined to water, as if all were but different manifestations of one and the same matter" (28). Another set of images from the same period depicts a dark sea: the ocean is now in nocturnal turmoil, the beach is gone, replaced by rocks or a buoy or a sea marker, but lacking solid ground entirely. Mirroring the roiling black sea, the stormy black sky swirls in the same violent wind that moves the waves. Again, the sea and sky are distinguishable, but only just. There is no horizon. There is only motion and darkness.

During his lifetime, Strindberg's paintings remained relatively obscure, showing only at a few exhibits, and never to acclaim. In fact, Strindberg's friend, the Swedish artist Carl Larsson, felt that the paintings lacked all artistic merit, and one of Stockholm's important galleries declined to lend their Strindberg canvases out during the commemoration of the founding of Sweden's National Museum in 1947. They did not want Sweden to be represented, they said, by a mediocre amateur painter. But by 1962, the fiftieth anniversary of Strindberg's death, the museum refused to lend out the paintings for another reason: the images had become indispensable to the museum's standing collection. In less than two decades, Strindberg had passed, in the eyes of the critics, from amateurish dauber to an important representative of Swedish modernism.[3] An exhibit of canvases toured Germany, Belgium, Paris, Copenhagen, Amsterdam, and London during that anniversary year of 1962, and subsequently Strindberg's paintings made their way to Leningrad and returned to Paris and London for extended single-artist exhibits. In 2005, London's Tate Gallery combined a staging of *Miss Julie* with a popular exhibit of Strindberg's paintings, pointing up the relationship between Strindberg's stripped-down gender and class drama and the proto-abstraction of his seascapes.

From the historical vantage of a century after Strindberg's death, it is now commonplace to describe his paintings, along with his plays and other writings, as standing on the threshold of modernism, and the paintings (and Strindberg's photographs) have taken their place as a significant aspect in his international image. But what precisely does this mean? The first time the paintings were exhibited in Stockholm in 1892, reviewers commented (disparagingly) on the difficulty of determining what it was that they were intended to represent—the color applied in textured layers, the difficulty, described above, of distinguishing between earth and sea and sky, the volatile nature of the applications of paint in the stormy images—these features lend themselves to association with abstraction, with impressionism or, in some cases, expressionism. Strindberg had written approving critical pieces for Swedish publications on the French impressionists when he encountered their works in France, and in 1894 he authored an essay on what he called "the new arts," art created by chance, art created by nature. The latter has been taken by many to forecast surrealism and found art (see for example Söderström, Kesting, and Robinson). Seen in the light of modernism, Strindberg's paintings, like the plays of his later period, could be regarded as reflections on his inner life, his psyche. Yet I would take them as something else as well.

First, as I stated earlier, these paintings are representations of the landscape Strindberg inhabited while writing *By the Open Sea*. The stormy images *The White Marker II* (*Vita Märrn II*) and *Broom Buoy* (*Stormigt Hav. Ruskprick*), both completed in 1892, depict navigational features described in *By the Open Sea* as part of the archipelago seacape, recognizable indicators of the setting for the paintings, even as the violent swirl of sea and sky seems to deny any firm grounding in an actual place. In the right-hand corner of an 1893 painting, Strindberg has depicted with great precision one of the most common of Sweden's poisonous toadstools, the *röd flugsvamp* (in English "fly agaric"; botanical name *Amanita muscaria*). And in the foreground of three other paintings from

1892 (*Purple Loosestrife, Beach on a Summer's Night,* and *The Solitary Thistle*) appear small, botanically correct renderings of flower species that grow in the Stockholm archipelago. A number of scholars have suggested that these isolated, well-delineated figures set against vast ocean and sky are meant to indicate the presence of the painter—that they are semi-comic portraits of the artist (Söderström, Kesting). But the almost Linneaen rendering of these flowers apparently evolved in style from detailed botanical pencil sketches Strindberg made while living on the archipelago island Runmarö and writing *By the Open Sea;* in the pencil drawings he labels each specimen: "Valerian, Corn Chamomile, and Sea Aster" (Hedström 26).

The scientific observation of nature is an important part of the optic developed in *By the Open Sea;* it is one of the ways Axel Borg, the novel's modern protagonist, perceives and describes the world of the archipelago. The term "optic" in Borg's case has unusual resonance. In one of the more memorable early scenes of the novel Borg goes out to sea with a boatsman and for hours leans over the side of their craft looking through a telescope into the water, which allows for a long meditation on the undersea life of the islands. This detailed and colorful portrait of an ordinarily invisible world of animal and plant life is filtered first through a modern optical tool, then through the scientific practices of taxonomy (giving the names of the fish and seaweed as Borg makes his observations) and a rather judgmental and emotionally colored form of evolutionary discourse:

> The inhabitants of the seabed dragged themselves along on their bellies, seeking darkness and cold, hiding their shame at having been left behind in the long struggle towards sun and air. (27/31)[4]

Borg's optic is set in opposition to two other ways of looking at nature depicted in *By the Open Sea,* one advocated by his father, who was an engineer, and the other typical of those Borg regards as dilettantes in nature: enthusiasts ("nature worshippers") and artists. Filtered through Borg's consciousness, the novel represents Borg's father in geological terms, as "mixed like a conglomerate blend of cemented splinters and refuse from preceding periods, gathered at random after the great eruption of the last century" (31/36). Borg's image of his father reflects the way in which natural and human realms are melded in Borg's perspective, and it is typical as well that the novel's protagonist envisions an individual person or landscape as containing traces of all ages, all landscapes. I will return to this, but will first examine more closely the father's optic:

> He became a distinguished topographer and took part in the building of the Göta Canal and the first railways. This preoccupation with a whole kingdom, which he was accustomed to have spread before him on the maps laid out on his table, taught him to view it from above, to survey it in a moment, and by degrees this developed in him a capacity to see things on a grand scale. . . . The map had to be altered, old waterways forgotten, and the straight, black lines of the new railways had to become the deciding factors. The uplands had to be made as fertile as the valleys. . . .
>
> A strong feeling of power resulted from this manipulation of the fates of countries and peoples, and his father had not escaped being gradually affected by the tendency to overrate his own ego, a thing which often follows the acquisition of power. He began to take a bird's-eye view of everything. Countries became maps and people tin soldiers. (33/37)

The father's topographic perspective allows for the modernization of Sweden, even as it causes a deformation of his psyche through an essential misunderstanding of his place within nature. The power to make fruitful valleys of the mountains and convert the sinuous waterway routes of the past into the straight black lines of the railways recalls the Lord's promise to Cyrus in Isaiah 45: "Själv skall jag gå framför dig, backarna skall jag jämna ut" ("I will go before you and will level the mountains"). The novel's description of the surge of power and growth of ego experienced by the father from his bird's-eye perspective begins to hint at a dangerous hubris engendered by the optic of modernity. The father's distance from the natural world allows him to see it in abstract, manipulable form, which leads to the father's eagerness to alter the very structure of the natural world, to shape it according to his needs and his inner vision.

When we are first introduced to Borg's father, he appears as a believer in "the pantheism of the Young Hegelians" (32/36), a system which posits the individual as the only reality, something that implies a unity of the human and nature, with humankind "as the highest link in the chain of the world's development" (32/36). Borg, too, embraces the idea of humanity (and more specifically, himself) as the pinnacle of creation, though his philosophical and scientific conviction derives not from Hegel, but from taxonomy, geology, and evolutionary biology (and a reading of race and culture derived from a kind of social Darwinism): "he realised that human beings could be classified like animals and plants in large classes, types, and families" (46/49), and his method of classification leads him to regard "children, most criminals, the majority of women, and some madmen" as "semi-mammalian" (46–47/49–50). Lower classifications are also prescribed for what Borg perceives as racial others: immigrant Germans, Walloons, Jews, and gypsies. If one attends carefully, however, the text hints that Borg's careful and orderly classification of the natural order contains a fatal inconsistency. The "semi-mammalian" tribe of children, women, madmen, and criminals are "unable to distinguish between subject and object" (47/50). But Borg himself uses nature as a kind of refuge, allowing himself to descend to the position of the lower classes; while observing the archipelago landscape, he can "fall back as it were in a healthy trance and feel at one with nature" (30/35).

At first flush, it would seem that Borg's scientific perspective on nature is nothing more than an outgrowth or evolution, so to speak, of his father's empirical and pragmatic gaze. After all, they draw similar conclusions about the preeminence of scientific man in the chain of creation. But Borg *looks* differently at the natural world. He moves through the natural world in an utterly transformed way as well. Unlike his father, who sets his scientific gaze on representations—maps—in the safety of his study, Borg goes out into nature and literally gets his feet wet, destroying his fine shoes and gloves on the initial stormy journey out to the archipelago. Even as he peers at the undersea world from above through a telescope, he enters into the natural world in his imagination, ascribing thoughts and feelings and sensations to the creatures he observes: the crow exhibits a "thievish bearing" and "criminal demeanour," making him the "object of hatred" to the more "industrious" birds. The reptiles hiss in a "first weak effort to express rage," the perch is "a bit of a philosopher and a bit of a pirate," the pike "dream[s] of the flowery meadows and birches up above which he can never visit" (26–27/32–33). Far from adopting a position above or outside nature in order to enforce the dominance of his subject position, Borg seeks to lose himself within the limitless sea and sky of the archipelago. When the natives of the island prove too much of an irritation, he gives up his scientific optic and takes his solace in union with the earth by lying on his back on the ground and staring up into the limitless sky: "all reminders of his fellow men, of the community, of laws and customs were swept away, and he allowed his thoughts to run riot. . . . By these means he intoxicated himself to the point of unconsciousness, like the Indian who gazes at his navel and forgets both heaven and earth in the contemplation of an unimportant external part of himself" (20/25). While the Indian gazes at his own body, however, the sky above functions as the "external part" of Borg's self as he rests in contemplation and releases himself from the bonds of conscious thought.

Sven Delblanc wants to argue that Borg's gaze is not scientific after all, but the gaze of an artist. He offers a number of persuasive arguments to show that the novel's protagonist is in fact an artist figure; but if he is an artist, he is a reluctant one. The text in fact expresses some resistance to the idea of Borg as an artist: "It was not with the dream-like imagination of the poet, or with vague and consequently disturbing emotions and confused perceptions that the beholder enjoyed this great spectacle. No, it was with the calm eyes of the scholar and conscious thinker that he detected order behind this apparent disorder" (29/34). When Borg attempts to instruct the object of his attraction, Maria, on the nature of the archipelago, she protests "but you are spoiling nature for yourself!" and he responds, "It puts me on intimate terms with nature: it soothes me to know that I have thereby freed myself from the poet's half-concealed dread of the unknown" (94/95). Borg's vision of his environment oscillates between the perspective he explicitly owns—the scientific optic—and the one he at every turn wants to disclaim: the artistic worldview. Sven Delblanc's argument that Borg is an artist figure is not entirely without grounds; but Borg is an artist despite himself, contrary to his stated intentions. Various scholars have noted the protagonist's dandyism, his excessive sensitivity, his proclivity for imposing an artist's vision on his living space and on the archipelago itself (Delblanc, Olsson). These features seem to point to a prototype for the decadence and decline of civilized humanity. When Borg creates his only actual artwork—the illusion of classical Italy with which he intends to delude the populace and charm Maria—he uses his scientific knowledge to bring about the artistic mirage. But when the illusion, by virtue of a trick of the sun's angle, takes on a reality he had not himself anticipated (since he had "never expected an otherwise law-abiding nature to produce such a monstrous phenomenon"), he "turned deathly pale himself from shock" (114/115). The power of the forces he has set in motion through his manipulation of the natural world exceeds his power to control them, and the position he wishes to maintain on the highest rung of the evolutionary scale receives a sound shaking as a result. It is his scientific belief that nature is "bound by laws" (essentially human constructions) that leads to his shock.

Marianne Kesting, reading the two archipelago texts "The Silver Lake" ("Silverträsket") and *By the Open Sea,* argues that Strindberg privileges the imagination over the landscape (the artistic subject takes preeminence, in other words), citing passages which she claims offer evidence of a projection of the self onto the landscape through the artistic process (174). The citations she chooses as evidence, however, are focalized through the protagonists of those narratives, and I would argue that the texts as a whole take up a critical position regarding these impositions of self onto the landscape. When she describes Borg's self-projection, for instance, it takes the following form in the novel: "This great expanse of water was like the embodiment of something emanating from the beholder, and only existing through him. *As long as he stood on land* he felt intimate with this *now harmless force,* superior to this immense source of power *now that he was out of its reach*" (16/21–22). I have emphasized the moments in the passage where the problem with Borg's optic becomes evident. The scene cited above occurs in the second chapter of the novel; in the first chapter, Borg just barely managed to survive the rage of the stormy sea on his journey out to the island. Now it is morning on the second day, the sea is calm, and Borg enjoys the security of distance and standing on solid ground. *Now* the sea is harmless, as long as he is out of its reach; but his sense of superiority, his notion that the sea is nothing more than something he imagines ("the embodiment of something emanating from the beholder"), is marked by the text as arrogant and misguided. By the end of the novel, the power of the sea will prevail, and Borg's assertion of preeminence will be entirely discredited, as is that of the narrator of "The Silver Lake."

One of the difficulties posed by Strindberg's prose text occurs in distinguishing among the various perspectives in the narrative; here I think that although, as Kesting points out, Borg's position at times closely parallels sentiments voiced by Strindberg in other, even nonfictional, texts, one must stay alive to the way in which the text undermines Borg's optic. It is precisely the critique raised against Borg and the other archipelago protagonists that makes an ecocritical reading productive.

Living in the Material World

I have noted that Borg enters into nature and merges with it through his gestures of anthropomorphization, self-erasure, and self-projection, but also by moving through the natural world, examining it at close quarters, exposing himself to the water, wind, sun, and rain. In the opening chapter mentioned above, the fragile, nattily dressed, and oversensitive Borg finds himself in a sailboat in rough seas, at the mercy of more experienced and coarser men as they attempt to navigate to their island through the gathering gloom. Borg's keen observational powers and scientific knowledge tell him that the boat's sail will not stand up to the high winds; he first offers advice, then commands the men to hand over the control of the boat to him. One of the more striking (if not entirely convincing) scenes of Strindberg's prose authorship follows:

> He soon taught himself the harmonics of the waves and he could even hear when danger was approaching by the tempo of the swell. He could tell by the pressure on his left eardrum when the wind was blowing hardest and threatening to whip the water up higher. It was as if he were improvising nautical and metereological instruments from his delicate senses, to which cords passed freely from his large brain-battery. (6/12)

The textual image of a "brain-battery" is more than mere metaphor. Wind and sound waves move through Borg's ear canals and set his eardrum into motion. Borg is literally "plugged in" to the raging sea. The cords and wires of his nervous system, which the narrative quite correctly describes as carrying electrical impulses, transmit messages to his brain for interpretation, and the brain sends out signals telling the body how to react—how to dance, as it were, with the storm. The process itself is no different from what occurs in the brains and bodies of the rougher sailors; the difference is that Borg's experience is converted into language and interpreted. And in fact, this same process of picking up the signals of the environment and reacting, converting them into energy and movement, is a description of how we live our everyday lives. The crisis moment of the storm merely throws light upon what is a normal circumstance and reveals also how Borg is abnormally conscious of something that usually occurs on an unconscious level. At the apex of excitement in this passage, Borg, sensing the presence of a dangerous barrier, strikes several matches at once and casts them up into the air, throwing into sudden illumination a devastating wave that is bearing down upon their boat. In this way the text creates an emblem of what the narrative itself performs; it lets us catch a glimpse of something that otherwise exists at the level of involuntary senses.

Borg's world is insistently material, and sometimes it can strike the reader that *By the Open Sea* enumerates in precise terminology the archipelago's each and every bird, fish, mineral, and form of sea life. But the text also lingers on descriptions of human artifacts and implements, pulling these, too, into relationship with the natural world:

> His inkwell, a large, glass cube cut in facets, shone with the pale blue light of water on ice. His porcupine-quill pen-holders, with their oily, indeterminate colours, produced a suggestion of animal life. The loud vermillion of the sealing-wax . . . the cold brillance of the steel scissors, the varnish and gold of the ash-trays, the bronze of the paper-knife. (22/27)

This passage highlights another fact that should strike us as quite ordinary, and yet it is something that does not receive much conscious attention: the items attached to "civilization" are also natural objects, made of the materials of the earth. The positions "nature" and "culture" are not opposed to each other in the way one often imagines, and even at his most cultivated—Borg lavishly decorates his room in order to combat what he classifies as the primitive simplicity of the islanders—the presence of the natural world is still preeminent in his life, and cannot be held at a distance, as he believes he can hold the sea and its power at bay.

If we return to the paintings now, we can see that Strindberg as painter attends with gusto to the materiality of his images. Marianne Kesting notes Strindberg's use of paint itself as a meaningful element; he uses a knife to slather the color on his image, making the viewer conscious of the texture of the paint, conscious of the painting as not just representation but a physical object. This is true especially in the dark and stormy paintings, where the paint re-creates the structure and movement of waves, but even the light and sunny seascapes usually include a textured line of horizon or indentations in the paint that are meant to represent human footprints in the sand. Oil paint is made up of natural components; some of the commonly employed pigments are among Strindberg's favorite color adjectives in his texts: cerulean, vermilion, cinnabar. During the period he painted, these pigments were made of entirely natural materials (today many are synthetic), and they were blended with plant oils, such as linseed, from flax. All of this is to say that the act of painting engages the painter's senses, of touch and smell as well as sight, with materials from the natural world. Like Borg's "brain-battery," the painter's sensory apparatus is plugged into the natural world in a way that is more palpable and conscious than it is for a writer (who also deals, though to a lesser degree of sensuality, with natural materials). Strindberg's texts, as has been noted by numerous readers, swarm with references to color (as evident even in the passage cited above); but in his paintings, he *produces* color in concert with nature.

At the end of his essay "New Directions in Art! Or the Role of Chance in Artistic Creation," Strindberg exults: "The art of the future (which will disappear, like everything else!): Imitate nature in an approximate way, imitate in particular nature's way of creating!" (cited in Hedström 182). In the context of the argument in this essay, we can take Strindberg to mean that nature creates by chance, unconsciously, as clouds take shape in the sky or coals burn down to peculiar shapes in a fire. But nature creates through the properties of the material world: the temperature, consistency, density, and so on of all the elements that make up the environment, in communion or conflict with one another. Strindberg places the artist's mind and eye and hand within that vast and complex assemblage as parts of the material world, plugged into the energies that move through it, and proposes to let the power of nature make his art. To the many forces of nature at play (light, air, wind, etc.) we can add the painter's unconscious, which will find a way to express itself in the painting as well. But it is not the dominant force in the assemblage, and certainly the conscious mind has to relinquish the commanding position imagined by a scientific figure like Borg, has to acknowledge how the human is fully embedded in nature, living in a permeable body, plugged into a network larger than itself. And it is important also to recall that Strindberg says of the new art that it, "like everything else," will disappear. The inevitable "melting of everything that is solid into air" Strindberg cites reflects a strong ecological consciousness, an implicit acknowledgment of the earth's status as living and mortal being, subject to the forces of erosion and decay.

By the Open Sea

I mentioned above that, in looking at the nearly abstract archipelago images Strindberg produces, some critics have fastened on the solitary toadstool or flower or buoy or sea-marker as an indication of Strindberg's presence—a self-portrait of the artist. Douglas Feuk takes a different, more intriguing view: "I myself tend to detect Strindberg's presence mainly in the strange horizon, a razor-sharp slash between water and the wider expanse of light above[, which] appear exactly alike. . . . Strindberg's intention . . . was not to create an illusion of reality but offer the horizon as an idea" (Feuk 47). Feuk goes on to explain that he feels that the stressed presence of the horizon (emphasized through a thicker application of paint) announces Strindberg's return to spirituality and his belief in dualism. While I would like to go along with Feuk in seeing the horizon as a compelling signifier, it seems to me that something else might be signified. The horizon appears as a threshold, not unlike the strand depicted in the foreground of these paintings. But the crossing over, which could be imagined, as Feuk does, in spiritual terms, might also indicate a crossing-over into oneness.

The archipelago paintings of 1892 depict, as Per Hedström has observed, a number of the motifs represented in the novel of 1890, *By the Open Sea*. Hedström suggests that "the novel could give us an indication of how Strindberg might have seen [the sea and the archipelago]" (40). It seems reasonable to posit, as Sven Delblanc and Ulf Olsson have done, that the archipelago setting is an allegorical as well as a real one; as

Olsson stresses, "the space indicated by the title is a border space" (244, my translation). The archipelago constitutes a border between delimited and open space, and I would say (drawing my own allegory) that this border separates, among other things, a delimiting and categorical way of thinking and seeing from an open and utterly integrated form of experience. If I were then to propose that the latter form, the world beyond the horizon, is the realm of the ecological subject, I would run into trouble, since in the final analysis of the novel, Borg sails off toward that (never reachable) horizon and into his death. The "oneness" implied in that union would mean the extinction of the human within the natural world, and that is not a productive ground for establishing an ecological subject. Rather, one should regard Borg's end as an outcome of his madness, which results from his insistence on the primacy of the individual and his refusal (or inability?) to accept connection to the human beings that make up the community in which he, after all, must live if he means to live. When he casts off the woman he meant to marry and begins instead to try to create his own homunculi children, a form of reproduction that privileges science and denies his nature as a human animal, it is clear that he has, ironically enough, lost the mind that he himself imagined to be the pinnacle of creation.

It is not an easy conclusion. In the sunny archipelago paintings, the clarity of the sea and sky beckon with a promise of openness and oneness and eternity in a shining blue and white realm, not unlike the one Borg sees as he lays on his back, gazing into the sky in order to break all connections to the human society that imprisons him. But Borg sets out on his last journey at night, and though the night is lit by stars, the reader understands that ultimately he will be engulfed in darkness, the darkness of the stormy paintings, the darkness without horizon. In Borg we find a model of science gone wrong, nature misunderstood. Despite his encyclopedic knowledge of the natural world that surrounds him, he has failed to grasp that the hierarchical model inspired in him by his reading of Darwin and natural history has left him in a position of isolation from his fellow humans and the network that gives him life. As he sails out onto the open sea he exults at sailing "out over the sea, the mother of all, the inexhaustible well of fertility and love, life's source, and life's enemy" (185/183). But in approaching the "mother of all," he bypasses the most proximate connection, the woman who could be the mother of the children he clearly wants to father, and instead loses his voice and claim to be part of the web of the living. In imagining Borg and in repeating again and again the threshold image of the outer islands, Strindberg brings our attention to the threshold space we all inhabit in relation to each other and to the natural world in which we are both subjects and material objects. And in this he exhibits a profoundly ecological consciousness, one that brings him into the ongoing global conversation about the human subject in a global environment.

Notes

1. www.asle.org/site/resources/ecocritical-library/intro/defining/glotfelty/; see also the various definitions offered at the Western Modern Language Association meeting in 1994: www.asle.org/site/resources/ecocritical-library/intro/defining/.

2. In insisting on the importance of setting in the novel and paintings, I am following the lead of Anna Westerståhl Stenport, who argues convincingly for the need to examine the geographic locations of modernist prose, and particularly in the prose of August Strindberg.

3. Grishka Petri has written on the modernist aspect of Strindberg's painting in a couple of essays, noting that what we consider "modernist" about the images probably emerges more from our expectations of what "modern" should be than any intent on Strindberg's part to produce what we would now call an "abstract" painting. But she does argue that Strindberg's method of painting falls into the camp of what would, in the years following the Second World War, come to be called "informal" art. Strindberg himself uses a different term: "This is natural art, where the artist works in the same capricious way as nature, without a set goal" ("New Directions," cited in Hedberg, 178).

4. I will give page numbers for the English translation of the novel, followed by a page number indicating the location of the citation in the Swedish edition.

Works Cited

Carlson, Harry. *Out of Inferno: Strindberg's Reawakening as an Artist.* Seattle: University of Washington Press, 1996.

Delblanc, Sven. *Strindberg—urtida, samtida, framtid: Texter av Sven Delblanc.* Ed. Lars Ahlbom and Björn Meidal. Stockholm: Carlssons, 2007.

Feuk, Douglas. *August Strindberg: Inferno Painting, Pictures of Paradise.* Hellerup: Edition Bløndal, 1991.

Glotfelty, Cheryl, and Harold Fromm, eds. *The Ecocriticism Reader: Landmarks in Literary Ecology.* Athens: University of Georgia Press, 1996.

Hedström, Per, ed. *Strindberg: Painter and Photographer.* New Haven, Conn.: Yale University Press, 2001.

Johannesson, Erik O. *The Novels of August Strindberg.* Berkeley: University of California Press, 1968.

Kesting, Marianne. "Das unbestimmte und der Zufall: Über Beziehungen zwischen Strindbergs Dichtung und Malerei." In *Dialog der Künste: Intermediale Fallstudien Zur Literatur des 19. und 20. Jahrhundert,* ed. Maria Moog-Grünewald and Christoph Rodiek. Frankfurt am Main: Peter Lang, 1989. 167–83.

Manes, Christopher. "Nature and Silence." In *The Ecocriticism Reader: Landmarks in Literary Ecology*, ed. Glotfelty and Fromm. Athens: University of Georgia, 1996. 15–29.

Naess, Arne. "Self-Realization: An Ecological Approach to Being in the World." In *Deep Ecology for the Twenty-First Century*, ed. George Sessions. Boston: Shambala, 1993.

Olsson, Ulf. *Levande död: Studier i Strindbergs prosa*. Stockholm: Symposion, 1996.

Petri, Grischka. "August Strindbergs Moderne Malerei und der Zufall im kunsthistorischen Schaffen." In *August Strindberg: Der Dichter und die Medien*. Munich: Wilhelm Fink Verlag, 2003. 83–112.

Robinson, Michael. *Studies in Strindberg*. Norwich: Norvik, 1982.

Söderström, Göran. *August Strindberg: "Underlandet."* Malmö: Malmö Konsthall, 1989.

———. *Strindberg och bildkonsten*. Stockholm: Forum, 1972.

Stenport, Anna Westerståhl. *Locating August Strindberg's Prose: Modernism, Transnationalism, and Setting*. Toronto: University of Toronto Press, 2010.

Strindberg, August. *By the Open Sea*. Trans. Mary Sandbach. London: Secker and Warburg, 1984.

———. *I havsbandet*. In *Samlade Verk* 31. Stockholm: Almqvist and Wiksell Förlag, 1982.

Paris, Laboratory of Modernity: Modernist Experimentation and August Strindberg's Search for "the Equation" in Paris

Sylvain Briens

As a writer in his Parisian laboratory, Strindberg places himself in the position of a scientific researcher. As a man of science his discourse is experimental in the sense that Émile Zola gives to this word in his essay from 1890 on *The Experimental Novel*: "Why does not literature itself become a science, thanks to the experimental method?" (Zola 81). Strindberg shares Zola's point of view when the latter explains that the experimental novel applies the methodology of the physician Claude Bernard and his protocol of scientific experimentation to literature. But contrary to Zola, whose fictional opus does not really in the end put this theoretical idea into practice, Strindberg introduces a scientific methodology in the *Inferno* cycle (1897) and thus experiments with a form of modernist writing, which plays with the aesthetic possibilities of a narration inspired by the *experience* of science. Paris becomes to him a double laboratory of a modernity that is both aesthetic and scientific.

Strindberg is not the only Scandinavian writer at the end of the nineteenth century to turn Paris into his laboratory. Sophus Claussen in *Antonius in Paris* (*Antonius i Paris,* 1896) and Johannes V. Jensen in *The Gothic Renaissance* (*Den gotiske renaissance,* 1901) also explore, through phantasmagorical forms of writing, the possibilities of Paris as *the capital of modernity* in Walter Benjamin's sense. In a more general way it is worth noting that the notion of modernity in Scandinavian literature is intimately linked with an attitude of the writer not as a witness to a present or past process, but as an experimenter turned toward the future. The term "modern" was introduced in Scandinavia by Georg Brandes as *the Modern Breakthrough* in his Copenhagen University lecture series of

1871. Brandes addressed the major currents of European literature in the nineteenth century in reaction to society's modernization, which he had recently discovered on a visit to Paris (at this period, Scandinavian society had only barely initiated these transformations). While in the rest of western Europe the modern project in the arts is a response to modernization, as shown by, among others, Stephen Kern in *The Culture of Time and Space: 1880–1918*, the *Modern Breakthrough* is in advance of the evolution of Scandinavian society. It heralds, rather than reflects on, the modernization of this society. In this way the Parisian experience sparks a cultural movement in which literature asserts itself more as an index for the future than as the echo of a present or recently past phenomenon. It is in this cultural movement that Paris affirms itself as a laboratory of Scandinavian modernity, conferring on the modern writer a function as a visionary pointing the way for society to follow.

At the end of the nineteenth century, Paris became an essential field of production and reception for the Scandinavian literatures. Historians of literature have given different labels to this phenomenon of international cultural concentration. Paris has been called a *cultural* or *literary capital;* Pascale Casanova has spoken of "the Greenwich meridian of literature" (127); Brigitte Munier has termed Paris "the workshop of modernity"; and Jean-Claude Villegas "the factory of literature" (215). I prefer the term *laboratory of modernity,* because of the experimental character of the artistic activities taking place there. Paris represents a laboratory in the original sense of the term (from Latin *labor*): it is a workplace where new products are elaborated. But Paris also functions as a *counter-field* for Scandinavian culture and, as such, is a laboratory in the full sense of the word. By definition it is a *counter-field* (a space outside of the traditional national field of culture, but which interacts with the national field) that is at the same time an enclosed space and a place of experimentation.

First, Paris is by necessity an enclosed space because of the geographical distance separating the city from Scandinavia. Like Italo Calvino a century later in his essay "Hermit in Paris" ("Ermita a Parigi," 1994), August Strindberg in effect describes his Parisian sojourn of *Inferno* in terms of withdrawal, retreat, and spiritual hermitage. The isolation of the Parisian context in relation to cultural life in Scandinavia is the exact image of how every laboratory works: it is enclosed unto itself. Second, Paris is a space of liberty, which invites Scandinavian writers to experience modernity and, in response, to experiment with new forms of expression. In Paris they make their personal discovery of the metropolis and of the artistic Bohemia; it is a social laboratory due to the liberality of its morals, its bohemianism, and paganism. They live through what

Walter Benjamin called "the experiment of shock" (207–8). Aesthetic innovation becomes an artistic imperative. Montmartre, Montparnasse, Saint-Germain-des-Prés, and the Latin Quarter are sites for the creation of modernity, sometimes revolutionary, often radical, but always innovative. Third, Paris constitutes a political laboratory as the site of the French Revolution and the Commune.

Paris establishes itself as a place where writers work in an experimental mode, where they make their observations and carry out their experiments; it constitutes a true laboratory of the arts. Scandinavian writers equip themselves with the critical apparatuses for carrying out their experiments, analyses, and calculations. The notion of laboratory is thereby not a metaphor: it describes the work of writers in the period of naturalism, which defined the work of the writer as equivalent to that of the scientist. Strindberg is without a doubt the Scandinavian writer living in Paris who takes this perspective most seriously.

Paris is indeed a scientific laboratory for Strindberg's literary creativity, I argue in this chapter, a hypothesis supported by his intense activity as scientific researcher in Paris in the 1890s in connection with Parisian research institutions like the Sorbonne (chemistry), the Jardin des Plantes (botany), and the Salpêtrière (psychology). This aspect of Strindberg's intellectual activities should be taken into account when studying the literary *Inferno* cycle as one that establishes a parallel between scientific experimentation and modernist literary experimentation, which Strindberg develops in his prose at the end of the nineteenth century (see also Stenport 88–123). This parallel appears clearly when studying the intersections between scientific reflection and aesthetic experiment in the Parisian laboratory of the 1890s and when analyzing the narrative function of Paris as a laboratory in Strindberg's writing.

Strindberg's Scientific and Literary Experimentation in His Parisian Laboratory

In a letter to the founder of the Alchemical Society of France, François Jollivet-Castellot, dated January 29, 1897, Strindberg writes, "This spring I hope to return to Paris where I have lived in spirit since my youth, and where I have gathered what little I know in the sciences and the arts" (Melberg, "Barbaren i Paris" 93; my translation). As an intellectual very much aware of developments in the natural sciences, Strindberg studied chemistry, botany, medicine, mathematics, astronomy, meteorology, optics, and zoology in Paris. From an early stage Strindberg had shown a lively interest in science, but he would wait for the triumph of his *Creditors* (*Fordringsägare,* 1889) on the Parisian stage on June 21, 1894, and then *The Father* (*Fadren,* 1887) on December 13, 1895, which brought him the international literary success he had aspired to for so many years, before he abandoned literature and realized what he considered as his principal vocation: to gain recognition as a scientist. In *Inferno* he bears witness to this vocation:

> The theater disgusted me like all things that one has mastered, and science attracted me. Having to choose between love and learning, I had opted for the supreme knowledge, and the sacrifice of my emotions had made me forget the innocent victim sacrificed on the altar of my ambition, or my vocation. (32)[1]

Beginning in 1894, Strindberg decides to dedicate himself almost exclusively to scientific research. For four years he writes no other work of fiction except the *Inferno* cycle, which recounts precisely this intense scientific activity, with its hesitations, its failures, and successes.[2]

One may ask whether this scientific activity is merely of anecdotal importance in relation to Strindberg's literary production and his aesthetic reflections. But as the essay "Deranged Sensations" ("Sensations détraquées," 1894) shows, Strindberg tries to create a bridge between his scientific activity and his literary work. Strindberg himself considered "Deranged Sensations" to be an experimental text that set out to renew literary forms (see also Ericsson 70). In a letter to Littmansson dated October 15, 1894, Strindberg explains how he is searching for an equation to connect naturalism and symbolism as a "symbolist, detraquist compromise of natural science, poetry, and madness" (*Brev* 10:278).

According to Strindberg, it is a question of combining science, poetry, and madness in order to find what he calls "min livsekvation" (the equation of my life). To stay with the scientific terminology, which Strindberg uses to describe his aesthetic endeavor, one might subsume his literary experimentation in an equation to which the parameters are naturalism and symbolism and the solution is modernism. The expression "equation" is interesting in the sense that it refers on the one hand to the notion of correspondence (between the two sides of the equation separated by the equal sign) and on the other hand to the idea of variable input (the parameters of the equation). His aesthetic quest is inscribed in an existential crisis, and he is faced with the observation that life is in constant mutation before a world and a subject which have lost all stability. This quest passes through a crisis of representation, which is the very foundation of modernism.

Strindberg shows at this point in his life affinities with the symbolism of Maurice Maeterlinck and Stéphane Mallarmé, as illustrated by the motif of fairy tales in "Funereal Studies" and in *Legends* (*Legender,* 1898). The motifs of roses, wisteria, and cypresses in "Funereal Studies" also recall Gerard de Nerval or Alfred de Musset. It might be thought that this sensibility to lyricism and musical melancholy would make Strindberg an atmospheric poet in the symbolist tradition. Yet Strindberg differs in his way of interpreting the symbols. Rimbaud moves into the domain of exalted hallucination, while Strindberg grounds his reflection in an observation of the minutiae of scientific reality. He never closes his eyes, and remains constantly awake. As Gunnar Brandell underlines: "A symbol is always something concrete, which contains something abstract, but for the Symbolists the emphasis is on the abstract element, for Strindberg on the concrete" (221). In *Inferno,* Strindberg describes "semi-visions" ("*halvvisioner*"): the beggar in the Closerie des Lilas, the individuals appearing on the Boulevard Saint-Germain while he is drinking an absinthe, and so on. Brandell incidentally reports that Strindberg thought of giving the subtitle *Conte symboliste* to the French translation of *By the Open Sea, Au bord de la vaste mer,* with one goal: "This would make me into a Modernist" (212).

Strindberg claims in a letter from January 22, 1888, that he has managed to solve the equation: "The young Frenchmen are still searching for the formula, but I have found it!" (quoted in Ericsson 74). What does this signify in terms of aesthetic innovation? Does Strindberg in his discourse on Paris find "the right formula"? Is Strindberg in Paris in the 1890s purely a scientist, who has forgotten all literary considerations? Or does he preserve a double identity, literary and scientific? The fact that Paris is the site of creation of so many works of literary and artistic innovation allows us to conclude, as do so many historians, that Paris is a workshop of modernity (see Munier) at the end of the nineteenth century. But the meeting of the literary and the scientific fields, in the same effort of understanding what is at stake aesthetically in modernity, transforms the workshop into a *laboratory.* More than a place of production, it is a place of experimentation, an experimentation which consists in effacing the artificial borders between sciences and humanities to find "the right formula."

In the *Inferno* cycle Strindberg uses the staging of Paris as a laboratory and the figure of a scientific researcher as narrator in order to blur the borders between science and literature. Elena Balzamo explains the continuity of style between his literary and scientific writings: "What is striking in the scientific writings of Strindberg is the absence of any kind of rupture with the tone and style of his literary writings" (223). On the contrary, Strindberg feeds off his activity as a scientist in his literary works. Per Stounbjerg terms this hybrid aesthetic identity "impure literature" (241–69). The literary discourse is impure to the extent that it is open to the world and transgresses the purity of art.

Strindberg's interest in the sciences and his quest for meaning are two determining elements in his literary development. As Brandell makes clear, the change in aesthetics is above all the result of a change in the conception of the world (204). The *Inferno* cycle contributes to the establishment of a theory of knowledge, a literary epistemology. Scientific and literary discourses intermingle in *Inferno* and *Legends.* Strindberg himself poses the question of literary genre in the conclusion to *Inferno:* is it fiction, an autobiographical journal, or a work of science? *Inferno* and *Legends* are certainly autobiographical, but what about the sections written in the form of scientific observations and proofs? How do we separate the scientific texts published in *L'Initiation* and *Sylva Sylvarum* from the fictional work when these texts are reintegrated as part of *Inferno*? Science and literature meet intentionally in Strindberg's work, at least in what concerns knowledge and logos. When he prepares scientific articles, Strindberg remains above all a writer. This may be the reason why he is eventually thwarted in his scientific work, but it is undoubtedly this interface of discourses that gives birth to an epistemology or noetics, which becomes essential to his literary production. This theory of knowledge appeared also in *Sleepwalking Nights on Waking Days (Sömngångarnätter på vakna dagar),* a poem written in 1883 which also describes Paris. Strindberg here introduces a reflection on rational theology (in Swedenborg's sense) and the notion of a divine signature and proposes a form of convergence between belief and scientific knowledge, for which the paradigm is his fascination with the Musée des Arts et Métiers in Paris, which houses its exposition of technical innovations in an old church.

The resonances of science in Strindberg's literary writings about Paris are numerous and operate at different levels. A first resonance is the influence of psychoanalysis and the doubling of the subject, in which Strindberg, with great precision, follows the methods of introspection in early forms of psychoanalysis (see Vogelweith). It is precisely in the staging of the double that a second scientific echo comes to express itself: that of theosophy. Asceticism, anamnesis, and somnambulism become central elements of Strindberg's Parisian narrations. The best example of this resonance of theosophy is the figure of the somnambulist in *Sleepwalking Nights on Waking Days*. The poem presents a fragmented chronotope due to a loss of temporal landmarks and an intermingling of places between Paris and Stockholm. During the first night the somnambulist experiences the separation of soul and body: while the body stays in the oppressive chaos of the train compartment, the spirit flies freed from gravity towards the north, in the opposite direction of the train. All these elements echo with the astral world of the theosophists. In a letter to Axel Lundegård from November 12, 1887, Strindberg writes:

> It appears to me as if I am sleepwalking; as if poem and life were blending . . . My peculiarity is that in a frequently recurrent nightly dream I feel myself to be flying, without gravity, finding this quite natural, just as equally all concepts of right and wrong, true and false seem to be dissolved for me, and everything that happens, no matter how unusual, seems to me to be just as it should be. (*Brev* 6: 157)

The narrative of the somnambulist finds its unity through Swedenborg's theory of correspondences, which proposes a set of relations between the physical world, the spiritual world, and the religious world. By this play of correspondences Strindberg stages the encounter between different levels of reality (material, oneiric, and religious) and advances a literary style which might be described (in the words of Jean Cocteau about the theater of Henrik Ibsen) as "unreal realism" (Cocteau preface).[3] The point is to introduce a description of "the unreal" in literature so that "the unreal" may extend the real, complement it, make it more intelligible. In a letter to Torsten Hedlund from 1896, the year *Inferno* was written, Strindberg confirms his method: "Hallucinations, fantasies, and dreams seem to me to contain a high level of reality" (*Brev* 11: 268).

It is no surprise to note Strindberg's fascination with the occult and his wish to become "the Zola of the occult" (*Brev* 11: 307). He is convinced that the occult is the new way of literature, that of the artistic avant-garde. His literary production around the turn of the century fed largely from the narratives of occult experiences, as illustrated in *Inferno* and *Legends* (as well as *The Occult Journal* to which they refer): telepathy, Buddhism, Hinduism, theosophy, alchemy, and the Kabbala are occult themes integrated in the literary discourse in a quest for meaning, which passes through the deciphering of invisible signs.

Strindberg attempts to manufacture gold scientifically in Paris, and his failure seems to lead him to synthesize another precious material, namely literature. The "alchemy of the word," in Rimbaud's term, is his real success. For it is through the literary resonances of the discourse of knowledge and the quest for meaning that Strindberg's manufacturing of gold gives the decisive impulse to Scandinavian modernism. By the application of rational theology, the theory of correspondences, and the notion of the divine signature, he introduces *unreal realism* to literature. Brandell proposes an analysis which confirms this interpretation:

> The scientific material has here been composed as a prose poem with a peculiar force of light. The argumentative form, which characterizes *Sylva Sylvarum* overall, has been replaced by a narrative presentation and the scientific demonstrations have been practically abandoned. It is the arabesque-like chain of association itself which interests Strindberg and which fascinates the reader. In this connection it is worth recalling that Strindberg a few months later read André Chevillon's description of the fantastic play of lines on an Indian vase and thought of giving the already planned *Inferno* volume the title "The Benares Vase." . . . According to his theories in *On the New Arts* the experience of a work of art should in itself consist in a sliding from image to image. In the original French text of *In the Cemetery* a section was included, in which Strindberg even more than in the saga of the death's-head hawk-moth lets his associations dance hither and thither in a Modernist confusion. (Brandell 217)

The scientific resonances in the literary work thus contribute a major innovation to the narration through an unexpected mediator, the gnosis. By the development of a theory of consciousness Strindberg proposes a form of literature in which a supra-sensible and supra-rational perception of the real liberates truth. The discrepancy from the real world, proper to the description of dreams, is certainly a necessary link in the process of knowledge, but it is also an essential stage in modern aesthetic renewal.

The *Inferno* Cycle as a Laboratory Novel

In *Inferno* and *Legends* Strindberg resorts to metafiction and describes his own scientific and aesthetic experiments. The narrator of the novel is acting as a scientific researcher mostly dedicated to chemistry and notes his comments in a book, which corresponds to the one we are reading. In that sense, *Inferno* and *Legends* can be considered as laboratory notebooks. Through this *mise-en-abyme* the fictional Paris here becomes a laboratory. The process is similar to the one that Primo Levi uses in *The Periodic System* (*Il sistema periodico*, 1975): the fact of writing a novel about a chemist permits the writer to resort to forms inspired by science. It is in this sense that one might call both of these novels *laboratory novels* (just as one might call Strindberg's *Occult Journal* a laboratory notebook). Just as Levi's novel follows a structure inspired by the periodic table for the classification of the natural elements, Strindberg's novel integrates his own previously published scientific articles. The discourse on Paris thus shows a separation in the text of Paris-as-laboratory between a literary prose text (the narrative of experiments) and a scientific prose text (the results, in the form of articles, of these experiments). The fictional world of Strindberg (like that of Levi) is thus fueled by the culture of science. And by reciprocity his scientific writings gain a literary value. Ulf Olsson perfectly sums up this endeavor: "The most modern drama proves to be that of science, the stage is formed by the spaces the wanderer can transform into laboratories" (376). The notion of the laboratory takes on three dimensions: scientific, psychological, and aesthetic.

The *Inferno* cycle is above all the portrait of Strindberg as scientist, who has chosen Paris as his laboratory. The sites of his experiments are the laboratory of the Saint Louis Hospital, Strindberg's chemistry laboratory, the laboratory of the Sorbonne, the Jardin des Plantes, the Montparnasse Cemetery, the Salpêtrière, and the hotels in which Strindberg stays (the Hotel Orfila, the hotel of the rue de la Grande-Chaumière, and the hotel of the rue de la Clef).

Paris appears in *Inferno* as the frame which contains Strindberg's scientific experiments. Already in the first chapter of *Inferno,* "The Hand of the Invisible," Strindberg narrates the installation of what he himself calls his "laboratory":

> Upon returning to my nasty student's digs in the Latin Quarter I searched my strongbox and brought out of their hiding place six containers of fine porcelain which I had taken care to buy by borrowing some money on my valuables. A pair of tongs and a packet of pure sulfur completed the installation of my laboratory. (*Inferno* 32)

Then he embarks on the narration of his experiments in this laboratory:

> A forge is lit in the fireplace, the door closed and the curtains drawn . . . Night falls, the sulphur burns in infernal flames, and towards morning I observe the presence of carbon in this body considered elemental, sulfur; and through this I believe I have resolved the great problem, reversed the reigning theories of chemistry, and gained the immortality accorded to mortals. (*Inferno* 32)

On receiving the results from the analyzing laboratory, of which he cites the contents, he concludes that pure sulfur contains carbon. This discovery confirms the theories on the nature of the elements which Strindberg had developed in his first collection of articles on chemistry, written in 1893 and published in German in 1894 under the title *Antibarbarus oder die Welt für sich und die Welt für mich.*[4] This book is a demonstration of the monistic theory of the unity of matter, which also takes into account the theories of Darwin and Haeckel.[5] It is composed of four booklets: the first on the nature of sulfur, the second on the transmutation of carbon, the third on water and air, and the fourth on the transmutation of metals. He takes a critical position in relation to modern chemistry, which in *Inferno* he calls "the outdated, deformed science" (56). The narrator further takes up an experimental activity at the Sorbonne: "Two days later I was enrolled at the Faculty of Sciences at the Sorbonne (at Saint Louis!) and authorized to work in the research laboratory" (47).

In 1896 he adds to his scientific production a work on botany, *Jardin des Plantes,* which is partially included in *Inferno.* The introduction and the article "The Cyclamen Throwing Light on the Infinite Disorder and Coherence" in fact make up chapter 5 with the title "Sylva Sylvarum"; and the article "Death's-Head Hawk-Moth" is included unabridged in chapter 6. This insertion of previously published scientific articles only concerns the French edition of 1898. The introduction to *Jardin des Plantes* (which forms the first part of the chapter "Sylva Sylvarum" in *Inferno*) states clearly the quest for meaning described in *Inferno:*

> And I no longer believed that the secret of the universe had been unveiled, and I departed, sometimes on my own, and sometimes in company, to reflect on the great disorder, in which I finished however by discovering an infinite coherence.
>
> This is the book about the great disorder and the infinite coherence. (60)

The reflections of the narrator in *Inferno* are thus concerned with the mysteries of the universe. And the scientific theory propounded in *Inferno,* which corresponds exactly to the one that Strindberg develops in all his scientific work in Paris, rests on three pillars: the universe has been created by God; the divine signature of the Creator is found in every element of creation; and creation is ordered mathematically.

> Leaving the minerals, I pass through the realms of plants and animals to arrive at Man, behind whom I discover the Creator. The Creator, this great artist who develops by creating, makes sketches, which He rejects, takes up again aborted ideas, perfects and multiplies the basic forms. (*Inferno* 141)

The work of the man of science consists of deciphering the rules of creation. The discourse on Paris in *Inferno* is thus at the same time a scientific and a Gnostic discourse. The scientific quest in the Parisian laboratory, put on stage here, is above all animated by a quest for meaning.

The third scientific article reprinted in *Inferno*, "Funereal Studies," belongs to the science of the occult. "Etudes funèbres" was published originally in French in 1896 in *La Revue des Revues*, then translated by Eugène Fahlstedt under the title "På Kyrkogården" ("At the Cemetery") and published the same year in *Vintergatan*. Strindberg here tells of his daily visit to the Montparnasse Cemetery and develops a chemical procedure for waking the dead:

> The souls, by which I mean to say the dematerialized bodies, thus held themselves floating in air: which brought me to the attempt to take them and analyze them. Armed with a small bottle filled with an acetate of liquid lead, I start this hunt for souls, which is to say bodies, and holding the uncorked vial in my closed hand I walk around like a bird-catcher who does not even have to go to the trouble of snaring his prey. . . .
>
> I pour a drop of acid on the microscope slide. The dead matter expands; it wriggles; it comes alive; it exudes a putrid odor; it calms down and dies. (*Inferno* 76)

Strindberg makes use of the latest scientific advances to try to demonstrate the irrational rationally, at a period where rationalism presented a number of faults. And inversely, he here uses literature to decrypt the invisible world.[6]

Strindberg's fascination for the occult sciences and their way of interpreting the world, which constitutes a rupture with religion and traditional science, contributes to the Gnostic character of his scientific discourse in *Inferno*. He vindicates the rational theology of Swedenborg and the botanist Carl von Linné (Linnaeus), according to which science is a hymn to Nature and the all-powerfulness of the Creator. He is carried by the conviction that there is a divine order behind the apparent confusion of the world.

Another scientific (and Gnostic) element in the Paris of *Inferno* is the recurrent mention of alchemy. It is in Paris that Strindberg begins his alchemical experiments and attempts to manufacture gold. Alchemy experienced a boom at the time: according to the journal *La Paix*, there were around 50,000 alchemists in Paris in 1893. The alchemists had an active review, *L'Initiation*, in which Strindberg published a number of articles on astronomy and optics. Strindberg was in the end nominated an honorary member of the Alchemical Association of France and a "master worker" at the Institute of this Association. Two works appeared in Sweden in 1896, *Contemporary Chrysopoiea* (*Nutidens Guldmakeri*) and *The Synthesis of Gold* (*Guldets syntes*). He also published in French a series of articles in *L'Hyperchimie* (1896–98) on gold and a variety of other subjects, notably on the synthesis of iodine as mentioned in *Inferno* (52). "So, by a supreme effort, I concentrate my will. I will make gold, by the dry method and by means of fire. The silver is there, the furnace, the containers, the bellows, the tongs" (137). The ambience of *Inferno* is that of an alchemical laboratory. The odors of chemical substances and electricity play a relatively important part. The hand of the invisible, as well as the enemies of the narrator, seem in fact to express themselves through odors and electrical currents. Thus when the narrator attempts to commit suicide, it is a smell of almonds which turns him away from his purpose (*Inferno* 59). He feels persecuted by electrical currents: "Then an alarming sensation glides through my body; I am the victim of an electrical current which passes through the two neighboring rooms. The tension heightens" (*Inferno* 139). Later in the story he feels the same phenomenon again: "Walking, an electrical shower falls on my neck and presses me to the ground" (146–47). Arne Melberg has rightly noted that electricity is a recurrent theme in Charles Baudelaire and Gérard de Nerval and that it is often associated with the flaneur (Melberg, "Strindberg stiger ner: *Inferno*" 238).

In its pursuit of alchemy and occult sciences, Strindberg's scientific discourse breaks with the scientific theories of the period and reveals a theosophical dimension. The notions of salvation by knowledge and of the unity of knowledge (via the correspondences) are elements, which contribute to the elaboration of a Gnostic theory of knowledge. All the time Strindberg mixes and blends belief and knowledge, and through their amalgamation he tries to reconcile them. His discourse on knowledge is above all a profession of a mystical faith, a quest for meaning impregnated by Gnosticism.

The narrator of *Inferno* does not stay behind the four walls of the laboratory of the Sorbonne and expands the geography of his laboratory to the streets and parks of Paris. His laboratory extends through all the space of Paris in which he develops through experimentation. In a work following *Inferno*, the drama *To Damascus* (*Till Damaskus*, 1898), Strindberg yet again puts on stage his scientific experiments in Paris, notably his research on the synthesis of gold. *Inferno* and *To Damascus* have a number of themes in common (Gravier 243–65). As in *Inferno*, in *To Damascus* Strindberg projects Paris on to a biblical place of reference:

Strindberg's quest follows the stages of Saint Paul's road to Damascus. *To Damascus,* like *Legends,* is composed of twelve stations (like the Stations of the Cross) and the two works are founded on the same idea: that Hell is on Earth. There is no reference to sites in Paris in the play, but the experiences it recounts are inspired by Strindberg's life in Paris: Strindberg only worked on the synthesis of gold in Paris; the scene in the asylum is inspired by his stay in the Saint-Louis Hospital; the denunciation for fraud recalls Strindberg's disappointment in Paris when he thought he had succeeded in synthesizing gold, but his work was not finally validated by the contemporary scientific community. The phenomenon of projection, staged through dreams, is complete, because the Parisian topography is effaced to leave in its place a universal topography.

The second dimension of experimentation takes place in the domain of psychoanalysis: *Inferno* is a scientific experiment where the object of study is the subject. Melberg highlights this aspect of Strindberg's narrative work:

> Perhaps it is possible to say outright that Strindberg on these promenades experiments with his self in order to sketch a new and modernized subject: a moveable self, without a center, but filled with its "connections." At all events, it is possible to affirm that Strindberg in *Inferno* through the figures of the labyrinth and the circle prefigures the strategies, which will become dominant when his writing returns to the Swedish language and passes over into its Modernist phase. (Melberg, "Strindberg stiger ner: *Inferno*" 237)

The Paris of *Inferno* is a psychological laboratory, at a period when Strindberg attends the lectures on hypnosis at the Salpêtrière (practically at the same time as Freud). The theories he develops in *Inferno* in the domain of "the sciences of the soul" are in effect close to the emergent thinking of Freud and Jung (see Vogelweith). His reading of French fin-de-siècle decadent writers like Paul Bourget and Joris-Karl Huysmans is important for Strindberg because of their psychological analyses. It is no surprise that he distances himself from Émile Zola and the Goncourt brothers and turns towards a more subjective mode of writing. In his celebrated essay "Skandinavische Litteratur" from 1890 Ola Hansson describes this tendency in Scandinavian literature at the turn of the century. Strindberg agrees with the conviction of the symbolists: that the world is only a projection of the self, and the subject is the only reality. The rest is only a dream. In 1894 he writes an essay entitled "Me" in which he states this conviction:

> It is the instinct for the expansion of the self, the tendency to pose oneself as the axis of the world, the tendency to enclose a clod of earth, to trace a horizon around the self, which is activated by the walking-stick, radius of the circle which each individual carries with him without any possibility of freeing himself from it. (quoted in Brandell 275)

The exploration of the subconscious is an essential dimension of *Inferno*. The term "vivisection" appears in this context: literature begins to concentrate on psychological writing and dissects the soul in a prolongation of the work of Flaubert.

"Deranged Sensations" is an essay which presents the scientific ideas of Strindberg in the form of a literary journal, which Strindberg had planned to present as the introduction to *Inferno*. Previous research (Olsson; Stenport) has shown how the psychological aspects can be considered as a passage toward modernity. The nervous state perturbed (or in his phrase "deranged") by a long journey by railway determines the perception for the narrator. The term "deranged" points to the idea of madness, of decadence, of a hallucinated state of mind, which is reminiscent of the psychological state of the poet described by Baudelaire in his writings on drugs—and reminiscent of what Verlaine wrote of Baudelaire as "a modern man, with his senses sharpened and vibrant, his spirit painfully subtle, his brain saturated with tobacco, his blood burning with alcohol" (Verlaine 599–600). Balzac had already in 1839, in his *Treatise on Modern Stimulants,* advocated the virtues of the artificial excitation of the senses. Coffee, alcohol, tea, tobacco, and sugar were for him the ingredients of modernity.

The sensations of Strindberg's narrator are, he claims, "deranged" by the modern environment, and the consequences in terms of perception of the sensuous environment are considerable. Strindberg has truly entered into an introspective exploration and he realizes that his brain has divided into two, exactly as it is described on the first night of *Sleepwalking Nights on Waking Days*.

In *Legends,* Strindberg here similarly develops the idea of the projection of the spirit as a chemical process. He recounts, "I have been seen on the Danube at the same time as I was in Paris" (*Légendes* 54). He affirms his belief in the theory of the double:

> Here I pause for a few moments to present the most current theories of the phenomenon known as the *double.*
>
> The theosophists recognize the fact, admitting that the soul or the astral body can leave the body and take on a quasi-material form, only

> visible to certain people under favorable circumstances. All telepathic phenomena are explained by this. The imagination has no reality, but visions and hallucinations possess a kind of materiality. This is why in optics one discerns virtual and real images, the latter susceptible to being projected onto a screen or fixed on a sensitized photographic plate. (*Légendes* 71–72)

He illustrates this phenomenon by an example and then gives a scientific explanation by reproducing the article "The Irradiation and Extension of the Soul: Observations from Nature," already published in July 1896 in *L'Initiation*. He recounts in this article an experience of the projection of the soul during a stay in Berlin: while he is seated with a wine merchant in Berlin, he suddenly found himself projected to the Brasserie des Saints-Augustins in Paris. Strindberg concludes:

> For several years I have been taking notes on all my dreams, and I have arrived at this conviction: that man leads a double existence; that imaginations, fantasies, dreams possess a reality. So much so that we are all spiritual somnambulists: in our sleep we commit acts which in their different nature we pursue in our waking state, with satisfaction or a bad conscience and a fear of consequences. (*Légendes* 78)

It is to be noted that during his stay in Paris, Strindberg is close to the circle of occultists around Albert de Rochas. He is inspired by Rochas's book on *The Exteriorization of Sensibility* (*L'extériorisation de la sensibilité,* 1895). Strindberg presents in a scientific manner the theory according to which the sensibility of the soul can separate itself, exteriorize itself, and extend itself.

The third dimension of Paris as laboratory is aesthetic. It is expressed in writing the metropolis. In "The Cities of Modernism," Malcolm Bradbury underlined the correlation between writing the city and the birth of modernism:

> Realism humanizes, naturalism scientizes, but Modernism pluralizes, and surrealizes. Where in much realist art the city is the emancipating frontier, the point of transition into hopeful possibilities, and where in much naturalism it is a vast system both throbbing with and passing beyond human will, a jungle, abyss or war, in much Modernism it is the environment of personal consciousness, flickering impressions, Baudelaire's city of crows, Dostoyevsky's encounters from the underground, Corbière's (and Eliot's) *mélange adultère du tout*. Modernist writing has a strong

> tendency to encapsulate experience within the city, and to make the city-novel or city-poem one of its main forms. (Bradbury 99–100)

In the big city Strindberg develops a specific apparatus of the senses, which opens for him more widely the way of the imagination. Paris invites the writer-flaneur to pursue a phenomenology of modernity, of which the resonances become decisive in the formation of Scandinavian modernism as an experience of modernity.

As Volker Klotz emphasizes in *The Narrated City* (*Die erzählte Stadt,* 1969), there exists a tension between realism's desire for linear writing and the labyrinthine structure of the modern city. Literature only comprehends this complexity of the city when it begins to aspire to a discontinuous mode of writing, in which the narration follows the psychological perambulations of the narrator. This is when "the narrated city," according to Klotz, becomes "city narration" (*Stadterzählung*). This threshold marks the advent of modernism: the city can no longer be narrated except through a fragmented and cut-up series of city experiences, following the modernist assertion that it is impossible to represent the city in its totality, what Emilie Hermant and Bruno Latour have called "the invisibility of the city," as the title of their book *Paris as Invisible City* indicates. The writer thus has to renew his narrative technique to face a new objective: no longer to represent the city, but to construct it. Frederik Tygstrup similarly highlights this epistemological challenge:

> The point of departure for the Modernist city novels is thus in a certain sense that the reality of the city can no longer be represented, inasmuch as it opposes itself to the traditional modes of representation. The metropolis as "undefined present" thus presents a double challenge: on the one hand a challenge to literary technique, a demand for the invention of modes of representation which may capture the essentially urban, and on the other hand, as an intensification of this, a challenge to thinking: how can we even think the city; how can we uncoil the patterns of its manifold impulses to the senses and the intellect, patterns which may make it possible for us to conceive of the city and perceive what life in the city does to human life. . . .
>
> The novels think the city; we must understand the representation as something other and more than a question of reference, which is to say not only a depiction of the city, but a construction of the city, the invention of a peculiar type of fiction—city narration—which thinks and depicts in the same gesture. (Tygstrup)

The aesthetics of urban montage, inspired by Paris, calls for a phenomenology of modernity. The city appears first of all as a text read by the flaneur whose horizon of perception transcends the visible as he hears the noise of the whole and takes an interest in the unread and excluded signs of the city. Paris thus becomes the reflection of a psychological landscape, a metaphor of consciousness: the city traversed mirrors the city in the mind.

Paris becomes a collection of textual spaces, which superimpose themselves on the places and give them meaning. The discourse on Paris breaks the continuous narration, transfers to the reader the task of organizing the textual fragments and thus turns towards modernism. This task of aestheticizing incomprehensible facts translates itself into a *de-realization* of the story. By reason of the complexity of the semiotic space, the city becomes a textual crossroads, the place for an intertextual hybridization.

The writing of Paris in Strindberg's *Inferno* is a hybrid, complex, heterogeneous, and nonlinear modernism in all its characteristic modes: collage, sensed rather than measured time, multiplicity of reality, fragmentation of the subject, dictatorship of the imagination, oneirism. *Inferno* and *Legends* explore a new aesthetics in response to the destabilization of representation: short phrases; narrative cut through by questions; aphorisms; brutal cuts in chronology, which creates tableaux rather than scenes; extracts from letters, from *journaux intimes,* and scientific articles; intertextual citations, and so on. The autobiographical prose here echoes the instability of modern life. Ulf Olsson explains in his analysis of *Inferno* the consequences of this writing from the point of view of literary history:

> The journey from the Danube to Paris is a journey from six-volume novels, with the type of psychology that they contained, to the hypersensitization of the nerves and a heightened sensitivity: towards the modern human being in "the great factory of the intelligences"—a journey from the stored six-volume novels of the lending libraries to the swiftly changing articles of the daily press, which characterize modernity. (Olsson 297)

Many scholars have shown the modernist nature of *Inferno* and *Legends*. Arne Melberg sums up his analysis in these terms: "The crisis of near-death is productive and what it produces is Strindberg's Modernism: a postmortem literary world with the same dreamlike paradoxical reality as, in its time, that of Kafka" (Melberg, "Strindberg stiger ner: *Inferno*" 240). Per Stounbjerg concludes: "*Inferno* is precisely an experiment in search of limits, which involves the soul as well as the form" (Stounbjerg 321).

The *Inferno* cycle is well described as a *laboratory novel*. Its experimental prose, which is fed not only by the author's scientific experiments, but also by its representation of a world projected into the imaginary of the narrator, corresponds to the transformation from realist and naturalist modes of writing, characteristic of *the Modern Breakthrough* to a supra-naturalist mode of writing, still termed at the time "subjective naturalism" or "unreal realism," but a premise of modernism.

Translation into English by Martin Leer

Notes

1. All quotes of *Inferno* refer here to the French version of *Inferno*, published in 1898 by Mercure de France, since *Inferno* was a work written originally in French by Strindberg. Note that the French original version contains some previously published scientific articles ("The Cyclamen Throwing Light on the Infinite Disorder and Coherence" and "Death's-Head Hawk-Moth"), which were removed in the Swedish version. The author of all translations in this article is Martin Leer.

2. The *Inferno* cycle refers here to the diptych composed by *Inferno* and *Legends*.

3. In the prologue to the French version of Henrik Ibsen's *A Doll's House*, "In the Saddle of the Real and the Dream," Cocteau says: "*Ghosts, A Doll's House, Love's Comedy*. By these three contrasts there begins a long procession, a veritable vanguard of *unreal realism*, which was to become the sign of our century."

4. The book subsequently appeared in French under the title *Hortus Merlini: Lettres sur la chimie: Sylva sylvarum première partie* in the journal *Hyperchimie* in 1896–97 and then eventually in a final form in 1897. It had to wait until 1906 before a publication in Swedish.

5. The subtitle of the Swedish edition refers directly to the theories of Darwin and Haeckel.

6. This literalist approach to spiritism is found in other Scandinavian writers, like Knut Hamsun in his text on the subconscious of the soul, which appeared in *Samtiden* in 1890, or Johannes V. Jensen in his novel *Madame d'Ora*, published in 1904.

Works Cited

Balzamo, Elena. *August Strindberg: Visages et destin*. Paris: Hamy, 1999.

Benjamin, Walter. *Charles Baudelaires: Ein Lyriker im Zeitalter des Hochkapitalismus*. Frankfurt am Main: Suhrkamp, 1955.

Bradbury, Malcolm. "The Cities of Modernism." In *Modernism: A Guide to European Literature*, ed. Malcolm Bradbury and James McFarlane. London: Penguin Books, 1991. 96–103.

Brandell, Gunnar. *Strindbergs Infernokris*. Stockholm: Bonniers, 1950.

Calvino, Italo. *Ermita a Parigi*. Milan: Mondadori, 1996.

Casanova, Pascale. *La République mondiale des lettres*. Paris: Seuil, 1999.

Claussen, Sophus. *Antonius i Paris: Valfart.* Copenhagen: Det danske Sprog- og Litteraturselskab, 1990.
Cocteau, Jean. Preface, "A cheval sur le réel et le rêve," to *Maison de poupée,* by Henrik Ibsen. Paris: Livre de poche, 1960.
Ericsson, Staffan. *Två drömspel: Från Strindbergs modernism till Potters television.* Stockholm: Symposion, 2004.
Gravier, Maurice. "Strindberg écrivain français." In *Actes du Colloque Strindberg à Paris: Université de Paris-Sorbonne octobre 1975. Revue d'histoire du théâtre* 3 (1978), 243–65. Ed. Maurice Gravier. Paris: Société d'histoire du théâtre.
Hansson, Ola. "Skandinavische Litteratur." *Das Magazin für die Literatur des in- und auslandes* 20, no. 17 (1890): 305–6.
Hermant, Emilie, and Bruno Latour. *Paris ville invisible.* Paris : La découverte, 1998.
Jensen, Johannes V. *Den gotiske Renaissance.* Copenhagen: Gyldendal, 2000.
Kern, Stephen. *The Culture of Time and Space: 1880–1918.* Cambridge, Mass.: Harvard University Press, 1983.
Klotz, Volker. *Die erzählte Stadt.* Munich: Hanser, 1969.
Melberg, Arne. "Barbaren i Paris." In *Strindbergs förvandlingar,* ed. Eva Adolfsson and Ulf Olsson. Stockholm: Symposion, 1999. 73–94.
———. "Strindberg stiger ner: *Inferno.*" In *Ästhetik der skandinavischen Moderne, Bernhard Glienke zum Gedenken,* ed. Annegret Heitmann and Karin Hoff. Frankfurt am Main: Lang, 1998. 231–43.
Munier, Brigitte. *Quand Paris était un roman: Du culte de Babylone au culte de la vitesse.* Paris: Différence, 2008.
Olsson, Ulf. *Levande död: Studier i Strindbergs prosa.* Stockholm: Symposion, 1996.
Rochas, Albert de. *L'extériorisation de la sensibilité.* Paris: Librairie générale des sciences occultes, Bibliothèque Chacornac, 1909.
Stenport, Anna Westerståhl. *Locating August Strindberg's Prose: Modernism, Transnationalism, Setting.* Toronto: University of Toronto Press, 2010.
———. *Making Space: Stockholm, Paris, and the Urban Prose of Strindberg and His Contemporaries.* Berkeley: University of California Press, 2004.
Stounbjerg, Per. *Uro og urenhed: Studier i Strindbergs selvbiografiske prosa.* Århus: Århus universitetsforlag, 2005.
Strindberg, August. *Antibarbarus.* Stockholm: Bröderna Lagerström, 1906.
———. *Brev.* Ed. Torsten Eklund. Stockholm: Bonniers, 1948–96.
———. *Inferno.* Paris: Mercure de France, 1966.
———. *Légendes.* Paris: Mercure de France, 1967.
———. *Ockulta Dagboken.* Stockholm: Gidlund, 1977.
———. "Sensations détraquées." *Le Figaro,* December 17, 1894; January 26, 1895; and February 9, 1895.
———. *Sömngångarnätter på vakna dagar.* Stockholm: Gernandt, 1900.
Tygstrup, Frederik. "Den litteraere by: Mellem system og sansning." 2005. Online.
Verlaine, Paul. "Charles Baudelaire." In *Oeuvres en prose complètes.* Paris: Gallimard, 1972.

Villegas, Jean-Claude. *Paris, capitale littéraire de l'Amérique latine*. Dijon: Éditions Universitaires de Dijon, 2007.
Vogelweith, Guy. *Psychothéâtre de Strindberg*. Paris: Klincksieck, 1972.
Zola, Émile. *Le Roman expérimental*. Paris: Garnier-Flammarion, 1971.

Voices and Visions in Fingal's Cave: Plato and Strindberg

Freddie Rokem

A Dream Play (*Ett Drömspel*) was published in 1902, more than a year after it was completed, and first performed with some additions in 1906. It is undoubtedly one of August Strindberg's masterpieces. The play has become a landmark within European theater history, with every detail of its open and seemingly random composition falling into a larger integrated totality, both thematically and aesthetically. The play set the stage for the major trends within twentieth-century drama and theater history, serving as a source of inspiration for numerous playwrights—most notably perhaps Samuel Beckett and Harold Pinter—but also for expressionism. It has been staged by major directors, including Max Reinhardt (1921) as well as more recently by Robert Lepage (1994) and Robert Wilson (2000). Ingmar Bergman, who integrated aspects of *A Dream Play* as an intertext in several of his films, directed the play itself several times, including as a TV film in 1963.

For Strindberg himself, it was no doubt a deeply personal play, which, like most of what he wrote, grew out of private concerns and anxieties, in this particular case reflecting a religious conversion as well as a confrontation with a mental crisis. It was also the outcome of his profoundly ambivalent relationship to women. The role of Indra's Daughter/Agnes was written explicitly for the young actress Harriet Bosse to whom he was married, but not living with, while writing the play. It is even possible to trace the idea and the basic structure of *A Dream Play* to a much earlier private letter that Strindberg wrote to his first wife Siri von Essen—who was an actress as well—twenty-five years before beginning to write *A Dream Play*, in 1876. In this letter, Strindberg recounts a dream he had about von Essen that he actually partly invented to impress her (see my discussion in Rokem, *Philosophers* 104–9). At the same time, the play is steeped in a broad range of cultural references to contemporary figures like Richard Wagner, to Oriental and Indian literature and religion, and to philosophical and religious notions like the transmigration of souls, which implies a particular reference to Buddhism and Platonic philosophy. It also relates in innovative ways to new technological inventions, in particular to photography and film. As an extension of this complex intertextual web, *A Dream Play* engages central thematic and aesthetic concerns of the time when it was written.

In the following, I draw attention to some of the broader issues of the international cultural debates at the time, focusing in particular on the multiple Platonic contexts of *A Dream Play,* which surprisingly have not received the attention they deserve by the play's critics. (Robinson's comprehensive *An International Annotated Bibliography of Strindberg Studies* does not mention a single item that deals directly with this subject.) The basic structure of the play as well as some of its concrete details, for one, draw directly on Plato's ideas of the transmigration of souls, which can also be found in several religious belief systems, but which in many cases—in particular in Christian belief—has deep roots in Neoplatonism. Throughout the chapter I address the intertextual references to Plato's philosophy within the larger weave of *A Dream Play,* with particular emphasis on the relation between the cave allegory in the beginning of book 7 in Plato's *The Republic* and the two scenes in *A Dream Play* that take place in Fingal's Cave.

My reading compares the representations of the sensory experiences in these two caves by discussing the relations between Plato's philosophical arguments involving the cave, focusing on the sense of vision, and Strindberg's poetic extrapolation on Plato's philosophical discourse, which includes visual as well as auditory experiences. The philosopher's role in Plato's cave offers a relevant counterpart to that of the poet in Strindberg's. This comparison demonstrates the type of figure that each author favors, for as Plato's philosopher is the figure in the cave who can break the illusion to reach the outside and then return to teach the others, it is Strindberg's poet who has the agency in Fingal's Cave to help Indra's Daughter return home to heaven from where she entered her earthly existence in the prologue of the play. Plato's cave narrative begins inside the cave of illusions, while Strindberg's begins with a descent from heaven to the illusions and suffering of earthly existence, within which there is a cave.

The comparison between the two caves draws attention to the complex relations between philosophy and poetry, a major issue within the classical Greek cultural context, in particular considering Plato's open hostility towards the arts, most prominently in *The Republic* itself, in which Socrates argues that the ideal state should banish the poets. In his play, Strindberg gives an interesting and complementary response to Plato by pointing at the redemptive role of the poet and creating an alternative scenario from Plato's exiling of the poets. Strindberg's figure of the poet in *A Dream Play*—as well as Strindberg himself, the poet who wrote this remarkable play and set the stage for some of the central cultural and critical agendas of the twentieth century—draws inspiration from world culture reverberating from far beyond the spatial borders of Sweden.

The visual experience in Plato's cave is primarily an exercise in epistemology, whereas the multisensory experience in Strindberg's cave allows for a representation of the complexity of human experience. The intertextual weave that Strindberg has created between the two caves—the Platonic, philosophical cave that foregrounds the visual experience and Fingal's Cave, offering a poetic dramatic expression that is both visual and auditory—reveals the full complexity of the cave in *A Dream Play.* Therefore a comparison between the two caves also offers a unique opportunity to closely examine the complex relations between the discursive practices of philosophy and poetry.

In order to discuss the complex relationship of the two caves, this chapter begins with the presentation of the play's greater international position in the tradition of the dramatic use of the deus ex machina. It then moves to a presentation of the play's structure and its relation to Plato's idea about the transmigration of souls. Subsequently, I move to a comparison of Plato's cave allegory in *The Republic* and Strindberg's presentation of Fingal's Cave in *A Dream Play.*

Indra's Daughter as Deus ex Machina and the Structure of *A Dream Play*

A Dream Play presents two simultaneous narratives—one overt and one more hidden or implied—that interact dialectically with each other. The more hidden narrative—which maps the three stages of a dream onto three sections in the play—contains a Platonic dimension. But I will begin with the more explicit narrative which presents the descent of Indra's Daughter to earth in order to examine if human suffering is really as relentless as the rumors coming from earth have indicated.

The play opens with the descent of Indra's Daughter to earth, being born as a human, but never forgetting or severing the ties with her divine origin. This opening scene, at the same time as it employs a method for ending plays used already during the Greek classical period, presents the basic iconographic, visual features of the deus ex machina from the baroque theater, where Indra's Daughter enters from above on back stage, and passes through the clouds in the centrally located focal point. This entrance is based on a visual regime that enables the supernatural to appear and to become materialized. In its ancient, classical use the deus ex machina is the mechanism through which the plot complications can be solved at the ending of the play through the intervention of a divine figure, which obviously, in Strindberg's case, also invites us to think of the redemptive functions of Jesus as an extension of God interacting directly with humanity. *A Dream Play* unifies pagan and Christian elements, situating the deus ex machina in the beginning of the play—as opposed to its classical use for ending the play—initiating the process through which Indra's Daughter can examine human suffering.

In order to carry out her mission on earth—finding out if human suffering is as unbearable as she has been told and perhaps even set it right—Indra's Daughter, now bearing the human name of Agnes, lives a "human" life: gets married, has a child, and experiences humiliation. The spectators follow her personal suffering as well as her exposure to the pain of others through different locations or stations—which could be described in cinematographic terms as a long shot—moving in a continuous space that is constantly transformed in front of our eyes. When she has reached a certain climactic point of her journey—actually located in a classroom where the laws of logic break down—she realizes that the rumors that she has heard about human suffering are actually true and that she can not do anything to change this. At this point she meets the Poet and decides to return to the heavenly sphere from where she came. On her way back to the place where she descended, and from where she can therefore also ascend, she passes through many of the same locations as on her way to this turning point. Fingal's Cave is one of the sites she passes through in both directions of her journey. The play ends with her ascent, returning to her supernatural existence. She is a "dea ex machina" unable to set things right again, finally saving herself, not humanity.

It is important to emphasize that the modern theater has preserved and transformed the ways in which the supernatural or its representatives enter into the human sphere, as I have argued elsewhere (Rokem, "Deus ex Machina"). Strindberg's use of the deus ex machina device has no doubt been extremely important for how the modern and our contemporary theater has related to the use of this device. Samuel Beckett's *Waiting for Godot* (*En attendant Godot*, 1953) is only one of the many examples relating directly to this device, showing that it does not function anymore, because Godot repeatedly does not appear, but in Bertolt Brecht's *Threepenny Opera* (*Die Dreigroschenoper,* 1928) and *The Good Person of Szechwan* (*Der gute Mensch von Sezuan,* 1943) the device still functions fully, though with a large measure of irony. Strindberg's play can be considered a model for the transformations of the deus ex machina in the modern theater, because it was such an early and paradigmatic example after Nietzsche had declared the death of God and the realistic/naturalistic theater had as a rule tried to abolish the supernatural in the theater. The issue is why the theater, after the death of God, has still been employing the theatrical machineries through which the divine figures make their appearance.

The more implicit narrative of the play presents the three stages of a dream: falling asleep (with the descent of Indra's Daughter), dreaming (through most of the play), and waking up (through the final ascent). Indra's Daughter is the main character of this dream, though not the dreamer. The play makes several references—in particular in the second scene in Fingal's Cave—to the impression that what Indra's Daughter has experienced during life on earth is like a dream based on delusions—like the life of the prisoners in Plato's cave—which we enter through birth and from which we wake up when dying, when our souls return to the true reality of the heavenly sphere, where the truth which we have forgotten during our earthly existence is again revealed to us. The most explicit mention of this meaning of the dream structure is actually Strindberg's own short introductory note, composed after he had completed the play, but basically not a part of the play itself:

> In this dream play . . . the author has sought to reproduce the disconnected but apparently logical form of the dream. Anything can happen; everything is possible and probable. Time and space do not exist; on a slight groundwork of reality, imagination spins and weaves new patterns made up of memories, experiences, unfettered fancies, absurdities and improvisations.
>
> The characters are split, double and multiply; they evaporate, crystallize, scatter and converge. But a single consciousness holds sway over them all—that of the dreamer. For him there are no secrets, no incongruities, no scruples and no law. He neither condemns nor acquits, but only relates, and since on the whole, there is more pain than pleasure in the dream, a tone of melancholy, and of compassion for all living things, runs through the swaying narrative. Sleep, the liberator, often appears as a torturer, but when the pain is at its worst, the sufferer awakes—and is thus reconciled with reality. For how agonizing real life may be, at this moment, compared with the tormenting dream, it is a joy. (192/7)[1]

What Strindberg's own interpretation of *A Dream Play* claims is that Indra's Daughter's visit to earth is actually a dream from which we wake up when dying. This idea is both similar to the experience of the men imprisoned in Plato's cave who are unable to perceive the true reality, as well as the Christian notion that life on earth is a temporary suffering from which we are released through death.

According to the dialectics between truth and illusion Strindberg presented in his introductory note, our life on earth is the dream from which we wake up to a higher reality when dying, liberating the humans from their earthly suffering. This belief also corresponds to Plato's ideas of the transmigration of the eternal souls introduced in particular in the Myth of Er which closes *The Republic*. Through her birth to earthly life, Indra's Daughter, who is such an eternal (and we must add) divine soul, becomes the protagonist of a dream that belongs to a subjective consciousness outside of, or "over" the play itself, a totality which at the same time examines itself from within through the characters. In poetic terms, the dream is a cave; or in reverse: the cave is a metonym for the dream, inside the more comprehensive dream of our lives. The two scenes in Fingal's Cave are a central location for developing these multidimensional figures of dream and reality, and they are important locations on the journey Indra's Daughter makes on her way into the heart of human suffering, in the first cave scene, and on her way toward liberation from this suffering, in the second cave scene.

Plato's Cave and the Ocular

The effect of entering a cave is one in which the sounds and voices of the everyday become transformed and obtain new dimensions. The cave creates a complex soundscape of auditory distortions and echoing effects, a kind of "*surround*" that we have probably all experienced and most likely enjoyed. The cave transports us into an acoustic experience where we perceive ourselves as being situated inside the sounds—immersed within our own voice and its echoes—rather than primarily perceiving it inside ourselves and as emerging from our own body, throat, and mouth. The cave experience sometimes creates confusions between outside and inside, partly reversing the relations between them. The cave also amplifies the voices of other speakers, enveloping us within their sounds, intensifying the experience that Jean-Luc Nancy has described as listening per se. According to Nancy, "to be listening is to be *at the same time* outside and inside, to be open *from* without and *from* within, hence from one to the other and from me in the other" (14).

When considering the auditory changes of perception and added self-awareness that the cave produces, it is quite remarkable that the parable opening book 7 of Plato's *The Republic* primarily draws attention to the cave as the primal scene of *visual* misrepresentations and distortions, but does not really take the unique auditory experiences that the cave produces into serious consideration. In what follows, I first want to examine Plato's preference for the ocular and his disregard of the auditory experience inside the cave, and subsequently compare it with a dramatic/theatrical rendering of the cave experience from the very beginning of the twentieth century which no doubt has been profoundly influenced by Plato's text: August Strindberg's *A Dream Play.*

When analyzing Plato's representation of the cave allegory in book 7 of *The Republic* it is no doubt tempting to project an auditory dimension onto it, as, for example, Nancy did, claiming that

> in Plato's cave, there is more than just the shadows of objects being moved about outside: there is also the echo of the voices of those who move them, a detail we usually forget, since it is so quickly set aside by Plato himself in favour of the visual and luminous scheme exclusively. (75, n. 42)

However, if we read Plato's own text carefully, the auditory experiences inside the cave are not only set aside, they are in fact (as the quotes below clearly show) depicted as an imagined possibility, a potential rather than something that we actually have to take into consideration within the philosophical context Plato sets up. For Plato it is the visual experience of the cave that serves as the allegorical testing ground for his philosophical system, drawing attention to the delusions caused by the senses—that is, vision—and for highlighting the necessity to recognize the world of eternal ideas beyond our everyday sensory modes of perception in order to attain true knowledge. But why have these potential sounds in Plato's cave not been integrated within the philosophical discussion triggered by the parable of the cave?

In order to answer this question I believe we first have to admit that the visual experiences and impressions no doubt serve Plato better within the ontological and epistemological contexts for which he mobilizes the picture of the human beings who have been confined to living in a cave from earliest childhood, "with their legs and necks in chains, so that they have to stay where they are, looking only ahead of them, prevented by the chains from turning their heads" (514b, 220).[2] It would obviously not be possible to monitor the perception of sounds in such an absolute and authoritarian fashion. The acoustic experience of the cave, and even sounds and voices in general, can probably not serve as the basis for the clear-cut distinctions between truth and illusion that Plato is interested in establishing. The ontological and epistemological elusiveness of voices and listening to them has no doubt influenced their conceptualization and cultural configuration within Western thought as expressions of emotion and subjectivity rather than rationality and truth. The cave provides a parable for seeing the truth, after the people kept chained in the cave have been freed from their imprisonment—no matter how painful this experience is—while the sounds of the cave, as we will learn from Strindberg, contain a poetic dimension which for well-known reasons, Plato unambiguously objected to. Following Plato as well as Aristotle (who I do not discuss here), Western culture has privileged the visual dimension. This has obviously also profoundly influenced our understanding of the theater, reminding us that the Greek word for theater, *theatron,* meaning a place to see or contemplate, has the same root as "theory," obviously privileging the sense of vision also in the arts.

However, we must admit that Plato, or rather his protagonist Socrates, does mention the sounds in the cave, and in particular the human voice (which is a necessity for making a dramatic performance) in the cave allegory, but only as a possibility that is not realized, foregrounding the unreliability of the curtailed visual experience of the hostages inside the cave. According to Socrates, "between the fire and the prisoners, at a higher level than them, is a path along which you must picture a low wall that has been built, like the screen which hides people when they are giving a puppet show, and above which they make the puppets appear" (ibid.). In addition to the images projected on the wall in this theatrical underground cave, Socrates adds that "as you'd expect, some of the people carrying the objects are speaking, while others are silent," to which Glaucon (the interlocutor) comments: "[a] strange picture. And strange prisoners" (515a, 220). But there is no explanation why some are speaking and others are silent while they are taking part in this unusual underground performance activity or what this means for the philosophical conclusions. *If* indeed there are voices, they do not really matter for Socrates's argument concerning his version of the cave experience, which, it seems, has some interesting features of a ritual initiation practice. And in such a context sounds and voices would of course be important, but not, even if ritual practices and philosophy have several features in common, for the epistemological consequences of the parable.

After an additional comment on the visual limitations of the prisoners, Socrates asks, "So, *if* they were able to talk to one another, don't you think they'd believe that the things they were giving names to were the things they could see passing?" (515b, 221). What Socrates clearly claims is that *if* the prisoners were able to speak it would only be to name the shadows passing on the wall, creating a language which points at what they see, but which is totally devoid of truth. And to further emphasize the complexity of these potential vocal "shadows," Socrates continues with an additional conditional question, again drawing attention to the visual dimension of this experience: "What *if* the prison had an echo from the wall in front of them? Every time one of the people passing by spoke, do you suppose they'd believe the source of the sound to be anything other than the passing shadow?" (515b, 221). "If"—Socrates asks—there is an echo from the wall in front of them, the prisoners would believe that the shadows on the wall are the source of these sounds. This is no doubt a possibility, but only if nothing but the echo could be heard and not the voices or sounds that have given rise to this complex echo effect—unless what Plato refers to as an echo is some form of ventriloquism.

Therefore the voices and the sounds in Plato's cave are both conditional and disrupted, and they are not an integral part of the philosophical significance of the parable Plato seeks to highlight. Instead, because the sounds are portrayed as potentials, which have not been realized, the emphasis remains on the ocular confusions and delusions created by the cave, even if these sounds had actually been there. The role of the poet, as a character in *A Dream Play,* and the aim of the poet (Strindberg himself) who has written that play, is to find a way to fully reintegrate the sounds and visions of the cave, creating a composite poetical image rather than a philosophical discourse.

Fingal's Cave and the Auditory

Rather than reinforcing the ocular basis for philosophical truth, as Plato does, Strindberg's text and its visual score explores the poetic, multisensory dimensions of the cave experience, where the auditory and the visual become amalgamated, interacting closely with each other. There are two scenes in *A Dream Play* that take place in the so-called Fingal's Cave, the name of a sea cave on the uninhabited island of Staffa in the Inner Hebrides of Scotland. By the time Strindberg wrote his play the odd echoes of this cave had already inspired Felix Mendelssohn's *Hebrides Overture* from 1829, known as the *Fingal's Cave Overture,* and it appears in later works as well, for example by the video artist Richard Ashrown, who spent several days recording the interior of Fingal's Cave in 2008 for a piece significantly called *Lament*. Also, one of the early songs by rock group Pink Floyd bears the name of Fingal's Cave.

Since the auditory field and its possibilities for interpretation seem to be much more ambiguous and multivalent than the visual field, the cave experience holds an interesting poetic and theatrical potential that can also realize the cave's sounds rather than more or less exclusively focusing on its visual aspects. *A Dream Play* has a Platonic deep structure with strong Neoplatonic and Christian elements. In his theatrical version of the transmigration of souls, Strindberg no doubt relied on later Christian developments of the conceptual framework stemming from Plato's thinking, but the fact that he also included the cave in his play no doubt shows he was referencing Plato's philosophy as well.

The first cave scene in *A Dream Play* takes place when according to the stage directions, "the organ [in the church] is changed to the wall of a grotto" by means of stage lighting (217). Looking at recent photographs of Fingal's Cave, it is quite obvious that Strindberg's pictorial imagination was activated both by the structure of the opening of this cave and the surrounding stone formations which look like huge organ pipes from which the roaring sea can supposedly be heard. Therefore it does not seem to be a coincidence that the first Fingal's Cave scene begins with a transformation of the church organ into the cave. In a short essay Strindberg published in *A Blue Book* called "Who Built Fingal's Cave?" ("Vem byggde Fingalsrottan"; *En Blå Bok,* 1907) he does not really give a clear-cut answer to this question, but implies that the cave is a place with divine origin because, he claims, it has exactly the same dimensions as the Notre Dame Cathedral in Paris. What matters for Strindberg is the poetic truth, rather than the geological facts.

Even if the visual aspects of the cave are obviously very important for Strindberg, the conversation between the Lawyer and the Daughter in the first of the two Fingal's Cave scenes focuses on the auditory experiences in the cave, the aspect of the cave experience which Plato had disregarded. First they hear the sounds of the cave, which they interpret as "the lamentation of mortals" that are echoed inside the cave. Their sudden decision at the end of the scene to get married constitutes a direct challenge to these lamentations, creating an alternative to the human anguish they have heard through the sounds inside the cave.

LAWYER: Where are we?
DAUGHTER: What do you hear?

LAWYER: I hear drops falling.
DAUGHTER: Those are the tears of mankind weeping. What more do you hear?
LAWYER: A sighing . . . a moaning . . . a wailing.
DAUGHTER: The lamentation of mortals has reached so far, no further. But why this endless lamentation? Is there no joy in life?
LAWYER: Yes. The sweetest which is also the bitterest—love! Marriage and a home. The highest and the lowest.
DAUGHTER: Let me put it to the test. (217/41)

The scene immediately following this sudden optimism shows a stifling marriage between Indras's Daughter and the Lawyer, gone sour in a claustrophobic home of distrust and bitterness, and with a newborn, crying child in the cradle. The sudden changes in the sequence of scenes from the church to the cave and then to marriage and acrimonious family life were perhaps triggered by the visual details of the cave, which can be interpreted as an amalgamated image of the church organ and the female genitals.

A Dream Play is no doubt an additional battleground for Strindberg in his ongoing struggle with (rather than battle against) the abstract principles of femininity as well as with concrete, particular women. This struggle can be followed like a red thread through much of Strindberg's writing, and *A Dream Play* is no exception, though here he shows a more balanced view of women than in most of his other writing. In a letter from July 23, 1903, after having completed the first version of *A Dream Play,* but while he was still occupied with its final completion for the first production, Strindberg informed his German translator Emil Schering that Otto Weininger had sent him a copy of his infamous misogynist book *Sex and Character* (*Geschlecht und Charakter,* 1903). Strindberg wrote that he found it "frightening" but that it had, as he formulated it, "probably solved the hardest of all problems" ("Brev till Emil Schering," my translation). He asks Schering to send Weininger a copy of two of his earlier plays, *The Father* (*Fadren*) and *Miss Julie* (*Fröken Julie*) from 1887 and 1888, respectively, which Strindberg implies actually anticipate Weininger's ideas about women. To Weininger himself, Strindberg sent a postcard offering heartfelt thanks for at last solving the "Woman Problem." This is exactly the same pattern Strindberg had exhibited in his correspondence with Nietzsche fifteen years earlier, that he had himself already expressed the major misogynist ideas in his own plays that the philosopher was propagating.

But even if Strindberg had strong sympathies for Otto Weininger's as well as for Nietzsche's view of women, *A Dream Play* arguably presents a more complex image of women. It is a tribute both to a female fictional figure as well as to the actress Harriet Bosse, Strindberg's third wife, who played Indra's Daughter in the first production of the play. If we collocate the significance of the cave as it emerges in *A Dream Play* with its visual features, I think it is possible to claim that for Strindberg the cave represents the potential redemptive power of the female principle, through which the visual and the acoustic closely interact. Some of Strindberg's own paintings from these years also elaborate in detail what the view from inside the cave or womb toward the illuminated sea looks like, showing how complex these visual metaphors are. It is perhaps even possible to argue that Strindberg views the feminine principle of the cave in similar terms as Luce Irigaray in her polemics with Plato will do almost a century later. In this context it is also worth noting that Strindberg and Freud, who published *The Interpretation of Dreams* (*Die Traumdeutung,* 1899) exactly at the same time as Strindberg was working on *A Dream Play,* were mutually unaware of each other. The fact that Freud's and Strindberg's efforts to interpret dreams in psychosexual terms coincide shows how closely connected Strindberg was, at least intuitively, to the major intellectual and cultural developments of his time.

The second cave scene takes place after Indra's Daughter/Agnes has left her oppressive marriage and is on her journey back to the heavenly spheres. The cave is the location where she encounters the Poet who assists her in her process of liberation, not only from her vindictive lawyer-husband who wants her to return to her domestic duties, but finally also from the shackles of earthly life, freeing her soul from its earthly suffering. While passing through Fingal's Cave again, they can see how "*A red bell-buoy rocks upon the waves, but gives no sound until later,*" as Strindberg indicates in his stage direction for this scene; then there is "*Music of the winds. Music of the waves*" (242/87). The Poet initiates the dialogue:

POET: Where have you brought me?

DAUGHTER: Far from the murmur and wailing of the children of men. To this grotto at the ends of the ocean to which we give the name *Indra's Ear,* for here, it is said, the King of Heaven listens to the lamentations of mortals.

POET: Why here?

DAUGHTER: Do you not see that this cave is shaped like a shell? Do you know that your ear is shaped like a shell? You know, but you have given it no thought. *She picks up a shell.* As a child, did you never hold a shell to your ear and listen to the whisper of your heart's blood, to the humming of thoughts in your brain, to the parting of a thousand little

> worn-out tissues in the fabric of your body? All this you can hear in a small shell. Think then what may be heard in this great one. (242/87)

They are in Indra's shell-formed ear where the sounds become amplified and through which the god can hear the lamentations of the humans. Each one of us can, she adds, take a small shell from the shore in our hands in order to listen to the blood of the heart, the rustle of the thoughts, through which the inner textures in the tissues of the human body can be heard. This ability apparently also makes all of us divine in some sense.

The structure of this scene, like many others in *A Dream Play,* is governed by an ostensive technique of "pointing" at a phenomenon—a sound or a visual image—creating a form of dialogue which is quite common in Strindberg's later work. According to Peter Szondi in *Theory of the Modern Drama* (1956), this dialogical structure is one of the signs of the dramatic disintegration which he argues leads to the development of epic storytelling in drama, lacking narrative cohesion and dramatic tension. This is a technique of exposition where one of the characters possesses some form of knowledge which he or she passes on to the other character, who passively acknowledges what the other has heard or seen. It is at the same time a poetic as well as a philosophical form of dialogue, actually quite closely related to the Socratic dialogue, where Socrates himself provides a detailed description of a phenomenon to which the interlocutor, who does not have any direct access to this knowledge, simply agrees by saying "yes."

Thus, when the poet says that he cannot hear anything but the sighing of the wind, the daughter continues to describe the soft music that she hears, serving both as interpreter and medium of these sounds, drawing attention to the metaphysical framework within which they have been created:

> Born under heaven's clouds,
> chased we were by Indra's fires
> down to the crust of the earth.
> . . .
> Indra, Lord of Heaven,
> Hear us!
> Listen to our sighing!
> Earth is not clean,
> life is not just,
> men are not evil
> nor are they good.
> . . .

> We, the winds, the sons of the air,
> bear man's lamentation.
> Thou hast heard us
> on autumn eves in the chimney stack,
> in the stove-pipe's vent,
> in the window cracks,
> as the rain wept on the tiles.
> . . .
> It is we, we, the winds
> who whine and whistle,
> woe! Woe! Woe!
> . . .
> It is we, we the waves,
> that rock the winds
> to rest. (242–44/88–90)

Now they suddenly see a shipwreck that has stranded on a rock in the sea, and the crew is singing "Christ Kyrie!" to which the daughter responds that "they are calling and the sea is calling. But no one hears" (248/96–97). If the cave opening is facing the audience, which is logical, the spectators are situated on the shipwreck. Then the daughter and the poet see someone that walks on the water, adding that this person wished "to set men free." Here Strindberg openly introduces the Christian dimension.

As its gets darker, it is time for the poet to take on the role of the *raisonneur,* beginning to escort Indra's Daughter back to her divine origins:

> The crew are screaming with horror because they have seen their Saviour . . . and now . . . they are throwing themselves overboard in terror of the Redeemer. *The crew shriek again.*
>
> Now they are screaming because they are going to die. They were born screaming and they die screaming. (249/98)

The last sentence—"They were born screaming and they die screaming"—could, like many other existential statements in *A Dream Play,* be from a Beckett text, showing that *A Dream Play* is in many ways a prototype for absurd drama, showing how influential this Strindberg play has been. And as the light changes, Indra's Daughter and the Poet are not sure anymore if they have actually seen a ship or if it has been an illusion. The poet continues:

> I do not think it is a ship. It's a two-storied house with trees around it . . . and a telephone tower—a tower reaching to the skies. It is the modern tower of Babel, sending up its wires to communicate with those above. (249/98)

Here Strindberg's Poet is articulating a quite possible reference to a material aspect of Stockholm's contemporary geography: the telephone tower erected in the city center in 1887, a little more than ten years before Strindberg wrote *A Dream Play.* This tower, which burned down in the early 1950s, immediately became an important landmark in the fast-growing city. For many years the 4,000 wires that originated from this "modern tower of Babel," which were later put underground, literally carried the voices of the inhabitants of the modern city. Strindberg's reference to technological inventions like the phonograph and the telephone were all directly related to sound. In a later play, *The Black Glove* (*Svarta handsken,* 1907), presenting a fairy-tale story about the appearance during Christmas of a puck-like otherworldly creature, a "tomte" in a modern apartment house, Strindberg even has the radiators for the newly invented central heating produce otherworldly sounds.

When the Poet adds that "it's not a house . . . not a telephone tower" (249/99) the daughter asks him what he sees, to which he gives a detailed answer, while the stage directions indicate that the set is gradually transformed from the cave to the opera corridor. The world of the theater as a site for extreme human suffering had already been exposed in detail in the first part of the play, and during the poet's description it returns. During this gradual transformation of the cave, the voices and the sounds completely disappear and the poet describes images that are completely mute:

> I see a snow-covered heath . . . a parade ground. The winter sun is hiding behind a church on the hill, so that the tower casts its long shadow on the snow. Now a troop of soldiers comes marching over the heath. They march on the tower and up the spire. . . . Now they are on the cross, and I seem to know that the first to tread on the weathercock must die. . . . They are drawing near it. It's the Corporal at their head who. . . . Ah! A cloud is sailing over the heath, across the sun. . . . Now everything has gone. The moisture of the cloud has put out the fire of the sun. The sunlight created a shadowy image of the tower, but the shadow of the cloud smothered the image of the tower. [Solens ljus skapte tornets mörkerbild, men molnets mörkerbild kvävde tornets mörkerbild.] (249–50/99)

This transformation of images described by the poet has the quality of a silent film, playing with light and shadow, with the snow-covered field serving as a screen on which the flickering images are projected like in Plato's cave parable. Here Strindberg describes a soundless image, indicating that Strindberg has integrated the Platonic cave in his poetic rendition. But rather than the delusions of the images on the wall in the cave as in Plato's case, the Poet's depiction contains a deeper truth consisting of threats and dangers that are suddenly revoked by mere chance. First the poet sees the shadow of the church on the snow-covered heath on which soldiers are marching. And because the tower is only such a shadow they can literally "climb" up the tower, and the first one who touches the weathercock on the top of the tower is doomed to die. But then a cloud covers the sun, casting an additional shadow, covering the whole scene, so that the shadow cast on the snow disappears, and the soldiers are saved. There is even something playfully childish in this narrative of salvation based on the purely visual images that gradually become the dominant mode of experience in Fingal's Cave.

Beginning already in the mid-1880s Strindberg had shown a great interest in photographic techniques and he frequently used the camera, primarily to document his own family, but he also very quickly realized that the new technology had far-reaching journalistic as well as poetic potentials. In *A Dream Play* the photographic play between light and shadow is used in a poetic context, where Strindberg shows his talents in creating poetry on the basis of technological innovations.

This spectacle of light and shadow, the dark-picture on the snow and its sudden disappearance, are also closely related to a specific photographic technique which Strindberg himself also practiced called celestography. Celestography, that is, photographing the sky, was carried out by exposing the photographic plate directly to the nocturnal sky for a certain time, without the use of camera equipment or lenses. It may perhaps seem that Strindberg has returned us to Plato's cave, where the flickering images on the photographic plate are like the delusions of the cave. But for Strindberg the sky and its cloud formations are actually photographic images of the earth. The basic principle of celestography, which is in principle like those of *A Dream Play,* is that living on earth, our senses are imperfect, enabling us only with great difficulty to interpret the truth behind our sense perceptions. But celestography, providing unmediated images of the sky, gives a much more exact picture of earth than those our eyes perceive. By photographing the clouds, which in turn are "photographs," we come closer to the truth.

A Dream Play can be read as a complex dialogue with Plato, where in particular the two scenes in Fingal's Cave are a development of the cave allegory in *The Republic,* adding sound to the silence in Plato's cave—where sounds were only a potential, unrealized dimension—but also experimenting with the flickering shadows from Plato's cave that create a silent film on a snow-covered heath. But beyond these concrete images, Strindberg is also taking up the challenge presented by Plato in arguing for a ban of the poets from his ideal state. Strindberg himself no doubt often felt that he himself had been subjected to such a ban, in particular by his own countrymen, and that his writings were considered by many to be subversive or the product of a madman. *A Dream Play* can therefore be read as a defense of poetry against suppression, pointing at the redemptive potentials of poetry that enable Indra's Daughter to return to the realm of eternal truth. Strindberg has accepted Plato's metaphysical framework, but his conclusions regarding the role of poetry are contrary to those of Plato. For Strindberg the cave is filled with beautiful poetry.

Notes

1. Excerpts from Strindberg's *A Dream Play* are quoted in English translation; page numbers to corresponding pages in the original Swedish in *Samlade Verk* follow in the parentheses.

2. All quotations from Plato's *The Republic* are from the translation by Tom Griffith. When there is emphasis it has been added. I want to thank Orna Harari for her help and insightful comments in reading the cave parable, and in particular for drawing my attention to its complex linguistic dimensions.

Works Cited

Nancy, Jean-Luc. *Listening*. Trans. Charlotte Mandel. New York: Fordham University Press, 2007.

Plato. *The Republic*. Trans. Tom Griffith. Cambridge, Eng.: Cambridge University Press, 2000.

Robinson, Michael. *An International Annotated Bibliography of Strindberg Studies*. London: Modern Humanities Research Association, 2008.

Rokem, Freddie. "Deus ex Machina in the Modern Theatre." In *Reconsiderations of Theatre History*, ed. Peter Holland and W. B. Worthen. Houndmills, Eng.: Palgrave/Macmillan, 2003. 177–95.

———. *Philosophers & Thespians: Thinking Philosophy*. Stanford, Calif.: Stanford University Press, 2010.

Strindberg, August. "Brev till Emil Schering. 21/7 1903." http://spraakbanken.gu.se/konk/?s=ovantill&soktyp=tab.

———. *A Dream Play*. In *Six Plays of Strindberg*. Trans. Elizabeth Sprigge. New York: Doubleday Anchor Books, 1955. 193–261.

———. *Ett Drömspel*. In *Samlade Verk*, vol. 46. Stockholm: Norstedts, 1988.

———. "Vem byggde Fingalsgrottan?" *En Blå Bok*.In *Samlade Skrifter*, 46–48 (http://runeberg.org/strindbg/blabok/0310.html).

Szondi, Peter. *Theory of the Modern Drama*. Trans. Michael Hays. Minneapolis: University of Minnesota Press, 1987.

Money Metaphors and Rhetoric of Resource Depletion: *Creditors* and Late-Nineteenth-Century European Economics

Anna Westerståhl Stenport

In Strindberg's works of the 1880s, money is a persistent concern. The short story collection *Getting Married* (*Giftas I,* 1883) outlines a number of domestic conflicts, many of which are centered around personal financial hardship and the allure of often unattainable merchandise consumption. Similar conflicts are brought up in the *The Father* (*Fadren,* 1887), *Utopias in Reality* (*Utopier i verkligheten,* 1885), and in *A Madman's Defense* (*Le plaidoyer d'un fou,* written in 1888; first official publication 1895 in France). The description of marital conflicts centered around money is not unrelated to the author's personal conditions—having left Sweden in 1883, he struggled as a professional writer to support his family while traveling and living internationally, often writing in less than ideal circumstances, always under deadline to produce, and barely satisfying his creditors.

Money concerns, especially in a domestic context and with clear gendered implications, are generally prominent in Scandinavian literature during the 1880s. Henrik Ibsen's *A Doll's House* (*Et Dukkehjem,* 1879) is, as I have argued elsewhere, fundamentally a play about the cultural and existential implications of money (see Stenport); Victoria Benedictsson's novel *Money* (*Pengar,* 1885) and Anne-Charlotte Edgren Leffler's play *True Women* (*Sanna Kvinnor,* 1883) are other well-known examples. What demarcates these examples from some of Strindberg's contemporary writing, especially his dramas, however, is that for Ibsen and Leffler, money and other financial instruments are central to the realistic intrigue of their plays. Money—usually a lack thereof, or in terms of complications of obtaining, maintaining, and increasing expendable funds—drives the plot, shapes characterization, and creates a discursive register that influences thematic interpretation. In addition, many of Ibsen's and Leffler's plays are clearly grounded in contemporary social conditions. They appear invested in realistically portraying gendered domestic economic arrangements while explicitly relating these to the public sphere in terms of banking and legal practices, limitations of and opportunities for wage-earning outside the home, industrial and capitalist wealth accumulation, and so on. Ibsen's and Leffler's plays seem to mediate value in the fashion suggested by Mary Poovey in her formidable work *Genres of the Credit Economy* (2008). Poovey argues that from the seventeenth century on, "one of the functions performed by imaginative writing in general was to mediate value—that is, to help people understand the new credit economy and the market model of value it promoted" (1–2). Though rarely studied in this way, Ibsen's and Leffler's drama thereby engage with some of the key changes of European economic theory at the end of the nineteenth century—particularly what has been called the marginal revolution. I will return to address the significance of these changes in a moment.

Strindberg's interest in and relevance for an understanding of economic theory throughout the major European economies in the late nineteenth century has been similarly understudied. Yet he uses a large number of economic, financial, and commercial metaphors in his writing during the 1880s. This interest reflects, as Karl-Åke Kärnell argues, the existing "economic conditions of the *Gründer*-period" (50) of Swedish history in terms of the accelerated industrial expansion of the 1870s and 1880s, and is evident in Strindbergian writing dealing with Swedish history and contemporary politics, including *Swedish Destinies and Adventures: Tales from all Times* (*Svenska öden och äventyr: berättelser från alla tidhvarf*, 1882–83), which takes a Marxist position with respect to the historical representation of workers' conditions, or *The Red Room* (*Röda rummet*, 1879), which can be understood as outlining an atomization of bourgeois life and the inequities of an increasing division of labor.[1] In writing set on the European continent, including *Among French Peasants* (*Bland franska bönder*, 1889), Strindberg's disdain shines through for what he saw as a streamlined and inflexible Marx-derived socialism, as sponsored by the prominent Social Democratic politician Hjalmar Branting. Strindberg, like others, called this industrial socialism, which they juxtaposed with a perception of what appeared then as its logical alternative, agrarian socialism. The first strand has subsequently been brought into close association with modernity, social progress, and the welfare state foundation, particularly in northern Europe. Late-nineteenth-century rhetoric over competing socialisms was also gendered—the Swedish independent farming couple was, for Strindberg and many of his contemporaries, construed as representative of a stable, primordial, and natural ideology of domestic distribution of labor (shared responsibility but different tasks). These gendered aspects perhaps made agrarian socialism attractive to Strindberg, but, what is more pertinent and relevant for my argument is that gender for Strindberg is not disassociated from political economy, which it has tended to be in the Marxist tradition. Yet there is a piece of the puzzle in Strindberg's writing from the 1880s that has been overlooked in terms of its connections to European economic history, including its gendered aspects: the play *Creditors* (*Fordringsägare*, 1888).[2]

Despite the title's obvious reference to credit, a key component of modern financial practice and economic theory, and a number of economic metaphors in the play, little attention has been directed to the significance of this discursive register. Strindberg had initially given the play a French-derived title for its first production, in Danish, at his own short-lived experimental theater in Copenhagen: "*Kreditorer.*"[3] The etymology of the terms "credit" (noun and verb) and "creditor," *fordringsägare*, in Anglo-French and Swedish contexts is significant. Credit has to do with credence, of having bestowed faith in someone—credibility in characterization is of course a factor significant to the development of modern drama at the end of the nineteenth century, as it was in the realist novel as it evolved earlier. In fact, since the middle of the sixteenth century, the attribute of credibility has in Swedish, English, and French been directly tied to money. *The Oxford English Dictionary*, for example, states that "credit" involves "trust or confidence in a buyer's ability and intention to pay at some future time." The term draws on double registers, which, like Strindberg's characters, vacillate between the psychological and economics as a system of exchange.[4] An analogy is the Germanic-derived term for *skuld/Schuld*, which combines the monetary with the ethical; *fordrande* in Swedish is also connected to having a demanding, *fordrande* personality. Strindberg's use of the title *Creditors* or *Fordringsägare* also reflects the playwright's interest in linguistic innovation at this time, particularly in terms of moving away from romanticism's and idealism's extended and convoluted metaphorical expressions toward a materiality of expression connected to a contemporary social moment (see also Kärnell 15–19). Yet, the title is, in fact, largely metaphorical in Strindberg's use. It describes the tangled sexual and marital relationship between the play's three characters; that is, how they are each indebted to one another.

The play's plot and characterization are rudimentary: Adolph is a failed artist who, in the absence of his wife Tekla (a novelist and New Woman figure), is joined at a seaside resort by Gustav, her former husband (this seaside resort is also where Tekla and Gustav went on their honeymoon several years earlier). Adolph, described as weak and appeasing, with character traits of a female hysteric of the late nineteenth century, falls under the apparent spell of Gustav. As a Faustian character, Gustav exerts pressure on Adolph in three ways, first by convincing him to relinquish painting in favor of sculpture, second by inducing in him the belief that his having sexual intercourse with Tekla is making him epileptic—partly because of Gustav's sexual transfusion into Adolph through Tekla—and third by leading Adolph to challenge Tekla's love and commitment to him. Upon returning from a shopping trip to town, Tekla suspects Adolph of having been manipulated by someone, guessing at Gustav's presence. While Tekla affirms her love for both her current and former husband, Gustav challenges her on the grounds that she has stolen his honor by leaving him and remarrying. The play ends with a dead Adolph, a distraught Tekla at his side, and a seemingly triumphant Gustav.

The title *Creditors* directs attention to the fact that the characters in this play express their emotional, intellectual, artistic, and sexual relationships in financial terms. For example, the dialogue reflects sentiments of being caught within a system of bookkeeping that allows no flexibility, as being trapped in a system of resources that risk depletion, and as wanting to believe in a system of fair bartering but being victimized by an inequitable system of supply and demand. Financial and economic metaphors are especially prominent in the first third and in the concluding scenes of the play. To give just a few examples, Adolph describes in bank terminology how he has "deposited" (277; "*deponerat*")[5] part of his brain and intellectual capacity into Tekla, but later laments that he has squandered his intellectual and emotional property, so to speak, to the extent that he becomes "finished, bankrupt, done for" (289). Adolph says, "But in inspiring her, I expired. I gave and gave for her sake—until there was nothing left for me to give" (288). . . . "Perhaps she has taken more from me—things I don't know about." (288). In a rhetorical turnaround, Tekla later asks Adolph, "you feel like a thief, don't you" (304); and he responds affirmatively while she continues, "You think you can steal women like you steal chicken or kidnap children. You think I'm his [Gustav's, her former husband's] personal property, chattel goods?" (304). Adolph responds, "No, I think of you as his wife. That's not the same as a piece of furniture. You can't buy another one" (305). In their discussions, Adolph continues in his discussion with Tekla to offer similar arguments. To "love means to give"; Adolph responds, to "love like a man means to give. To love like a woman is to take" (306); he describes

Tekla as wanting to "sneak away like a thief in the night" . . . "I tried to remind you of what you owed me. And in an instant I was transformed into the troublesome creditor who wouldn't go away. You wanted to tear up the IOU's. And to avoid getting deeper into debt, you stopped dipping into my wallets and went to others instead" (307). At the end Gustav and Tekla also describe their relationship in monetary terms. Gustav sees himself as "the plaintiff," telling Tekla her debts may not be forgiven: "sooner or later the bill collector shows up" . . . "I have come to collect what you stole, not what I gave you as a gift" (324). As the examples above convey, the imagery of *Creditors* illustrates Strindberg's interest in representing human relationships through a vocabulary culled from contemporary economic and financial practices. Expressions like the ones above exemplify the "knowledgeable application of terms derived from the commercial sphere onto the relationship between the sexes," for which Kärnell argues with respect to *Getting Married* (50). This argument would also seem to pertain to *Creditors*.

Economic Abstraction and the Marginal Utility Revolution

There are indeed two significant characteristics of the recurring financial and economic metaphors in *Creditors*' dialogue: their abstraction and their connections to developments in contemporary European economic theory. First, characters speak about financial and economic matters nearly exclusively metaphorically. The material consequences of money, or economic ability to extend a loan or repay a debt, are strikingly absent in the play. For example, no one in *Creditors* is concerned with actual money to spend or invest; it is as if these characters, and particularly Gustav, exist outside revenue streams. This abstraction correlates with the fact that in *Creditors*, characters are dislodged from a domestic setting and located in the transient space of a contemporary resort hotel, a *pensionat*. This is in sharp contrast to Ibsen's and Leffler's contemporary plays, for example, in which income, debt, and expenses actually matter on a material level and are closely associated with the perceived instability of a bourgeois domestic space as "home." In *Creditors*, Tekla is the only one who makes money (thanks to novel writing) and who returns to the resort after spending money on a shopping trip. The economic discursive register complements several other metaphorical registers in the play, which previous scholarship has addressed in detail (see Lönngren 79–82 for a recent overview of previous scholarship; see also Robinson 944–950). These registers pertain to psychology, anatomy, biology, sexology, racism, and colonialism, with specific references to hypnosis, cannibalism, heredity, predatory behavior, telegony,[6] slave-master dialectics, infantry tactics, and more. Like these other discourses, the financial and economic discursive register is neither systematic nor seemingly grounded in everyday or contemporary socioeconomic practices. This abstraction correlates with a gendered representation we have come to expect from Strindberg's writing in the late 1880s, with women characters figuring as incapable of any substantial achievements on their own, as parasitic on men, or, to keep with the play's economic metaphors, as gold-diggers. Tekla is, for example, described by Gustav and Adolph as stealing intellectual resources or borrowing emotional capital without any intent of returning what they express they did not give her freely.

The second significant aspect of the financial and money metaphors in the dialogue is that characters relate to an idea of scarcity, including of intellectual capacity, emotions, artistic merit, and sexual prowess: their resources are finite. At the same time, they seek to want to ascribe some kind of value—emotional as well as aesthetic—to their existence. In this way, they are also concerned with a relationship between production and consumption. Their discussions bridge two primary explanatory models of political economy during the late nineteenth and early twentieth century. First, the focus on the valuation of human capacities in the dialogue between the small cast of characters in *Creditors* seems to reflect Alfred Marshall's well-known statements in the seminal *Principles of Economics* (1890) about economics as the study of peoples' everyday interactions: "economics is a study of mankind in the ordinary business of life; . . . on the one side a study of wealth; and on the other, and more important side, a part of the study of man" (1). Second, their references to a scarcity of resources seem to gesture to Lionel Robbins's identification of economics as a science of "human behavior as a relationship between ends and scarce means" (16) in *An Essay on the Nature and Significance of Economic Science* (1932).[7] *Creditors* is not interested in a scientific or societal formulation of economics; scarce resources are discussed only as they pertain to the experiences of the three individuals in the play. In this way, the abstract economic register employed by Strindberg seems to correlate Marshall's understanding of economics as a study of humanity with Robbins's emphasis on scarcity.

In fact, the concept of scarcity was central to the development of modern economic theory at the end of the nineteenth century. In this way, the economic and financial metaphors in *Creditors* serve as conduits—albeit in sometimes opaque ways—for understanding a transitional moment in economic history during the 1870s and 1880s. This transition has been called the marginal utility revolution and involved, in basic terms, a shift in the explanatory model for economic value from one based on production to one based on consumption.[8] The standard explanatory model of classical political economy—the beginnings of the free market/supply and demand model—as developed from the mid-eighteenth century onward by Smith, Ricardo, Mill, and Marx—emphasized a labor or production theory of value in which the price of a good is ascribed depending on the unit of labor that goes into it. This free market model is also geographically and historically specific. For example, natural resources (geography; think colonialism) as well as the possible division of labor among the population (history; think industrialization) shape both supply and demand. This model, in contrast to the one subsequent to it, has clear ethical potential—"once society had developed its [optimal] productive forms, humanity could progress ethically and politically" (Gagnier 2; see also 40); similarly, the model allowed for comparison between population groups (*x* number of labor hours equals *y* compensation); and between classes of goods produced (*x* good as a contributor toward productivity in ways different from good *y*).

In contrast, the marginalist model, developed in the 1870s nearly simultaneously by European economists of the marginal utility revolution such as Jevons (in Manchester), Menger (in Vienna), and Walrus (in Lausanne) and fully popularized by Marshall (Cambridge), proffers a model of value based on individual consumer demand. This transition in economic explanatory paradigms has been called the marginal utility revolution and occurs concurrently to Strindberg's writing *Creditors*. What is so striking about the revolution is that it measures only the perceived additional utility of each good or service with respect to an individual consumer, whose perception of its marginal utility is decoupled from concrete labor or material resources constitutive of it.[9] The marginal revolution thereby gives us a way to understand a turn toward subjectivity, individualism, and aesthetic abstraction at the end of the nineteenth century. Literary scholar Regenia Gagnier neatly summarizes some of the socio-cultural implications of the marginal utility revolution transition in the field of economic theory that appeared concurrently with Strindberg's *Creditors:*

> Political economy's theory of the productive relations between land, labor, and capital thus gave way to the statistical analysis of price lists or consumption patterns. . . . Consumer choice ceased to be a moral category: it did not matter whether the good desired was good or bad, just that the consumer was willing to pay for it. Value ceased to be comparable across

> persons: it became individual, subjective, or psychological. The theory of economics became more psychological than sociological. The psychological bias transformed the modern concept of *scarcity*. . . . Under marginal utility theory, scarcity was relocated in the mind itself, as a consequence of the insatiability of human desires. [Gagnier 4, emphasis added] Political economy was also historical and progressive: it seized as its domain the distant past as well as the distant future. And it was realist. [40]. . . . [The shift to a neoclassical paradigm was also] a shift from macroeconomics to microeconomics, the theory of the consumer and the firm. . . . It represents a turn from economic man as producer to economic man as consumer, from labor or pain to pleasure, and from the substantive to the formal. (41)

In brief, and drawing on Gagnier's succinct interpretation above, I posit there to be three aspects of particular relevance to Strindberg's play *Creditors* in the marginal revolution. One, the emphasis on subjectively perceived scarcity and the changing assumptions of Economic Man (a concept dating as far back as Adam Smith to describe people as beings that act in their own rational self-interest) and emergent formulations of nineteenth-century Economic Woman; two, the abstraction of geographical and historical factors; and, three, a transition in the perceived value of art and aesthetic production—including performative dramatic arts. In the remainder of this chapter, I will focus on aspect one and two and gesture in the conclusion toward the third.

Creditors and the Marginal Revolution I: Scarcity, Economic Woman, and the Inadequacy of Money

The spirit of the marginal revolution is complemented by other concurrent economic paradigms in Strindberg's play. As an experiment, we may map the characters Adolph, Gustav, and Tekla onto three respective economic paradigms: mercantilist, classical/liberal, and marginal. Adolph and Gustav appear to operate on mercantilist or classical/liberal systems of supply and demand, with Adolph more closely aligned with mercantilism and Gustav closer to the classical/liberal paradigm; while Tekla seems to embody the idea of an individual consumer, what we can call a marginalist Economic Woman. Adolph and Gustav both see emotional and intellectual capacity as limited, as constantly at risk of depletion, especially by Tekla's seemingly insatiable wants.[10] The mixed metaphors and competing discursive registers brought up in Gustav's and Adolph's initial conversation have one thing in common, which is the idea that interpersonal relationships are supposed to be productive (whether in terms of a marriage contract, children, camaraderie, or artistic partnership) and that actual human resources (intellectual, emotional, aesthetic, or sexual) going into the relationship are limited. These resources need to be carefully managed in order to optimize the desired outcome. Adolph's expressions, in particular, appear to operate on a mercantilist, zero-sum, model in which there is no possibility of dynamic or mutual gain without another person's loss. Having given too much, his resources are depleted, the play seems to suggest, to the point of his own extinction (Adolph dies at the end). Adolph's character reflects an idea of giving and receiving according to a preset social or political protocol and thereby correlates with the principles of nation-based mercantilism. This was a dominant pragmatic during the period 1500–1800. As theories of classical liberal economics took over, mercantilism died out. In *Creditors,* this process correlates with Gustav's success and Adolph's demise.

In Adolph's expression, the mercantilist model is also gendered: to "love means to give"; Adolph says, to "love like a man means to give. To love like a woman is to take" (306). In practice, mercantile economics assumed that a country should try to amass the largest possible amount of gold/valuables and expend with the least possible amount of gold. So, to be successful, a country must export goods for gold, and consume goods at home, without expending the gold for imports; this also assumes a colonial plundering paradigm (new sources of valuables can be identified and resituated in the economy without high expense) as well as an understanding of a stable nation-state, including one in which military power over another state should increase the possession of gold/valuables. Adolph is like a country gone bankrupt: he has given away all his "gold"; there is no possibility of a jointly assumed common good with either Tekla or Gustav; he is weakened and susceptible to colonial or military invasion by Gustav. For Adolph, there is a limited pool of resources and once his intellectual, sexual, aesthetic, and emotional capacity is depleted he cannot recuperate.

Yet, in this play, financial and economic metaphors indicate modern commercial activity used to overcome the rigidity of the mercantilist system: debt and credit, in particular. Gustav represents, at least partially, this model. Though resources also remain scarce and finite for him—he expresses, for example, a need to recapture what he believes Tekla took from him (324)—this character can be seen as operating on a classic model of supply and demand liberalism, in which a commercial exchange is not a zero-sum activity but rather mutually beneficial. Participants in a transaction must find the goods or services received at last minimally more valuable than the ones delivered. Gustav indeed sets out with the idea that he can rationally manipulate both Adolph and Tekla to gain leverage in ways for him to benefit from the transaction. He seeks revenge for having been cheated and cuckolded: "You stole my honor, my reputation," Gustav says to Tekla and continues, "How could I get it back without taking yours? Wasn't I right?" (324). In line with the classical/liberal paradigm, Adolph's and Gustav's discussion, and their accusations leveled toward Tekla, operate on the assumption that value can be defined in absolute units of labor: in this case their respective intellectual, emotional, aesthetic, or sexual input into their relationship with Tekla.[11] Underlying Adolph's and Gustav's discussion, moreover, is the search for a unit of value of interpersonal relationships, and particularly for men and women in relation to marriage and divorce. Both characters indeed assume that value can be measured and that it is dependent on the input—the labor—each party dedicates to the relationship (what the male characters state they give to Tekla to maintain the relationship). Moreover, Gustav is a productive and rational capitalist in the classical paradigm: he has identified what he wants from Adolph and Tekla; he has both a desire and a strategy to produce an objectively measurable result: Adolph's suicide and Tekla's misery.

Tekla, on the other hand, is a character whose emphasis is on individual consumption and for whom the ethical implications of goods consumed are presented as irrelevant; she has sought to consume both Adolph and Gustav, it appears, in an attempt to increase her own utility as a woman in a marriage game and her perceived social stature as a novelist. Similarly, she is a creature of insatiable wants: "I think only *of* myself. I am a frightful egotist" (298); she values less Adolph's sculpture of her (the product of his labor) than the experience of being desired it appears to produce in her (298–99); she flirts with others for sexual stimulation and because she wants to be "liked and admired" (302, 304); she laments she cannot maintain emotional and/or sexual relationships with both Gustav and Adolph (325); and, as described by Gustav, seeks "freedom, broad horizons, fast company" rather than "monotonous daily routine" or "dull work" (314). When Adolph recaps his impression of his and Tekla's courtship and relationship, he formulates this as contributing to her perception of her own increased utility, while his utility becomes substitutive or subtractive (Pribram 278). For example, he recalls how he made her, how he "advertised her" and how "in making you, I had undone myself. . . . I became ill. . . . My illness embarrassed you and sometimes I felt that what was behind it was a desire to get rid of me, the creditor" (309). In the play, Tekla is a consumer, one concerned with aesthetics, how she looks and how her companion appears; she is perhaps embarrassed by unsightly illness. Similarly, the more help she receives in becoming a novelist, the less valuable each individual unit of help. And, Adolph affirms, she becomes less creative, that is, less *productive,* as time passes; she is satisfied to be consuming on credit, never wanting to "pay your own debts" (310). Gustav sees her in similar ways, as an insatiable consumer, while his perspective remains based on the scarcity of resources: "you have only taken, and what you have taken, you've consumed, so there's nothing left to give back" (325).

Tekla's second line in the play indeed situates her as a consumer, and as one who is willfully subjective: "I've been spending money like mad" (297). Because this line is never concretized, it remains an abstract use of a financial term, and we do not know what Tekla has bought (the product) or how much she has spent (the labor theory of value). Tekla is only partially a *Doll's House* or *True Women* figure—in these plays, Ibsen and Leffler concretize and materialize consumption by tying it to a labor theory of value (we know that hours of nighttime handicraft or copying goes into buying a good). In Strindberg, these aspects of concretion are not known. Consumption is abstract, formal, and detached from labor in *Creditors.*[12] At the same time, Tekla is the one who appears to have an income, just as her allegiances do not seem quite as rigid or static as those of her male counterparts. Though we may follow an established line of criticism about the play and read Adolph's manipulability and Gustav's departure from stage as examples of threats posed to a weak "patriarchy," indeed by the threat of a Tekla as what appears to be a resourceful New Woman figure, Tekla does not conform to standard femininity roles of the nineteenth century.

Another way to express the interpersonal relationships in *Creditors* involves rethinking the influential model of Economic Man, which in the late nineteenth century shifted from "Economic Man as producer (Smith, Ricardo, Mill, and Marx) or reproducer (Malthus) to a view of Economic Man as consumer," Gagnier writes; as "first and foremost an individual whose aesthetic, or taste, is revealed by the choices he (or she) makes" (2). The concept of Economic Man was coined by Adam Smith in *The Wealth of Nations* (1776) and further developed by J. S. Mill. It involves a model of human behavior that always involves acting out of rational self-interest, even when this self-interest is governed by, as Smith described it, an Invisible Hand leading all human behavior toward more productive wealth accumulation.[13] For our purposes, it is worth mentioning that though the aesthetic representation of Economic Man has been analyzed in particular by scholars of the English novel, this figure is also like a Dramatis Persona—a character as part of a script. Michèle A. Pujol provides a basic definition of what we can call a late-nineteenth-century Economic Woman (she does not use this term), as promoted by the views of women in an economic system expressed by European late-nineteenth-century marginal utility economists Edgeworth, Jevons, Walras, and Pigou:

> These flaws [of the marginal paradigm] can be seen more clearly when we analyze the five elements which characterize [the marginal economists'] views of women: 1. All women are married, or, if not yet, they will be. Similarly, all women have or will have children. 2. All women are (and ought to be) economically dependent on a male relative: father or husband. 3. Women are (and ought to be) housewives, their reproductive capacities specialize them for that function. 4. Women are unproductive (whether absolutely or relative to men is not always clear) in the industrial workforce. 5. Women are irrational, they are unfit as economic agents, they cannot be trusted to make the right economic decisions. (21)

Gustav and Adolph appear to operate on the assumption that Tekla should want to operate according to Pujol's definitions 1 to 4 and that she is acting according to 5; i.e., that she should be what we can call an Economic Woman. On closer inspection, Tekla's characterization in *Creditors* seems not to correlate with this view, however. Strindberg may be pointing out not only the gendered assumptions underlying contemporary economic theory, but also its flaws as pertaining to women wage-earners. It is clear what Gustav gains (revenge) and what Adolph loses in *Creditors* (his life); but it is not clear what Tekla gains or loses, though her despair at the end can be interpreted as a loss of utility. Yet, Tekla is certainly both a central and a dynamic character; the two men talk about her, she is the bridge between them, and she is the last person to remain on stage. Is whatever Tekla has learned and experienced in fact what Strindberg wants to show as the final moment of the play? This final moment reveals, most explicitly, that her actions and expressions are characterized by subjective individualism. In this way, Tekla's character may show the inherent problem in trying to calculate utility objectively; regardless of gender, she offers a critique of the theory of utility and points out its limitations. Indeed, money may have appeared as an objective form of evaluation at the end of the nineteenth century, yet utility is not calculated in money and is not money. This formulation may apply especially to human perception of one's own experiences: "You can get richer without becoming more satisfied," as *The Economist* puts it in its definition of utility. Indeed, *Creditors* shows that money does not capture utility.

The money metaphors in *Creditors* do not capture the economy between the characters and neither do the many references to debt and IOUs, not least because of the abstract nature of these discussions. The play's abstract economic language thereby correlates to and goes beyond what Mary Poovey describes as an economic naturalization process preceding and concurrent with the marginal revolution:

> Nineteenth-century Literary writers repeatedly—and after 1845, increasingly—appropriated economic and financial themes and real-life situations for fictional treatment. . . . Most of these Literary appropriations were only incidentally concerned with the explanatory function that was central to writing about money and finance; imaginative writers' tendency to mine contemporary financial events for characters and plots paradoxically cultivated in readers a tolerance for ignorance about the very financial mechanisms political economists sought to explain, and this strange symbiosis both underscored the differences between the two kinds of writing and bound them together in an increasingly complicated, increasingly misrecognized relationship of mutual indebtedness, masked by mutual disavowal and misunderstanding. (9)

Strindberg's use of money metaphors in *Creditors* goes one step further than the "strange symbiosis" that Poovey describes, in that Strindberg mines economic terms strictly for use in an abstract register divorced from "economic and financial themes and real-life situations for fictional treatment." In fact, Adolph, Gustav, and Tekla all express themselves by drawing on the terminology of classic bookkeeping while financial accounting in itself plays no role in the plot. In an argument with Tekla, Adolph challenges her interpretation by drawing on an analogy: "You can't reduce a lifetime of experiences to one number," and Tekla responds, "It was the sum total of what you said, the bottom line"; and Adolph retorts, "(*in a wild rage*) There can't be a bottom line if you don't add" (310). This interchange reflects both how pervasive economic discourse is conceived to be for the representation of human experiences and relationships, and also that Adolph in particular appears to recognize this discursive register's limitations. He gets angry, presumably in frustration at not being understood. In a similar use of economic rhetoric, Gustav construes himself at the end of the play as the creditor in the triangular constellation, as someone who has come to claim explicitly from Tekla but also implicitly from Adolph repayment of a debt, from having been deceived as a husband. On the one hand, the economic rhetoric conjured up in the play seems detached, mediated, and entirely symbolical, a "system" used to cover up, it appears, both a difficulty of expressing human emotions and forces of sexual attraction and the embodied practices of those, including numerous references to blood, cannibalism, dissection, and animal desire. On the other hand, *Creditors* obviously does not encapsulate any simplistic economic interpretive models; the play is far too complex to allow such schematization. Though stripped down in terms of intrigue, set, and characterization, this is a messy, difficult, idiosyncratic, and incoherent play. There are many contributing aspects to this complexity, and I have alluded to several of them in the discussion above. Yet I wish to highlight one aspect in particular: its unabashedly subjective protagonists—particularly Tekla—whose actions and utterances appear inexplicable and at times far removed from the naturalist paradigm the play supposedly adheres to. Tekla, in particular, is a thoroughly modern, if not pre-expressionist, character based on contingency and subjectivity.

Creditors and the Marginal Revolution II: Economic Implications of Spatiotemporal Abstraction

Just as the financial metaphors and implicit references to economic theory have gone unnoticed in *Creditors*, the significance of the setting has been overlooked by scholars. In fact, its anonymity—the transience and impermanence implied by an unspecified seaside *pensionat* (a boarding house, or an inexpensive resort hotel) that could be imagined as anywhere in Europe—is significant on several levels that relate to the marginal utility revolution in economic thought at the end of the nineteenth century. First, *Creditors* is a play conceived to be international. The nondescript seaside *pensionat* could be anywhere in Europe—though two geographical markers in the dialogue of the script situate it for a Swedish reader on a vacation island off the west coast of Sweden near Strömstad, translations have often removed this specificity or masked the cultural connotations of this location (Sprinchorn provides a literal [mis]translation of the town's name and makes it a generic "Rivertown" [300]). Not only are national identificatory markers largely absent in the play, but the dialogue also avoids most references to any specific cultural context. Similarly, there are no descriptions of a distinctive landscape or other geographical features. It is as if the characters, possibly like the playwright himself who penned the play at a borrowed residence in Danish Skovlyst, exist in a transient limbo, marked by displacements and shaped by implications of impermanence. The set is unstable in its metaphorical implications too; within it, none of the characters feel at home but instead trapped. We know little of the characters' personal background. At the beginning of the play, Gustav has just arrived, Tekla has recently departed, and Adolph languishes on his own while he at the end insists that he wants to leave. Neither are the characters ever on stage together; instead they occupy the performance space in pairs, so that any sense of collectivity is deemphasized.

Indeed, the characters seem on the one hand to be searching for permanence and stability in an existence marked by impermanence and displacement. A yearning for a utopian notion of permanence, or stability, is a well-known reaction to the perceived impermanence of accelerated modernity at the end of the nineteenth century and hardly unique in period literature. What *Creditors* has to offer this complex of ideas is its multifaceted and at times contradictory interest in incorporating a discourse shaped by contemporary economic theory in order to challenge precisely such a nostalgic search for permanence, transcendence, or continuity. Having just completed *Miss Julie,* August Strindberg describes his subsequent play *Creditors* in a letter as a ninety-minute psychological examination that is "better than *Miss Julie,* with three persons, one table, two chairs, and no Sunrise" (letter Aug. 21, 1888, cited in Sprinchorn, "Introduction to Creditors" 270; see also Ollén 158). It appears that the playwright understands his play as ascetic both formally and thematically—abandoning a Sunrise, it would seem, to imply that time stops for the characters on stage: there is no continuation, no morning after when life presumably goes on. *Creditors* relinquishes the setting of a bourgeois domestic space so common in many late-nineteenth-century plays whose plots foreground money matters, including Ibsen's *A Doll's House* and Leffler's *True Women.* As such, the play also suggests an ahistoricity, a renunciation of both past and future, which according to both Gagnier and Poovey are constitutive of the marginal revolution: it not only delocalized economic thought; it also dehistoricized it.

Creditors' many references to debt and credit may be largely abstract, as I have argued above, yet there is one significant feature to the process of extending credit or being a creditor that cannot be ignored: the temporal component. There must be a time limit to credit. It needs to be paid back at a certain time. And there is something very peculiar going on with respect to temporality in *Creditors.* For instance, there appears to be several different temporal dimensions coexisting within the diegesis.

In *Creditors,* time passes very quickly—relationships and events are sped up—and seem unrealistically accelerated. Gustav and Adolph befriend each other immediately. Though they say they have spoken for six hours, they seem to have known each other for years. The play lasts only about ninety minutes. At the same time, Gustav has been in residence near the resort for many days before he goes to see Adolph. All three characters are described in metaphorical language that equates them with a clock, or a clock-like machine, an electric generator, or even an automaton who is wound up for a period of time (see, for example, *Creditors* 278–79, 286, 292–93, 306; see also Heitmann). These references link the characters not only to modernity and industry, but also to a perception of them as mechanical, as perhaps not quite human.

The play also postulates a difference between interior and exterior time, in which it is clear that the specter of Gustav and Tekla's divorce, including its financial implications, is distorting their sense of time. As Gustav and Tekla at the very end of the play stand talking on the veranda, two ladies pass by, and as they see the couple, they whisper and giggle (319); it appears as if the play suggests both a challenge to diegetic time, and a throwback to when the two were staying there first as newlyweds. Another assumption could be that the ladies' laugh implies that the two are now lovers and cheating on Adolph. Similarly, spatiotemporal distortion affects the end of the play, as Gustav describes the parlor room in the hotel, where he had spent time with Adolph before Tekla's arrival. It turns out that this room was once the couple's bedroom. "How about the time when we were just married and we lived in this very room. It wasn't the lounge then and it was furnished differently." Washbasin, and so on, and over "there, there was the bed. . ." (317). The play relinquishes pretensions of home as a space of belonging or rootedness; indeed, Gustav declares at the end that he will never have a home, nor will he seek to get one. In the space of the anonymous hotel boarding house, it seems like time passes quickly, but also that this semi-public space becomes the site of a psychological struggle that ends up being conceived at the end in economic rhetoric that at first appears realistic but remains abstract.

The final lines between Gustav and Tekla further thematize the temporal disjunctures of the play and emphasize the temporal limitations to credit. "You stole my honor, my reputation. How could I get it back without taking yours?" (324). As Gustav makes arrangements to check out, he responds that he hasn't "got a home" to return to and that he never will (324). Tekla at this point asks for reconciliation, but Gustav refuses. In an interchange that seems tinged with ironic references toward Ibsen's

Doll's House, Strindberg's play appears to satirize the idea of "forgiving debts," tearing up "IOUs," or "canceling debts" (324). Instead, Gustav urges Tekla to "settle your accounts with your husband" (325). Gustav's next-to-last words to Tekla are "Settle up with him"; then he leaves. Adolph dies, with Tekla caressing him and wanting "little brother" to return. Credit is limited in time: it must be repaid. Similarly, the play offers no "Sunrise" and no indication of a continuation. Every character in this play can occupy the position of creditor, yet at the end Adolph appears bankrupt: the depletion of his intellectual, emotional, sexual, and aesthetic resources appears to be the source of his death. Similarly, Adolph does not seem capable of making money anymore; he appears to be living off his wife, and were she to go back to Gustav, he would be left without a source of livelihood. In this vein, the play addresses questions of ownership and of value. Adolph, Gustav, and Tekla cannot produce anything of lasting value. Consumption—whether in the form of a holiday at a seaside resort or the increased marginal utility of marriage—is only tokens of perceived value. For Adolph, credit has been extended to its ultimate end point: the death of the debtor.

Conclusion: The Marginal Revolution and the Production and Consumption of Art

The characters in this play repeatedly address questions pertaining to art and aesthetics. Discussions are often abstract, yet the play is a work of art for consumption, and the characters are also involved in both aesthetic production and consumption. Gustav and Adolph's discussion about visual and plastic art in the first part of the play is significant (279–80), as this discussion illustrates a transition from two-dimensional (painting) to three-dimensional (sculpture) to four-dimensional aesthetic production (performance). The performance part is meta-theatrical: Gustav acts out his own/his supposed brother's epilepsy, with Adolph copying the movements. The discussion on realist painting and sculpture which moves toward a validation of live performance can be argued to illustrate the accelerated socio-cultural implications of Scandinavian transitions into modernity: it is exemplified in this play's aesthetic rhetoric as a transition first from realism to impressionism and subsequently toward a meta-theatrical performance-within sequence. The preface to *Miss Julie,* written after the completion of that play and right before *Creditors,* famously shuns the use of a two-dimensional painted backdrop on stage to advocate for a naturalism that is three-dimensional, embodied, and multi-sensory (real artifacts on stage, smelly sausage frying, and bodies choreographed in a mime that preempts an overt staging of sexual intercourse).

The meta-theatrical performance-within sequence of *Creditors,* in which Adolph copies Gustav's enactment of his brother's convulsions and thereby comes to exhibit them as his own, indeed marks an ever further radicalization of the possibility of theater. This sequence stages a process of subjectification that is both modernist and expressionist. It also illustrates the accelerated temporality of the play: Adolph becomes sick, immediately, by *performing* the supposed bodily movements of a to him unknown epileptic. His concept of his own self, psychological as well as physical, is instantly transformed. This can also be seen as a meta-theatrical gesture, with Strindberg advocating for performance arts as the most modern and ultimately transformative in terms of their representation. The transition in this play from valuation of two- to three- to four-dimensional art is accelerated. It thereby allows us to posit the argument that Strindberg is writing specifically for a contemporary audience, one who he, as an aspiring avant-garde playwright, might imagine as particularly susceptible to a formulation of performance as the most transformative art form. Indeed, Strindberg translated the play himself into French as *Créanciers* for an 1894 production at Lugné-Poë's Théâtre de l'Oeuvre in Paris and envisioned it as a vehicle for his breakthrough in French culture.

Creditor's meta-theatrical interest in staging the power of performance is significant also with respect to the economic discourse traced in this chapter. The play's sparse set design and few characters have economic implications. The play is not written for a repertory theater or a national stage, but explicitly for the kind of small and often ad hoc companies with limited budgets that began to shape new European experimental drama at the end of the 1880s. Indeed, *Creditors* is well suited for speedy and inexpensive production in unconventional venues and with a cast on the move. There is another potential argument to be made in this respect, however. Adolph's performance of epilepsy and subsequent embrace of Gustav's diagnosis also illustrates from another angle the sophisticated movement between realistic and abstract layers in this play. The disjuncture between Adolph's performance and his subsequent rapid decline into ill health and ultimate death parallels the disjunctive levels of economic discourse in the play. A set of extended money metaphors and a repeated invocation of economic discourse seem to indicate the centrality of commercial and economic practices in the play, yet this level remains abstract only, separated from the diegesis or the performance materiality of the play. In this play, male characters are configured to fit a classical political-economic paradigm that actually does not quite map on to the aesthetic program of intense character subjectivity and individualism that Strindberg is exploring in his drama around this time. It seems the playwright tries to get complex psychological reactions to adhere to a static economic model.

In this way, the economic references in the play seem metaphorical, as replacements for a language that can address human emotions and measure value in human relationships. This is consistent with the increasing *naturalization* of economic discourse into literature at the end of the nineteenth century, as shown in the discussion above. The abstract nature of this discursive register in *Creditors* thereby also maps onto the marginal revolution's increasingly abstract explanatory models. *Creditors* thus appears interested in exploring a concept like marginal utility, but it appears also as if the play is reluctant to embrace the theory; it appears to want to hold out for a nostalgic notion of non-commercialized or zero-sum potential for the evaluation of human relationships. Concurrent with the Europe-wide development of economic theory at this time, the play's economy of human emotions is only approximated by money terms; just like in the theory of marginal utility. Though the economic references in *Creditors* operate on a number of additional levels, several of which reflect contemporary changes in economic theory at the end of the nineteenth century, Strindberg's primary interest appears to be in correlating economics with changing conceptions of subjectivity, spatiotemporal abstraction, and aesthetic abstraction. In this way, *Creditors* is much less a naturalistic play than a modernist one.

Notes

1. Gunnar Ahlström's *Det moderna genombrottet i nordisk litteratur* contextualizes some of these aspects with respect to developments in Scandinavian literature in the 1870s.

2. There is also a one-act short play *Debit and Credit* (*Debet och Kredit*, 1892).

3. The play was first published in a Danish translation in 1889. In Swedish, it was first published in *Tryckt och otryckt*, 1890.

4. *The Oxford English Dictionary* defines the noun "credit" first: "Belief, credence, faith, trust. To give credit to: to believe, put faith in, credit"; subsequent definitions include "trust or confidence in a buyer's ability and intention to pay at some future time, exhibited by entrusting him with goods, etc. without present payment"; "Reputation of solvency and probity in business, enabling a person or body to be trusted with goods or money in expectation of future payment"; "The acknowledgement of payment by entry in an account"; and, in bookkeeping: "A sum entered on the credit or right-hand side of an account; this side itself (abbreviated *Cr.*)."

5. I generally quote *Creditors* from Sprinchorn's translation into English.

6. Telegony refers to a theory of heredity in belief until the nineteenth century. According to the *Oxford English Dictionary,* it involves the "(hypothetical) influence of a previous sire seen in the progeny of a subsequent sire from the same mother."

7. Robbins notably defined economics as "the science of how a particular society solves its economic problem" and that "an economic problem exists whenever scarce means are used to satisfy alternative ends" (cited in Arnold 2). According to the *Macmillan Dictionary of Modern Economics,* economics is "the study of the way in which mankind organizes itself to tackle the basic problems of scarcity. All societies have more wants than resources (the factors of production), so that a system must be devised to allocate these resources between competing ends" (121).

8. This shift has been studied by numerous economic historians (see Black 777; Negishi 24–28) and cultural critics. Regenia Gagnier's presentation in *The Insatiability of Human Wants* is particularly relevant for literary studies, though she, like her colleagues Catherine Gallagher and Mary Poovey, focuses nearly exclusively on the English novel.

9. R. D. Collison Black defines "utility" in *The New Palgrave: A Dictionary of Economics* as such: "Utility is a term which has a long history in connection with the attempts of philosophers and political economists to explain the phenomenon of value. It has most frequently been given the connotation of 'desiredness,' of the capacity of a good or service to satisfy a want, of whatever kind" (776). Utility is a hard concept to grasp because unlike money, which is easily measured, it is difficult to measure "desiredness." The Economist.com's directory of "Economics A–Z" writes, "A tricky question is how to measure utility. Money does not (entirely) capture it. You can get richer without becoming more satisfied." Utility can therefore only be approximated by money to a certain extent, without capturing its essence. A second characteristic of utility is put forth by the marginal economics that introduced the concept of "diminishing marginal utility." This is "the phenomenon whereby it is assumed that the additional utility attached to an extra unit of any good diminishes as more and more of that good is purchased" (*Macmillan Dictionary of Modern Economics* 106). According to diminishing marginal utility, then, the first good consumed is worth more utility than the second, the second more than the third, etc.

10. Although there is not much existent secondary literature on non-Marxist economics and Germanic and Scandinavian drama around 1900, the German scholar Sol Gittleman detects a similar relationship between Frank Wedekind's insatiable character Lulu on the one hand and the cool rational Homo Economicus male characters of *Erdgeist* and *Die Büchse der Pandora* in his article "Sternheim, Wedekind, and Homo Economicus." For Gittleman, Lulu occupies "the role of representing uninhibited pleasure and gratification in the face of society's need to control, to limit, and to restrain" (25). Gittleman demonstrates that "[Wedekind] finds in the male, conversely, the restrictive, rational powers of a civilization which in order to survive had to control the threatening potency of Lulu . . . in Wedekind, this is Economic Man" (25, my translation).

11. As Pribram shows, the marginal revolution removed the value of a good from the work put into it, that is, the "cost of production" as defined in the classical, Ricardian cost theory, and emphasized the good's relation to other goods and the consumer (278).

12. Even if the theory of marginal utility developed unevenly around Europe, at least one strand accounted for the psychological components of perceived gains in utility, i.e., that just as supply and demand dynamics can have a psychological component, an individual's understanding of increases or decreases in marginal utility has psychological and thereby also subjective components (Pribram 290–91).

13. Definition from the *Macmillan Dictionary of Modern Economics:* "Economic man. The name given to the 'construct' in economics whereby individuals are assumed to behave as if they maximize utility, subject to a set of constraints of which the most obvious is income. Economic man is then 'rational' if he pursues this objective although he may face obstacles, such as imperfect information, which prevent him actually achieving the goal. Rational man in economics may however pursue objectives other than the maximization of utility, in which case he is rational if he pursues that goal in a self-consistent manner" (120). Adam Smith, the classical economist and Enlightenment thinker, began defining economic man in *The Wealth of Nations* (1776): "It is not from the benevolence of the butcher, the brewer, or the baker that we expect our dinner, but from their regard to their own interest" (97). Later, the neoclassical economist J. S. Mill also defined a similar model in his essay "On the Definition of Political Economy, and on the Method of Investigation Proper to It" (1836): "[Political economy] does not treat the whole of man's nature as modified by the social state, nor of the whole conduct of man in society. It is concerned with him solely as a being who desires to possess wealth, and who is capable of judging the comparative efficacy of means for obtaining that end" (97).

Works Cited

Ahlström, Stellan. *Det Moderna Genombrottet i Nordens Litteratur.* Stockholm: Kooperativa Förbundets Bokförlag, 1947.

Arnold, Matthew A. *Macroeconomics, Concise Edition.* Southwestern College Publications, 2006.

Black, R. D. Collison. "Utility." In *The New Palgrave A Dictionary of Economics.* Vol. 4. London: Macmillan, 1987.

"Diminishing Marginal Utility." *Macmillan Dictionary of Modern Economics.* 4th ed. Ed. David W. Pearce et al. Basingstoke, UK: Palgrave Macmillan, 1992.

"Economic Man." *Macmillan Dictionary of Modern Economics.* Ed. David W. Pearce et al. 4th ed. Basingstoke, UK: Palgrave Macmillan, 1992.

"Economics." *Macmillan Dictionary of Modern Economics.* Ed. David W. Pearce et al. 4th ed. Basingstoke, UK: Palgrave Macmillan, 1992.

Gagnier, Regenia. *The Insatiability of Human Wants.* Chicago: University of Chicago Press, 2000.

Gallagher, Catherine. *The Body Economic.* Princeton, N.J.: Princeton University Press, 2006.

Gittleman, Sol. "Sternheim, Wedekind, and Homo Economicus." *German Quarterly* 49, no. 1 (1976): 25–30.

Heitmann, Anne-Gret. "August Strindberg's *Fordringsägare* and/as Media Studies." In *Strindberg and His Media,* ed. Kirsten Wechsel. Leipzig: Edition Kirchof & Franke, 2003. 13–31.

Kärnell, Karl-Åke. *Strindbergs bildspråk*. Stockholm: Geber, 1969.

Lönngren, Ann-Sofie. "Att röra en värld: En queerteoretisk analys av erotiska trianglar i sex verk av August Strindberg." Ph.D. diss., Uppsala University, 2008. Lund: Ellerströms, 2008.

Magnusson, Lars. "Introduction" to *Mercantilism*. London: Routledge, 1995.

Marshall, Alfred. *Principles of Economics*. 8th ed. London: Macmillan, 1972.

Mill, John Stuart. "On the Definition of Political Economy, and on the Method of Investigation Proper to It." In *Essays on Some Unsettled Questions of Political Economy.* Kitchener, Ont.: Batoche Books, 2000. Online: http://www.efm.bris.ac.uk/het/mill/question.pdf.

Negishi, Takashi. *History of Economic Theory.* Amsterdam: Elsevier Science, 1989.

Ollén, Gunnar. *Strindbergs dramatik*. Rev. ed. Stockholm: Sveriges Radios förlag, 1982.

Oxford English Dictionary. Online.

Poovey, Mary. *Genres of the Credit Economy: Mediating Value in Eighteenth- and Nineteenth-Century Britain.* Chicago: University of Chicago Press, 2008.

Pribram, Karl. *A History of Economic Reasoning.* Baltimore: Johns Hopkins University Press, 1983.

Pujol, Michèle A. "Into the Margin!" In *Toward a Feminist Philosophy of Economics,* ed. Drucilla K. Barker and Edith Kuiper. London: Routledge, 2003. 21–37.

Robbins, Lionel. *An Essay on the Nature and Significance of Economic Science.* 3rd ed. London: Macmillan, 1984.

Robinson, Michael. *An International Annotated Bibliography of Strindberg Studies, 1870–2005.* 3 vols. London: Modern Humanities Research Association, 2008.

Smith, Adam. "On the Division of Labour." In *The Wealth of Nations.* New York: Penguin Classics, 1986.

Sprinchorn, Evert. "Introduction to *Creditors.*" In *Selected Plays,* vol 2., ed. and trans. Evert Sprinchorn. Minneapolis: University of Minnesota Press, 1986. 269–72.

Stenport, Anna Westerståhl. "The Sexonomics of *Et Dukkehjem:* Money, the Domestic Sphere and Prostitution." *Edda* 106:4 (2006): 339–53.

Strindberg, August. *Creditors.* In *Selected Plays I,* ed. and trans. Ever Sprinchorn. Minneapolis: University of Minnesota Press, 1986.

"Utility." In "Economics A–Z." The Economist.com. Online, n.d.

A Nineteenth-Century Long Poem Meets Modernity: *Sleepwalking Nights*

Massimo Ciaravolo

Sleepwalking Nights on Wide-Awake Days: A Poem in Free Verse (*Sömngångarnätter på vakna dagar: En dikt på fria vers,* 1884, 1890)[1] is one of August Strindberg's texts that deals most explicitly, both in terms of its form and content, with questions of international late-nineteenth-century modernity—including aspects of displacement and disjuncture both private and public. The poem details the experiences of a Swedish poet who travels from his hometown of Stockholm to France, stops in Grez-sur-Loing at an international colony of artists, and thereafter continues to a prolonged stay in Paris. The idea expressed in the title reveals the structure of the plot; the protagonist is a sleepwalker in the sense that he, during his journey and stay in France, dreams, or daydreams, of revisiting Stockholm. The poem thus juxtaposes several distinct geographical locations and mediates these through the practices of dreaming and subjective recollection. The multiple Stockholm places recalled by the poet include a church, a museum, a library, an academy of science with astronomical observatory, and other emblematic locations. These refer, concretely or symbolically, to his life and development. The flashbacks are connected to the exile motif that runs through the poem and provide a vehicle to intertwine autobiographical references with a modernity critique that links the personal with the public as part of a proto-modernist European poetic idiom.

Although eminent Strindberg scholar Gunnar Brandell has defined this work as "undoubtedly one of the most important in his production" (18, my translation), *Sleepwalking Nights* still occupies a minor position in Strindberg's oeuvre, internationally as well as in Sweden. Poetry is not this writer's best-known genre; in addition, the hybrid form of the long poem used in *Sleepwalking Nights* is difficult to place within a predominantly lyrical modern standard. Swedish anthologies of poetry seldom include *Sleepwalking Nights,* with the one exception of the self-contained prologue lyric "At Avenue de Neuilly" ("Vid avenue de Neuilly"),[2] which is, in fact, one of Strindberg's best-known poems. *Sleepwalking Nights* was composed when Strindberg left Sweden for France in the autumn of 1883. A later section, "The Fifth Night," also called "The Homecoming" or "The Awakening," was written in the autumn of 1889, when the author had returned to Stockholm after his first period abroad (Spens, "Kommentarer" 407). In this fifth section of the poem, the poetic speaker, too, is physically back in his hometown. As he did in Paris, he strolls around, gazes, and reminisces. By interpreting the new signs of the city, he guesses what has happened there during his absence, while places and circumstances still evoke memories of events prior to his departure from Stockholm. *Sleepwalking Nights* is an innovative, hybrid long poem which is at the same time a travelogue, a *flânerie,* a reportage, and an autobiography in verse. In this work, lyrical subjectivity is interwoven with reflections on religion, art, philosophy, society, and politics as well as with recurring references to myth (Prometheus, Lucifer, the Wandering Jew, Faust, the Descent into Hell, and the Apocalypse). In his dislocation in Paris, while meeting modernity in the streets, the poetic speaker is engaged in an ambitious existential quest, which makes him critically reconsider his origin and past stages in life, and reflect on the meaning of development and progress, both on a personal and on a socio-historical level. This is a poem about European modernity, communicated in a voice both skeptical and enticed.

Divided into five sections, five "Nights," *Sleepwalking Nights* develops a coherent narrative despite its formal and thematic heterogeneity (Bellquist 73–114).[3] In fact, the heterogeneity of this poem—as well as its relation to forms of contemporary prose narrative, including that of the urban novel, the reportage and the autobiography, its insistence on temporal and geographical displacements, its voicing of a modernity critique, and its explicit juxtaposition of Paris with Stockholm as mediated by dreaming and subjective recollection—suggests the radical modernity expressed in and through it. In this chapter, I seek to address these aspects by focusing on two specific traits. First, I address the significance of Strindberg's adaptation and mixing of the *knittel* verse form, the nineteenth-century European long poem, and the contemporary forms of city life representation in literature. This mélange creates a poetic synthesis capable of transmitting a modernist experience in line with and in anticipation of Benjaminian modernity. Second, I propose a consecutive reading of the five "Nights" in light of the poem's autobiographical elements and relate these to the political critique and modernity critique implicit within the poem's thematic emphasis. This political position takes its cues both from Sweden's political situation and from multiple international thinkers and is fostered in the physical locations of Grez, Paris, and Stockholm, as well as in the dreamed and subjectively constituted transnational space that connects them. This poem, as I propose to show, reveals that an emerging modernist experience goes hand in hand with, indeed, can be seen as inseparable from, an intertwining of the personal and the political, of autobiography and modernity critique. Finally, by considering these two traits, I aim to demonstrate that *Sleepwalking Nights*—in spite of its multiplicity, complication, and fragmentation—has a coherent structure and plot.

What can be perceived as dissonant and "ugly" verses are deliberately used by Strindberg to reshape traditional verse in Swedish poetry. Specifically, Strindberg adapts the medieval and originally German *knittel* verse form to his poem set in Paris and Stockholm. The *knittel* line has a rather free form, consisting normally of four stressed syllables and a varying number of unstressed ones. Moreover, a *knittel* poem has no stanzas, as either very few or many lines can form a unit. This form had been employed in important literary works preserved in Old Swedish, such as the translations of courtly romances and the historical chronicles, and was commonly used for epic, didactic-religious, and historical-political purposes even into the beginning of the seventeenth century. In particular, this verse became a popular form in the late Middle Ages and during the Reformation, adaptable to the spoken language and easy to memorize thanks to its rhymed couplets. When the normative rules of classicism introduced "higher" verse forms in Swedish literature, the *knittel* survived in the popular history of the *folkböcker* and in the ballads (Ståhle 12–57).

Strindberg's use of the *knittel* is provocative. He had already practiced it in 1876, in the verse version of his first masterpiece, the historical drama *Master Olof* (*Mäster Olof,* 1872) about Olaus Petri, the Swedish humanist of the Reformation period; but with *Sleepwalking Nights* he went a step further. His new strategy of actualization must be related, as James Spens has pointed out, to the ongoing fight in Swedish literature of that time between tradition and innovation, and the conservative and the radical ("Kommentarer" 360–70; "*I Musernas bidé*" 15–22). The writers and artists of the radical front were struggling for their right of expression, and for a more open and democratic society. Strindberg, the most talented among them, wanted to provoke his literary and political enemies of the academy, whose faultless poetic exercises were only apparently innocent from an ideological point of view, while aiming to preserve the good old "idealistic" values against the purported disreputable literature of realism and naturalism (i.e., aimed at the social and political status quo).[4]

Through the popular *knittel* form Strindberg could show that he was aware of the poetic traditions, but that he actualized them for his own purposes. Not only did he vary the fixed rhyme pattern (besides *aabb,* also *abba* or *abab*), but he recontextualized the verse toward a modern freethinker's "poetry of ideas" (*tankedikt*), which could deal with high metaphysical and philosophical questions, while lowering the gaze to the level of ordinary and prosaic life, making him travel by train, walk on the crowded boulevards, and see the machines at work. In this respect, the poet's experience of Paris is not depicted by chance, since this big city in particular was playing an important role in determining what Sylvain Briens, with reference to Bourdieu, defines as the cultural counter-field of the Scandinavian writers and artists of the so-called *Modern Breakthrough* (*Paris* 41–108).

In fact, we can think of Strindberg's deliberate use of an old-fashioned verse form as one way to accentuate, if not announce, the modernist impetus of his poetic strategy in *Sleepwalking Nights.* By molding his *knittel* into "free verse," Strindberg could embed the tradition and, at the same time, prefigure twentieth-century modernism. His verses, with their "deliberately prosaic poetic mode" (Bellquist 82), convey the signs of the big city and the industrial age, their cacophony and restless movement. Gunnar Ekelöf, the great voice of Swedish poetic modernism, confesses that he has learned to hear the noise of Paris in *Sleepwalking Nights:* "Behind these free, unpredictable and yet rhythmically bound verses I think I can actually hear something of the world city's never ceasing street noise and traffic murmur, penetrating into the hotel room day and night and creating its atmosphere, whether your balcony door is ajar or not" (215, my translation).

Lyric poetry prevailed as a highly significant literary form in Europe during the second half of the nineteenth century. With Charles Baudelaire it became a sign of the modern.[5] Baudelaire's urban poems—his lyrical as well as his prose poems—offer a model by which poetry can specifically cope with the new reality of big cities and the experience of modernity in the age of capitalism (Benjamin, "Das Passagen-Werk" 54–56). At the same time the modern novel gives writers (Strindberg among them) more resources than the long poem, which has been inherited in the course of the nineteenth century but seems now less adequate and adaptable as a narrative form. In *Sleepwalking Nights* Strindberg moves boldly against this trend and experiments with a long, narrative form of poetry that still belongs to a post-romantic tradition. The German author Heinrich Heine was important to Strindberg's development as a poet (see Sjöstedt 450–51; Spens, "Kommentarer" 275, 334–35, 374). If we compare *Sleepwalking Nights* with Heine's long poem *Germany: A Winter's Tale* (*Deutschland: Ein Wintermärchen,* 1844), we see the connections: the radical and democratic tendency; the satiric and ironic modes that contradict national indisputable truths; the public, political poem that expresses concern for the destinies of one's nation, combined with an autobiographical "confession"; the peculiar position of the nostalgic exile as oppositional patriot who returns to his country; Paris and France as the exile's external viewpoint; the travelogue; reality interwoven with dreams and visions (whereby the soul can even depart from the body); and, last but not least, a basically continuous narrative.

The comparison also shows, however, the differences from that model. In *Sleepwalking Nights* the traveler's speed and anxiety are characteristic of the new age of the train, the big city, and machines; the modern subject's identity is multilayered, contradictory, and thoroughly questioned by the distant standpoint offered by the Parisian dislocation, and it ultimately resists completion and definition. The urban experience produces a particularly restless encyclopedic effort, whereby the poem aims to solve life's riddle. Without yet being the fragmented and heterogeneous form of a long poem that plays such an important role in twentieth-century modernism, especially in North American poetry (see Dickie; Kamboureli), *Sleepwalking Nights* announces some of its traits. These proto-modernist fragmentation techniques include the effort to "embody the whole knowable world" and search "the great theme of historical interpretation" (Dickie 13) and the reshaping of traditional and modern elements into a new text, which "tempts us with a lyric, epic or documentary reading," but "breaks free from their specifications" and "lies within and beyond the grammar of the various genres it includes" (Kamboureli, *On the Edge of Genre* xiv). *Sleepwalking Nights* also thematizes the impossibility of escaping the shock and disorientation of the big city as fundamental existential condition, and includes a will to express, in the mode of the public poem, a criticism of Western modernity's dream of progress.

It is interesting to observe that these cultural processes belong to the increasing sense of transition and crisis in the early phase of modernism, during the last two decades of the nineteenth century and the beginning of the twentieth century. Malcolm Bradbury and James McFarlane argue that this perception reached in Scandinavia "a much higher degree of self-consciousness, of articulateness, of documentation than perhaps any other part of Europe" (37). And they consider Strindberg's work, primarily as a dramatist, a strong evidence of this cultural atmosphere. Strindberg's poetry is an important, if overlooked, part of the self-reflexiveness we associate with European modernism and which Bradbury and McFarlane see as critical to Strindberg's oeuvre. Indeed, the years between the first four sections of *Sleepwalking Nights* and the final one include, among other things, Strindberg's fundamental theory of the discontinuous subject formulated in the preface to *Miss Julie* (*Fröken Julie,* 1888). Historically and in an international context, a poem like *Sleepwalking Nights* becomes even more significant if related to Heinrich Heine, Charles Baudelaire, and the modernist long poem.

Section after section, *Sleepwalking Nights* builds up a network of strictly related themes. In the prologue lyric "At Avenue de Neuilly" the psychical interplay that characterizes the structure of the long poem is offered in short form. The subject is walking in the streets of suburban Paris and a detail he observes passing by makes his thoughts fly back home; the gutted heart in a butcher's shop corresponds metaphorically to the exposed book in a bookshop window in central Stockholm. The scene can be connected to the categories proposed by Walter Benjamin in *The Arcades Project,* in which the condition of modern literature as commodity to be sold on the market is examined.[6] Benjamin stresses the particular vulnerability of poetry in the new historical conditions that arose in the nineteenth century and Charles Baudelaire's heroism to face the challenge in the big city of Paris. Baudelaire's poet, who chooses the low, prosaic perspective of the streets in his pursuit of authenticity and beauty, is interpreted as a last version of the urban flaneur (Benjamin, "Charles Baudelaire" 537–69; Benjamin, *Das Passagen-Werk* 54–56, 301–489, 524–69). The raw and naturalistic image in Strindberg's lyric stresses his intention to write "ugly" verses in opposition to the academic poets, but at the same time works as an intimate and idealistic reminder about the subject as artist and nostalgic exile. Placed on the threshold of the long poem (Genette, *Seuils* 150–60, 183–94), this short poem also serves as a form of autobiographical contract proposed to the reader as buyer, implied in the picture of the shop window, a *captatio benevolentiae* and a guarantee of authenticity: the article being sold is my book, my heart, my life.

Henry Olsson stressed already in 1931 that *Sleepwalking Nights* is Strindberg's first more outspoken autobiographical text (329), written before the works that, from a generic point of view, must be considered his "real" autobiographies (e.g., *The Son of a Servant, Tjänstekvinnans son I–IV,* 1886–87, 1909). The structural interaction in the poem between the present time of action (France, Paris) and the past stages (Stockholm) illustrates how the reconstruction of the past through several analepses exists as a pragmatic function of the present state (Genette, *Figures III* 90–105). Through this use of analeptic technique, the protagonist is facing a critical moment and needs self-scrutiny—including a reassessment or reintegration of the past into the present—to make a new start. From "The First Night" to "The Fourth Night" anachrony's reach (Genette, *Figures III* 89–90) diminishes, so that a dialectical and approximately chronological process in the subject's development is represented. This process involves a move from religious faith to art, from art to the idea of a more useful form of knowledge that must serve justice and human progress, to a criticism of the model of Western material progress, and, finally, to a public position that corresponds to the poet's present standpoint and his need to search for future perspectives.

Strindberg uses several suggesting devices to create an autobiographical space in the poem, and thereby propose an autobiographical contract to his readers (Lejeune, *Le pacte* 165–96). For example, the art museum and the library, visited by the poet's spirit respectively in "The Second Night" and "The Third Night," are made to correspond to the National Museum and the Royal Library in Stockholm (where Strindberg pursued his studies and worked as a librarian), without being explicitly named in the text.[7] On the whole, the reader never doubts the identity between author, narrator, and protagonist, which Philippe Lejeune considers as the primary condition to recognize a text as autobiographical (Lejeune, *Le pacte* 7–46). At the same time, the unity of Strindberg's subject is made up of different layers and fragmented. The character's personality is split in a Parisian body and in a spirit visiting Stockholm. These two subjects are alternatively represented in the first and in the third person, and on some important occasions (such as the conclusion of "The Fourth Night") in the second person. Again Lejeune has explained this uncommon but existing autobiographical strategy as a way to stage identity as multiple and oscillating, caught as we are in a paradoxical condition, between the impossible unity of our ego and its intolerable division ("L'autobiographie" 38).

As an autobiographer, Strindberg adopts Kierkegaard's method of experimenting with his contradictory points of view and different stages in life, and although this method aims to reach a point of synthesis, it consciously develops into a process that is always in the making (Robinson, *Strindberg and Autobiography* 1–18, 87–88). This is the case of *Sleepwalking Nights*. The end of "The Fourth Night" was in fact left open, without closure, in the version published in 1884. Coming back to Stockholm in 1889, Strindberg appears to have felt a need to take up that narrative and conclude it with a fifth section. What is particularly fascinating about this last section, published in 1890, is that it respects the stylistic, formal, and thematic markers of the previous four sections, but reconsiders these from a new personal and political standpoint. The peculiar genesis of the poem illustrates therefore what Per Stounbjerg has termed the "reluctance to conclude" in Strindberg as an autobiographical writer ("Between Realism and Modernism" 52). An interesting circumstance is that while Strindberg was introducing his autobiographical space in 1883, he had considerably enlarged it by 1889, and his Swedish model reader had consequently a different, wider encyclopedia regarding his private and public life and could cooperate even more to "fill in the blanks" of the text (Eco, *Lector* 5–11, 50–85; Eco, *Six Walks* 8–25, 109–16).

The thematization of modernity—including its technologies—is present from the very beginning of the poem. In "The First Night" the motion of the train and its effects on the body define the speed and the rhythm imposed by modernity (Briens, *Technique* 40–43, 153–57, 179–80).[8] The "First Night" presents a prosaic, everyday world in which the subject's quest for meaning must necessarily be situated. Ironically, the spirit separates itself from material reality and begins its flight in the opposite direction. This opening of the poetic sequence also determines the kind of mood which characterizes the first four "Nights": the serious existential quest coexists with the peculiar sorrow and nostalgia of exile, but also with an expression of self-irony, sardonic comments, and a sense of humor, which seem to have been learned from Heine.

As the traveling protagonist falls asleep, his freely soaring spirit moves back to Stockholm to take farewell from his childhood's faith, represented by the church where he used to go with his family. The confrontation with Christianity is complex, because it includes a triple characterization of Jesus. He represents the dogmatic, oppressive tradition that the poet, as a skeptical freethinker, wants to get rid of; he also embodies, however, the martyr, the victim of his ideas, who had to be sacrificed (as the protagonist as a young man was sacrificed during confirmation in that church; as the gutted heart, or book of poetry, is exposed in the prologue lyric). Christ is finally also a revolutionary leader who has defied authority on earth and taught the value of doubt. The protagonist sympathizes with the revolutionary leader and martyr, and they reinforce the exile motif. The interesting aspect is that Strindberg tends to juxtapose historical, social emancipation and metaphysical redemption, a "horizontal" and a "vertical" dimension. This interaction, which was already characteristic of Strindberg's archtypical hero Master Olof, will continue to work throughout his literary and intellectual oeuvre (Carlson 42–48,

83–87, 107–11) in the most contradictory and peculiar ways, to be sure, but until the very end of it.

"The First Night" ends with a paradoxical comparison between two doubters: Jesus and Decartes (reliefs of both of them are placed almost side by side in Adolf Fredrik's Church, the temple visited by the spirit). They are opposed and akin at the same time, according to what connotation Jesus is given: dogmatic authority or critical spirit.

Strindberg, as often in his literary works, juxtaposes the rural and the urban in order to examine the contemporary moment. In the "Second Night," the characterization of the rural environment in Grez indirectly conveys the political theme of the poem. Moving to France to enjoy more freedom of expression had become almost a necessity for many Scandinavian oppositional intellectuals and anti-academic writers and artists (Söderström 82–95).[9] The joy of being together and sharing life in a less conventional manner, freed from the compelling social roles and closer to nature, is stressed in the opening of this section. This understanding of nature's creative or even utopian potential—entertained by many of the European artists who left cities to paint or write about nature in rural surroundings at the end of the nineteenth century—frames the representation of an existential quest in the second section of the poem.

In the "Second Night," the relentlessly questioning protagonist addresses a series of problems. First, he reflects on the complex relationship between nature and culture. Second, he is concerned with an understanding of the process of mimesis in connection with his doubts about the usefulness of art. The poetic speaker asks: Is the nature seen in the orchard really "natural"? Isn't it created and constricted by human culture? Aren't the artists who, in the plein air environment of Grez, have fled Paris, still conditioned, especially in their urge to produce art, by the nearby big city? Isn't art just artificial, a useless urban privilege? Isn't it the imitation of an appearance (the divine creation)? And what is this human desire to imitate? These stances reveal Strindberg's dialogue with the negative conceptions of art expressed by Plato in *The Republic* (79–102, 344–62), and by Jean-Jacques Rousseau, especially in *Discourse on the Arts and Sciences* and *Discourse on the Origin and Basis of Inequality Among Men* (*Discours sur les sciences et les arts,* 1750, and *Discours sur l'origine et les fondements de l'inégalité parmi les hommes,* 1754) (Poulenard 17–21, 75–85). At the same time, however, Strindberg's political motivation in the mid-1880s is never straightforward. In these years he also tries to convince himself that it is necessary to write non-artistically, in a kind of pure, "useful" social prose that has to serve the cause of justice, but at the same time he cannot help writing literature.

The visit of the poet's spirit to the art museum in "The Second Night" parallels his previous flight to the church. As a new temple, a place loaded with sacred social value, the museum becomes the target of the spirit's mocking criticism. Art—as the Canon of Beauty—proves to be something void of meaning for the searching spirit now. The spirit encounters mainly statues from classical antiquity, probably because sculptures are, figuratively speaking, easier to demolish for the iconoclast. An epiphany occurs, however, when he sees the statue of the Knife-Grinder: it is the revelation of art from the streets representing low reality, in contrast with the idea of art as leisure activity for the upper, ruling classes; and it is, again, an anticipation of the political theme of the poem, the need for social emancipation and democracy. The apparition of the Knife-Grinder is related to Strindberg's naturalistic program in his first collection of poems, *Dikter* of 1883, by which truth must of necessity be ugly, as long as beauty is false appearance (*Poems;* see *Samlade Verk,* vol. 15:23–24). This program is in its turn linked to the modern, urban motif in *Sleepwalking Nights,* to the reality of the streets we find especially in the prologue lyric, "The Third Night" and "The Fifth Night." The juxtaposition of high culture and perspective from the streets is one of the strategies that marks the proto-modernism of *Sleepwalking Nights.*

The concluding part of "The Second Night" returns to the Swedish writer in Grez, who ironically, in complete (and conscious) contradiction with his thoughts about the uselessness of art—and in competition with his fellow artists—writes poetry. He can't help it, driven as he is by the utmost pleasure and his holy fire:

> Då går författarn på ett avsides rum
> Och vid sitt skrivbord sätter sig krum.
> Han gör poesi, om ock ej så poetisk,
> Och skriver om konst, som vanligt, frenetisk.
> Det kan ju kallas helt enkelt en sofism—
> Inkonsekvens är kanske det rätta—
> Jag tror att Darwin kallar det atavism!—
> Och att utvecklas jämt är icke det lätta.
> Nå, fabula docet: gör som jag lär
> Och ej som jag lever! Har man hört på maken!
> Ja visst, det din egen lära ju är:
> Giv fan personen, men tänk på saken! (189)
>
> Then goes the author to a room not too near,
> seats himself at his desk, bent over,

> there concocts poetry, though not so poetic,
> writes about art—in a frenzy as usual
> (it might be labelled as simple sophistry,
> though the right word may be irrelevancy;
> I think Darwin has christened it atavism!).
> To be ever at one's best is not so easy. . . .
> Well, *fabula docet:* do as I teach
> and not as I live! Have you heard such inanity!
> I certainly have—I taught it myself:
> To hell with the person—it's the subject that matters!
> (*Sleepwalking Nights* 36)

Strindberg's poem presents a meta-poetic *mise en abyme,* the "signature" of the poem within the poem, and therefore also of the autobiographical contract with the reader, as the protagonist coincides with the author of the written text and with his narrator in the first, second, and third person (all three persons being summed up in this passage).[10] It appears moreover as the proud affirmation of the protagonist's existence, an adaptation of the Cartesian ego's motto—I write, therefore I am.

Strindberg's statements can also be seen as an apology of poetry and imagination against his own doubts and against Plato's authority. Strindberg draws on a dialogic function of another threshold of the text (Genette, *Seuils* 134–49): an epigraph taken from the beginning of chapter 4 in Aristotle's *Poetics* (34), where the philosopher argues that the origin of poetry is in humankind's tendency to imitate nature, as we, from childhood onwards, understand through mimesis and find instinctive pleasure in it. "The Second Night" proves in fact to be a piece of fiction, as only few of the sculptures the spirit encounters are really at the National Museum in Stockholm. As Aristotle writes in chapter 9 of *Poetics,* "the poet's task is to speak not of events which have occurred, but of the kind of events which *could* occur, and are possible by the standards of probability and necessity" (40).

The dialogue with the Aristotelian concept of mimesis should finally be related to another important question in *Sleepwalking Nights.* Strindberg's biblical and Christian roots are not only a religious and cultural matter, but also a matter of style. In *Mimesis,* Erich Auerbach famously explains how the Jewish and Christian heritage, especially the Gospels, changed the concept of representation of reality in Western literature, since the earthly experience of God's son represents the highest and most sublime questions of our life in a humble and "low" style, in contrast with the classical principle of the division of styles, by which serious things need "high" style and low things can only make us laugh (in particular 5–52). Jesus's story also shows how the problem of redemption is entangled in history and society, interwoven with the problems of emancipation and social justice. In this respect, even Auerbach's analysis of nineteenth-century naturalism is relevant (460–87), although his study does not include Strindberg and his poetics of "ugliness."[11]

"The Third Night" and "The "Fourth Night," the two longest sections in the poem, display the interaction between Paris and Stockholm anticipated in the prologue lyric. These are also the most explicitly political sections, which engage with Strindberg's modernity critique. In Paris, the protagonist appears as a hectic version of the flaneur of mid-century Paris, either reporter or poet (Köhn 42–62). He walks and observes, and although he is disturbed by the traffic, the crowd, and the artificiality of social behavior, his gaze is participating. Moreover, he cannot but feel a strange kind of admiration against all odds for the spectacular, ceaseless phantasmagoria of modernity, the dreamlike (or nightmarish) quality of its reality.

"The Third Night" opens with a description of the street, with its dirt, noise, and movement:

> Ute på strövtåg hela dagen
> I det dimmiga höst-Paris;
> Häpen väl, men icke betagen,
> Och beundrar på eget vis.
>
> Genom tunnlar av kalk och tegel
> Mänskor knuffa sig rastlöst fram;
> Våta gatan som söndrig spegel
> Ligger solkig av dy och slam;
> Speglar ännu av himlen flikar,
> Ger en vrångbild dunkel och svag
> Av den fallna människans drag. (190)
>
> Strolling about in the town all day
> in the haze of autumn-Paris. . . .
> full of wonder, but not enthralled,
> yet I like it in a way.
>
> Inside tunnels of mortar and brick
> people restlessly jostle their way;
> rain-dampened street, like shattered mirror,
> now lies begrimed by slush and sludge,
> still reflecting patches of heaven,

with a distortion, dark and dim,
of the fallible human's features.
(*Sleepwalking Nights* 37)

Only fragments of the sky can be reflected on the wet street; humanity has fallen, as if it had lost its origin. This metaphysical dimension is suggested in the middle of a frenetic horizontal movement:

Lastad kärra dundrar och skräller,
Kuskens piska som bössan smäller,
Tramwaysklockan varnande gnäller,
Omnibussen blåser trumpet. . . .
(190)

Loaded cart rumbles ricketing by,
the driver's whip cracks loud like gunshot,
the street-car tinkles its warning shrilly,
the bus now trumpets a blaring sound. . . .
(*Sleepwalking Nights* 37)

What Marshal Berman has written about Baudelaire's "loss of halo" in his seminal book about the experience of modernity implies choices of poetics and style, but also a fundamental ethical question concerning the responsibility of the writer. It can be applied to Strindberg's stance in *Sleepwalking Nights,* with its poetics of "ugliness":

> The new force that the boulevards have brought into being, the force that sweeps the hero's halo away and drives him into a new state of mind, is modern *traffic*. . . . The archetypal modern man, as we see him here, is a pedestrian thrown into the maelstrom of modern city traffic, a man alone contending against an agglomeration of mass and energy that is heavy, fast and lethal. . . . One of the paradoxes of modernity, as Baudelaire sees it here, is that its poets will become more deeply and authentically poetic by becoming more like ordinary men. If he throws himself into the moving chaos of everyday life in the modern world—a life of which the new traffic is a primary symbol—he can appropriate this life for art. The "bad poet" in this world is the poet who hopes to keep his purity intact by keeping off the streets, free from the risks of traffic. (158–60)

Echoes of Rousseau are heard in Strindberg's lines, when they refer to miserable and hungry people, and a crying child. The poet's gaze notices that the indifferent city is a place of injustice, where wealth and poverty may be side by side, but are in fact at the greatest distance from each other.

A spiritual need—or at least a need to step out of the infernal rhythm—manifests itself when the protagonist sees, in the labyrinth of streets, a Gothic church. Its spires suggest again an upward movement; its statues of saints and martyrs remind the poet of his condition as exile. His entering a church creates a parallel with "The First Night," but this time, he assures, he does not want to pray, but simply recover from the city shock.

The former church of St. Martin des Champs, in central Paris, was transformed into a museum of technology and science after the French Revolution, the Musée des Arts et Métiers. During the second half of the nineteenth century, in the heydays of positivism and the great world exhibitions, it became a symbol of modern progress. A spectacular hall, with machines in function and motion, was created in the nave. It operated between 1882 and 1885 and is the one Strindberg refers to in *Sleepwalking Nights*.

The mimetic quality of Strindberg's language undoubtedly reveals the ambivalent fascination of machines on his modern spirit (compare Kärnell 52–66; Kylhammar 28–46). The point of this description is a polemic confrontation with the idea of utilitarianism, also as an idea nourished by the protagonist who, in his development, takes leave from the illusion of art to look for a more useful and practical kind of knowledge that can contribute to the advancement of mankind. The way in which progress is unmasked as the great illusion of modernity contributes to the near-Nietzschean energy that Perrelli (40–41) and Bellquist (101–2) have observed in *Sleepwalking Nights*. In the nave of St. Martin, progress seems to have become a deity in its own right, modernity's own god; and its ceaseless noise, its materialism, have conquered the altar. But is material progress real development? Besides, the advancement of science and technology has mainly served the capital and not the causes of general welfare. Another temple has thus been entered, another authority questioned and found faulty. The industrialization of space has proved to be ubiquitous, and no peace can be obtained in that church. On the contrary, the rhythmic noise of machines determines our quest; modern speed is a permanent existential condition, here as much as on the boulevards.

The spirit's flight to the library in Stockholm proposes, at this point, a confrontation with another "temple." The inadequacy of books is rendered with an irreverent and hasty examination of religion, philosophy, history, and law. The idea of getting rid of books as a useless burden, with which "The Third Night" ends, does sometimes appear in Strindberg's works; the question is, however, whether the inadequate solutions given by the humanities throughout the centuries to the fundamental questions of existence should not be read, here, as a way of creating a contrast with the complacent show of progress in St. Martin des Champs, so as to reinforce the criticism against it. Not only does the spirit's survey mention, especially in the field of philosophy, some of the authors who play an important role in Strindberg's oeuvre, and in *Sleepwalking Nights* in particular, but the recurring situation of the iconoclast in different "temples" can be read as the way in which the modernist writer paradoxically saves the past against a materialistic present time without memory. George Steiner has precisely described this condition:

> The sense of a persistent authority of the classical and Hebraic precedent has been one of the principal forces—perhaps the principal force—during some two millennia of Western sensibility. It has largely determined the Western image of reason and of form. The new design, the new utterance, are tested within and against the exemplary legacy. We move forward from quotation, explicit or not, of the classic formula. . . . We know now that the modernist movement which dominated art, music, letters during the first half of the century was, at critical points, a strategy of conservation, of custodianship. . . . In twentieth-century literature, the elements of reprise have been obsessive, and they have organized precisely those texts which at first seemed most revolutionary. "The Waste Land," *Ulysses*, Pound's *Cantos* are deliberate assemblages, in-gatherings of a cultural past felt to be in danger of dissolution. . . . The apparent iconoclasts have turned out to be more or less anguished custodians racing through the museum of civilization, seeking order and sanctuary for its treasures, before closing time. (488–90)

"The Fourth Night" completes the criticism of our model of progress. The city park, Bois de Boulogne, is presented as a form of amputated and falsified nature, an extension of the urbanized room as stage and artificiality. Moreover, the protagonist's gaze at the Jardin Zoologique d'Acclimatation emphasizes how our rationality has ended up manipulating and exploiting the natural resources. The standpoints echo more directly Rousseau, but the setting is that of the industrial society. The spirit's following flight to the Academy of Science in Stockholm coincides with an attack against the authority of the natural sciences and the whole cultural hegemony of positivism. They give an illusion of exact answers but do not answer the fundamental questions about the meaning of life; they can measure the material world but cannot consider our spiritual need; last but not least, their advancement does not operate for the common good but is most often allied with the interests of capital and of the few who hold power.

By moving to the near hill of the observatory, the spirit takes on a viewpoint which allows him, as it happened during the flight in "The First Night," a panoramic gaze on the city of Stockholm. Anna Westerståhl Stenport has pointed out the role and recurrence of this overview position in Strindberg's urban prose (29–47). In *Sleepwalking Nights* it also seems connected to the function of the public long poem (Dickie 1–17), as the writer, through his spirit, addresses the citizens of the sleeping polis from above, trying to awaken their conscience. In this part of "The Fourth Night" the writer makes an apology of his necessary role as uneasy conscience of Swedish society; by stressing his bond with Stockholm and his nostalgia, he also reminds the reader of his condition as an exile—an indirect act of accusation throughout the poem.

Watching the moon in the sky, the spirit has a series of fanciful visions in which his concern for a global unsustainable development and his pleading for social justice merge. Utopian tones follow the apocalypse, as the catastrophe on earth, a new ice age, will one day give a chance of rebirth. When Sweden, then, gets rid of all the privileged and their oppressive structures, it will learn the virtues of a simple, natural, and equal life.

The political function of this long poem proves finally to be the unmaking of old Sweden and the making of a new, fairer one. We must not forget that it was written in a time when the outcome of the conflict between the conservative ruling powers and those who fought for formal and substantial democratic rights was not at all decided. In order to cope with this struggle, the protagonist must first stop doubting, because even though doubt is a fundamental critical tool, it can become paralyzing. At the end of "The Fourth Night," what we can consider the provisional ending of the poem, the writer encourages himself to feel as an active part of the collective force that is already changing Sweden. Against all odds, he needs a "heroic" faith in progress.

Considered from the point of view of cultural history and with this conclusion, the poet wants to be faithful to the program, launched by the Danish critic Georg Brandes, of a literature that has a socially reforming potential and is able to "discuss the problems." The stance was reinforced in Strindberg by his meeting, in Paris during the autumn and winter of 1883–84, with the Norwegian fellow writers Bjørnstjerne Bjørnson and Jonas Lie, to whom *Sleepwalking Nights* is also dedicated, a further, significant threshold of the text (Genette, *Seuils* 117–27). In the perspective of today, the author of *Sleepwalking Nights* appears as the committed writer advocated by Edward Said in *Representations of the Intellectual:* the one who does not flee complexity and contradiction, but still dares to tell power the truth and interpret humanism as a struggle for democracy. Only by this stance can the protagonist of *Sleepwalking Nights,* in the end, defeat the doubt "that your work is merely writ in water" (67/223), which is the second reminder of the act of writing in the poem.

Hjalmar Branting—Strindberg's friend, journalist and literary critic, radical intellectual, eventual founder and leader of the Swedish Social Democratic Party, and, as such, a founding father of modern Sweden—reviewed *Sleepwalking Nights* in 1884. His article is an important response, because Branting does not hesitate to consider the author an evident member of the Swedish progressive movement, but at the same time he cannot help emphasizing that his hatred of industrialism and modernity is an obstacle and a problem: in that respect Strindberg seems to move against the current of history.

The doubt whether this Western progress of ours is any good is, as a matter of fact, particularly shaking for a writer who claims a progressive role and works for social emancipation, and seems to form the most complex of the Gordian knots tied in *Sleepwalking Nights,* as well as in the other socially committed works written by Strindberg between 1883 and 1887. Yet, it can be argued whether the writer's preoccupations with the dilemmas and shortcomings of an absolute faith in civilization, sharply expressed in *Sleepwalking Nights,* are only a sign of conservative views or, rather, partake in a long Western intellectual tradition of criticism and questioning of the idea of historical progress.[12]

"The Fifth Night" functions as a section on its own, as well as the new epilogue of the whole cycle. The perspective is altered here: it turns gloomier, resigned. The gap of the six-year-long ellipsis (Genette, *Figures III* 139–41) is first filled with an internal analepsis—a quick, almost cinematic summary of the protagonist's experiences abroad—but more space of this section is dedicated to external analepses, which—as the protagonist is walking in Stockholm and coming across places connected to his married life—recall the time of great expectation before 1883, even his wedding. The personal and political themes are interwoven; the protagonist is confronted with a feeling of a "big chill" in his hometown: his old friends have vanished; the radical front has lost its battle; political repression dominates the atmosphere; the protagonist suspects that he is now considered a "heretic," and he is not even physically recognized as the one he is and was: the most talented writer of that group.

By making the reader wonder what has happened in the meantime, the text activates an implicit encyclopedia concerned with Strindberg's complicated paths, which include, between 1884 and 1889, political essays such as "On the General Discontent, Its Causes and Cures" ("Om det Allmänna Missnöjet, Dess Orsaker och Botemedel," 1884); the short stories of *Getting Married I–II* (*Giftas I–II,* 1884, 1886); the trial for blasphemy and, at the same time, the rupture between the writer and his political comrades owing to his (truly heretical) position concerning women, sexual roles, and marriage; the need to show that he could still direct his writing towards social and political themes and be an even more advanced radical writer, for example in *Utopias in Reality* (*Utopier i verkligheten,* 1885) and *Among French Peasants* (*Bland franska bönder,* 1886); a growing distance from democratic ideals in the autobiography *The Son of a Servant;* an even more outspoken orientation toward "aristocratic radicalism" in the short novel *Tschandala* (1889); the complications in the marriage between Strindberg and Siri von Essen and the coming divorce.

Back in Stockholm, the protagonist admires the city from above, again from a panoramic viewpoint on a hill. The city appears at first surprisingly beautiful and modern; it has changed and acquired even more evident signs of material progress and modernity that make it look like a "Paris of the North" (Stenport 1). The interaction between these two cities is both part of Strindberg's experience—as life experience as well as textual strategy—and of the architectural history of the last decades of the nineteenth century, when Baron Haussmann's conception of the city plan is exported all over Europe. However, the unifying overview is eventually contradicted when the protagonist actually walks in the city, at street level, and a new reality is revealed behind the fascinating façade. The splendid buildings (which quite clearly refer to the new parade boulevard Strandvägen) become a sign of the victory of the big capital over all hopes of change. This vision also implies an indirect, denying reference to Strindberg's own poem "The Boulevard System" ("Esplanadsystemet," 1883), in which the making of the new boulevards rather appeared as the symbol of the young forces of history and of the necessary progress of society (*Samlade Verk,* vol. 15:37–38).

The interpretation of the ideological dimensions of "The Fifth Night" is particularly difficult, because Strindberg seemed by 1889 to have moved away from his democratic standpoint and found support in Nietzsche's ideas. *Tschandala* had already been published in Danish and the novel *By the Open Sea* (*I havsbandet,* 1890) was being composed. In a letter to Georg Brandes, written in April 1890, only a few months after the composition of "The Fifth Night," Strindberg dated back his detachment from deism and democratic principles to 1885, adding that even his socialism was an experiment he had gone through (Strindberg, *Brev* 8:26). Still, in a speech he gave in Stockholm on March 15, 1890, he could point out that he was not a renegade with respect to the radical fights of the 1880s (Söderström, 138–40). Was Strindberg mystifying when he represented his alter ego in "The Fifth Night" as the homecoming radical, the last survivor, the unrecognized heretic? Or do we rather have to accept—here as much as elsewhere—his different voices and moods on the same subject? Was Strindberg finally objectifying, as an autobiographer, a critical turn and a past stage of his life? As Elena Balzamo has argued, an ideological crisis compels Strindberg to relocate the previous elements of his Weltanschauung in a new order (223, 302–3), which implies an inclusion with modifications, more than a rejection, of his past stages within an increasingly complex *system* of contradictions.

The disillusioned radical writer also observes that one of his former comrades is now sitting in jail. It is true that Branting was in prison for some months in 1889 (Spens, "Kommentarer" 557, 560), and in a certain sense the paths of Branting and Strindberg part here: one is the pragmatic, political man who successfully starts the Social Democratic movement that will "make" modern Sweden (the progress of history was beginning just then, one could argue from this point of view); the other one is the tormented intellectual, whose political commitment has proved unpractical and unusable, also because the integrity of the artist, with all his contradictions, is the dearest thing to him. In 1889, when the victorious history of the Swedish workers' movement is beginning, Strindberg pessimistically turns his back on "progress" and, similarly to Walter Benjamin's Angel of History, sees it only, retrospectively, as a landscape of failures and ruins at all levels ("Über den Begriff der Geschichte" 697–98). His life's investments—marriage, family, and mission as socially committed writer—have collapsed.

The writer's sorrow is devastating in the end. The act of writing is evoked, for the third time in the poem, in a nightmarish vision of his younger self sitting and writing in what once used to be his working room:

> Bläcket lämnar ej spår på raden
> Pennan löper synbart på lek
> Nej han skriver, han tror sig skriva,
> Se nu lyfter han handen opp
> Liksom ville han tankar giva

Ordets levande luftiga kropp,
I sitt bläckhorn han ivrigt doppar—
Se nu—vänder han ansiktet till—
Dödmans ögon stora som koppar
Stirra mörkt som en enda pupill,
Och mot namnen bekant han nickar
Pekar tankfull på verket sitt;
Och ur halsens kotor han hickar:
"Ser du jag börjar att skriva vitt!"
(232)

Not a trace of ink is seen on the page;
the man seems merely to toy with the pen.
No—now he is writing—thinks he is writing;
look, now he raises his hand as if he
would shape his thoughts with meaning and substance,
a living, airy form of the word.
Dipping fervidly in his inkwell
he turns his countenance toward me now—
the eyes of a dead man, large as cups,
staring darkly, like a single pupil,
as he familiarly nods to the names
and pensively points to his work;
then from the depths of his entrails he hiccups:
"Look—you see I am starting to write white!"
(*Sleepwalking Nights* 75)

The image is annihilating. The integrity of the subject, guaranteed by his writing (Robinson, *Strindberg and Autobiography* 47–83), is denied and dissolved. The narrator (and writing author) is doubled, mirrored, and confronted with his narrated (and also writing) younger self. The writer's progress seems to have left only burnt ground behind, and the "unfair" conclusion is that what he has accomplished as a writer is worthless. As Lotta Löfgren Casteen observes, "The Fifth Night" is written "only a few years away from the Inferno crisis" (180) and its author "teeters on the brink of Inferno" (187).

Readers of *Sleepwalking Nights* are confronted with the difficulties and fascination of a fundamentally political poem, which claims a public role for the writer, but at the same time uses autobiography to admit uncertainty, fragmentation, anxiety, the need to dissect the different layers of the poet's personality, his contrasting viewpoints and the innumerable impulses coming from an enormous encyclopedia. *Sleepwalking Nights* has in this respect a tentative and prismatic quality that makes it rather unique in Strindberg's oeuvre (Lamm 115).

The compelling autobiographical elements in Strindberg's work are a resource and a problem. They do not allow his readers much freedom to interpret his texts while ignoring his life. An important effort has been made in the last decades to read Strindberg's autobiographical urge in terms of fictional and textual strategies, so as to avoid the fallacies of the previous and more traditional biographical readings, whereby Strindberg's life appeared immediately reflected in his literary texts, and the literary texts were used as evidence of the writer's life and as psychological documents of his personality.[13] On the other hand, the necessary results of the postmodern critical approach should not prevent us from seeing the referential function in Strindberg's texts, also because Strindberg used his life and his "destiny" to represent a reality that we still can recognize as ours, something more universal than just his life.

Strindberg's ability to describe the existential reality of the modern self in *Sleepwalking Nights* can be considered in light of what contemporary sociology has observed in relation to modernity and self-identity in our late modern age. Anthony Giddens identifies in doubt "a pervasive feature of modern critical reason" and a "general existential dimension of the contemporary social world" (3). This basic uncertainty of ours has many reasons. Modernity is a condition that "produces *difference, exclusion* and *marginalisation.* Holding out the possibility of emancipation, modern institutions at the same time create mechanisms of suppression, rather than actualisation, of self" (6). Giddens furthermore describes our typical apocalyptic attitude, "now that nature . . . has in a certain sense come to an 'end'—as a result of its domination by human beings" and "the risks of ecological catastrophe form an inevitable part of our horizon of day-to-day life" (4). Modernity's extreme dynamism—he continues—makes chronic revision in the light of new information inevitable (16–20). It also affects the way in which we interpret our lives, as "the existential question of self-identity is bound up with the fragile nature of the biography," and our identity is to be found "in the capacity *to keep a particular narrative going*" (54). "The reflexive project of the self" becomes, in this sense, "the sustaining of coherent, yet continuously revised, biographical narratives" (5).

As it always happens in autobiography, silence talks. What is concealed or implied is at least as important as what is revealed. Gedin (290–317) argues that the debates in the wake of *Getting Married I* became the point of rupture between Strindberg and the radical front, and to a large extent determined the general retreat of the radical in the second half of the 1880s. This gives a relevant context for a proper understanding of "The Fifth Night," of the structural gap between 1883 and 1889 in *Sleepwalking Nights* and on the general "turn" of this long poem, taken as a coherent whole. *Sleepwalking Nights* proves, in conclusion, to be intriguing and engaging thanks to the way the personal dilemmas are interwoven with the public dimension and become political. The prismatic quality of the text enables us to read in it many of the issues that characterize Strindberg's intellectual and social commitment during the 1870s and 1880s, but also an anticipation of the writer's later dilemmas. The questioning feature of the poem combines a critique against the conservative Swedish establishment of that time and a critique against the complacent faith in modernity. This combination becomes problematic in *Sleepwalking Nights,* as one pleads for "progress" while the other one attacks "progress." Moreover, the multiplicity and fragmentation of the text witness a new perception of the ego's impossible unity and consistency, but at the same time the conditions of displacement and recollection are rendered through a finely tuned structural use of space and time, whereby the poetic text keeps its formal coherence and does not dissolve. Strindberg's original genius has created an experimental poetic form, by him defined "the modern poem" (Strindberg, *Brev* 9:366–67; Strindberg *Brev* 10:140–41), in which a penetrating modernity critique takes place. I argue that it can be interpreted as a proto-modernist form of long poem.

Notes

1. I use the recent critical edition of Strindberg, *Samlade Verk,* vol. 15:161–234, for citations of *Sleepwalking Nights.* Translations of the title into English vary. I adopt the (main) title used by Arvid Paulson in Strindberg, *Sleepwalking Nights,* though there is no general agreement regarding the English title of several of Strindberg's works (Robinson, *Cambridge Companion* xxxii). Michael Robinson proposes *Sleepwalking Nights in Broad Daylight* (*Cambridge Companion* xxxiv); Lotta Löfgren Casteen translates the work as *Sleepwalking Nights on Awake Days* (678–870). John Eric Bellquist uses *Sleepwalker Nights on Waking Days* (73). Michael Meyer calls it *Somnambulist Nights* (120). The first four sections, "Nights," were published in February 1884 (Stockholm: Bonniers). Another section, a "Fifth Night," was eventually added in 1890 and has been a recognized part of the text since the second edition of its publication in 1900 (Spens, "Kommentarer" 407).

2. This lyric is actually without a title. "Vid avenue de Neuilly" is its first line.

3. Another relevant close reading is Spens, *"I Musernas bidé"* 71–118, although its conclusions are that the plot is too chaotic and tends to disintegrate. See also Löfgren Casteen 150–87.

4. See also Gedin (especially 36–56, 102–19). Although it does not directly deal with *Sleepwalking Nights,* Gedin's analysis, which is carried out with the help of Pierre Bourdieu's theory of "field," provides important elements to understand how this literary and aesthetic conflict during the 1880s had social, political, and ideological implications.

5. It must be pointed out that Baudelaire is not among the names and "influences" that define Strindberg's declared intertextuality. He was introduced late in Sweden, and Strindberg must have known at least some of his works, but surely after the 1880s. One of Strindberg's friends in later years, the younger writer Emil Kléen, was one of those who introduced Baudelaire in Sweden. See Sjöblad, in particular 130–56.

6. See Ulf Olsson, "I varans inferno"; Ulf Olsson, *Levande död* 25–26; Stenport 45–46.

7. They are named in a letter: Strindberg, *Brev* 3:329.

8. See also Schivelbusch's classical study on the railway journey and on the general change of perception it provoked.

9. The character of the young painter Osvald Alving in Henrik Ibsen's play *Ghosts* (*Gengangere,* 1881) is paradigmatic in this respect.

10. To render the subject's inner debate, Paulson should have translated literally "I certainly have—you taught it yourself." See also Löfgren Casteen's version: "Have you heard such nonsense? / Of course, that is your very own teaching" (748).

11. For a similar approach to Strindberg, Harry G. Carlson uses Bakhtin's concept of "carnevalization" (97–100). On the importance of Auerbach and his *Mimesis* see Said, *Humanism* 85–118.

12. A leitmotif in Benjamin's *Arcades Project* is the criticism of the late-nineteenth-century bourgeoisie's illusion of linear and continuous progress (in particular *Das Passagen-Werk* 570–611); see also Benjamin, "Über den Begriff der Geschichte." On the crisis of the myth of progress, considered from today's perspective, see Nordin, especially 107–23; and Wright, especially 7–90.

13. See in particular Robinson, *Strindberg and Autobiography;* Dahlbäck; Ulf Olsson, *Levande död;* Behschnitt; and Stounbjerg, *Uro og urenhed.*

Works Cited

Aristotle. *Poetics.* Trans. Stephen Halliwell. London: Duckworth, 1987.

Auerbach, Erich. *Mimesis: Dargestellte Wirklichkeit in der abendländischen Literatur.* 1946. Bern: Francke 1964.

Balzamo, Elena. *August Strindberg: Visages et destin.* Paris: Hamy, 1999.

Behschnitt, Wolfgang. *Die Autorfigur: Autobiographischer Aspekt und Konstruktion des Autors im Werk August Strindbergs.* Basel: Schwabe, 1999.

Bellquist, John Eric. *Strindberg as a Modern Poet: A Critical and Comparative Study.* Berkeley: University of California Press, 1986.

Benjamin, Walter. "Charles Baudelaire: Ein Lyriker im Zeitalter des Hochkapitalismus." In *Gesammelte Schriften,* vol. 1, II. Frankfurt am Main: Suhrkamp, 1974. 509–690.

———. "Das Passagen-Werk." In *Gesammelte Schriften,* vol. 5, I–II. Frankfurt am Main: Suhrkamp, 1982.

———. "Über den Begriff der Geschichte." In *Gesammelte Schriften,* vol. 1, II. Frankfurt am Main: Suhrkamp, 1974. 691–704.

Berman, Marshall. *All That Is Solid Melts into Air: The Experience of Modernity.* 1982. New York: Penguin, 1988.

Bradbury, Malcolm, and James McFarlane. "The Name and Nature of Modernism." In *Modernism: A Guide to European Literature 1890–1930,* ed. Malcolm Bradbury and James McFarlane. 1976. London: Penguin, 1991. 19–55.

Brandell, Gunnar. *Strindberg—ett författarliv.* Vol. 2, *Borta och hemma 1883–1894.* Stockholm: Alba, 1985.

Branting, Hjalmar. "Strindbergs Sömngångarnätter." In *Tal och skrifter.* Vol. 11, *Litteraturkritik och varia.* Stockholm: Tidens Förlag, 1930. 17–21.

Briens, Sylvain. *Paris: Laboratoire de la littérature scandinave moderne 1880–1905.* Paris: L'Harmattan, 2010.

———. *Technique et littérature: Train, téléphone et génie littéraire suédois.* Paris: L'Harmattan, 2003.

Carlson, Harry G. *Genom Inferno: Bildens magi och Strindbergs förnyelse.* Stockholm: Carlssons, 1995.

Dahlbäck, Kerstin. "Strindberg's Autobiographical Space." In *Strindberg and Genre,* ed. Michael Robinson. Norwich: Norwik, 1991. 82–94.

Dickie, Margaret. *On the Modernist Long Poem.* Iowa City: University of Iowa Press, 1986.

Eco, Umberto. *Lector in fabula: La cooperazione interpretativa nei testi narrativi.* 1979. Milan: Bompiani, 1994.

———. *Six Walks in the Fictional Woods.* Cambridge, Mass.: Harvard University Press, 1995.

Ekelöf, Gunnar. "Strindbergs dikter." In *Skrifter.* Vol. 7, *Blandade kort och annan essäistik.* Stockholm: Bonniers, 1992. 213–17.

Gedin, David. "Fältets herrar: Framväxten av en modern författarroll: Artonhundraåttitalet." Ph.D. diss., University of Stockholm, 2004. Stehag: Symposion, 2004.

Genette, Gérard. *Figures III.* Paris: Éditions du Seuil, 1972.

———. *Seuils.* Paris: Éditions du Seuil, 1987.

Giddens, Anthony. *Modernity and Self-Identity: Self and Society in the Late Modern Age.* Stanford, Calif.: Stanford University Press, 1991.

Heine, Heinrich. *Deutschland: Ein Wintermärchen.* Stuttgart: Reclam, 1982.

Kamboureli, Smaro. "The Long Poem's Race away from Modernity." In *Krysninger: Nye perspektiver på moderne nordisk lyrikk,* ed. Ole Karlsen. Oslo: Unipub, 2008. 185–209.

———. *On the Edge of Genre: The Contemporary Canadian Long Poem.* Toronto: University of Toronto Press, 1991.

Kärnell, Karl-Åke. *Strindbergs bildspråk.* Stockholm: Gebers, 1969.

Köhn, Eckhardt. *Straßenrausch: Flanerie und kleine Form: Versuch zur Literaturgeschichte des Flaneurs bis 1933.* Berlin: Das Arsenal, 1989.

Kylhammar, Martin. *Maskin och idyll: Teknik och pastorala ideal hos Strindberg och Heidenstam*. Ph.D. diss., University of Linköping, 1985. Malmö: Liber, 1985.

Lamm, Martin. *August Strindberg*. 1948. Stockholm: Aldus/Bonniers, 1968.

Lejeune, Philippe. "L'autobiographie à la troisième personne." In *Je est un autre: L'autobiographie de la littérature aux médias*. Paris: Éditions du Seuil, 1980. 32–59.

———. *Le pacte autobiographique*. Paris: Éditions du Seuil, 1975.

Löfgren Casteen, Lotta. "The Poetry of August Strindberg: A Translation and Commentary." Ph.D. diss. Ann Arbor, Mich.: UMI, 1990.

Meyer, Michael. *Strindberg*. New York: Random House, 1985.

Nordin, Svante. *Från tradition till apokalyps: Historieskrivning och civilisationskritik i det moderna Europa*. Stockholm: Symposion, 1989.

Olsson, Henry. "Strindbergs Sömngångarnätter." *Nordisk Tidskrift* (1931): 329–50.

Olsson, Ulf. "I varans inferno: Utkast till en strindbergsläsning." *Bonniers litterära magasin* 59, no. 1 (1990): 22–28.

———. *Levande död: Studier i Strindbergs prosa*. Stockholm: Symposion, 1996.

Perrelli, Franco. *August Strindberg: Il teatro della vita*. Milan: Iperborea, 2003.

Plato. *Republic*. Trans. Robin Waterfield. 1993. Oxford: Oxford University Press, 2008.

Poulenard, Elie. *Strindberg et Rousseau*. Paris: Presses Universitaires de France, 1959.

Robinson, Michael, ed. *The Cambridge Companion to August Strindberg*. Cambridge, Eng.: Cambridge University Press, 2009.

———. *Strindberg and Autobiography: Writing and Reading a Life*. Norwich: Norvik, 1986.

Rousseau, Jean-Jacques. *Discours sur les sciences et les arts. Discours sur l'origine et les fondements de l'inégalité parmi les hommes*. Paris: Garnier-Flammarion, 1971.

Said, Edward W. *Humanism and Democratic Criticism*. New York: Columbia University Press, 2004.

———. *Representations of the Intellectual:The 1993 Reith Lectures*. London: Vintage, 1994.

Schivelbusch, Wolfgang. *Geschichte der Eisenbahnreise: Zur Industrialisierung von Raum und Zeit im 19. Jahrhundert*. 1977. Frankfurt am Main: Fischer, 1989.

Sjöblad, Christina. "Baudelaires väg till Sverige: Presentation, mottagande och litterära miljöer 1855–1917." Ph.D. diss., University of Lund, 1975. Lund: LiberLäromedel, 1975.

Sjöstedt, Nils Åke. "Strindberg och lyriken." *Bonniers litterära magasin* 38, no. 6 (1969): 450–56.

Söderström, Göran. "Strindberg och bildkonsten." Ph.D. diss., 1972. Stockholm: Forum, 1990.

Spens, James. "'I Musernas bidé': En essä om Strindbergs 'fula' poesi omkring 1883." Ph.D. diss., University of Stockholm, 2000. Stockholm: Almqvist & Wiksell, 2000.

———. "Kommentarer." In August Strindberg, *Samlade Verk*. Vol. 15, *Dikter på vers och prosa; Sömngångarnätter på vakna dagar; Och strödda tidiga dikter,* ed. James Spens. Stockholm: Norstedts, 1995. 269–578.

Ståhle, Carl Ivar. *Vers och språk i Vasatidens och stormaktstidens svenska diktning*. Stockholm: Norstedts, 1975.

Steiner, George. *After Babel: Aspects of Language and Translation*. 1975. Oxford: Oxford University Press, 1998.

Stenport, Anna Westerståhl. "Making Space: Stockholm, Paris and the Urban Prose of Strindberg and His Contemporaries." Ph.D. diss., University of California, Berkeley, 2004. www.cafepress.com/stenport.

Stounbjerg, Per. "Between Realism and Modernism: The Modernity of Strindberg's Autobiographical Writings." In *The Cambridge Companion to August Strindberg,* ed. Michael Robinson. Cambridge, Eng.: Cambridge University Press, 2009. 47–57.

———. *Uro og urenhed: Studier i Strindbergs selvbiografiske prosa*. Ph.D. diss., Aarhusuniversitet. Århus: Aarhus universitetsforlag, 2005.

Strindberg, August. *Bland franska bönder: Subjektiva reseskildringar.* In *Samlade Verk,* vol. 23, ed. Per Erik Ekholm. Stockholm: Almqvist & Wiksell, 1985.

———. *Brev.* Vol. 3. Ed. Torsten Eklund. Stockholm: Bonniers, 1952.

———. *Brev.* Vol. 8. Ed. Torsten Eklund. Stockholm: Bonniers, 1964.

———. *Brev.* Vol. 9. Ed. Torsten Eklund. Stockholm: Bonniers, 1965.

———. *Brev.* Vol. 10. Ed. Torsten Eklund. Stockholm: Bonniers, 1968.

———. *Dikter på vers och prosa; Sömngångarnätter på vakna dagar; och strödda tidiga dikter.* In *Samlade Verk,* vol. 15, ed. James Spens. Stockholm: Norstedt, 1995.

———. *Fadren; Fröken Julie; Fordringsägare.* In *Samlade Verk,* vol. 27, ed. Gunnar Ollén. Stockholm: Almqvist & Wiksell, 1984.

———. *Giftas I–II: Äktenskapshistorier.* In *Samlade Verk,* vol. 16, ed. Ulf Boëthius. Stockholm: Almqvist & Wiksell, 1982.

———. *I havsbandet.* In *Samlade Verk,* vol. 31, ed. Hans Lindström. Stockholm: Almqvist & Wiksell, 1982.

———. *Mäster Olof: Prosaupplagan; Mellandramat; Versupplagan.* In *Samlade Verk,* vol. 5, ed. Hans Sandberg. Stockholm: Norstedts, 1994.

———. "Om det Allmänna Missnöjet, Dess Orsaker och Botemedel." *Likt och Olikt I–II samt Uppsatser och tidningsartiklar 1884–1890.* In *Samlade Verk,* vol. 17, ed. Hans Lindström. Stockholm, Norstedts, 2003. 9–83.

———. *"Sleepwalking Nights on Wide-Awake Days" and "Biographical."* Trans. Arvid Paulson. New York: Law-Arts, 1978.

———. *Sömngångarnätter på vakna dagar: En dikt på fria vers.* Stockholm: Bonniers, 1884.

———. *Tjänstekvinnans son I–II.* In *Samlade Verk,* vol. 20, ed. Hans Lindström. Stockholm: Norstedts, 1989.

———. *Tjänstekvinnans son III–IV.* In *Samlade Verk,* vol. 21, ed. Hans Lindström. Stockholm: Norstedts, 1996.

———. *Tschandala.* In *Samlade Verk.* Vol. 14, *Svenska öden och äventyr II: Berättelser från alla tidevarv,* ed. Bengt Landgren. Stockholm: Norstedts, 1990. 170–281.

———. *Utopier i verkligheten: Fyra berättelser.* In *Samlade Verk,* vol. 19, ed. Sven-Gustaf Edqvist. Stockholm: Norstedts, 1990.

Wright, Georg Henrik von. *Myten om framsteget: Tankar 1987–1992 med en intellektuell självbiografi.* Stockholm: Bonniers, 1993.

By the Open Sea—A Decadent Novel? Reconsidering Relationships Between Nietzsche, Strindberg, and Fin-de-Siècle Culture

Tobias Dahlkvist

By 1900, Friedrich Nietzsche was one of the most widely read and discussed philosophers in the world. Just one decade before the turn of the century, however, he had been all but totally unknown. Perhaps he was occasionally remembered for the controversy that some of his first books had stirred up in the early 1870s; perhaps the passionate Wagnerism of his youth would be remembered by some. But on the whole, he went from complete obscurity to a position as one of the most famous (and infamous) thinkers in the world in just a few years during the 1890s. Ironically, Nietzsche himself was unaware of this development, for in the beginning of January 1889 he suffered a mental breakdown from which he never recovered.

Scandinavian intellectuals played an important part in Nietzsche's rise to fame in these years. The Danish critic Georg Brandes had begun a correspondence with Nietzsche in 1887 and encouraged August Strindberg and Nietzsche to read each other's books and to strike up a correspondence of their own (see Rokem 87–104; Perrelli, "Eine Zimelie"). This correspondence, however, was cut short after about a month by Nietzsche's breakdown. Brandes and the Swedish writer Ola Hansson both published essays in German on Nietzsche that belonged to the first attempts to take Nietzsche's thinking seriously (see Fambrini; Brantly).

On Strindberg's part, the encounter with Nietzsche inspired him to write the novel *By the Open Sea* (*I havsbandet*), published by the prestigious Swedish publisher Albert Bonnier in 1890.[1] The novel tells a story about the fishery inspector Axel Borg, a frail aesthete and programmatically modern spirit who is given the task of finding alternative fishing methods for the fishermen of the Stockholm archipelago. Borg makes his appearance in the novel as a dandy, dressed with consummate elegance and wearing a golden bracelet in the shape of an ourobouros, a serpent biting its own tail. From the outset, his arrogance and cosmopolitan manners provoke fear in and hostility from the fishermen. After the unhappy end of a love affair with a young woman who spends the summer at the island, Borg finds himself totally isolated and gradually descends into madness. The novel ends with Borg, after a moment of clarity, setting out in his boat to take his life on a stormy Christmas night.

For a long time after its publication, *By the Open Sea* was generally considered an interesting but all in all a failed book. It has, however, been valued higher and higher over the years, not least because it is one of Strindberg's works testifying most clearly to the author's deep involvement with the great intellectual and artistic debates of his day. Indeed, I believe it stands in such an intricate relation to these debates that it is still not properly understood. In the following, I attempt to clarify one important aspect of how *By the Open Sea* relates to its contemporary European intellectual context. I seek in particular to reexamine the implications of one flawed starting point in the research about Nietzsche and *By the Open Sea,* which positions the character Borg as a Nietzschean *Übermensch.* I find this position to be an example of what Ulf Olsson has described as "the typical fear of Nietzsche" (Olsson 455) within Strindberg scholarship, and propose a new reading of the novel that focuses on a completely different aspect of Nietzsche's philosophy, namely the concept of *décadence.*

The *Übermensch* Question and an International Critical Legacy

In an article on *By the Open Sea* from 1929, Swedish literary scholar Torsten Eklund came to the conclusion that Nietzsche's influence on Strindberg generally was limited, and when applicable extended primarily to the concept of the *Übermensch.* Eklund additionally found Borg to be a flawed portrait of a Nietzschean superman ("Strindbergs I havsbandet" 119; compare Stern 24). This conclusion has remained the point of departure for most analyses of *By the Open Sea* ever since.[2] Yet, the *Übermensch* is a concept with a very specific meaning to Nietzsche. The purpose of the *Übermensch* is to make the absolute meaninglessness of existence bearable by presenting the reader with someone who can affirm life even when one's existence is repeated eternally. The *Übermensch* is thus not an ideal person in Nietzsche's eyes, but someone who can give a new meaning to life even when its inherent meaninglessness is increased infinitely. In the words of Mazzino Montinari, perhaps the most important of all Nietzsche scholars, the *Übermensch* is "nothing else than the man who is capable of saying yes to life as it is, in eternal repetition" (Montinari 125; see also Haase, "Der Übermensch"). With this background, the character Axel Borg emerges as much more complex than previous scholars have assumed. In addition, a comparison of the protagonist of Strindberg's novel to the *Übermensch* only makes sense if Strindberg was familiar with Nietzsche's use of the concept.

We know with some certainty which of Nietzsche's books Strindberg read. In a letter to Georg Brandes from October 2, 1888, Strindberg acknowledges the reception of *The Wagner Case* (*Der Fall Wagner,* 1888). Sometime in November 1888, Nietzsche had his publisher send *Twilight of the Idols* (*Götzen-Dämmerung,* 1889) to Strindberg, and somewhat later *On the Genealogy of Morality* (*Zur Genealogie der Moral,* 1887) and *Beyond Good and Evil* (*Jenseits von Gut und Böse,* 1886). We can assume that Strindberg did read these books: they contain marginal comments in Strindberg's hand, and there are transparent allusions to their contents in letters and books from this period. Also, in the spring of 1889, Strindberg's friend Ola Hansson (himself one of the key figures in Nietzsche's early reception in Germany as well as in Scandinavia) lent him *Human, All-Too-Human* (*Menschliches, Allzumenschliches,* 1878; see Stern 15). To achieve plausible results, any discussion of Nietzsche's relevance to Strindberg around 1890 will have to be based on themes and questions put forward in these works. Hence, if the *Übermensch* were to be a relevant concept to Strindberg in that period, it would have to be a concept used in Strindberg's own writing.

But the fact is that in the books with which Strindberg was familiar, Nietzsche only uses the term *Übermensch* twice: once in *Twilight of the Idols* and once in *On the Genealogy of Morality;* and he uses it ironically. Under the heading "Whether we have become more moral" in *Twilight of the Idols* he discusses the image of himself in the press, characterizing the description of his position by the journalists as a presentation of Cesare Borgia as an *Übermensch* (101/136).[3] In this passage he uses the term to stress how unreasonable the interpretation of his philosophy is that advocates the right of the strong to oppress the weak. Also, in *On the Genealogy of Morality* there is an equally ironic reference to Napoleon as a synthesis of a non-human (*Unmensch*) and an *Übermensch* (36/288), which Walter Kaufmann takes as a sign that Nietzsche was "evidently not charmed by Napoleon's inhuman qualities" (315).

The *Übermensch* is a concept that Nietzsche uses almost exclusively in one book: *Thus Spoke Zarathustra* (*Also sprach Zarathustra,* 1883–86). Circumstances indicate that Strindberg had not read *Zarathustra* by the time he wrote *By the Open Sea.* There is no trace of the book in the catalog of Strindberg's libraries (see Lindström, *Strindberg och böckerna* vol. 1). He did attempt to borrow it from Ola Hansson in the spring of 1889, but Hansson had himself borrowed the book and had already sent it back to its owner (Hansson and Strindberg, *Brevväxling* 52). For what it is worth, Strindberg claimed not to have read the book in 1894 (Strindberg, "Mitt förhållande till Nietzsche" 104). But the most important circumstance is the fact that Strindberg does not use the term *Übermensch* anywhere, either in his works or in his correspondence, and neither in Swedish nor in German, until several years later. In particular, one would assume Strindberg to comment on the *Übermensch* in letters to Nietzsche if that theme were his principal interest in Nietzsche's philosophy, but there is in fact not a single reference to it. Though Strindberg may have been familiar with the *Übermensch* from a secondary source, neither Georg Brandes's nor Ola Hansson's essays on Nietzsche (both of which Strindberg had read when he wrote *By the Open Sea*) contain any discussion of the *Übermensch;* they both use the term once in passing (Brandes 595–96.; Hansson 23), but neither of them explicates the concept.

One thing, and to my mind one thing only, speaks in favor of the relevance of the *Übermensch* to *By the Open Sea.* In a 1909 addition to the autobiography *Son of a Servant* (*Tjänstekvinnans son,* 1886), Strindberg describes *By the Open Sea* with reference to this concept: "Nietzsche's philosophy influences, but the individual is ruined in the striving towards absolute individualism. Begins the 90s: Übermensch" (*Tjänstekvinnans son* 265). But this addition really has very little explanatory value: it was written almost twenty years later, and furthermore on the other side of a religious crisis that had Strindberg reinterpret his own past, and in particular his atheist period of the 1880s and early 1890s. So it seems that the *Übermensch* was not a relevant concept for Strindberg in the early 1890s.

The *Übermensch* would, however, eventually become relevant to him. In *Inferno* (1897), as well as in *The Gothic Rooms* (*Götiska rummen,* 1904) and *Black Banners* (*Svarta fanor,* 1907), Strindberg clearly associates Nietzsche with this concept. In these books, the term *Übermensch* is used more or less whenever Nietzsche's name is mentioned (see *Inferno* 290, 308; *Götiska rumen* 215; *Svarta fanor* 29).[4] In these books, and particularly in *Inferno*, Strindberg tries to find a new meaning of existence. Though the religious framework of *Inferno* is markedly different from a Nietzschean one, it appears that Strindberg realized a connection between the *Übermensch* concept and the task of finding a meaning of existence. If anything, Strindberg's use of the term *Übermensch* in these books implies that he at least understood the meaning of the concept much better than the scholars who have tried to interpret Axel Borg as a failed portrait of an *Übermensch*.

But if Strindberg was uninterested in—and possibly even unaware of—Nietzsche's notion of the *Übermensch* when his interest in Nietzsche's philosophy was at its peak around 1890, the question of which aspects of his philosophy were relevant to Strindberg must be addressed. The concept of *décadence,* which encompasses Nietzsche's critique of the modern, was in fact highly important to Strindberg at that time. This is evident in Strindberg's correspondence with Nietzsche; I argue that *décadence* is also a key element in *By the Open Sea.*

Strindberg as a Reader of Nietzsche

As many commentators have noted, the principal theme in Strindberg's and Nietzsche's correspondence was translations and translators: Nietzsche even asked Strindberg to translate *Ecce Homo,* Nietzsche's forthcoming autobiography, into French. Though less prominent, their discussion on the question of degeneration provides a fuller understanding of Nietzsche's relevance to Strindberg. (Strindberg uses the French term *dégénérescence;* Nietzsche uses the German *Entartung* as well as the French *décadence*).[5] In the first letter to Nietzsche, Strindberg attacks Nietzsche's notion of the criminal as a person too strong for society to handle. Strindberg's letter is apparently a comment to paragraph 45 of the section "Skirmishes of an Untimely Man" in Nietzsche's book *Twilight of the Idols,* which Strindberg had just read. For in that paragraph, Nietzsche defines the criminal type in just those terms that Strindberg attacked: "The criminal type is the type of the strong human being under unfavorable conditions, a strong human being made sick" (*Twilight of the Idols* 110/146; see also Campioni, *Les lectures françaises* 239). Strindberg finds this notion to be misinformed, and by referring to the photographs that accompany Lombroso's *Criminal Man* (*L'uomo delinquente,* 1876), he seeks to convince Nietzsche that he was mistaken about the nature of the criminal type. According to Strindberg, the criminal is a degenerate, an inferior animal, who lacks the faculties to understand the mechanisms of society and morality (*Letters* 294; *Brev* 190; see Lindström, *Strindberg och böckerna* 1:186). Nietzsche answers, politely, that although the hereditary criminal is indeed a decadent, the studies conducted by Francis Galton demonstrate that the criminals tend to have an ancestor that was expelled from society due to his dangerous strength: “The *hereditary* criminal a décadent, even an idiot—no doubt! But the history of the criminal families, of which the Englishman Galton (‘the hereditary genius’) has collected a vast material, always leads back to a person who is *too strong* for a given social level” (*Briefe* 508; for Nietzsche’s knowledge of Galton, see Haase, “Friedrich Nietzsche liest Francis Galton”). A letter to Ola Hansson from February 19, 1889, shows that Strindberg was not convinced by Nietzsche’s reply, but also that the question of criminality as a symptom of degeneration was very much on his mind: “Galton (and Nietzsche) believe the criminal is a strong type, who has not found his right place. I don’t. The strong intelligence bends, is supple, bears adversity, endures, waits. . . . The strong criminal is weak in intelligence (= stupid) but strong in emotion (= an animal)” (*Letters* 305; *Brev* 248). This, clearly, is the aspect of Nietzsche’s philosophy to which Strindberg responded. The threat of degeneration to modern culture (and modern culture’s response to that threat); not the *Übermensch*.

Other contemporaneous sources also indicate that Strindberg associated Nietzsche with the degeneration question. In a letter to Georg Brandes from December 4, 1888, shortly after the first letter to Nietzsche, Strindberg writes, for instance, that Nietzsche announces the fall of the Occident: “For me, Nietzsche heralds the downfall of Europe and of Christianity” (*Letters* 295; *Brev* 191). This was apparently Strindberg’s first impression of Nietzsche’s philosophy: a prophecy of a decline of the West. Also, the preface to *Miss Julie* (*Fröken Julie,* 1888) shows that Strindberg’s mind was steeped in the degeneration theme at this time. In the preface, written after the play itself and generally considered one of the texts where Nietzsche’s influence on Strindberg is most visible, Strindberg seeks to refute the criticism that the Brandes brothers, among others, had directed against the play. In reply to the allegation that Miss Julie’s suicide is not motivated enough, Strindberg gives a list of factors that motivate the act. Together with her upbringing and faulty instincts inherited from the mother, Strindberg lists “the suggestive effect of her fiancé upon her weak and degenerate brain” (*Miss Julie* 93, 103). Somewhat later (95, 106), he also discusses Julie’s androgynous type, “the half-woman” (“*halvkvinnan*”), as a degenerate type that unfortunately succeeds in attracting degenerate men and therefore often mates successfully.

So it is clear that around 1890 Strindberg was very much preoccupied with the idea that man is undergoing a physiological degeneration in modern Western society. He sought to discuss this matter in his literary work, and he obviously saw a kindred spirit in Nietzsche. Not least, it seems to me, because of the common interest in degeneration and its cultural symptoms.

The question of degeneration, its causes and symptoms, is one of the most important themes in Nietzsche's later phase. It is also an extremely important subtext to Strindberg's works of the 1880s and 1890s. This is a context to their works that is all too often forgotten. Both of them dedicate considerable effort to the question of the artistic manifestation of degeneration: decadence. Nietzsche develops a critique of decadent art, whereas Strindberg stages his critique in his novels of this period.

By the Open Sea and Decadence

Let us first of all establish that *By the Open Sea* is a decadent novel. It represents a break with the naturalistic aesthetic of *The Father* (*Fadren,* 1887) and *Miss Julie,* and was clearly conceived within a decadent horizon of expectations. It displays, as I will seek to demonstrate in what follows, a number of the typical characteristics of this genre, an important literary trend around 1890, in France as well as in Scandinavia.[6] The correspondence with Ola Hansson, himself a programmatically decadent writer at this time, testifies to Strindberg's interest: not only do they discuss the likes of Huysmans and Bourget, but the degeneration of modern man is also a topic of debate, and Strindberg gives his younger friend advice on what scientific works to read (see Hansson and Strindberg, *Brevväxling* 25–26, 91; Strindberg's letter of February 19, 1889, *Letters* 304–6/*Brev* 247–48). But, as I will also seek to demonstrate, Strindberg seems in particular to have drawn on Nietzsche's conception of *décadence* for the decadent theme in the novel.

In a manner typical of the decadent literature, *By the Open Sea* uses the connotations of a number of psychopathological phenomena that were in vogue at the end of the nineteenth century. In particular, *By the Open Sea* contains a protagonist who is described as particularly modern by virtue of his nervousness. The central female character is defined by her hysteria, which also is presented as a quintessentially modern illness. Both hysteria and nervousness (neurasthenia) were widely associated with the degeneration of modern man in the late nineteenth century (see Micale).

In the third chapter of the novel, Borg meditates on his past. He describes himself as suffering from nervousness, but in the eyes of Borg himself, this is because his generation is a transitory stage to a new variety of human being:

> But having been brought up in the era of steam and electricity, when the pace of life had quickened he, like the rest of his generation, was inevitably afflicted by bad nerves. . . . It was the creation of a new race or at least of a new type of human being. Consequently it appeared to the old type sick and unhealthy, because it was in process of being formed. This the old type was reluctant to admit. It wanted to be the healthy norm itself, though it was in fact in a state of disintegration. (*By the Open Sea* 40; *I havsbandet* 44)

Borg is thus a representative of a typically modern type of man: he exhibits a nervousness that might border on being pathological and that is caused by the rapid changes in modern society. The novel illustrates Borg's nervousness on several different levels.

In the medical literature of the late nineteenth century, the alleged pathology of genius was something of a specialty. To a number of doctors, anthropologists, and so on, genius (in the arts and philosophy mainly) was considered a symptom of degeneration comparable to insanity and to a lesser degree to innate criminal tendencies.[7] There were different theories as to what disease genius was related to—Lombroso considered it a neurosis, caused by a form of epileptic degeneration—but it was generally considered to be a form of hyperesthesia, an extreme sensitivity of the nervous system. Borg's sensitivity and nervousness are fairly transparent allusions to this medical discourse.

Borg's extreme intelligence—he claims to work as quickly as twenty normal people thanks to his unusual intelligence—is a result of his typically modern nervousness, and as we shall see he nurtures his sensitive nerves with the help of various luxury items; indeed, his refined taste has become second nature to him. In all these respects, *By the Open Sea* is a decadent novel; and Borg's nervousness as well as his aestheticism and his modernity contribute to this. But these elements of the novel are not only decadent: they are furthermore reminiscent of a particular notion of decadence, namely that of Nietzsche.

Nietzsche's Concept of *Décadence*

Decadence—Nietzsche usually prefers the French form *décadence*—is an extremely important theme in Nietzsche's last books. Particularly in *The*

Wagner Case and in *Twilight of the Idols,* two of the books that Strindberg read in the fall of 1888, Nietzsche discusses this theme in great detail. In *The Wagner Case,* Nietzsche draws on Paul Bourget's definition of decadence from his essay on Baudelaire in *Essays on Contemporary Psychology* (*Essais de psychologie contemporaine,* 1883–85), describing literary decadence as a style where the elements of a work of art gain independence in relation to the whole: "the page becomes independent of the book, the sentence becomes independent of the page, the word becomes independent of the sentence" (Nietzsche, *Der Fall Wagner* 27; compare. Bourget 14; the importance of Bourget's *Essais* for Nietzsche is discussed by a number of Nietzsche scholars: Campioni, *Les lectures françaises de Nietzsche,* deserves special mention). One of the central characteristics of a decadent work of art is in other words its fragmented form. Nietzsche regards decadent art, Wagner being his prime example, as a symptom of a physiological degeneration of modern man (see the chapter on Nietzsche in Bauer). He developed these ideas in connection with his wide reading in modern French psychology and psychologically oriented literary criticism. As the recent, philologically oriented Nietzsche scholarship has also made clear, his reading in these fields was extensive (for Nietzsche's French orientation, see Campioni, *Nietzsches persönliche Bibliothek;* Lampl; Brobjer, "Nietzsche's Reading").

Nietzsche was highly French-oriented in all cultural matters. This is important to bear in mind. After he resigned from his chair at the University of Basel (he was appointed professor of classical philology at the tender age of twenty-four, but was forced to resign for health reasons ten years later) he would travel extensively through the south of France, Switzerland, and Italy in search of a location with a climate that would suit his frail physiology.[8] His interest in French literature grew deeper, spreading from the classical moralists to modern literature and criticism; in particular Stendhal and Mérimée became great favorites, but he was familiar with, for example, the brothers Goncourt, Flaubert, and Zola too, as well as the critical works of Bourget, Taine, and Brunetière (see *Beyond Good and Evil,* 110–11/153; Campioni, *Les lectures françaises de Nietzsche*).

Nietzsche holds the preoccupation of modern art with psychopathology to be unhealthy, an obsession that in itself is a symptom of the degeneration of modern man and that furthermore contributes to that degeneration. Particularly in *The Wagner Case,* the violent attack on his former mentor and friend Richard Wagner, Nietzsche uses Wagner as an example of this tendency; and he accuses him of contributing to a pathological nervousness of his adherents (for Nietzsche's rhetorical use of allusions to medical conditions, see Moore). But in the preface to this book, Nietzsche characterizes himself as a *décadent* (*Der Fall Wagner* 11). He writes that he is a decadent who had the ability to defend himself against his decadence. By overcoming his decadence, he has reached insights into the nature of decadence that would be unavailable to a person not afflicted by decadence at all. This is a central aspect of Nietzsche's philosophy: the overcoming of a negative influence is always more valuable than not having been subjected to that influence at all. The greater the threat to be overcome, the greater the achievement in overcoming it. This means that Nietzsche's ideal—be it with regard to humans or to ideas—is always very close to utter disaster. This is a fact to be taken into consideration when trying to determine Nietzsche's relevance to Strindberg's *By the Open Sea.*

Aestheticism and Asceticism in *By the Open Sea*

When reflecting on his own past in the third chapter of *By the Open Sea,* Borg touches briefly on the foundation for his ethics: "Unlike the weak Christian, who postulates a support outside himself in God, he grasped the tangible present in his own personality and tried to create out of it a perfect type of human being—a man whose conduct and actions would not infringe anyone's rights and who knew that the fruits of a highly esteemed tree could not fail to be of profit and comfort to others" (*By the Open Sea* 40/43). Borg's refined sensitivity and the intelligence that accompanies it is the result of a conscious striving to become a perfect type of man. His is a virtue ethic of sorts. His aestheticism and his proud distance from the population of the island are functions of his strategy to make himself a better person. This is in fact a notion of morality that is very close to that of Nietzsche (for Nietzsche's philosophy as a virtue ethics, see Brobjer, *Nietzsche's Ethics of Character*). It is close to Nietzsche as far as the ambition is concerned, that is; Borg's means to achieve his ambition are faulty.

It is by meticulously carrying out his duties as a fishery inspector that Borg can help the fisher community of the archipelago. He does not care about the fishermen: on the contrary, he consciously keeps his distance from them, believing that their friendship would bring him down to their level. But in keeping with his individualistic ethics, he maintains that by doing his work—finding new fishery methods, in particular how to fish salmon in the Baltic Sea—he can help the islanders. However, his ethics collide with the more conventional morality of Maria. After a failed attempt to have a chapel built on the island, Borg fears that poverty will strike the island. To Maria, poverty would be an opportunity to take part in some charity work and thus prove herself to be a compassionate person, and so she hints that Borg should initiate such a project. He refuses:

> "I have not come here to practice charity, but to teach the people to live without it."
> "You are at bottom a heartless person though you make yourself out to be otherwise."
> "And you want to show off your great heart at my expense, without being willing to sacrifice one metre of the pleats in your dress."
> "I hate you! I hate you!" the girl burst out with a horrible expression on her face. (*By the Open Sea* 131/132)

Both protagonists are fundamentally indifferent to the plight of the fishermen. But whereas Maria—a typical Strindbergian woman: sentimental and highly erotic, cruel, and egoistic—sees the poverty of the fishermen as an opportunity to demonstrate her compassion, Borg has a wish to help them. Not because he cares about the fishermen—they are his enemies—but because it is his job to help them.

Borg's meditation on his past makes it clear that he has consistently tried to take advantage of his nervousness, tried to mold his mind into a precise instrument. His attempts to do so are ethically motivated: his wish to become a more intelligent scientist is his contribution to a better world. His considerable intelligence is a result of his extreme sensitivity; and he has done his best to increase his sensitivity through a surprising combination of asceticism and luxurious habits. It is really this combination that testifies to Nietzsche's relevance to the novel.

In some memorable sequences in the early chapters of *By the Open Sea,* Borg is distressed by the austere rooms in a fisherman's hut that he is entitled to as representative of the government. He soon sets about decorating his quarters. Borg's decoration is decadent in the sense that it displays a preference for the artificial over the natural by mimicking nature rather than incorporating it. The color scheme of the room, with "flesh-coloured" (*köttfärgade*) Persian curtains and tablecloths and rugs in various shades of green is an attempt to imitate nature, complemented by the mock ice of the various glass objects and the animal tones provided by a set of pens made from porcupine spines. In particular, his lamp is of interest: on his desk he places a strange art-nouveau lamp, sculpted in the form of a hunting scene, complete with a hunter, a fox, and a hare (this tendency to design objects in the form of something else was interpreted as a symptom of degeneration by a contemporary of Strindberg:

see Nordau 1:19–22). Not only is he an aesthete, but Borg's aestheticism furthermore displays a typically decadent liking for the artificial. It is not an accident that Borg is often compared to Des Esseintes (for example Olsson 266), the hero of Huysmans's *Against Nature* (*À rébours,* 1884) and an archtypical decadent.

But there is more to this than just mere aestheticism in the typically decadent fashion. The descriptions of these objects, the lamp, the rugs, the bookcases, as well as of the various species of fish in the Baltic Sea in the third chapter expand into a series of small essays or at times prose poems. This is in no way called for by the action of the novel: on the contrary, Strindberg seems to attribute to them an intrinsic worth, independent of the novel. This is typical of the decadent literature; Max Nordau, that arch-critic of decadence, was less than impressed by the essayistic digressions of the decadent novels, describing them as "the diary outpourings of an upper-class daughter" (Nordau 2:110). But what is more important, the fragmentation that these poetic digressions cause is in consonance with Nietzsche's notion of decadence.

Furthermore, Borg's despair when confronted with the bare white walls and cheap furniture of the rooms is a result of his being used to "having his eyes sated by impressions" (*By the Open Sea* 12/18). This is a highly significant expression when it comes from a writer with an outspoken interest in Nietzsche. When decorating the room, it is apparent that Borg's first priority is to provide stimulation for his senses. His books are arranged according to color; he litters the floor with small colorful rugs to break up the monotony of the pale floorboards; and the glass objects and the bizarre lamp also serve the purpose of providing him with visual stimuli (*By the Open Sea* 21ff./26ff.; see in particular 22/27). Borg has an obvious need to have his senses constantly stimulated. Indeed, he lacks the ability not to respond to stimuli. This is evident from other scenes as well; it is in fact a character trait that Borg displays throughout the novel. The dark color of a volcanic cliff encountered when rowing between the islands makes Borg uneasy; when he has rowed past it he feels relief:

> When he returned to the boat and had the mournful scene behind him, he rejoiced again at the infinite purity of the water, the empty blueness which, like a blank sheet, lay before him, soothing, because it could not arouse any memories, could not call forth any ideas, could not squeeze out of him any strong sensations. And when he approached a rather larger island, he greeted it as a new acquaintance who would speak to him of something else and erase the feelings he had recently experienced. (*By the Open Sea* 57/60)

If this inability to resist stimuli is the source of Borg's intelligence, it is to an even higher degree the source of his fragility.

To Nietzsche, the inability to resist reacting to stimulus is a clear sign of degeneration. In *Twilight of the Idols,* which as we remember was one of the books that Strindberg read in 1888, he defines it as a source of lacking spirituality as well as a pathological symptom:

> All unspirituality, all vulgarity, is due to the incapacity to resist a stimulus—one *has* to react, one obeys every impulse. In many instances, such a compulsion is already morbidity, decline, a symptom of exhaustion—almost everything which unphilosophical crudity designates by the name "vice" is merely this physiological incapacity *not* to react. (*Twilight of the Idols* 76/109)

We have seen that Borg's superior intelligence is a function of his sensitivity. Apparently, his aestheticism is a means to take advantage of this sensitivity. Since he is unable to resist stimuli, he makes sure that he is surrounded with beautiful objects that have a positive impact on his senses. Conversely, he seeks to avoid situations that damage his sensitive nerves. The narrator observes that Borg has found physical movement ("violent exercise") to be "harmful for his nerves and mental life, as the delicate instruments enclosed in his brain-box could no more endure being shaken than a building in which the precision instruments of an astronomer were housed" (*By the Open Sea* 54/58).

This is a key passage for Strindberg's relation to Nietzsche. It is important because it shows that the body and the mind stand in an antithetical relation in Borg's eyes. His intelligence is a result of his fine senses, and they in their turn are a result of Borg's weak physique. This is a notion that is very distant from Nietzsche. To him, it is no less important to find the diet and way of life that provide the best conditions for one's thinking than it is for Borg; but Nietzsche stresses time and time again that this means that the body needs strengthening. In *Twilight of the Idols,* Julius Caesar's austere lifestyle is presented as the best means to protect a genial mind:

> *Another problem of diet.*—The means by which Julius Caesar defended himself against sickliness and headache: tremendous marches, the simplest form of living, uninterrupted sojourn in the open air, continuous toil—these, broadly speaking, are the universal preservative and protective measures against the extreme vulnerability of that subtle machine working at the highest pressure which is called genius. (*Twilight of the Idols* 96/130)

A certain amount of asceticism is fundamental to any creative person, Nietzsche holds (in particular this is an important theme in *On the Genealogy of Morality* 82–85/351–56). He regarded, for instance, Wagner's inability to sublimate both detrimental to his art and dangerous to his health. But asceticism must be used with caution. When it becomes an ideal as opposed to a tool it is dangerous—this, according to Nietzsche, is what has happened within the church (this is the central tenet of the third section of *On the Genealogy of Morality*). It is dangerous not least because suffering is an essential element to life.

In particular Borg's asceticism is a means to handle painful experiences. This is evident after the engagement to Maria has been broken off. Rather than experiencing the pain, Borg tries to block it out:

> The inspector had had to work for a month before he succeeded in healing his soul from the gunshot wound he had sustained during the game he had played with love. By means of potassium bromide and a reduced diet he had cured his desire, and when the misery of his loneliness took hold of him, he made himself a dose of laughing-gas from ammonium nitrate, as he had long ago discovered that alcoholic intoxication was simple-minded, and was followed by dejection and suicidal mania. (*By the Open Sea* 168/167)

Borg is constantly trying to avoid things that are painful. When he hears the fishermen gossip about his father, he tries to make himself deaf and indifferent (*By the Open Sea* 53/57). This is a consistent feature of the novel. In some scenes it is even mirrored in the very language of the novel. When Borg thinks back upon his life, it is obvious that his father played an important role in his life; and various aspects of their relation are described in some detail. But the death of the father is mentioned in passing, as if it were an occasion too painful to remember: "When after seven years of painful service, he inherited the estate of his father, who had just died, and resigned his post to travel abroad in private capacity, he had to hear people saying that he had betrayed his calling, that it was a pity he had come to nothing or, alternatively, that he had been dismissed" (*By the Open Sea* 44/48). Although the narrator of *By the Open Sea* is not identical to Borg, the latter's ideas and perceptions are mirrored in the imagery of the novel and the narrator's voice (as demonstrated in Kärnell 225ff.). The great difference between the verbose descriptions of the discussions with the father on women and on politics and the laconic description of his death is therefore important to note. The description of the death of the mother is equally terse: "This father was to his son, whose mother had died early, both an example and a teacher" (*By the Open Sea* 34/38). Borg's mother is totally absent from the novel until he dreams of her as he is losing his sanity in the final chapter. The death of the mother at an early age, and of the father, the great role model, is mentioned only in passing, and in remarkably neutral words: it is as if Borg were forcing himself not to think about them. The book contains a third example of a loved one whose death is mentioned only once, with seemingly forced distance. When treating Maria for a fit of hysteria, Borg wears his golden bracelet, which captures her attention:

> "You are looking at my bracelet," said the inspector, breaking the silence.
> "No, I'm not," contradicted the girl.
> "It was given to me by a woman, who is of course dead, since I have not given it back." (*By the Open Sea* 106/106)

This is the only instance that this woman, who obviously was Borg's fiancée, is mentioned in the novel. No further details about her fate are given: the conversation immediately changes to a discussion of the nature of love. It is in other words a clear pattern that whenever a painful experience such as the death of someone close to the protagonist of this very verbose novel is mentioned, the language changes to a laconic, neutral mode. It is as if the narrator were forcing himself not to think about that which causes pain. This is completely consistent with Borg's behavior.

We observed that Borg's ethic has a certain resemblance to Nietzsche's in that it is not primarily concerned with matters of right and wrong, but with developing one's person with the aim of improving the conditions for one's thinking. But there is an enormous difference when it comes to their attitude to pain. Borg strives to increase his sensitivity and therefore seeks to avoid painful experiences. To Nietzsche the ability to overcome adversity and painful experiences was always the highest ideal. The ability to do so was what in Nietzsche's eyes enabled him to defend himself against his *décadence* and was thus what distinguished him from Wagner and the like. Borg on the other hand lacks this ability, and instead he carefully nurtures his pathological nervousness. He is someone who could have lived up to Nietzsche's ideal—his superior intelligence is a clear sign—but whose failure to do so illustrates the Nietzschean notion of the extreme proximity of the highest ideal to utter disaster. We saw earlier that Strindberg considered Nietzsche an announcer of the demise of Europe (*Brev* 191). If we take this interpretation seriously, then the story of Axel Borg, Strindberg's portrait of a quintessentially modern man, becomes a warning that whatever is valuable in modern Western culture is also infinitely fragile. But if we take this interpretation seriously, then it is also clear that far from being an *Übermensch,* Borg actually represents a far more important Nietzschean figure: he is a *décadent.*

Notes

1. I am using Hans Lindström's edition of *I havsbandet* in the national edition of Strindberg's collected works; as for the English translation, I rely on Mary Sandbach's edition of the novel. When quoting Strindberg and Nietzsche, I give page references first to the English translation, then to the original.

2. Eklund repeated his discussion of Borg as a superman in his large 1948 study *Tjänstekvinnans son;* and his view of Nietzsche was taken for granted by an entire generation of Strindberg scholars, such as Martin Lamm, Hans Lindström, and Walter Berendsohn. (See Eklund, *Tjänstekvinnans son* 414; Lamm, 1:419; Berendsohn, "August Strindbergs 'I havsbandet'" 110; Berendsohn, "Strindberg och Nietzsche" 31; Lindström, *Hjärnornas kamp* 153.) Among later scholars too, the *Übermensch* is more often than not accepted as the point of reference for discussion of Strindberg's reception of Nietzsche (Perrelli, *Strindberg e Nietzsche* 125; Sprinchorn). Furthermore, in the studies of the Scandinavian Nietzsche reception in general the situation is no different (Strecker 53; Beyer 2:60; Borland 39; Schimanski 38). There are some exceptions, of course, but on the whole the *Übermensch* is the aspect of Nietzsche's philosophy with which *By the Open Sea* has been, and indeed still is, associated (for exceptions see Brandl; Stern; Dahlkvist).

3. I am using the German standard edition of Nietzsche's collected works and letters, the *Kritische Studienausgabe* edited by Giorgio Colli and Mazzino Montinari.

4. Michael Meyer's hypothesis that Strindberg might have read *Zarathustra* together with Anders Eliasson when he was a guest at his home in Ystad in the south of Sweden during the summer of 1895 therefore makes perfect sense (Meyer 323).

5. See Pick for a brilliant discussion of the degeneration question in fin-de-siècle Europe.

6. There are three book-length studies of the Scandinavian decadence literature: Andersen, Ahlund, and Lundberg. None of them discusses Strindberg in any detail.

7. Cesare Lombroso wrote several books on genius as a form of "higher degeneration": *Genio e follia* (1864), *L'uomo di genio* (1888), *Genio e degenerazione* (1897), and *Nuovi studi sul genio* (1901/02); and other prominent members of the medical professions such as Moreau de Tours, P. J. Möbius, Francis Galton, and Henry Maudsley discussed it as well.

8. The 800 pages of the second volume of Janz's biography of Nietzsche cover his erring life from his retirement from the University of Basel to his mental breakdown in great detail.

Works Cited

Ahlund, Claes. *Medusas huvud: Dekadensens tematik i svensk sekelskiftesprosa.* Uppsala: Uppsala University, 1994.

Andersen, Per Thomas. *Dekadanse i nordisk litteratur 1880–1900.* Oslo: Aschehoug, 1992.

Bauer, Roger. *Die schöne Décadence: Geschichte eines literarischen Paradoxons.* Frankfurt am Main: Vittorio Klostermann, 2001.

Berendsohn, Walter. "August Strindbergs 'I havsbandet.'" *Samlaren* 26 (1945): 101–16.

———. "Strindberg och Nietzsche." *Samfundet Örebro Stads- och Länsbiblioteks Vänner Meddelande* 16 (1948): 9–37.

Beyer, Harald. *Nietzsche og Norden.* 2 vols. Bergen: Universitetsforlag, 1958–59.

Borland, Harold H. "Nietzsche's Influence on Swedish Literature: With Special Reference to Strindberg, Ola Hansson, Heidenstam, and Fröding." Ph.D. diss., Cambridge University, 1954. Göteborg: Wettergren & Kerbers förlag, 1956.

Bourget, Paul. *Essais de psychologie contemporaine: Études littéraires.* 1883–85. Ed. André Guyaux. Paris: Gallimard, 1993.

Brandes, Georg. "Aristokratisk Radikalisme: En Afhandling om Friedrich Nietzsche." *Tilskueren* 6 (1889): 565–613.

Brandl, Horst. "Persönlichkeitsidealismus und Willenskult: Aspekte der Nietzsche-Rezeption in Schweden." Ph.D. diss., Frankfurt University. Heidelberg: Carl Winter, 1977.

Brantly, Susan. "Creating an Alternative to Naturalism: Ola Hansson's Assimilation of Nietzsche." *Orbis Litterarum* 42 (1987): 44–57.

Brobjer, Thomas H. "Nietzsche's Ethics of Character: A Study of Nietzsche's Ethics and Its Place in the History of Moral Thinking." Ph.D. diss., Uppsala University, 1995.

———. "Nietzsche's Reading and Private Library, 1885–1889." *Journal of the History of Ideas* 58, no. 4 (1997): 663–93.

Campioni, Giuliano. *Les lectures françaises de Nietzsche.* Trans. Christel Lavigne-Mouilleron. Paris: Presses universitaires de France, 2001.

———. *Nietzsches persönliche Bibliothek.* Ed. Paolo D'Iorio, Maria Cristina Fornari, Francesco Fronterotta, Andrea Orsucci, and Renate Müller-Buck. Berlin: Walter de Gruyter, 2004.

Dahlkvist, Tobias. "Vad kan Borgs armband säga oss? Nietzsche och *I havsbandet.*" *Samlaren* 125 (2004): 92–111.

Eklund, Torsten. "Strindbergs I havsbandet." *Edda* 29 (1929): 113–44.

———. "Tjänstekvinnans son: En psykologisk Strindbergsstudie." Ph.D. diss., Stockholms högskola, 1948. Stockholm: Bonniers, 1948.

Fambrini, Alessandro. "Ola Hansson und Georg Brandes: Einige Bemerkungen über die erste Rezeption Nietzsches." *Nietzsche-Studien* 26 (1997): 421–40.

Haase, Marie-Luise. "Der Übermensch in *Also sprach Zarathustra* und im Zarathustra-Nachlass 1882–1885." *Nietzsche-Studien* 13 (1984): 228–44.
———. "Friedrich Nietzsche liest Francis Galton." *Nietzsche-Studien* 18 (1989): 633–58.
Hansson, Ola. *Friedrich Nietzsche: Seine Persönlichkeit und sein System.* Leipzig: E. W. Fritsch, 1890.
Hansson, Ola, and August Strindberg. *Brevväxling 1888–1892.* Stockholm: Bonniers, 1938.
Janz, Curt Paul. *Friedrich Nietzsche: Biographie.* 3 vols. 1978. Frankfurt am Main: Büchergilde Gutenberg, 1994.
Kärnell, Karl-Åke. "Strindbergs bildspråk: En studie i prosastil." Ph.D. diss., Lunds University. Stockholm: Almqvist & Wicksell, 1962.
Kaufmann, Walter. *Nietzsche: Philosopher, Psychologist, Antichrist.* 1950. 4th ed. Princeton, N.J.: Princeton University Press, 1974.
Lamm, Martin. *August Strindberg.* 2 vols. Stockholm: Bonniers, 1940–42.
Lampl, Hans Erich. *Flair du livre: Friedrich Nietzsche und Théodule Ribot: Eine Trouvaille.* Zürich: Am Abgrund, 1988.
Lundberg, Johan. *En evighet i rummets former gjuten: Dekadenta och symbolistiska inslag i Sven Lidmans, Anders Österlings och Sigfrid Siwertz lyrik 1904–1907.* Stockholm: Symposion, 2000.
Lindström, Hans. "Hjärnornas kamp: Psykologiska idéer och motiv i Strindbergs åttiotalsdiktning." Ph.D. diss., Uppsala University, 1952.
———. *Strindberg och böckerna.* 2 vols. Uppsala: Svenska litteratursällskapet, 1977–90.
Micale, Mark S. *Approaching Hysteria: Disease and Its Interpretations.* Princeton, N.J.: Princeton University Press, 1995.
Meyer, Michael. *Strindberg: A Biography.* London: Secker and Warburg, 1985.
Montinari, Mazzino. *Che cosa ha detto Nietzsche.* 1975. Ed. Giuliano Campioni. Milan: Adelphi Edizioni, 2003.
Moore, Gregory. "Hysteria and Histrionics: Nietzsche, Wagner and the Pathology of Genius." *Nietzsche-Studien* 30 (2001): 246–66.
Nietzsche, Friedrich. *Beyond Good and Evil.* Ed. Rolf-Peter Horstmann and Judith Norman. Trans. Judith Norman. Cambridge, Eng.: Cambridge University Press, 2002.
———. *Briefe: Januar 1887–Januar 1889. Briefe: Kritische Studienausgabe in 8 Bänden.* Vol. 8. Ed. Giorgio Colli and Mazzino Montinari. Munich: Deutscher Taschenbuch Verlag and Walter de Gruyter, 1986.
———. *Der Fall Wagner.* 1888. In *Sämtliche Werke: Kritische Studienausgabe in 15 Bänden.* Vol. 6, ed. Giorgio Colli and Mazzino Montinari. Munich: Deutscher Taschenbuch Verlag and Walter de Gruyter, 1999.
———. *Götzen-Dämmerung.* 1888. In *Sämtliche Werke: Kritische Studienausgabe in 15 Bänden.* Vol. 6, ed. Giorgio Colli and Mazzino Montinari. Munich: Deutscher Taschenbuch Verlag and Walter de Gruyter, 1999.
———. *Jenseits von Gut und Böse.* 1886. In *Sämtliche Werke: Kritische Studienausgabe in 15 Bänden.* Vol. 5, ed. Giorgio Colli and Mazzino Montinari. Munich: Deutscher Taschenbuch Verlag and Walter de Gruyter, 1999.

———. *On the Genealogy of Morals*. Ed. Keith Ansell-Pearson. Trans. Carol Diethe. Cambridge, Eng.: Cambridge University Press, 1994.

———. *Twilight of the Idols and The Antichrist*. Trans. R. J. Hollingdale. Harmondsworth, Eng.: Penguin, 1990.

———. *Zur Genealogie der Moral*. 1887. In *Sämtliche Werke: Kritische Studienausgabe in 15 Bänden*. Vol. 5, ed. Giorgio Colli and Mazzino Montinari. Munich: Deutscher Taschenbuch Verlag and Walter de Gruyter, 1999.

Nordau, Max. *Entartung*. 2 vols. Berlin: Carl Duncker, 1892–93.

Olsson, Ulf. *Levande död: Studier i Strindbergs prosa*. Stockholm: Symposion, 1996.

Perrelli, Franco. "Eine Zimelie: Der Briefwechsel zwischen August Strindberg und Friedrich Nietzsche." In *Friedrich Nietzsche: Rezeption und Kultus*, ed. Sandro Barbera, Paolo D'Iorio, and Justus H. Ulbricht. Pisa: Edizioni ETS, 2004. 163–83.

———. *Strindberg e Nietzsche: Un problema di storia del nichilismo*. Bari: Adriatica, 1984.

Pick, Daniel. *Faces of Degeneration: A European Disorder c. 1848–c. 1918*. 1989. Cambridge, Eng.: Cambridge University Press, 1996.

Rokem, Freddie. *Philosophers & Thespians: Thinking Performance*. Stanford, Calif.: Stanford University Press, 2010.

Schimanski, Folke. "Nietzsche im Norden." In *Widersprüche: Zur frühen Nietzsche-Rezeption*, ed. Andreas Schirmer and Rüdiger Schmidt. Weimar: Böhlaus, 2000. 35–51.

Sprinchorn, Evert. "Strindberg and the Superman." In *Strindberg's Dramaturgy*, ed. Göran Stockenström. Minneapolis: University of Minnesota Press, 1988. 14–26.

Stern, Michael. *Nietzsche's Ocean, Strindberg's Open Sea*. Berlin: Nordeuropa-Institut der Humboldt-Universität, 2008.

Strecker, Karl. *Nietzsche und Strindberg: Mit ihrem Briefwechsel*. Munich: Müller, 1921.

Strindberg, August. *Brev: Februari 1888–December 1889*. In *August Strindbergs brev*, vol. 7, ed. Torsten Eklund. Stockholm: Bonniers, 1961.

———. *By the Open Sea*. Trans. Mary Sandbach. Athens: University of Georgia Press, 1985.

———. *Fröken Julie*. 1888. *Fadren/Fröken Julie/Fordringsägare*. In *Samlade Verk*, vol. 27, ed. Gunnar Ollén. Stockholm: Almqvist & Wicksell, 1984.

———. *Götiska rumen*. 1904. In *Samlade Verk*, vol. 53, ed. Conny Svensson. Stockholm: Norstedts, 2001.

———. *I havsbandet*. 1890. In *Samlade Verk*, vol. 31, ed. Hans Lindström. Stockholm: Almqvist & Wicksell, 1982.

———. *Inferno*. 1897. In *Samlade Verk*, vol. 37, ed. Ann-Charlotte Gavel Adams, trans. Eugène Fahlstedt. Stockholm: Norstedts, 1994.

———. *Letters: 1862–1892*. In *Strindberg's Lettters*. Vol. 1, ed. and trans. Michael Robinson. London: Athlone, 1992.

———. *Miss Julie*. In *Plays: One: The Father, Miss Julie, The Ghost Sonata*, trans. Michael Meyer. London: Methuen, 1991.

———. "Mitt förhållande till Nietzsche." 1894. *Viviseektioner II*. In *Samlade Verk*, vol. 34, ed. Gunnel Engwall and Per Stam. Stockholm: Norsteds, 2011. 104.

———. *Svarta fanor*. 1907. In *Samlade Verk*, vol. 57, ed. Rune Helleday. Stockholm: Norstedts, 1995.

———. *Tjänstekvinnans son III–IV*. In *Samlade Verk*, vol. 21, ed. Hans Lindström. Stockholm: Norstedts, 1996.

“The Spoken Word Is All”—“Ordet det talade är allt”: Translating Strindberg for the International Stage

Anne-Charlotte Hanes Harvey

“Translation theory” and “Strindberg’s oeuvre” are both vast topics of ongoing and intense exploration. In this chapter I will limit my investigation to the convergence of two specific subfields—theory of translation for the theater on the one hand and Strindberg’s dramatic oeuvre on the other. I will discuss how theater translation theory applies to the practice of translating Strindberg’s dramas into English for production, how translating for specific productions has resulted in my development of *platform translation*—a theory-based practical approach to theater translation and dramaturgy—and how the specifics of Strindberg’s language may underscore, foster, even demand a certain approach to performance text.

I focus on the above-mentioned convergence—translating Strindberg for the stage—for three reasons: (1) the international scope of Strindberg’s audience, who globally, outside of Sweden, can access Strindberg’s works only in translation and who are most familiar with Strindberg as a dramatist, rather than a novelist, poet, or essayist; (2) the relative newness of theater translation theory as a field of study, with some areas of inquiry still terra incognita, intriguingly unexplored; and (3) the breadth of my own experience as a Strindberg translator, dramaturg, director, and performer in professional and academic contexts. Examples will be taken from plays I have translated, translated/dramaturged, or translated/dramaturged/directed, particularly *Miss Julie* (*Fröken Julie,* 1888).[1]

Clearly one cannot discuss translating Strindberg without acknowledging the unique characteristics of his language, specifically the language in his dramas, which has also been examined and written about at length.[2]

Yet nobody addresses the fact that translating Strindberg the dramatist is a different matter from translating Strindberg the novelist, poet, or essayist. *The People of Hemsö* the novel and *The People of Hemsö* the play (*Hemsöborna,* 1887 and 1889, respectively) have the same author, and to some extent the same language, but they present different challenges to the translator. Why and how do the translators' tasks differ? What characterizes a translation for the stage as compared with a translation for the page?

My task in this chapter is threefold: first, to contribute to a discourse that recognizes current theater translation theory, including neglected or contested areas; second, to describe Strindberg's dramatic language with the kind of specificity and aptness that is helpful to a translator; and third, to arrive at some guiding principles for translating Strindberg for production based on the preceding discussion and my own practical experience. The article (a) begins with a discussion of my assumptions about the nature of dramatic works written for stage production and how they inform my concept of platform translation, then (b) discusses the major challenges Strindberg's language poses for a translator, (c) proceeds to examples of these challenges from *Miss Julie,* and (d) concludes with a list of principles and recommendations for translating Strindberg for production.

Platform Translation and Two Assumptions on Translating for Theater Production

In proposing platform translation as the most fitting translation method for Strindberg's plays, I make two fundamental assumptions: plays are, on the whole, written to be performed, and the playwright's "voice" is important.[3] Both assumptions are general, not Strindberg-specific. Though seemingly simple and noncontroversial, when pursued to their logical conclusion, they do have ramifications which are both controversial and of central importance for my continued discussion and advocation of platform translation. I will therefore examine these assumptions and their significance for my definition of platform translation before going on to discuss the nature of Strindberg's language and the translation of his dramas.

Plays are written to be performed. There is a functional distinction between literature and drama which has wide implications for playwrights, translators, dramaturgs, theater practitioners, audiences, publishers, and the general public. For various reasons, some of them practical and economic, Western theater remains logocentric to the point of continuing to treat theater translation as the translation of words, while anyone creating a work of theater knows that theater translation is "the product, not of a linguistic, but rather a dramaturgical act" (Pavis 140). A play script is, like a composer's score—a comparison made already by Harley Granville-Barker in 1924—a blueprint or "commanding form" (Susanne Langer's term) for completion by other artists in performance. As Rafael Spregelburd so poetically puts it, "the theatrical text is barely a kernel, lacking apparent real life yet mysteriously containing it and capable of being seen to grow and flower on stage" (373). The work of art is not the words or notes on the page; the work of art is the "art symbol" (Langer's term) created by the actors or musicians guided—"commanded"—by the "form" or "kernel" set down by the playwright or composer. The flower, not the kernel, is the work of art. The interlingual translation of a play script is not a question of re-creating a finished work of literary art for a different culture, but of transmitting "commanding" impulses for the creation onstage of a finished work of theater art. (The fact that these impulses are almost always transmitted via written language is the source of persistent confusion, especially in view of the fact that plays are overwhelmingly published, marketed, and consumed as literature.)

A play is not a novel. It is in the nature of a written play to be incomplete, demanding completion in performance through the dozen other, nonverbal theatrical sign systems operating on stage.[4] Even when lavishly supplied with *Nebentext*—set and character descriptions, stage directions, and introductory essays à la G. B. Shaw—in relation to the full production onstage, the play text is still a skeleton, a blueprint, or "commanding form." Santa Cruz Shakespeare veteran Paul Whitworth describes his work as an actor: "The lines is all you got; you dive from it, go way under it and come up with all the rest and that informs what you then actually do with that text, how you say it" (research interview). This means that all the words in the script—*Haupttext* (dialogue) and *Nebentext*—work together to transmit to the theater practitioners the original world of the play, while the *Haupttext* is doing double duty, transmitting the original world of the play but also contributing to the new world created in the mise-en-scène by being part of the aural/verbal sign system that reaches the audience's ears in performance. Playwrights, like Strindberg, who want to be "heard" know this, and know what words to choose and why.

If plays are written to be performed, the words of the dialogue are written to be spoken and heard. But, as noted, before they can be spoken and heard, they must be read. Paul Whitworth refers to this as the double function of a play text. It must first serve to fully inform the theater practitioners, who at this point relate to the text as readers. After they have studied and absorbed the text and "translated" it into action and images for the stage, the words of the dialogue must live as spoken and heard. The double function of the play text obscures the fact that the primary function of dialogue is to be heard by an audience. That is why almost all discussion of play translations carried on in writing, in print—serious, informed discussion, comparing translations and their different solutions to particular problems—is beside the point. The absurdity of this situation is easily seen if a play script is likened to a music score. No one would dream of judging Handel's *Messiah* merely by reading about it, or declare one set of violin variations superior to another based solely on a comparison of their respective manuscripts.

It is true that some nineteenth-century playwrights successfully wrote for both page and stage. The plays by G. B. Shaw—famously prefaced and studded with stage directions aimed at a reader—as well as the plays by Strindberg and Ibsen were "prepared for the reader but written to be spoken" (Ewbank, "Translating Ibsen" 60). Their dramas do double duty superbly—in the original. But in translation, the translator had better know what creature he is producing: a scholarly edition, a director's platform script, an edition for a book club? All serve different purposes and require different approaches.[5] To repeat, plays are not novels, whatever they look like and however well they "read." The printed word is only a conduit: "the lines is all you got." The play is a commanding form that needs to be filled out by other sign systems on stage.

In translating for the stage, authorial voice (what the author says and how he says it) rather than authorial intent (what we think the author may have thought he wanted to say) does count, and is clearer in its original form—the words he himself wrote—than couched in any other language (i.e., translated). Therefore, a prospective director/producer of *Miss Julie,* presumably finding its "invariant core"—Susan Bassnett-McGuire's term for the immutable core of a drama in translation (26)—of value, wants to transmit his or her[6] staged vision of it to a theater audience and should have maximum access to the original. (If he, on the other hand, as often happens, is only interested in the play as a marketable classic, an excuse for sex on stage, or a showcase for the leading lady, the original "voice" is willfully ignored.)[7]

Yet as is well known, a series of disruptions and interventions occur in all translation, not only from language to language but also from culture to culture ("world" to "world"), and—in the case of translation of text for performance—from page to stage. Some of these "translations" and their concomitant disruptions are inevitable; others, though not avoidable, can be minimized. Inevitable—if you want to reach other than Swedish speakers—is the reductive linguistic one.[8] Likewise inevitable—if you want to reach a theater audience—is the additive one from page to stage, in which scenic signs complement and amplify the spoken word in the "basic transposition" from source text to target performance (Törnqvist, *Transposing Drama* 7–8) or "intersemiotic translation or *transmutation* . . . an interpretation of verbal signs by means of signs of nonverbal sign systems" (Jakobson 145). Whatever term is used, the move from page to stage is a potentially enriching one, which skillful playwrights count on for the full effect of the final work of art, their play in performance. Strindberg himself almost reluctantly admits that the playwright "vet i allmänhet vad han har skådespelaren att tacka för" ("usually knows what thanks he owes the actor") and that he has "sett roller som voro bättre och vackrare än mina original" ("seen characters better and more beautiful on stage than in my original [text]") (*Teater och Intima teatern* 15).

The "updating" or modernizing of plays, so popular today, is not an issue. (We have heard the arguments: make the play more "relevant," give the director a reputation for daring and creativity, limit the costume budget, save the leading actor from having to speak/move with period decorum. . . .) If the producer/director wants to produce a modern version or adaptation of the play, there is still a need for an interlinguistic translation by which the original can be accessed. If, after accessing the original fully, the director/company devises a new version or adaptation with a new script, so be it.[9] But there is no point is trying to coax an orchid out of a corn kernel.

Unless the director speaks the language of the original script, he reads the translated script like any other script: for plot, character, dramatic potential, and central images, envisioning the sign systems suggested, thinking of casting, audience reaction, technical challenges, marketing—all the things that may go through the head of the practiced director reading any script for potential production. He is judging the script's theatrical potential, not the quality of the translation or its relationship to the original. It is entirely possible that our hypothetical director reading translations of *Miss Julie* is most captivated by a translation that fails to transmit the author's voice fully; for example, one in which the translator has added explanations and clarifications galore, or made numerous cuts and transpositions. The unsuspecting director does not realize that there is anything added or missing. Either way, he does not have optimal access to the original when he makes his own cuts and changes. But if he likes the translation, is this a cause for concern? Yes—the author's voice is twice removed.

The ramifications of the two assumptions that began my argument—that plays are meant to be performed and that the author's voice matters—inform my definition of platform translation, the method of translation that I propose as most fitting for Strindberg's dramatic works. Platform translation—my term—differs from standard play translation in that it aims to transmit as much as possible of the original commanding form's options, possibilities, associations, overtones, potential, and "flavor" to the theater practitioners. Doors are opened to the original instead of closed. It is not up to the translator to make final choices, but rather to provide access, present options, and contextualize them. Final dialogue choices are made by the director and dramaturg, sometimes including the actors in the process.[10]

Platform translation can be used in conjunction with Patrice Pavis's theater translation model to enhance the transition from page to stage. Pavis's model—from the idea/impulse of the original artist (playwright) to his written text (script in language A), to the translator's text (script in language B) via the dramaturg's explication (research) to the director's reading (interpretation), the resultant scenic creation (mise-en-scène), and finally the receptive senses/minds of the target audience—implies at each step a certain discontinuity, disruption, or loss of communication (Pavis 136–59; and Harvey, "Translating Scandinavian Drama" 26). But this model also suggests how one can downplay the inevitable disruption in language-to-language translation. In fact, this disruption can serve to enrich the "basic transposition" from page to stage in all its aspects—the spoken word, the acting, and the mise-en-scène—by conflating steps in the latter process along with using platform translation.

The platform process highlights two implications of interest for theater translation theory. First, *Nebentext* and dialogue—*Haupttext*—may well warrant different translation approaches and strategies. There is a tendency among literary translators to ignore or downplay the original's *Nebentext*. It is treated cavalierly, cut, modified, "improved," or simply overlooked.[11] The tendency to neglect the *Nebentext* may reflect the non-theatrical background of many theater translators—they simply do not understand it—or they may feel it is not couched in language worthy of their effort and talent. Perhaps it is encouraged by the modern directorial practice of routinely cutting all stage directions from classic play texts before handing actors their scripts. Nobody seems to respect old stage directions. As verbal content constitutes at most 15 percent of the total communication on stage—the actual word spoken is always subverted by the more powerful subtext and the other sign systems—the translator has an obligation to both subtext and text. Since the *Nebentext* harbors commanding form for all theatrical sign systems other than the words spoken, it should be carefully transmitted. It guides us to the subtext. And since the *Nebentext* never reaches the audience, there is no reason why it cannot be lavishly explicated, footnoted, and discussed by the translator.

The *Haupttext,* the dialogue, on the other hand, cannot be explicated, footnoted, or elaborated. It must be reined in, delimited by the constraints of the original. There is good reason to speak of a commanding "form," as duration, meter, shape, and sound values of the original dialogue are of crucial significance and should be preserved, as far as possible, in the translated dialogue. (Substantive footnotes may of course be attached to the dialogue, but these are in the nature of additional *Nebentext* for the benefit of the actors. The content of such notes never reaches the audience directly. If the dialogue itself is to carry additional information, lines must be rewritten—a step not lightly taken.) In other words, there are two different aims for the translation: the *Nebentext* should be as full and rich as possible, the *Haupttext* should convey the form of the original.

A note here: the platform script is by definition aiming to retain the formal aspects of the original (punctuation, emphases, meter) but due to its double duty—fully explicating the *Nebentext* as well as offering choices for the *Haupttext* and commenting on the nature of the *Haupttext*—the length of the platform script will never be able to suggest the original's length.[12]

The second implication of the platform process concerns the impact of rehearsal on the translation of the dialogue. In platform translation, doors are closed not by the translator working alone before rehearsals begin but during the rehearsal period, and changes—well-motivated, actor-supported changes—can be made almost up to opening night. The fluid, shifting character of the dialogue demands and promotes continued probing of character, subtext, relationships, and power balances, as well as repeated consultation of both the original text and the platform text. In other words, the platform process differs from Pavis's linear path of intercultural transmission on which I originally modeled my description of the progression from playwright in language A to audience in language B. In reality, the process is anything but linear, continually looping back on itself in a complex and erratic way, resembling a "two steps forward—one step back" shuffle. The impact of this phase of rehearsals—*chaos is come again*—on the translation of a play from page to stage is rarely acknowledged, much less documented and studied.[13]

What actually happens in rehearsal definitely deserves more study and analysis. It is understandable that scholars have shunned this part of the process from page to stage: it implies access to the private sphere of the actors at work (and how many scholars are welcome to sit in on rehearsals?); it is an unpredictable, messy activity, often carried out by instinct or habit, certainly not according to any neatly laid out guidelines; it is difficult to describe, whatever theory and tools you make use of; and the results of such study may seem less than spectacular. (Wherein lies the significance of a deleted comma? a move to another chair? the change in the length of a pause? the shortening of a line from five words to three?)

Setting aside the old saw of *traduttori traditore,* what is a translator from language A to B—a chameleon? A shape-shifter? A person with "double horizons" (Delblanc 14)? Walter Benjamin provides the most enduring—because most enigmatic and most open to interpretation—fundamental discussion of the soul of translation.[14] Benjamin affirms the pre- or supra-linguistic nature of thought, the plane on which true translation takes place. Since "original" and "translation" are manifestations of the same core, "the unfathomable, the mysterious, the 'poetic' something" (70), "not as reproduction but as harmony" (79), they complement rather than duplicate each other. Their kinship denotes common origin, not similarity. They are so much akin that it is only the accident of earlier birth that sets the original apart from its translations. But, according to Benjamin, only works with that certain poetic core have translatability. Translation undertaken only to convey meaning is not translation. Benjamin disdains all mere "information" as untranslatable—a statement bound to irritate the casual reader, though Benjamin argues it elegantly on his own premises. Equally controversial or paradoxical is his claim that the purpose of translation is to express the central reciprocal relationship between languages, not to provide access for readers who do not understand language A. Surely translation can do both, and to perversely argue this point seems to unnecessarily muddy the whole discussion, at least when it comes to theater translation. For the purpose of theater translation is to provide the foundation for the "'poetic' something" of the original to be expressed in a new way, in language B and embedded in scenic signs.

However evocative and compelling Benjamin's vision of translation may be, it has one major flaw when it comes to translation for the stage: he rejects the significance of the recipient of the end product; a translation undertaken to serve the reader is merely "inaccurate transmission of an inessential content" (Benjamin 70). Very few theater practitioners in Western theater today can afford not to consider their intended/hoped-for/expected audience.[15] And in the theater, reception theory addresses the very core of the art-making process. Rather than ask whether a theater translation is "literal" or "free," whether a translation, version, or adaptation—terms more viable as legal distinctions in commercial theater than true genre descriptors—it would make more sense to inquire about the impact of the performed play on its audience, since that is "what it is all about." Because of Benjamin's disregard for the recipient of the end product, his translation model is not ideal for the translation of any plays. Rather, the platform translation method, which takes both the recipient and the author's voice into account, provides an approach to drama translation more suited to successfully producing a Strindberg play for an international audience.

Characteristics of Strindberg's Language

Strindberg's language is characterized by concreteness, even when dealing with mental or psychic processes; a wealth of metaphors of all kinds, private, conventional, and lexicalized (van den Broeck's categories); literary invention; and great naturalness and ease. It shares many features with spoken language. It is fluid and flexible. Scholars comment on his abrupt switching of styles, the contrast between laconisms, on one hand, and floods of precise, factual data, on the other; what Nils Svanberg calls "[denna] ryckiga, ständigt spårväxlande Strindbergsrytm" ("this fitful, continually track-switching rhythm of Strindberg's") (119). Michael Billington in *The Guardian* refers to it as "that peculiar Strindbergian mix of the material and the numinous" (Robinson, Aldrig längre än till Gravesend 119).

Beyond the acknowledgment of Strindberg's original writing style, it is also generally agreed that Strindberg's language is challenging to translate. Frederic Fleisher—with a nod to British translator Edward Fitzgerald's "a live sparrow is better than a stuffed eagle"—states "hans örnskri har förts vidare av sparvar" ("his eagle's cry has been transmitted by sparrows") (384). Who are these sparrows? With regard to Strindberg's dramas, three crucial characteristics of his language are all too often ignored or overlooked by his translators: tautness, innovation, and track-switching. Translators of Strindberg's dramas who elaborate on the dialogue to make it easy to grasp, who smooth over Strindberg's idiosyncrasies, and who impose a uniform style (single "track") on the whole, are "sparrows."

In order to see how the above observations about theater translation apply to Strindberg's drama, we must look at Strindberg's language.

Drawing on my experience as a dramaturg and translator of Strindberg, I shall focus on Strindberg's idiosyncratic language as it functions in his plays, and examine it from the point of view of the translator committed to transmitting a maximum of August Strindberg's voice to the director and *metteurs-en-scène*. The main question to keep in mind is this: which characteristics of his dramatic language must be especially noted in order to provide the most helpful, rich, and accessible (platform) translation? Four main language-based challenges make the translation of Strindberg's plays difficult: (1) the lengthening of a text when translating from Swedish into English; (2) his creative syntax and innovative use of the Swedish language; (3) his noted track-switching; and (4) the difficulty of retaining the impact of his sound and rhythm.

The tautness of Strindberg's language makes lengthening an ever-present and particular danger in translating it for the stage. In addition to the already naturally occurring lengthening between Swedish and English, many translators are tempted to elaborate. (I am not referring to substantive footnotes included for the benefit of the *metteurs-en-scène* but to material added in the dialogue itself.) An example from *Ett drömspel* (*A Dream Play,* 1901):

> Den där blåa Stormhatten där ute! Den har jag sett sen jag var barn . . . Är det samma en? . . . Jag minns i en prästgård, då jag var sju år . . . det sitter två duvor, blåa duvor under den där hatten . . . (*Ett drömspel* 23)

> . . . that blue flower out there—that monkshood. I remember it from the time I was a child. Can't be the same one, can it? . . . It was at the parsonage, I remember, the minister's house—the garden. I was seven years old. . . . Fold back the top petals—the pistil and stamen look like two doves. We used to do that as children. . . . (*A Dream Play,* Sprinchorn trans. 662)

Note the lengthening (77 vs. 49 syllables), the paraphrase, the elaboration, the deemphasis on the color, the unstressed position of the pronoun referring to the flower.

Some theater translators, trusting neither the author nor the translation's intended audience, insist on adding material, clarifying, and "improving" the original; some add material because they are tempted by the paucity of stage directions in the original to give in to their own directorial impulses.[16] Yet lengthening is deadly on stage and must be consciously resisted at every turn. "Aim to retain the original length" is a strong guiding principle. Retain, as far as possible, the original breath/

duration. Above all, be sensitive to whether the point of a particular utterance lies more in the "how," including the duration, than in the lexical load, the "what."

When it comes to Strindberg's innovative language and syntax, the translator's dilemma would seem to be whether to sacrifice the original's creative features or to risk being accused of writing poor English or being a poor translator. Again, the specter of the reader's script, the play printed for a reading public, raises its head and proposes to dictate the rules for "good" translation. The normalizing influence of an editor's red ink is familiar. We are taught what English should look like—on the printed page. But we also know that that is not how people speak, either in real life or on stage. Fortunately, the translator creating a platform script is creating something that is by definition "bad English," simply the commanding form for the actual lines eventually spoken by the actors. A play translation should be judged by how it functions on stage, not on how it looks in print.

Actually, the question is not whether the translation should be "good" English or "bad," it is whether Strindberg's language was "good"—standard—Swedish or not. And since it was not, neither should the language of his translation be. If someone argues, "But you don't say that in English!" the reply should be, "You don't say that in Swedish, either!" or "Nobody other than Strindberg says this in Swedish, either!" One Italian publisher goes so far against popular "wisdom" as to state, "A good translation is NOT recognized by its even flow, but by its unusual and peculiar turns of phrase—things you just don't say—which the translator has had the courage to translate and protect. Down to the smallest punctuation sign" (Delblanc 15). In fact, well aware both of his own originality and the tendency of translators to normalize, Strindberg asked his friend Leopold Littmanson to help him find somebody who could translate him "utan att hyfla kanterna af min styl [*sic*] som skola vara qvar" ("without shaving the edges off my style for they must remain") (*Brev* 10:112). Strindberg himself thus gives us a second guiding principle for translating his unique language, including that in his dramas. Considering the crucial contribution of every word to the theater script as commanding form, it follows that retaining the foreign riches, the unshaved "edges," is far preferable to domesticating the play and "making it flow."

Some of the edges to be preserved are not Strindberg's innovations, simply interlingual discrepancies. A case in point is the third-person address commonly used in Strindberg's day (in Stockholm as late as the 1950s, in some parts of Sweden still in use) to denote a certain deliberate distance—out of respect, disdain, lack of breeding or etiquette—between speaker and the person addressed. Functioning throughout Strindberg's oeuvre, prominently and centrally in *Miss Julie,* it is often brought up as a thorny issue, an unsolvable problem in translation. Though "impossible" in print, it has worked well on stage since I first tried it in 1988.[17]

Strindberg's innovative language is also marked by the fact that he changes tense mid-sentence and slides back and forth across grammatical borders with the greatest of ease: adjectives become nouns, nouns become adjectives or verbs, verbs become nouns or gerunds (Kinnander 51–57). Syntactically, his language is also characterized by inverted word order, asyndeton, and dependent clauses, creating a complex syntax that nevertheless results in a free and impulsive—though somewhat frenetic—style. The impression of heedless speed is heightened by the notable lack of adjectives and the wealth of verbs, especially the abundance of verbs pertaining to seeing and hearing. In his play dialogue he capitalizes on the hesitant, incomplete, yet urgent nature of normal discourse and makes frequent use of aposiopesis—breaking off in mid-sentence—as well as interruptions, pauses—within or between lines—and a wealth of exclamation points.[18] These originalities and innovations must be preserved in a Strindberg production translation, as they contain messages in code from playwright to theater practitioner. Strindberg's punctuation—and Ibsen's—are gold mines of subtextual information and, in addition, are easily retained in translation.

A third major challenge in translating Strindberg's dramas is the pervasive track-switching. Yet here the nature of theater translation is actually a natural fit for Strindberg's own language. The continual reprioritization advocated by Antoine Vitez in theater translation as well as mise-en-scène, "the art of making choices in the hierarchy of signs" (cited in Vitez 128), Strindberg makes use of already in his language. By closely observing Strindberg's track-switching—in other words, again paying attention to *how* he says something instead of *what* he says—you have expanded the guiding principle of "not shaving the edges" to encompass all the unusual characteristics of his language, including track-switching.

Thus the overriding principle for the translating brain is to transmit as much as possible of the commanding "form" in language A—length, sound values, rhythm, punctuation, level of formality, type of speech act, track-switching, oddity, innovation, irregularity, and so on—to language B. As Laurence Senelick sums up,

> Do not assume it is your job to correct or improve the author. . . . Preserve the peculiarities of a character's speech. . . . I am always bemused when reviewers who . . . have not read a play in the original commend a

> translation for sounding "smooth." The best playwrights . . . do not write smooth dialogue. . . . Trust the author's punctuation . . . [which serves to] score the dialogue. . . . Rhythm, rhyme, and meter should be preserved as much as possible. . . . When the playwright places an operative word at the beginning or end of a phrase, don't lose it in the middle of the sentence. . . .
>
> Where a phrase seems odd, out of place, or grotesque, try to ascertain if it is a quotation or cultural reference. (371–72)

For the translator there is a crucial difference between Vitez's continual "making choices in the hierarchy of signs" and making choices based on a specific directorial image or concept. In platform translation, the translator's first responsibility is to transmit as many of the choices as possible to the prospective director. It is not up to the translator to make choices, "direct" the play, close doors. It is especially detrimental to the process when the translator decides to edit or cut the text. Then doors are irrevocably closed.

> If the stage director . . . feels impelled to indulge in a little face lifting in order to enhance a foreign playwright's appearance in front of a domestic audience, we realize that no amount of plastic surgery can restore to truthful communication what the translator has committed to extinction by amputation, and it is precisely for the reason that his cuts are so final and irrevocable and rob the director of information which, if he had it, might conceivably influence his interpretation, that the translator's concern ought to be to preserve the original in its entirety in order to give the director more to go on. . . . Let not the translator, however well intentioned, cut away parts of the original, for no amount of cosmetic surgery can restore what has been removed by amputation. (Amble 268)

In other words, try to avoid lengthening, but above all do not cut or edit, and retain the form as much as possible. The platform translation must be inclusive and open, as it is the foundation for the definitive translation by director, translator/dramaturg, and perhaps actors. Then, paraphrasing Vitez, the theater practitioners are the ones to "make choices in the hierarchy of linguistic signs," while they, in the same process, "make choices in the hierarchy of scenic signs."

The above recommended principles for translating August Strindberg for production lead to the consideration of one final, crucial aspect of the text performed, namely its sound, the impact of the spoken word. Even when eloquent, using many words, Strindberg's language is characteristically concentrated. There is no chat, no mere conversation, no "straw in the mouth," as Sir Laurence Olivier called it (Meyer 71). Few if any lines are casual, leisurely, relaxed. The sound tends to be intense, with distinct rhythms and rhythmic emphases. This characteristic is often unnoticed or ignored by translators, but, if preserved, it is certainly noted by actors as it directly affects their speech on stage.

With the motivation that "jag som författaren bäst vet hur rolen menats! och pjesen" ("I as the author know best how the role/character was intended! and the play") (*Brev* 16:171), Strindberg advises his actors at the Intimate Theater—individually or as a company—in notes subsequently published in *Open Letters to the Intimate Theatre.* He addresses acting, role interpretation, tone and mood, but above all speech (diction) and voice production as crucial in reaching the audience.

His recurring fundamental argument is that the spoken word has priority. In a letter to Anna Flygare, February 3, 1908, he envisions acting with

> det talade ordet som hufvudsak; men inga sårande understrykningar som publiken finner förolämpande, om Ni nemligen talar så tydligt att hvarje ord höres. Detta kan endast ske, om Ni håller frasen bunden (legato) och icke staccato.
>
> Tag det bredt som en sångare, njut af att höra Er egen röst. . . . (*Brev* 16:174)

> the spoken word as the chief thing; but no insulting emphases, which the public finds offensive, that is if you speak clearly enough for every word to be heard. This can only happen if you keep the phrase together (legato) and not staccato.
>
> Take it expansively like a singer, enjoy hearing your own voice. . . . [19]

In a letter to August Falck, May 9, 1908, Strindberg argues for the word and against scenery:

> Med enkla dekorationer kommer huvudsaken fram: personen, rolen, talet, minen, åtbörden. Ofta är det bortkastad möda att dekorera om för en kort scen; åskådaren . . . har all möda att höra och uppfatta det talade ordet! "I begynnelsen var ordet!" Ja, ordet, det talade är allt. (*Brev* 16:304–5)

> With simple scenery the main thing is foregrounded: the actor, the character, speech, facial expression, gesture. It is often a wasted effort to change scenery for a brief scene; the spectator doesn't have time to take it all

> in, is fully occupied trying to hear and comprehend the spoken word! "In the beginning was the word!" Yes, the spoken word is all.

The spoken word is all—and yet he admits, "Jag har även sagt mina skådespelare: tumma gärna på repliken, om ni får den ligga bättre i munnen! Skarva, om ni vill, men laga det blir svar på tal" ("I have also said to my actors: you're welcome to fiddle with the line, if that makes it fit your tongue better! Splice, if you wish, but make sure you speak up clearly") (*Teater och Intima teatern* 115). This statement is not to be taken as proof that Strindberg did not care for his own words or was browbeaten by a troupe of young actors into making concessions. (Rewriting lines to accommodate actors is unnecessary with first-rate actors—based on her experience with prominent Strindberg productions in London, Inga-Stina Ewbank observes that "the greater the actor or actress, the less he or she questions the translation" ["Translating Ibsen" 56].) Rather, *Open Letters* suggests that Strindberg is so concerned that "the word, the spoken word" should reach his audience that he agrees to almost anything that would strengthen the connection between the actor's speech and the audience's ear. In this case he promotes the spoken word by allowing the rewording of a line, in other instances he modifies his scenic vision, sacrificing visual schemes to gain aural presence.[20] The point of the text in question is the subtext—the specific words spoken are less crucial.[21]

Rhythm was important to August Strindberg. He advises Manda Björling in *Miss Julie,* July 16, 1908: "Ni skulle . . . föredraga som vers, ty det finns en hemlig rytm i denna prosa, der hvarje ord gäller. Hennes berättelse för Jean . . . var bra, nyanserad, pauserad. . . ." ("You should . . . deliver it like poetry, for there is a concealed rhythm in this prose, where every word counts. The story she tells Jean . . . was well told, with vocal nuances and pauses. . . .") (Falck 175). The original Strindberg sound and rhythm are of course impossible to retain, but the formal qualities of the original must be recognized, not routinely dismissed or sacrificed to some ideal to lexical "faithfulness." Rhythm and sound hold an undeniable clue to "meaning," something clearly seen in the translation of poetry and, most clearly, lyrics set to music.

But for many translators the quality of the original sound appears to be irrelevant; for others, the sound is reluctantly set aside as impossible to retain. Birgitta Steene is one of the few scholars to consider the transfer of sound values. In her discussion of *The Pelican* (*Pelikanen,* 1907) she calls for a translation sensitive to specific vowel sounds as well as the duration of lines (Steene 56–57). In "Translating Scandinavian Drama—for Whom?" I discuss the rhythm/meter in fourteen different translations of the crucial line "Det är synd om människorna" in *A Dream Play*, calling for rhythm/meter analysis when comparing play translations (48–49).

That sound values, duration, and rhythm are extremely important in performance and should be prime considerations in translation is clearly borne out by opera director Göran Järvefelt. When he was invited to direct not an opera but a stage play, at the Adelaide festival in 1988 celebrating Australia's bicentennial, he chose Strindberg's *A Dream Play*. His cast was Australia's top actors. He describes the process:

> The difference between rehearsing spoken drama and music drama became clear to me: in an opera the rhythm, pauses, tempi, *et cetera*, are given and learnt [known by the performers] from the beginning. The work consists of finding the motivations behind the musical terms. You seek from the outside in. With a spoken play you go in the opposite direction. You seek from the inside out. From nothing [the printed commanding form] you slowly intuit and produce rhythms and pauses and create your own score. The text [in performance] becomes a symphony in which each note must be in tune. (65, my trans.)

Järvefelt describes the two different approaches, to spoken drama and music drama respectively, as clear opposites.[22] (There are of course genres combining the two: operetta, musical comedy, revues, and so on.) In reality, the distinction is less clear, the process more looping than linear. My point is that playwrights of spoken drama also craft commanding form for sound and do their best to indicate duration, pauses, volume, and so on with the narrow repertoire of tools available to them (*Nebentext*, punctuation, capitalization, type style, font, layout, meter, rhythm, rhyme, repetition, choice of sounds). Strindberg certainly does: he uses musical terms to describe/direct sound in his individual notes to the actors at the Intimate Theater and gives the general advice that "musiktermer borde skådespelaren hålla i minnet och ha till hands, ty de säga nästan allt" ("the actor ought to keep musical terms in mind and ready at hand, for they say almost everything") (*Teater och Intima teatern* 106). Strindberg scores his plays; his plays are scores.

The rhythm of a work results not only from stress patterns in words spoken, but also from the repetition of words, expressions, gestures, situations—a fact naturally expanded into other sign systems on stage, for example, by the identical placement onstage of two characters in different scenes, recurrence of certain scenic elements, repetition of sound and lighting effects, and so on. Any repetition that is an express feature of the original should be retained in translation, particularly repetition of spoken words. And yet, many translators proudly strive for verbal variety, rich vocabulary, and a wealth of synonyms.

Some repetitions are clearly significant. In *A Dream Play,* Indra's Daughter's recurring "Det är synd om människorna"—at first a response to a situation, over time a confirmation of fact and a summing up of a stance—acquires more weight with each repetition. Its translation may be thorny, but the significance of its repetition is not questioned—it sounds too "important" to be reworded with each recurrence.[23] Other less important-sounding repetitions are often killed by translators who have been taught that repeating words is poor English. They ignore the fact that the point may lie not in the lexical meaning but in the fact of repetition. Strindberg is clearly ringing variations on a theme when the root *smuts,* "dirt," "filth," recurs at key moments in *Miss Julie,* as *smutsiga, smuts, smutsig, smuts,* and *smutsig,* respectively. As Egil Törnqvist points out, the theme is lost when the translator uses different words: dirty, filth, dirt, mud, dirty (Edwin Björkman); filthy, filth, filth, mud, dirty (Elizabeth Sprigge) ("Translating Strindbergian Imagery for the Stage" 10–11).

We can study the various inventive ways in which Strindberg, the playwright, tried to "command" the impact of the spoken word on stage (idiosyncratic punctuation, the words and sounds chosen, rhythm, meter, duration, pauses, staccato, legato, repetition, theme and variations, and so on). We can produce additional evidence in his correspondence and other writings that the spoken word was at the core of his communication in the theater. But aside from his own instructions we have remarkably little description by reviewers and audience members of how his sound was or should be produced, what the impact was or should be, and how the structure and nature of his dialogue characterized or should characterize, through sound, the virtual human beings created onstage.

Perhaps it is understandable that little has been written on this subject—nuances of spoken Swedish—which immediately excludes all non-Swedish-speaking scholars and theater practitioners from the investigation. Others, who know spoken Swedish well—actors, singers, voice coaches and teachers, directors, conductors, composers, acousticians, radio and TV announcers, therapists, pedagogues, speech communication and remedial speech teachers—are not necessarily interested in studying, analyzing, and reporting on how Strindberg's language sounds. And Swedish Strindberg scholars appear to have other targets than the sound of Strindberg's language.[24]

One person who was interested, and who also recorded his impressions of Strindberg's language as spoken, was Ture Rangström, the early-twentieth-century composer of the music for *Kronbruden* (1915) and of a symphony based on Strindberg's life.[25] In imagery worthy of Strindberg himself he describes the musical nature of Strindberg's language, including

> dess tonfall av urtid och nutid i snabb och kärv förening, där gick det inte att musicera med den blonda svenska romansens blyga tonfall, knappast heller med folkvisan, ty Strindberg talade granitspråk och blandade granbarr i sin vers, redan det var uppfriskande och svårlöst som problem. . . . Det var lyrik för karlfolk, musik för salongen kunde det aldrig bli. (Hellqvist n.p.)[26]

> its sounds of ancient times and the present in rapid and stringent union, there it would not do to make music with the shy sounds of blonde Swedish romance, hardly even with folk song, for Strindberg spoke granite and mixed pine needles in his rhymes; that in itself was refreshing and problematic. . . . It was poetry for real men, music for the [feminine] salon it could never be.

"Strindberg spoke granite"—a metaphor that says more than many linguistic analyses, evoking Strindberg's choice of words as well as their sound and solidity.

An equally eloquent evocation of the intended impact of Strindberg's language in performance—on the actor as well as the audience—is Göran Järvefelt's, speaking of directing *A Dream Play:*

> To begin with the actors were alienated by Strindberg's directness. They were more used to Ibsen. . . . Strindberg is . . . spontaneous and irrational. In him there is no polite conversation and no hidden meaning. His lines must be spat out. They must be vomited up! He must be acted with stomach and guts! (65)

The resultant advice to the translator? The translated words should invoke "granite" and allow "vomiting"! The commanding form clearly cannot sound like chitchat or Olivier's "straw in the mouth."

In conclusion, the Strindberg translator is responsible for recognizing and retaining tautness, signifiers of sound values (duration, musical terms, punctuation, spelling, rhythm, meter, pattern), unshaved edges, and track-switching—all characteristic features of Strindberg's language. This is in addition to what is assumed, namely that he will transmit the work's lexical content, be thoroughly familiar with the world of the play as well as the world of the projected audience, and thus be able to truly bridge the gap between them if necessary.

The Example of *Miss Julie*

A case in point from *Miss Julie:* to gain Julie's sympathy, and perhaps to impress her with his inborn yearning for beauty, Jean tells of his ill-fated childhood fascination with the Count's estate ("the Garden of Eden") and its wonders. He describes how, curious about the estate's fancy *utedass* (outhouse)—"the Turkish pavilion"—he once dared to enter but was accidentally trapped inside by someone approaching, and ended up avoiding discovery by dropping down through the hole onto the excrement below,[27] crawling out and running off through the garden and across the fields.

The passage in question contains no contested, ambiguous, or untranslatable words. The difficulty lies in the cultural associations and images conjured by the words, especially the image of little Johan escaping through the privy hole.[28] The point of the image is the utter degradation suffered. I will look specifically at how different translations recognize that Jean is relating the incident in order to have an impact on Julie, as Strindberg's stage directions make clear.

> JEAN: . . . En gång kom jag in i lustgården med min mor för att rensa löksängarne. Bredvid trägårdslanden stod en turkisk paviljong i skuggan av jasminer och överväxt med kaprifolium. Jag visste inte vad den kunde brukas till, men jag hade aldrig sett en så vacker byggnad. Folk gick där in och kom ut igen, och en dag stod dörren lämnad öppen. Jag smög dit och såg väggarne klädda med tavlor av kungar och kejsare, och det var röda gardiner för fönstren med fransar på—nu förstår ni vad jag menar. Jag—[*bryter en syrenblomma och håller under näsan på Fröken*]—jag hade aldrig varitinne i slottet, aldrig sett annat än kyrkan—men det här var vackrare; och hur mina tankar lupo, så gingo de alltid tillbaka—dit. Och så småningom uppstod en längtan att en gång få erfara hela behaget av—*enfin,* jag smög därin, såg och beundrade. Men då kommer det någon! Det fanns bara en utgång för herrskapsfolk, men för mig fanns det en till, och jag hade inte annat än att välja den!
>
> FRÖKEN: [*som tagit syrenen, låter den falla på bordet.*]
>
> (*Fröken Julie* 140–41)

> JEAN: . . . Once I came into the Garden [of Eden] with my mother to weed the onion beds. Next to the vegetable garden was a Turkish pavilion in the shadow of jasmines and overgrown with honeysuckle. I didn't know what it might be used for, but I had never seen such a beautiful building. People went into it and came out again, and one day the door was

> left open. I snuck in and saw the walls covered with pictures of kings and emperors, and there were red curtains in the windows with fringe and—now you understand what I mean: I—
>
> [*Breaks off a lilac cluster and holds it under* MISS JULIE*'s nose.*]
>
> I had never been inside the manor, never seen anything other than our church—but this was more beautiful; and wherever my thoughts would roam, they would always come back—there. And by and by I had such a longing to once experience the whole pleasure of—*enfin,* I snuck in, saw, and admired. But then someone is coming! There was only one way out for finer folk, but for me there was yet another one, and I had no choice but to take it!
>
> [MISS JULIE, *who has taken the lilac from* JEAN, *drops it on the table.*]
>
> (Harvey, *Miss Julie* translation 19)

To underscore the first part of his story and mark a kind of rest—a hesitation, a moment to regroup—in his storytelling, Jean breaks off a cluster from the lilacs Kristin has stuck in a large Japanese spice jar on one end of the kitchen table and holds it under Julie's nose. He may be softening the impact, deodorizing the image, as it were, or simply flirting (lilacs = aphrodisiac). This is a significant stage direction. (Modern directorial practice of erasing all original *Nebentext* certainly shortchanges the actors in *Miss Julie.*)

We don't know exactly when the lilac is transferred from Jean to Julie—it could be anywhere before the stage direction indicates that she drops it—and we don't know whether Jean offers it and she accepts it, or she takes it from him (perhaps to cover up her embarrassment). If I were to direct the scene, I would have Jean offer it, soothingly setting the scene, creating the image by the choice of words ("vackrare," "more beautiful," or "längtan," "longing"), maybe by a long caressing vowel sound ([i:] in "dit," "there," or [ɔ:] in "småningom," "by and by"), or—depending on how much pleasure Jean takes in speaking French—the very word "*enfin,*" "in conclusion, to sum up." Julie would accept the flower as a sign that she accepts the image he is painting and has understood what building he is talking about.

Then he continues the story: impossible dream! bold action! fear, drama, trapped! the exit for better folk—the door—blocked! what to do? But a second exit—the privy hole—possible for the boy! To add to the urgency, Jean switches tense from the imperfect to the historic present:

> JEAN: . . . Och så småningom uppstod en längtan att en gång få erfara hela behaget av—*enfin,* jag **smög** därin, **såg** och **beundrade**. Men då **kommer**

någon! Det **fanns** bara en utgång för herrskapet, men för mig fanns det en till, och jag hade inte annat än att välja den! (140) [boldface added]

Miss Julie has been carried along, sees the picture—and drops the lilac.

Jean has just told how he lowered himself down the privy hole. He has managed to affect Julie. She is not disgusted by Jean, rather (according to plan) moved by his misfortune. But the story is clearly not finished yet. Jean goes on to relate how he ran off, saw her—now reduced to "a pink dress and a pair of white stockings"—on the rose terrace (where else?). He, himself filthy and smelly, lay down under some weeds on the dank foul-smelling earth and reflected on the fact that a thief could join Christ in Heaven while a laborer's child could not get into the castle park to play with the Count's daughter. Jean's conclusion to the story has the desired effect: Julie is pulled firmly into the sphere of maudlin sympathy, evidenced by the stage direction ("elegiskt," "in an elegiac tone," or "elegiacally") before her verbal response:

FRÖKEN [*elegiskt*]: Tror ni alla fattiga barn haft samma tankar som ni i detta fall? (141)

MISS JULIE [*in an elegiac tone, sentimentally*]: Do you think all poor children have had the same thoughts as you in this case? (Harvey 20)

Julie's response recharges his story:

JEAN [*först tvekande, sedan övertygande*]: Om *alla* fattiga—ja—naturligtvis! Naturligtvis!

FRÖKEN: Det måtte vara en gränslös olycka att vara fattig!

JEAN [*med djup smärta, starkt chargerat*]: Åh, fröken Julie! Åh!—En hund kan få ligga i grevinnans soffa, en häst kan bli smekt på nosen av en frökenhand, men en dräng. . . . (141)

JEAN [*hesitating at first, then with conviction*]: If *all* poor—yes—of course! Of course!

MISS JULIE: It must be an enormous misfortune to be poor!

JEAN [*with deep pain, quite exaggerated*]: Oh, Miss Julie! Oh!—A dog may lie on the Countess' sofa, a horse can be patted on the nose by a young lady, but a hired hand— (Harvey 20)

Jean then goes on to tell how he went to church to get a glimpse of Julie, realized the unbridgeable gap between them and tried to commit suicide by sleeping on a bed of elderberry blossoms in an oats bin—an event he later dismisses as "bara prat," "made up," inspired by a newspaper notice of a chimney sweep in a wood bin with lilacs. Miss Julie is surprised and impressed:

> FRÖKEN: Ni berättar charmant, vet ni. Har ni gått i skola? (142)

> MISS JULIE: You are a charming storyteller. Have you gone to school? (Harvey 20)

Jean is not giving information, he is telling a story to invoke Julie's sympathy by sentimentalizing his own background. As he is telling the story, he is watching her carefully to judge the impact he is having, weaving his tale only long enough to achieve his end. His French "*enfin!*" momentarily interrupts the fictional flow—he needs say no more in that particular direction.

But *enfin* (French = deodorized) here also has another function, which is usually overlooked even in Swedish productions. In the line "Och så småningom uppstod en längtan att få erfara hela behaget av—*enfin. . . .*" ("And by and by I had such a longing to once experience the whole pleasure of—*enfin. . . .*"), Jean stops himself and lets the single refined "*enfin*" replace some crude words left unspoken but understood, something like *hela behaget av att få skita som fint folk,* "the whole pleasure of being allowed to shit like gentry," or *skita vackert,* "shit beautifully." In other words, the boy would have been about to use the privy when he was surprised, which adds to the adrenaline of the trap. Julie understands from the very beginning what building Jean is talking about, and he makes doubly sure she is following his narrative. But Little Johan's fascination with the pavilion, even his desire to use it, produces at most amused condescension in Miss Julie. It is not until the graphic image of the trapped boy about to use the privy jumping down onto a pile of excrement that she really reacts—signified by the dropping of the lilac branch—with revulsion.

Now comes the question: if the point of Jean's story is manipulation of Julie's feelings leading up to revulsion, pity, and sentimental sympathy for "the poor"—what must the translation do? First, the translation must retain Jean's manipulation—which Strindberg heightens by Jean alternating between the imperfect and the historic present.

Yet not one of thirteen published translators of *Fröken Julie* observes this tense change,[29] although nothing prevents the use of the historic present also in English, particularly as spoken by an actor:

> JEAN: . . . By and by a longing was born to once experience the whole pleasure of—*enfin,* I **snuck** in, **saw**, and **admired**. But then someone**'s coming**! There **was** only one way out for the gentry, but for me there was one more, and I had no choice but to take it![30]

Second, the translation must make the audience fully understand the image Jean paints of the "pavilion" and how the boy escapes. To a Swede, the image of the fancy outhouse, on the grounds of an estate before the advent of indoor plumbing, is enough to conjure its layout and function. A non-Swedish audience, on the other hand, does not necessarily interpret velvet curtains and portraits of kings and emperors as signifying "outhouse."[31] I once taught *Miss Julie* in California to a large general education class of two hundred undergraduates. Their anthologized translation of the play explained nothing. When, as an experiment, I asked them what the Turkish pavilion was, only two of them had understood its function—both, interestingly, foreign students. What to do to make a non-Swedish audience able to follow Jean's story along with Julie and understand both the depth of the boy's degradation and Julie's reaction?

Strindberg expected his audience to visualize the privy without difficulty, just as he expected them to understand Kristin's threat to "move come October 24" and the magic of "sleeping on nine midsummer flowers." But a translation into another culture and age is "an active reconstitution of the foreign text, mediated by the irreducible linguistic, discursive and ideological differences in the target-language culture" (Venuti 10) for another audience entirely.[32] Here the translator has two choices: either add a footnote that informs the reader as well as the theater practitioner and trust that the actors can convey—through their understanding of the situation and their acting—what the boy Johan did; or add words to the dialogue that inform the audience directly.

The fact that "active reconstitution" is aided by explanations is consistently proven by Inga-Stina Ewbank's exemplary footnotes, which are "primarily aimed at the directors but may also help readers" ("Introduction" 9). A platform translation—that fluid script between original and translated performance text which demands "active reconstitution"—by definition incorporates footnote-like comments on the original, but can also be annotated with substantive footnotes. But in exceptional cases—switching tracks à la Vitez—the translator may have to prioritize verbal communication of a pivotal image and add a word or two to the dialogue.

Either way, in footnote or dialogue, the word(s) used to describe the function of the building is crucial. It cannot be "bathroom," "toilet," "W.C.," or "lavatory" (Meyer), since no water is involved and the boy jumps through the hole down onto the excrement. Better is "latrine or earth toilet" (Robinson, note), though the first term may evoke military camps and the second is foreign to an American ear. Far preferable is Sprinchorn's "privy" (note, 200; dialogue, 234) or simply "outhouse."

Of the above-mentioned eleven published translations of *Fröken Julie*, only two (Robinson, Sprinchorn) add a note to enlighten the reader/director. (Ewbank never translated *Fröken Julie*.) Though directors may in rehearsal add an explanatory couple of words to a line spoken onstage by an actor, only two translators (Sprinchorn, Martinus) have taken the step to add an explanation to Jean's line in print:

> —nu förstår ni vad jag menar. Jag—*(bryter en syrenblomma och håller under näsan på Fröken)*—jag hade aldrig varit inne i slottet . . . (*Fröken Julie* 140)

> Recognize it? **Yes, the count's private privy.** . . . I—*(He breaks off a lilac and holds it under Miss Julie's nose.)* I had never been inside a castle . . . (Sprinchorn 234)[33]

> you know what I mean . . . **yes, the privy**—I . . . *(Breaks off a twig of lilac and holds it under LADY JULIE's nose.)* I'd never been inside the manor . . . (Martinus 115)

The last two productions of *Miss Julie* I worked on as translator and dramaturg had the option of added words,[34] indicated by an asterisk in the script and the footnote "Words in bracket inserted for clarity in production, if desired." (Both directors included the addition.)

> —now you understand what I mean [: yes, the outhouse*]. I—*(Breaks off a lilac cluster and holds it under* MISS JULIE's *nose.)* I had never been inside the manor . . .
> (Harvey 19)

Unless the translator and dramaturg is certain that the theater practitioners for whom the translation is intended will understand the meaning of the Turkish pavilion, he had better err on the side of being informative. The director is then the one to decide whether to transmit the original's words or their impact.

A final word about this passage. Strindberg's punctuation is indeed a treasure trove of information. Take, for example, the period in the quote above at the end of the words "—nu förstår ni vad jag menar."

Jean is stating what he has just observed—namely, that Julie has somehow shown that she fully understands the place he is talking about. (The description—portraits of kings and emperors and red curtains with fringe—unmistakably identifies the place to her.) The period caps Jean's setting up of the story with the subtext: "You know the place—now I can go on to what happened there. . . ." If, with Sprinchorn and Martinus, you replace Strindberg's period with a question mark or *points suspensifs,* you add a sardonic twist by adding a teasing or testing subtext to Jean's storytelling. But Jean is here mock sincere, appealing to Julie's sentiment for the young boy, and cannot afford to take any detours into reactions—personal or shared—to the idea of a privy. It is not the outhouse that is disgusting—a part of everyday life for practically everyone in Sweden in 1888—it is the victimization of the laborer's boy and the pointlessness of his striving for social equality.

Principles and Recommendations for Translating Strindberg

Based on my experience as Strindberg translator, dramaturg, and director, as well as the fundamental assumptions that plays are written to be performed and that the playwright's voice is important, I advocate the platform translation as the most fitting method for translating Strindberg's dramas for production. What is at stake for an international audience—which can only know Strindberg in translation—is Strindberg's sound and rhythm, as well as the form of the original version of the play. The platform translation method aims as far as possible to retain these elements of the original plays. In conclusion, a list of principles and recommendations for translating Strindberg for production and the tasks of a Strindberg translator/dramaturg might read as follows:

1) Advocate a new translation for each new production.
2) Be thoroughly sensitized to Strindberg's personal and linguistic idiosyncrasies, "the edges"!
3) Be thoroughly versed in the world of Strindberg's plays, recognizing traditions and modernity, social capital and cultural markers of power relationships (Sweden's four estates; cotters [*statare*] vs. landowners; servants vs. masters).
4) Minimize interventions between original text and final recipients (audience) by combining the functions of translator and dramaturg and working in close collaboration with the director; *or* combining all three functions (translator, dramaturg, and director).

5) Maximally transmit the original by providing the theater practitioners with a platform script translation, especially sensitive to and clearly identifying:
   a. the track-switching taking place in the original language, yet leaving all choice-making regarding the staging—including the final decisions regarding words spoken on stage—to the director (possibly with the help of the actors)
   b. duration and tautness
   c. the sound values—test the original and the translation by reading both aloud
   d. the *Nebentext*
   e. anything that needs glossing/explanation by providing additional notes (footnotes)
   f. the original punctuation and layout and, as far as possible, preserving them
   g. the original's rhythm, meter, and rhyme schemes and, as far as possible, preserving them
6) Serve in the rehearsal process as the director's auxiliary brain, and assist (through further verbal explication of the original) in making the final choices of words to be spoken onstage.
7) Serve the production and the play in performance in the various tasks usually assigned to production dramaturgs: write program notes, edit the program, arrange lobby displays, write publicity releases, conduct talk-backs and actor's forums, and so on, that is, facilitate contact between the production (and the theater company) and its audience.

The translator of Strindberg's plays must in other words be thoroughly familiar with the world of Strindberg, his times, and his language, but equally with the target language and culture and—ideally—the theater practitioners and audience for whom the translation is being done.

If he in addition has the skills of a dramaturg, the persistence of a terrier, the patience of Job, the openness of a collaborator, love of "psychic pay," and invisibility, you have a translator who might be able to evoke more of the eagle than a sparrow.

Notes

1. I have translated ten Strindberg plays, collaborated on the translations of six, dramaturged eight, and dramaturged/directed seven. For example, my *Miss Julie* credits include translator/dramaturg/director, San Diego State University 1988; translator/dramaturg, Stone Soup Theatre, San Diego 2008, and North Coast Repertory Theatre, Solana Beach 2010.

2. For comprehensive overviews of scholarly works about Strindberg's language, see Egil Törnqvist, *Det talade ordet: Om Strindbergs dramadialog* (2001) and my "Problems in Translating Strindberg's *Kronbruden* for Production" (1973).

3. Excepting "closet dramas" never intended for the stage (Seneca) and scripts written only as documents of a particular performance, most works in dialogue form—"plays"—are written to be embodied and performed. Academic/pedagogical discourse in dialogue form (Plato, Hrosvitha, Boleslavsky) may document actual rhetoric, or simply present information in an emotionally heightened, persuasive way.

4. Semiotician Tadeusz Kowzan identifies thirteen semiotic categories onstage in all, including speech (73). Included are lights, sound, sets, properties, costumes, makeup, movement, gesture, proximity, voice, and so on. (The one category Kowzan omits is progression of scenic images, that is, the significance of a progression of sets as, for example, in *Ghost Sonata,* which moves from an expansive exterior into gradually smaller interiors.)

5. For a fuller discussion of this point, see my paper in *Tijdschrift.*

6. In the following, the director, the translator, the dramaturg will for simplicity's sake all be referred to as "he."

7. One example of such a use is the Canadian Native American adaptation *Miss Julie: Sheh'mah* by Tara Beagan. The relationship of master to servant is replaced by a relationship of white colonials (Julie and her British father) to Native American tribal members ("Jonny" and "Christie Ann"). The sex is primary and graphic, ingratiatingly framed onstage like a shot in a pornographic movie. Jonny and Christie Ann speak tribal languages (Shuswap and Thompson River Salish respectively) with each other, emphasizing their mutual bond and weakening Jonny's striving to emulate his masters. The play pivots around Christie Ann's resentment about the way she was treated on the "rez," while we understand little about Julie's life. In addition to full intercourse on stage—always a staging challenge—the play ends with an impossible feat: Julie slashes her wrists and bleeds to death in a washbasin facing front center stage.

8. Discussions of literary translation focus almost without exception on the translator's woes: the problems of translating from language A to B, the obstacles, the sacrifices, the difficulties, the inevitable losses. *Traduttori traditore*—the translator is by definition a traitor. Very few mention, much less analyze, the joys, the unexpected gains in translating from A to B. Literary translators in the United States today are living testimony to the importance of this mental activity as reward ("psychic pay") for their labors. As Strindberg himself put it, "det knastrar i hjernan när det rätta ordet ska födas på det främmande språket, men denna ansträngning ger full vision af det upplefvade" ("the brain crackles when the right word is about to be born in the foreign language, but this effort produces a vivid image of the experience [portrayed]") (letter to Axel Lundegård, January 28, 1888, *Brev* 6:389).

9. My argument is not with updating or modernizing a play, or with versions or adaptations perse, but with high-handed superficial "takes" on the

original which—for lack of time, expertise, or directorial perspective—do not fully access the original they purport to represent, yet ride on the coattails of the original's reputation and name recognition. One example of such a "take" is the above referenced Canadian Native American adaptation *Miss Julie: Sheh'mah* by Tara Beagan.

10. The first play for which I provided a platform translation was *Hedda Gabler*. This platform has subsequently been used by six different directors and productions, among them South Coast Repertory, Costa Mesa; Annette Bening's Hedda at the Geffen Playhouse, Los Angeles; Kate Burton's Hedda and Mary Louise Parker's Hedda, both on Broadway. I have also done platform translations of *Dance of Death I, Ghosts, Miss Julie, The Stronger,* and parts of *A Doll's House*. To my knowledge, only three other translators have created something like my "platform translation": May-Brit Akerholt in Australia and, in Great Britain, Janet Garton and the late Inga-Stina Ewbank. Working on *A Doll's House* at Watford Palace Theatre in 1987, Garton produced what she terms a "director's script," a "translation full of alternative renderings, notes and explanations, and which I spent a couple of days going through . . . explaining the connotations and the background" (97). Ewbank worked with Peter Hall on several Strindberg productions, for which she created what she called a "base script." Translating the Chamber Plays, her aim was "to be as faithful as possible to Strindberg, that is to try to preserve a sense of his style and use of language; not to explain or clarify his sometimes apparently irrational associations and incoherent sentence structures and dialogue patterns. Where explanations seemed necessary, they have been placed in the notes, which were primarily aimed at the directors but may also help readers" (Ewbank, "Introduction" 8–9).

11. Not paying attention to Strindberg's praxis or specificity in indicating directions onstage leads to confusion. Sprinchorn's incorrect use of the term "downstage right" (739) reverses part of the opening set description in *Ghost Sonata;* Sprigge simplifies and Paulson reverses the kitchen floor plan in *Miss Julie*.

12. It would today be possible to construct a platform script using hypertext for all *Nebentext* as well as for all commentary on the *Haupttext*. This would slim the platform text down. But the platform will still not even approach the slimness of the original until all choices have been made and the final performance *Haupttext* has been arrived at—at which point the text is no longer a platform.

13. For one notable exception, see Kristine Cala's description of the impact of looping in the bilingual rehearsal process preparing the translated text *Pluie Oblique* for production in Nantes, France, in January–February 1993, published in *About Performance: Translation and Performance* in 1995.

14. Benjamin's seminal preface "The Task of the Translator" (written in 1923) has done for translation what Antonin Artaud's *Théâtre et son double* (1938) has done for theater: provided a statement of such visionary power and lack of concrete particulars that each successive generation embraces it as a touchstone and beacon.

15. Perhaps Jerszy Grotowski's Polish Laboratory Theater came close to pure theater disinterested in how it was received.

16. Evert Sprinchorn's translations of Strindberg's plays run approximately 40 percent longer than the originals. Michael Meyer does not lengthen the plays as much; on the other hand, he edits, rewrites, changes names of characters, and so on.

17. A program note explained: "Since this is a translation for production, not for publication, the director has made the interesting experiment to retain this third person address—Kristin, for example, never addresses Jean as "you," always as "Jean" or "he"—which, though it looks impossible on the printed page, functions on stage" (Harvey, translator's note 3).

18. See Göran Lindström, "Dialog och bildspråk" 170–71. The chamber play *Pelikanen* (*The Pelican,* 1907) has no less than 430 exclamation points. The full-length *Kronbruden* (*The Crown Bride,* 1901) has over 900 exclamation points and some 300 question marks but only a little more than 100 periods. *Fröken Julie* (*Miss Julie,* 1888) has 710 exclamation points. (Compare Sprinchorn's *Miss Julie,* which has 318.)

19. Unless otherwise noted, all translations are my own.

20. He reluctantly gives up his pet scheme of double prosceniums (in *To Damascus* at the Royal Dramatic Theatre, Stockholm) because voices would be lost behind them; he favors the Perfall-inspired shallow "Shakespeare stage" because it helps project actors' voices.

21. Note that the letter in which Strindberg gives what appears to be carte blanche to change his words to make a line more speakable was directed to Manda Björling playing the role of Miss Julie. I doubt he would have allowed the same treatment of one of his lyrical passages, for example, the "Song of the Waves" in *A Dream Play.*

22. In a sense, Järvefelt unwittingly describes the interlinguistic translation process: the opera score is the original work, in which the form is laid down, the motivations found behind the music are Bassnett-McGuire's "invariant core," the printed stage play is like a translation, another manifestation of the "invariant core," which as commanding form guides the bringing forth of all sound, the whole "symphony."

23. Yet Strindberg used three variations of this phrase in *Rêverie,* his own translation into French of *Ett drömspel* (Engwall 45).

24. Törnqvist's valuable *Det talade ordet* acknowledges the difference between drama text to be read and to be spoken, but does not specifically address the sound values of the spoken text.

25. *August Strindberg In Memoriam* (1914).

26. Quoted in Per-Anders Hellqvist, "Lidholms långa väg till tonsättning av Strindberg," *Svenska Dagbladet,* November 12, 1998.

27. The privies of large estates often had multiple holes within the same structure. Although the famous eighteenth-century Ekstedt manor in Värmland has a multi-holed privy decorated with a charming painting of the entire family sitting there together, the practice of having several holes was actually dictated by a rotating schedule of on-site composting. One-hole outhouses generally

require a container that can be carried away and emptied. Clearly the Turkish pavilion in *Miss Julie* did not have such a container fitted under the hole—Jean would have been trapped in it—so was presumably a multi-holed privy.

28. "Johan" or "Johannes" would have been Jean's Christian name, before he adopted or was given the French form of the name, Jean. Either form links with Midsummer, the day of St. John the Baptist, the time of the action.

29. There are more; the ones referred to here are (British) Sprigge, Meyer, Martinus, Watts, McLeish, Robinson, Molton, and (American) Oland, Paulson, Sprinchorn, Carlson, Johnson, and Southerington.

30. The choice of words describing his exit is also crucial. McLeish manages to suggest the boy did not know the layout of a privy and had to search for the hole through which to exit: "For fine folk there was only one way in or out. But I found another, and I did use it!" (16)

31. No French audience member or reader would associate pictures of kings and emperors with an outhouse, a point made by Suzanne Jenner in "Fröken Julie i fransk översättning—ett drama i förvandling" (55–56). French translators have translated the words, not the play.

32. Even a Swedish audience today needs "active reconstitution"—the new national edition of *Fröken Julie* has 113 explanatory notes, including 61 substantive ones (*Fröken Julie* 344–49).

33. Sprinchorn goes on to add to the already clear image—and the length of the dialogue—by elaborating on the exit available to the boy: "But for me there was one more—a lower one" (234).

34. Stone Soup Theatre, San Diego, 2007; Stone Soup and North Coast Repertory Theatre, Solana Beach, Calif., 2010.

Works Cited

Amble, Kjell. "The Spirit of Ibsen: Problems of English Translation in Three of His Plays." Ph.D. diss., Northwestern University, 1964.

Bassnett-McGuire, Susan. *Translation Studies.* London: Routledge, 2002.

Benjamin, Walter. "The Task of the Translator" (1923). In *Illuminations,* ed. Hannah Arendt, trans. Harry Zohn. New York: Harcourt, Brace and World, 1968. 69–82.

Broeck, Raymond van den. "The Limits of Translatability Exemplified by Metaphor Translation." *Poetics Today* 2, no. 4 (1981): 73–87.

Cala, Kristine. "*Pluie Oblique:* A Case Study." In *About Performance: Translation and Performance,* ed. Tim Fitzpatrick. Vol. 1 (1995): 99–108.

Delblanc, Aimée. "Att förstå är att översätta." *Sverigekontakt* 95, no. 4 (2008): 14–15.

Engwall, Gunnel. "'Det knastrar i hjärnan': Strindberg som sin egen franske översättare." In *August Strindberg och hans översättare,* ed. Björn Meidal and Nils Åke Nilsson. Stockholm: Kungl. Vitterhets Historie och Antikvitets Akademien, 1995. 35–51.

Ewbank, Inga-Stina. Introduction to *Three Chamber Plays by August Strindberg,* by August Strindberg. Trans. Inga-Stina Ewbank. Leeds: Alumnus Playtexts in Performance, 1997. 5–9.

———. "Translating Ibsen for the English Stage." *Tijdschrift voor Skandinavistiek* 19, no. 1 (1998): 51–74.

Falck, August. *Fem år med Strindberg*. Stockholm: Wahlström & Widstrand, 1935.

Fleisher, Frederic. "Den misshandlade Strindberg." *Bonniers Litterära Magasin* 31 (1962): 384.

Garton, Janet. "Translating Ibsen—From Page to Page—to Stage?" In *Drama Translation and Theatre Practise,* ed. Sabine Coelsch-Foisner and Holger Klein. Oxford: Peter Lang, 2004. 89–91.

Granville-Barker, Harley. "On Translating Plays." In *Transactions of the Royal Society of Literature: Essays by Divers Hands* 5. London: H. Mulford, Oxford University Press, 1925.

Harvey, Anne-Charlotte Hanes. "Translating Scandinavian Drama—for Whom?" *Tijdschrift voor Skandinavistiek* 19, no. 1 (1998): 25–49.

———. Translator's note. Theatre program. *Miss Julie.* San Diego State University, 1988.

Hellqvist, Per-Anders. "Lidholms långa väg till tonsättning av Strindberg." *Svenska Dagbladet,* November 12, 1998.

Jakobson, Roman. "On Linguistic Aspects of Translation." In *Theories of Translation,* ed. Rainer Schulte and John Biguenet. Chicago: University of Chicago Press, 1992.

Järvefelt, Göran. *Opera Regi.* Stockholm: Bonniers, 1990. Print.

Jenner, Suzanne. "Fröken Julie i fransk översättning—ett drama i förvandling." In *August Strindberg och hans översättare,* ed. Björn Meidal and Nils Åke Nilsson. Stockholm: Kungl. Vitterhets Historie och Antikvitets Akademien, 1995. 53–60.

Kinnander, Bengt. "Ordstudier i Strindbergs prosa." In *Strindbergs språk och stil,* ed. Göran Lindström. Stockholm: Gleerups, 1964. 47–70.

Kowzan, Tadeusz. "The Sign in the Theatre: An Introduction to the Semiology of the Art of the Spectacle." Trans. Simon Pleasance. *Diogenes* 61 (Spring 1968): 52–80.

Langer, Susanne. *Feeling and Form.* New York: Charles Scribner's Sons, 1953.

Lindström, Göran. "Dialog och bildspråk i Strindbergs kammarspel." In *Strindbergs språk och stil,* ed. Göran Lindström. Stockholm: Gleerups, 1964. 167–79.

Meyer, Michael. "Strindberg in England." In *Essays on Strindberg,* ed. Carl Reinhold Smedmark. Stockholm: J. Beckman, 1966.

Pavis, Patrice. "Toward Specifying Theatre Translation." In *Theatre at the Crossroads of Culture,* trans. Loren Kruger. London: Routledge, 1992. 136–59.

Robinson, Michael. "Aldrig längre än till Gravesend." In *August Strindberg och hans översättare,* ed. Björn Meidal and Nils Åke Nilsson. Stockholm: Kungl. Vitterhets Historie och Antikvitets Akademien, 1995. 109–21.

———, ed. *Strindberg's Letters.* 2 vols. Trans. Michael Robinson. Chicago: University of Chicago Press, 1992.

Senelick, Laurence. "Semper Fidelis." In "What's at Stake in Theatrical Translation?" *Theatre Journal* 59, no. 3 (October 2007): 369–72.

Spregelburd, Rafael. "Life, of Course." In "What's at Stake in Theatrical Translation?" *Theatre Journal* 59, no. 3 (October 2007): 373–77.

Steene, Birgitta. "Sommarlovets hägring är inte nödvändigtvis översättarens vision: Om *Pelikanen,* Kulturspråk och Författarspråk." *Strindbergiana* 4 (1989): 56–66.

Strindberg, August. *Brev.* 22 vols. Ed. Torsten Eklund, Gunnar Ollén, and Björn Meidal. Stockholm: Bonniers, 1948–2001.

———. *A Dream Play.* In *August Strindberg Selected Plays 1,* trans. Evert Sprinchorn. Minneapolis: University of Minnesota Press, 1986.

———. *Ett drömspel.* In *August Strindbergs Samlade Verk,* ed. Lars Dahlbäck et al. Vol. 46. Stockholm: Bonniers, 1981–2009.

———. *The Father—Lady Julie—Playing With Fire.* Trans. Eivor Martinus. London: Amber Lane, 1998.

———. *Fröken Julie.* In *August Strindbergs Samlade Verk,* ed. Lars Dahlbäck et al. Vol. 27. Stockholm: Bonniers, 1981–2009.

———. *Miss Julie.* Trans. Anne-Charlotte Hanes Harvey. Unpublished translation for production, San Diego, 2007.

———. *Miss Julie.* In *Strindberg Plays One,* trans. Michael Meyer. London: A&C Black, 2003.

———. *Miss Julie.* In *August Strindberg Selected Plays 1,* trans. Evert Sprinchorn. Minneapolis: University of Minnesota Press, 1986.

———. *Miss Julie and Other Plays.* Trans. Michael Robinson. Oxford: Oxford University Press, 1998.

———. *Miss Julie by August Strindberg.* Trans. Kenneth McLeish. London: Nick Hern Books, 1995.

———. *Strindberg: Three Experimental Plays.* Trans. F. R. Southerington. Charlottesville: University Press of Virginia, 1975.

———. *Teater och Intima teatern.* In *August Strindbergs Samlade Verk,* ed. Lars Dahlbäck et al. Vol. 64. Stockholm: Bonniers, 1981–2009.

———. *Vid högre rätt.* In *August Strindbergs Samlade Verk,* ed. Lars Dahlbäck et al. Vol. 40. Stockholm: Bonniers, 1981–2009.

Svanberg, Nils. "Ur Strindbergs prosautveckling." In *Strindbergs språk och stil,* ed. Göran Lindström. Stockholm: Gleerups, 1964. 16–34.

Törnqvist, Egil. "Bildspråket översatt." *Strindbergs dramatiska bildspråk.* Amsterdam Contributions to Scandinavian Studies 7. Amsterdam: Amsterdam University Press, 2011. 229–41.

———. *Det talade ordet: Om Strindbergs dramadialog.* Stockholm: Carlssons, 2001.

———. "Translating Strindbergian Imagery for the Stage." *Tijdschrift voor Skandinavistiek* 19, no. 1 (1998): 7–23.

———. *Transposing Drama: Studies in Representation.* London: Macmillan, 1991.

Venuti, Lawrence, ed. *Rethinking Translation.* London: Routledge, 1992.

Vitez, Antoine. "The Duty to Translate." Interview by Georges Banu. In *The Intercultural Performance Reader,* ed. Patrice Pavis. London: Routledge, 1996.

Whitworth, Paul. NEH Translation Institute, Santa Cruz. Research interview. July 20, 1989.

The Art of Doubt: Form, Genre, History in *Miss Julie*

Leonardo F. Lisi

Miss Julie: A Naturalistic Tragedy. The definition contained in the subtitle to Strindberg's play has exercised a continuous fascination on the secondary literature, not least, it seems, because the adjective and noun share an uneasy coexistence. If critics such as Madsen (70–98), Harrison (89–90), or Greenway are correct in viewing *Miss Julie* (*Fröken Julie*, 1888) as a strictly naturalist play, one in which all action is determined by scientific laws, there would appear to be little space for free will.[1] Without the latter, however, Templeton (470), Stockenström ("Dilemma" 40), Sprinchorn (34), and Dahlström (5) have argued, tragedy cannot arise, and the pretensions of the subtitle would have to be rejected. On the other hand, if the subtitle is rehabilitated by identifying aspects of free will in the play alongside its crudely naturalist mode, the contradiction between the principles of determinism and freedom is either seen to constitute a failure (Stockenström, "Dilemma" 52–54; Delblanc 8–9; Dahlström 18), or to make *Miss Julie* tragic only in the weaker sense of staging the ultimately deplorable victory of naturalism's un-tragic view of life (Templeton 479–80).

In the discussion that follows, I would like to propose a solution to this interpretative dilemma by simultaneously deepening and widening the implications of its relevant terms. With respect to its deepening, I argue that, contrary to strictly naturalist readings, the contradiction between objective modes of determination and the freedom of particular individuality is indeed present in the play, but also, and against the other dominant interpretation, that this contradiction is far from being a failure of sorts but rather constitutive of the aesthetic structure of the text at large. This structure consists in the dialectical interrelation of two opposed representational logics and provides the central organizing principles of the play, not only at the level of its characters, but at those of its events and discourse as well. With respect to the widening of the implications of this formal contradiction, I show that it is this same structure that Strindberg in fact associates with tragedy and repeatedly points to as the play's dominant feature in the notorious preface to *Miss Julie.* I then place this particular notion of tragedy in the context of discussions on the genre from the late eighteenth to the early twentieth century, and elucidate how it conflates the sharp distinction repeatedly drawn between its modern and ancient forms. Only Søren Kierkegaard appears to hold a view of tragedy compatible with Strindberg's play, thereby suggesting that the combination of ancient and modern characteristics into a single form provides a particularly fruitful model for Scandinavian drama during its period of transition into European modernity.

Form

That *Miss Julie* centers on the conflict between classes and genders is a commonplace in the reception of the play. The importance of these categories as structural principles lies in their determination of individuals and events in terms of characteristics that exceed their particularity and which they share with other members of their group. It is this level of abstraction that has served to equate these modes of determination with the play's naturalism, given that the scientific method central to the latter by definition also operates with categories applicable to more than just one entity. In the play, the lower classes are repeatedly described in terms of their cowardly nature, as is visible both when Jean accuses the approaching peasants of hiding behind the obscure lyrics of their song (85/145),[2] and in Jean's own repeatedly expressed fear of the Count (87/150, 108–10/189–90). This submissiveness also finds expression in the lower classes' collective obligation to accept orders (e.g., 74/124, 81/138) and is coupled to their religiosity (96/165, 107/184). Further, the lower classes are clearly expected to be uncultured (76–77/128–29) and have pragmatic rather than romantic notions about sex, as is made clear in Jean's explicit claim that "for us love's a game, when work allows" (97/167), in his plan to convert romance into a business operation on Lake Como (95–96/165), or in the implication that Kristin and he have premarital intercourse (77/130).

Inversely, the upper classes are associated with the power to give orders, as is shown in Julie's various successful and unsuccessful attempts to do so (e.g., 77/130, 81/138), as well as in her use of social markers as a means of verbal violence: "Lackey, servant, stand up when I speak to you!" (91/156). The assertion of social divisions on the part of the upper classes is similarly visible in Jean's suggestion at the opening of the play that Julie's fiancé would not have been considered up to par with her class due to his lack of wealth (71/119), as well as Julie's plan to have her bitch abort after it has had sex with the gatekeeper's mutt (73/121). This superiority of the upper classes is strongly figured in Jean's fictional story about his stay in the Turkish Pavilion, in which the luxury and opulence of the latter contrast starkly with the poverty associated with his own childhood (82–83/140–42). Contrary to the pragmatism of the lower classes, moreover, the representatives of the upper classes are supposed to be free from the vulgar speech and motives of their inferiors (84/142), and instead repeatedly draw on romantic notions, such as Julie's invocations of love (87/149, 89/151, 97/167), or, most important, the code of honor that ultimately dictates her suicide (107/186).

The distinction between gender roles, what the play itself refers to as "the difference between a man and a woman" (107/186), is drawn in similarly stark terms. Women are presented through a spectrum of interrelated stereotypes that stretch from their supposed virtue (they should not be seen drinking with men [78/133]) and quiet acceptance of men's escapades (Kristin will make a good wife because she does not get jealous over Jean's dance with Julie [75/127]), through their naive preoccupation with their future husbands (74/123) and infatuation with clichéd love stories (90/155), to their coquettish flirtation (80–81/136–37) and ultimate submission to the sexual superiority of their male counterparts. As Jean makes clear with respect to the last of these points, women always invoke love as an excuse for their sexual promiscuity (84/143), while Julie seeks to explain women's sexual subjection through what she calls "the lure of the weak to the strong" (89/153).

The weakness and inferiority of women in the play's sexual dynamics that this points to is further stressed by the aggressiveness of male sexuality. When Jean warns Julie, "*Attention! Je ne suis qu'un homme!*" (80/136), for example, he immediately follows up by trying to force a kiss on her (81/138). Later, Jean confesses that all boys have dirty thoughts about girls (91/155) and refers to his relation with Julie as a "conquest" ("segern"), even if a disappointing one (91/157). The verbal aggressiveness that the upper classes can exercise against their servants is in turn available to men against women, as is visible in Jean's rebuttal to Julie's above quoted insult: "Lackey's whore, servant's tart, shut your mouth and get out of here!" (91/157).

For all their seeming stability, the capacity of these general categories of classification to explain the central characters of the play is clearly challenged from the outset. Julie is not properly aristocratic given that she attempts to "act common" (73/122), nor is Jean merely a servant since he acts like an "aristocrat" (79/134). On the other hand, Julie is clearly not common either, given that she cannot shed her upper-class ideals of love and honor, nor does Jean's aristocratic behavior become adequately naturalized: his knowledge of wines merely stems from being a sommelier (76/129), his sophisticated language from the theaters (77/129), and his luxurious meal is simply stolen (72/120). Moreover, the very information concerning the positive attributes pertaining to each class or type (upper/lower, male/female) primarily derives from the particular characters' transgression of their specific norms. Julie's deliberate rejection of class boundaries and sexual codes from the outset of the play in fact places her beyond the confines of social classifications. As Jean puts it, "Unfortunately the law says nothing about a woman who seduces a man" (96/166).[3] The presence of a gap between individual agency and socially defined functions that this statement reveals is again explicitly evoked, although with the opposed intention, in Julie's famous exclamation toward the end of the play: "I haven't a thought I didn't get from my father, not an emotion I didn't get from my mother, and this last idea—that everyone's equal—I got from him, my fiancé—which is why I called him a swine! How can it be my own fault, then?" (108/187). A similar moment is found in Jean's warning that Julie should not tempt him, "not because I'm me, but because I'm a young man" (81/138). In both cases, the very negation of individual agency points to the presence of a separate self that is not identical to the determining forces of society and gender.

Both Jean and Julie are in this way represented as containing aspects to their personality not reducible to those attributes and principles that are derived from their participation in a larger group. To the extent that such aspects exceed the explanatory power of general social categories, they are conceived as individual and particular, and constitute a form of transgression of objective rules that shows these to be relative. The highest representative of such negation of the logic of objective determination that is usually associated with naturalism is found in Julie's mother. As Julie explains,

> My mother was a commoner, from a very humble background, you see. She was brought up according to contemporary theories about equality, women's emancipation, and all that. . . . My mother decided to bring me up as a child of nature and, what's more, I was to learn everything a

> boy has to learn, so that I might serve to demonstrate that a woman was just as good as any man. I had to wear boy's clothes and learn to handle horses, but not to go into the barn; I had to groom and harness them, learn about farming, and go hunting, even how to slaughter the animals. Ugh, that was horrible! And on the estate the men were put to women's work, and the women to men's—so that everything went to the dogs, and we became the laughing-stock of the neighbourhood. Finally, my father must have woken up from his bewitchment and fought back, for everything was now done his way. (93/160–61)

The confusion and transgression of social and sexual categories that the mother implements clearly reflect the side of Julie and Jean's personalities that seeks to free itself of externally imposed determinations. More important still, the emphasis on "equality" ("jämlikhet") in this passage gestures toward a positive dimension in this realm of subjectivity, which is crucially elaborated at three further moments in the play. In the first, Julie insists that Jean dance a schottische with her, to which the latter reluctantly agrees: "JEAN. As your Ladyship commands. I am at your service. / MISS JULIE [*softly*]. Don't take it as a command. This evening we are all just enjoying ourselves together, and any rank is laid aside. So, give me your arm" (74–75/125). This notion of equality underlying the distinctions set up by social determinations reappears a few pages later, when Julie begs Jean to tell her of his childhood love: "JEAN. You can't make me tell you. / MISS JULIE. Suppose I ask you as an equal [*jämlike*], as a—friend! Who was she?" (82/139). The third time occurs after the pair's sexual intercourse, when Jean persists in addressing Julie with the formal "ni," to which the latter replies, "Miss! Call me Julie. There are no barriers between us now. Call me Julie!" ("Ni! Säg du! Mellan oss finns inga skrankor mer! Säg du!"; 87/150). In all three instances, the rejection of social determinations is accompanied by the assertion of an opposed equality that is also an expression of the desire for physical and emotional intimacy. The logic of transgression thus serves not only to do away with the socially constructed distinctions but also provides a new equality and proximity, different from the sexuality of the gendered realm discussed above. In her tirade against Jean following his slaughter of her bird, Julie explicitly points to this kind of difference in the modes of relation between people: "You think I love you because my womb desired your seed; you think I want to carry your brood beneath my heart and nourish it with my blood—to bear your child and take your name—by the way, what is your surname?—I've never heard it—you probably haven't got one" (103/178). The association, in this instance, of her self with the romantic notion of love, the hatred of men and her superiority over Jean due to his lack of surname, all make it clear that the antagonism between them is framed in terms of the social logic that sets up distinctions between individuals. Opposed to this, however, stands the desire of biology, her womb's for his seed, which binds people together in spite of their overt differences and socially determined wills.

On the one hand, then, *Miss Julie* organizes its characters and their relations through socially constructed categories, such as class and gender, which distinguish between them and keep them apart. On the other, the play draws on a realm of subjectivity that transgresses and negates these structures and which establishes positive relations of equality between individuals. Prima facie, the conflict of the play would seem to consist in the brute incommensurability of these two different spheres, in the fact that the relation at the level of individuality that draws people together cannot coexist with the relation at the level of social determinations, which keeps them apart. Upon closer examination, however, it is clear that the relation at stake is not simply one of contradiction, but rather of a dialectical interdependence, of the fact that the one does not merely negate the other but also depends on it for its existence.

The point finds clear expression in Jean's desire to escape the influence of the Count immediately following the peasants' ballet:

> JEAN: . . . [*Kicks the boots*] Superstition, prejudices, dinned into us from childhood—but they can easily be forgotten, too. Some other country, as long as it's a republic, and people will bow down before my porter's livery—bow down, you'll see. But *I* shan't! I wasn't born to bow and scrape, there's something to me, I've got character, just let me get hold of that first branch, and you'll soon see me climb! I may be a servant today, but next year I'll have my own place, and in ten years I'll be a landed gentleman. Then I'll go to Romania and get myself a decoration; why I might—only *might,* mind you—end up a count! (87–88/150)

Jean desires to escape the confinement to social roles for the sake of a political system in which their very structures are absent and in which his individuality can find proper expression. But that freedom from social constraints is ironically envisioned simply as a means to re-inscribe himself in a new objective type, that of the Romanian count, making the moment of transgression yield a new stabilizing structure. Significantly, the same process of transformation is seen to be at work in the origins of Julie's own noble lineage. As Jean asks somewhat later in the play: "Do you know who your earliest ancestor was? A miller who let the king spend the night with his wife during the Danish war" (96/166). As with Jean's desire for nobility, the distinctions and divisions implemented by Julie's social class have their foundation in the transgression of social boundaries which the king rewarded with a title.

The logic of transgression in this way does not merely negate social categories, as at first appeared, but also generates them. Inversely, the logic of social categories not only seeks to confine and restrict moments of transgression, but in fact produces them. The latter point is clear not only from the previous example, where it is the king who encourages the transgression, but also from the way the corruption and subversion of the social system within the play's present is not in fact limited to Jean and Julie, but rather encompasses the fictional world at large. Not only is the Count, too, victim of an irrepressible passion when crossing social boundaries to marry Julie's mother (93/160–61), but toward the conclusion of the play the subversive drive is expanded even further: "JEAN. You're all right, you've got yourself a fine man. / KRISTIN. Oh yes, so fine he sells his lordships oats from the stables . . . / JEAN. You can talk, you take a slice on the groceries and bribes from the butcher!" (106/183–84). As the butcher and Kristin are also brought into the sphere of corruption and deceit, the subversion of social norms decisively shifts from being an individual occurrence to an inevitable counterpart to the logic of those norms themselves. Rather than mere opposites, the logics of order and transgression are intimately linked: the one leads to the other in a dialectical process that can in principle go on forever.

In the play's construction of its characters and their relations we in this way encounter a simultaneous opposition and interdependence of two opposed organizational systems: one centered on individuality and transgression, the other on types and semiotic stabilization. The same structure, significantly, can be located at the level of the play's events, or plot. This is most immediately apparent in the way the adherence to specific social types generates certain necessary events and outcomes. Most obviously, this is the case with Julie's suicide at the end, which is explicitly linked to the nobility's code of honor (107/186), and which her mother clearly did not follow when she found herself in an analogous situation (94/161). Indeed, toward the conclusion of the play, the inability of either Jean or Julie to free themselves from the social determination of their personalities is the most immediately apparent aspect. As Julie exclaims in despair, "Do me this last service, save my honour, save his name!" To which Jean replies, "I don't know why—but now I can't either—I don't understand—it's just as if this coat made me—I can't order you. . . ." (108–9/188). The point of no return that leads to this conclusion is likewise determined by social forces, given that the decision to escape into Jean's room is framed in terms of the attempt to protect Julie's aristocratic reputation, and is presented as an inevitability: "Necessity knows no law" ("Nöden har ingen lag"; 86/146). This same sense of an objective structure imposed upon the characters from outside and independent of their wills is further generated by the play's very symmetry and formal unity, which sets a clear limit to variations that an individual might produce: one time and space for all action; one central pantomime at the play's moment of crisis (86/147), flanked by two smaller ones on each side, one with Kristin (75/126) and another with Jean (98/170); clear signs of when events begin and end, such as Jean's change from livery into coat and back again (76/128 and 108/187), or the references to the start and end of magic spells (74/123 and 101/176).

Within this rigid formal structure, however, the play also deploys a number of counter-strategies. Most significantly, the very setting of midsummer night constitutes a ritual context in which all social and objective determinations can be subverted. As the anthropologist Victor Turner has described such liminality, "this condition and these persons elude or slip through the network of classifications that normally locate states and positions in cultural space. Liminal entities are neither here nor there; they are betwixt and between the positions assigned and arrayed by law, custom, convention, and ceremonial" (95).[4] This condition of course resonates with the logic of transgression and individuality traced above,[5] and the connotation of such states with magic is also emphasized in the description of Julie's mother cited previously, where the Count was precisely said to "have woken up from his bewitchment" ("ha vaknat ur förtrollningen"; 93/161). Similar references to magic or the supernatural occur throughout the play (73/121, 74/123, 80/136, 101/176),[6] further emphasizing that within the social and formal codes that impose certain necessary events, the play also carries another logic where, in principle, anything can happen.

It is important to note that this inherently anarchic dimension to the play is not merely symbolic or thematic but rather also directly determines its plot. In addition to the conclusion being an outcome of Julie's and Jean's adherence to the social codes that govern them, it is, after all, also described as a product of the inescapability of the sexual/biological bond between them that makes any such adherence impossible:

> MISS JULIE: I've been mad, I've been crazy, but does that mean there's no way out?
>
> JEAN: Stay here, and say nothing. No one knows.

MISS JULIE: Impossible! The servants know. And Kristin.
JEAN: Not for sure, and anyway, they'd never believe it.
MISS JULIE [*hesitating*]: But—it could happen again!
JEAN: That's true!
MISS JULIE: And the consequences?
JEAN [*frightened*]: Consequences!—What on earth have I been thinking of?—All right, there's only one solution.—You must leave! At once! (97/168)

The option of leaving is discarded because its social implications would kill the Count (98/169), but the alternative solution of staying is equally impossible due to the sexual/biological consequences that it carries and the transgression that these constitute. Julie's suicide is thus an outcome of both these factors, rather than simply the former, and therefore caught in a dialectical relation that mirrors the one identified at the level of characters above.

The same can be shown to be the case with respect to the prior turning point in the plot, the decision to escape into Jean's room. If at first sight the overt motivation is to avoid social humiliation, it is equally clear that the play is asking us to read this concern as simply the characters' excuse to satisfy their transgressive sexual desire. Explicitly, Jean insists that they must escape because the song the peasants sing is about the two of them, but the lyrics to this "little-known singing game" ("mindre känd danslek"), as Strindberg admits in the preface, "do not hit home precisely" ("ingefär och icke på pricken"; 65/111). In fact, they do not seem to carry much of a relation to Jean and Julie's situation at all, and how they can qualify as "an obscene song [*nidvisa*]! About you and me!" is difficult to see at best (85/145). The deliberate theatricality of their escape—Jean's promise to shoot any intruders and his exuberant genuflection, with its echo back to his previous playful kiss of Julie's foot (78/132)—all add to this incongruity between cause and effect and suggest that a motive distinct from the overtly social one must be at work as well. In other words, if "necessity knows no law" this is not only because it can substitute a set of higher obligations (protection of the family's honor) for a lower one (propriety of behavior), but because "necessity" can refer to the brute force of sexual desire, which cannot be resisted and which ignores all social codes and limits.

Both catastrophe and resolution are in this way determined in two different directions. On the one hand, by the laws of society and classic form that dictate what the necessary order and outcome to any event should be on the basis of principles that exceed its particular manifestation. On the other, by the forces of desire and liminality, in which the sequence of events is never certain in advance but at every moment open to changes not to be controlled by pre-established rules. Both aspects are operative and equally constitutive of the trajectory of the play: neither one nor the other in isolation, but both at once.

Characters and action, then, exhibit similar structures. One last example of the same from the sphere of discourse follows. As critics have frequently bemoaned, in *Miss Julie* Strindberg makes use of a number of heavy-handed symbolic motifs, which seem to threaten the otherwise naturalistic constitution of the play. Among these, the most frequently invoked are Jean and Julie's account of their dreams (79–80/135), with its related imagery of hawks (82/140, 90/156) and branches (88/150, 90/156); the relation between Julie's bitch Diana and the gatekeeper's mutt, which mirrors that of Julie and Jean (73); and the topic of beheading, which recurs with the execution of Julie's bird Siskin (102–3), the sermon on St. John the Baptist (99/170), and finally, of course, Julie's suicide (110/190).[7] The function of such symbolic elements, however, has not yet been adequately considered. What is striking about them, in fact, is that they extend far beyond these more obvious instances, into an entire network of prefigurations at the level of discourse of what subsequently occurs in the realm of action. The suicide with which the play ends is thus invoked not only in the topic of beheading, but also in the account of Jean's youthful attempt to take his life (83/142), followed by that of the Count's failure to do the same (94/163, 107/186). The imagery of slaughtering animals, which converges with that of beheading in the killing of Siskin, is likewise repeatedly invoked (93/161, 95/164, 102/177–78). Julie's disgrace is already announced not only in her dream, but also earlier, when Jean warns her that if she chooses to "step down," "people will always say you fell [*faller*]" (79/134), which is subsequently confirmed when Julie herself refers to her fate in those same terms: "And now you despise me!—I'm falling [*faller*], I'm falling" (89/153). Similarly, at the opening of the play, when Julie assures Kristin that "I shan't run off with your fiancé" and explains to Jean that she needs someone "who won't make me look ridiculous," her statements carries a clear dramatic irony that transforms their schottische into a dance of death. When Julie responds to Jean's warning that "it's dangerous to play with fire" by stating that "I'm insured" (81/137), this seemingly playful exchange echoes the story Julie later tells of the fire on her father's farm, for which there also was no insurance and where her mother's affair with another man was likewise involved (94/161). Even Jean's submission to the Count's demand for his boots and coffee just prior to the end (108/188) is announced already at the outset, when Kristin mutters an identical order in a similarly hypnotic state (78/133).

The presence of such a continuous stream of announcements of what will happen later on gives the action of the play the appearance of a mere literalization of what the audience already knew, and thereby generates the sense of inevitability and fate. The network of intra-textual references, that is, overdetermines the action, making it amply clear in advance what will unquestionably happen next.[8] To that extent, in fact, and contrary to what the secondary literature has claimed, the symbolic aspects of the play do not so much contradict the naturalistic ones as reinforce them, since both the discourse and the categories of class and gender perform the same function of fixing the sequence of events along necessary laws.[9]

Opposed to this principle of determination, however, *Miss Julie* also displays a continual randomness in its discourse, which directly contradicts it. To take but one example, following the peasants' ballet, Jean initially enters the stage giving expression to his "slave mentality" (62/108) through his fear of consequences and his desire to escape: "JEAN. There you see! And heard! Do you think it's possible to stay here now? / MISS JULIE. No. I don't. But what can we do? / JEAN. Leave, travel. Far away from here" (86/148). These short, assertive statements nevertheless quickly cede to the long, fast-paced passages that describe his planned hotel in great detail and rhetorical exuberance, and which in turn further morph into the punctuated, paratactic enumeration of the abstract names of cities on the way: "Malmö at six-thirty; Hamburg at eight-forty tomorrow morning; Frankfurt to Basel takes a day, and Como via the Gotthard Pass, let me see, three days. Three days!" (87/149). This rhythmical shift then leads back to his previous expression of fear, now directed explicitly against the Count, which in turn gives way to the flight of fancy about acquiring a title of his own in Romania (87–88/150). As previously, the poetic vision is transformed into pragmatic matter-of-factness, when Jean proceeds to enumerate the steps necessary to realize their plans (88/151), and is again replaced by a new tone of growing brutality towards Julie once he realizes that she is unable to provide the required economic backing (88–89/152). Within this new emotional and rhetorical register, Jean's voice progresses from a modified disdain that still shows some support for Julie ("Fall down to me, and I'll lift you up again" [89/153]), through a growing verbal violence in response to Julie's own changing mood ("And a whore is a whore!"), to the destruction of all previous illusions ("That was just talk"; "Women always fall for pretty stories" [90/155]), and the explosion of a brute destructive will:

> Lackey's whore, servant's tart, shut your mouth and get out of here! How dare you go and call me crude? No one of my sort has ever behaved as crudely as you have this evening. Do you think any of the girls around here would approach a man the way you did? Have you ever seen a girl of my class offer herself like that? I've only seen the like among animals and prostitutes. (91/157)

But even here the shifts continue. Immediately after this violence, Jean repents and changes tone completely: "No. Forgive me for what I've just said. I don't hit someone who's down, least of all a woman." After this, he again voluntarily refers to his own status as servant and speaks with an increasing familiarity, until he is finally overcome with desire for Julie once more and tries to seduce her to have sex a second time (92/158–59). Julie declines, and the plan to escape together is reintroduced, leaving us where we began a short moment before.

One sequence, one character, and at least thirteen different emotional and mental states, each with their own mode of discourse, diction, and rhetorical structure, and each related to the others without any apparent logic or necessary development, but simply as a product of Jean's interaction with the contingent circumstances of his shifting surroundings. If, according to Mikhail Bakhtin, Shakespeare's plays do not qualify as truly polyphonic works because "each play contains only one fully valid voice, the voice of the hero, while polyphony presumes a plurality of fully valid voices within the limits of a single work" (34), then Strindberg appears to have overcome this problem by giving us not only a world in which no single voice can claim authority, but even one in which no single character possesses a unified perspective. As Strindberg rightfully points out in the preface to the play, "I have avoided the symmetrical, mathematical artificiality of French dialogue and allowed my characters' brains to work irregularly as they do in real life, where no subject is ever entirely exhausted before one mind discovers by chance in another mind a cog in which to engage" (63/109).

If the discursive sphere of the play generates an overdetermination of events so intense that the audience would seem to learn the outcome from the start, it thus also contains a fluctuation and randomness so vast that the unity of characters and actions threatens to dissolve. That the play avoids both of these extremes is due precisely to its combination of both within a single space, as equally constitutive aspects of the fictional world. The polyphony of voices places the overdetermination of symbolic patterns within a lived immediacy that lends it flexible relativity, while the overdetermination of symbolic patterns in turn confines the polyphony of voices within strict bounds. As with characters and action, so with discourse too: not the one or the other of organizing structures, but both at once.

Genre

Miss Julie, then, is structured around the opposition and dialectical interdependence of two opposed representational logics, which repeat themselves at the level of characters, action, and discourse: one, the stabilizing principle associated with the deployment of class and gender types, prefiguration and overdetermination; the other, the destabilizing principle associated with individuality, liminality, and anarchy. One of the remarkable aspects of this formal organization is that it returns in Strindberg's famous discussion of the genre of the play in his preface, even though the secondary literature has long insisted that these two texts contradict each other (a view that Strindberg elsewhere could be taken to encourage [see "Césarine" 118]).[10] Arguably, this point has been obscured by the fact that Strindberg in his discussion in the preface makes use of the term "naturalism" in two radically opposed ways. The first use occurs in the opening discussion, when Strindberg explains that "naturalists, who know how richly complicated the soul is," must reject the traditional notion of character as "a man who was fixed and set, who invariably appeared drunk or comical or sad" (59/104). Instead, Strindberg claims, his own characters are depicted "as more split and vacillating" (59/105), "conglomerates of past and present stages of culture, bits out of books and newspapers, scraps of humanity, torn shreds of once fine clothing now turned to rags, exactly as the human soul is patched together" (60/105). As Strindberg explains further in a famous section worth quoting at some length,

> Every event in life—and this is a fairly new discovery!—is usually the result of a whole series of more or less deep-seated motives, but the spectator usually selects the one that he most easily understands or that best flatters his powers of judgment. Someone commits suicide. "Business worries," says the business man. "Unrequited love," say the ladies. "Physical illness," says the sick man, "Shattered hopes," says the failure. But it may well be that the motive lay in all of these things, or in none of them [*allestädes, eller ingenstädes*], and that the dead man concealed his real motive by emphasizing quite a different one that shed the best possible light on his memory.

> I have motivated Miss Julie's tragic fate with an abundance of circumstances: her mother's "bad" basic instincts; her father's improper bringing-up of the girl; her own nature and the influence her fiancé's suggestions had on her weak, degenerate brain; also, and more immediately: the festive atmosphere of Midsummer Night; her father's absence; her period; her preoccupation with animals; the intoxicating effect of the dance; the light summer night; the powerful aphrodisiac influence of the flowers; and finally chance that drives these two people together in a room apart, plus the boldness of the aroused man. (58/103)

It is important to point out that the notion of "fate" ("öde") at play in this passage is clearly not the traditional one of a *singular* logic of events that we can fully recognize but which will manifest itself in the world no matter what the hero does. Rather, fate is here linked to an opposed *excess* of possible causes for events, which are beyond our control not primarily because we cannot stop them, but because their number and complexity exceeds our grasp. Further still, the epistemological conditions of this universe are highly problematic. The set of circumstances underlying any event are not only unique to every individual (their particular past, biology, context, etc.), but also subject to contingency ("chance"). More importantly, as the first paragraph makes clear, whatever observations we might make about it are inherently subjective, either because the observer only perceives those aspects that resonate with his or her own personality, or because the object of investigation might well have manipulated appearances.

If this notion of "naturalism" would seem to correspond quite neatly with the play's destabilizing strategies identified in the previous section of this chapter, it seems clear that it fits only uneasily with the kind of "naturalism" that is usually understood to rest on the method of scientific investigation. The latter, after all, establishes general principles and rules for phenomena, and for that reason not only presupposes the possibility of an objective and detached mode of observation, but also abstracts from the particularity and uniqueness of experience that Strindberg emphasizes here. That these aspects of the scientific method are central to naturalism is clear from Zola's definition in his seminal manifesto, "The Experimental Novel," from 1880: "The end of all experimental method, the boundary of all scientific research, is then identical for living and for inanimate bodies; it consists in finding the relations which unite a phenomenon of any kind to its nearest cause, or, in other words, in determining the conditions necessary for the manifestation of this phenomenon" (3/325). Such knowledge of conditions becomes possible, moreover, when the scientific observer "accepts only facts conformable to the determinism of phenomena" (12/329), rejecting "the supernatural and the irrational" (26/335), and thereby providing "a complete knowledge of the truth" (12/329). Naturalism, that is, not only assumes that the world of experience is in principle open to an exhaustive explanation by scientific means, but also subordinates the particularities of that experience to aspects compatible with such objective and universal rules. As much is in fact also visible in Strindberg's own statement, in his essay "On Modern Drama and Modern Theatre," from 1889, that Zola has "sought the truly significant and from ordinary reality has extracted the essence, demonstrated the prevailing laws of nature and placed the detail in context, as befits a subordinate part of the machine" (76).

This apparent contradiction between Strindberg's notion of naturalism in the preface and the more familiar one from other contemporary sources, however, is partially canceled by his second use of the term in this same text. If, in the opening pages of the preface, Strindberg goes out of his way to emphasize the inherent multiplicity of human beings and the complexity of their fate, a sudden shift occurs as soon as he begins to speak of his heroine as a representative of the "type" described as "the man-hating half-woman." What is intriguing in this shift is that Strindberg's clear misogyny makes him abandon his previously nuanced attitude and delve into the very kinds of reductive stereotypes that he has just rejected. Rather than being subject to the uniqueness of circumstance and chance that make each individual a particular and irreplaceable occurrence, we are now told that women are "governed by the laws of propagation," and for that reason,

> will always be born stunted and can never catch up with the one in the lead, according to the formula: A (the man) and B (the woman) start from the same point C; A (the man) with a speed of, let us say, 100 and B (the woman) with a speed of 60. Now, the question is, when will B catch up with A?—Answer: *Never!* Neither with the help of equal education, equal voting rights, disarmament, or temperance—no more than two parallel lines can ever meet and cross. (60/105–6)

In Strindberg's crude scientific analogy we find the very conception of natural law and biological determinism so frequently associated with naturalism and absent from the initial pages of the preface.[11] From this perspective, no change in contexts or particular distinctions can modify differences between genders, the a priori laws of which determine the fate and constitution of each individual in universal terms. Strindberg himself, in fact, makes the link between such a determinism and naturalism explicit in the following paragraph:

> The type [half-woman] is tragic, offering the spectacle of a desperate struggle against nature, a tragic legacy of Romanticism which is now being dissipated by Naturalism, the only aim of which is happiness. And happiness means strong and sound species. But Miss Julie is also [*även*] a relic of the old warrior nobility that is now giving way to the new aristocracy of nerve and brain; a victim of the discord which a mother's "crime" has implanted in a family; a victim of the errors of an age, of circumstances and of her own deficient constitution, which together form the equivalent of the old-fashioned concept of Fate or Universal Law. (61/106)

The impossibility of breaking free of the scientific formula for the superiority of man is here equated with the impossibility of escaping nature, and the acceptance of this fact is identified with naturalism. The fate ("öde") at stake in this passage is thus radically distinct from the previous one, no longer a sheer excess of determinants that cannot be objectively known and understood, but rather the univocal laws of gender and class which are explicable and comprehensible as easily as A, B, C.

To the extent that individuals in this second notion of naturalism are significant merely in terms of their qualities as types and subject to objective laws beyond their control, it clearly resonates with the principles of stabilization previously identified in the play itself. What is particularly interesting in this last passage, however, is the definition of tragedy as the struggle against such principles. The identification of the agency of that struggle with romanticism, and its opposition to naturalism's concern with the species, makes it clear that Strindberg here has in mind something like the romantic notion of genius, which is precisely fully individual and beyond the universal laws of science. That condition is closer to the first than to the second kind of naturalism discussed by Strindberg, and resonates with Kant's famous definition: "Genius is a *talent* for producing something for which no determinate rule can be given . . .; hence the foremost property of genius must be *originality*" (175/307). As Jeffrey Cox has argued, romantic tragedy is characterized by the revolt of this kind of individuality against the social categories of state, family, and church that confront it (427; see also Cooper 454). But where this struggle is inevitably unequal in romantic drama, Strindberg goes one step further by insisting on the contradiction's *internal* rather than merely external status: Julie is not only romantic individuality *but also* ("även") subject to the categories "of Fate or Universal Law" that exceed her particularity. The tragic conflict, that is, consists in the opposition of two equally constitutive representational principles within the same fictional space.

The dialectical relation identified within the play at the levels of characters, action, and discourse in this way repeats itself in the combination of two opposed conceptions of naturalism in the preface, and becomes the centerpiece of Strindberg's notion of tragedy. No doubt the terminology is faulty here; not only is naturalism described in contradictory terms, but the definition of romantic individuality as a "type" is problematic too. The point, however, is not whether Strindberg had a consistent idea of tragedy clearly formulated in his mind, but rather that the very confusions of the conceptual discussion in the preface implicitly give voice to the same creative impulse as the play.[12]

History

One striking aspect of this implicit notion and praxis of tragedy in *Miss Julie* is that it contradicts a dominant strain in the theory of the genre during the long nineteenth century. What Strindberg joins into a single dialectical relation is in fact traditionally kept strictly apart, as the features of sharply distinct historical periods: the drama of the ancient Greeks, in which only abstract social, moral, or religious principles are at work, and the drama of the moderns, where the conflict is between particular individuals, in all their contingent specificity.

This contrast is clearly drawn already in Friedrich Schlegel's 1795 essay *Über das Studium der Griechischen Poesie*, in which modern literature is defined as "anarchic" (219), subject to "chance" rather than principles and rules (221), and as seeking to represent only the particular, characteristic, and interesting (228). The culmination of these features is found in the modern's predilection for "philosophical tragedy," which stands in direct opposition to the "aesthetic tragedy" of the ancient Greeks that, like all classical art, aims at beauty, universality, and objectivity (246; see also 277, 283, 396). The same characterization recurs in the influential *Vorlesungen über dramatische Kunst und Literatur* by Friedrich's brother August Wilhelm Schlegel, first published in 1809–11. As the older Schlegel explains there, where Greek art "proceeded with scientific rigor from the most universal concepts," so that "the individual is by far the last thing to which it would decline," "for us [moderns] it is exactly the other way around" (1:54). Greek tragedy represents the "idea," "fate," or "myth," and lacks the immediacy and color of everyday life (1:61, 62, 66), while the moderns provide the experience of reality, although as chaos rather than nomos, fragments and particulars that cannot be exhausted by conceptual determination (2:111–12, 130). The association of the art of the moderns with the invention of particular characters opposed to the universal principles found in the ancient world is similarly at work a decade earlier, in F. J. W. Schelling's *Philosophie der Kunst,* from 1800. In ancient tragedy, so Schelling explains, it is the conflict and identity of necessity and freedom as transcendental principles that is at stake, meaning that the characters operate simply as symbolic representations of these forces, not as specific individuals that would leave room for empirical and contingent motivations (518). In modern tragedy, however, reality and character become central (551), and the conflict is transformed from a mythical or metaphysical one to a historical one, a struggle between particular individuals rather than abstract principles (528). The most important contribution to the theory of tragedy in the nineteenth century, Hegel's concluding discussion to his *Vorlesungen über die Ästhetik,* delivered mainly during the 1820s, elaborates on this same line of thought. The heroes of ancient tragedy, we are again told here, are merely individual embodiments of substantive principles of state, morality, or religion, and therefore act with absolute necessity. But, "in modern, or romantic, poetry, on the other hand, the principal topic is provided by an individual's passion, which is satisfied in the pursuit of a purely subjective end, and, in general, by the fate of a single individual and his character in special circumstances" (1206/536). Where the conflicting principles in ancient tragedy are both equally justified moments of the absolute idea that underlies them both, modern tragedy is ruled merely by accidents, and at most retains necessity in the notion of a Providence that simply destroys the subjective hero in his or her illegitimate particularity (1208/537–38, 1230–32/565–67).

The terms of the discussion on tragedy that dominate Germany during the early decades of the nineteenth century are disseminated throughout Europe in the years that follow, not least by Madame de Staël's influential *De l'Allemagne,* from 1810. Like her German contemporaries, de Staël distinguishes between ancient drama's emphasis on necessity and fate as opposed to the modern's focus on the merits and actions of particular characters (162–63). Seventeen years later, in Victor Hugo's seminal preface to *Cromwell,* the binary can be recognized anew in the opposition between "l'idéal" of the ancients and the "réel" of the moderns (67). Still in the twentieth century, at the birth of another literary movement, Walter Benjamin relies on the same historical narrative in an early essay from 1916: "Classical tragedy . . . deals with the tragedy of fate, Shakespeare with the tragic hero, the tragic action. Goethe rightly calls him Romantic"

("*Trauerspiel*" 56). A few years later, in his influential *Ursprung des deutschen Trauerspiel,* from 1925, the division is again operative in Benjamin's claim that classical tragedy takes myth as its material, the conflict with God and fate, whereas *Trauerspiel* uses history, where everything is secularized, contingent, and subject to the radical instabilities of meaning (44–45). At almost the same time, in 1923, Ludwig Marcuse reiterates the point in his *Die Welt der Tragödie:* the characters of ancient tragedy are not there for the sake of their particular psychologies, but as the exemplifications of the universal categories of fate and divine necessity (27–28). In modern tragedy, on the other hand, the individual is everything, and thereby generates the loss of objective frameworks that brings with it a world of chaos and anarchy devoid of all previous unity (115, 145–46).

The opposed representational principles that Strindberg in *Miss Julie* joins in a dialectical struggle are in this way traditionally kept strictly separate, as two modes of organizing and viewing the world that belong to wholly different historical periods. Indeed, the very centrality of this distinction is not merely a question of theoretical pedantry, but rather, as Hans Robert Jauss has argued in a different context, is grounded in the fact that it arises during the *querelle des anciens et des modernes* as part of the initial formulation of the very notion of modernity.[13] More than just a question of form and genre, in other words, the structure at work in *Miss Julie* appears to put into play the nature of history itself.

In this light it is particularly suggestive to note that Strindberg's isolation in the debate about tragedy is not in fact absolute. A view similar to his is expressed by his Danish near-contemporary, Søren Kierkegaard, in a short essay from the first half of *Either/Or,* published in 1843: "The Tragic in Ancient Drama Reflected in the Tragic in Modern Drama." Kierkegaard's essay is extraordinarily rich and complex and cannot be done justice in the present context, where only a few points need be emphasized. Most important among these is the fact that Kierkegaard defines tragedy precisely in terms of a conflict between two opposed but equally justified principles akin to those in Strindberg. Kierkegaard's analysis is divided into three areas: first, action ("Handling"); second, guilt ("Skyld"); and third, mood ("Stemning"). Tragic action, Kierkegaard explains, is the product not only of the hero's individual choices ("Handling"), but also "suffering" ("Lidelse"). Suffering is an event ("Begivenhed"), which in the Danish already contains the idea of receptivity, of being given something: "Be*given*hed." What the hero is given are the "substantial determinations," that is, those aspects of character and action that are determined not by the individual's freedom, but by his or her participation in larger, inter-subjective structures, "the state, the family, in fate," as Kierkegaard writes (143/143). Oedipus's fall, in this way, is a product both of the particular decisions that he takes and the curse placed upon his family. Tragic guilt, for this reason, so Kierkegaard explains, is both individual, what he terms "Skyld," and the product of a general condition that exceeds the hero's subjectivity, "Lidelse." The mood of tragedy, finally, which arises from this combination of objective and subjective guilt is likewise a mixture between, on the one hand, pain ("Smerte"), which reacts to the individual's responsibility, and, on the other, sorrow ("Sorg"), which is a product of the objective dimension of action and guilt.

Up until this point it is clear that Kierkegaard shares with Strindberg's tragedy the idea of a dialectical relation between representational principles otherwise associated with distinct historical periods. However, it should be noted that, to Kierkegaard, this tragic form is in fact common to the genre in all its historical manifestations. What distinguishes the modern from its ancient versions is accordingly found not at the level of the elements that constitute it, but rather at the level of relation to that structure. The point is summarized most clearly in Kierkegaard's imagination of a modern version of *Antigone* in the essay's second part:

> The Greek Antigone participates in her father's guilt through her childish piety, and so does the modern. But for the Greek Antigone the Father's guilt [*Skyld*] and suffering [*Lidelse*] are an external fact, an unshakeable fact, that her sorrow does not move (*qoud non volvit in pectore*); and to the extent that she personally suffers, as a natural consequence, under her father's guilt, then this again is in all its external factuality. But for our [modern] Antigone it is different. I imagine that Oepdipus has died. Already when he was alive, Antigone knew this secret, but did not have the courage to confide in her father. . . . But one thing she does not know, [namely] whether or not her father knew it himself. Here is the modern element: it is the restlessness in her sorrow, it is the amphiboly in her pain. . . . While the father was living, she could not confide her sorrow to him, for she indeed did not know whether he knew it, and consequently there was a possibility of throwing him into a similar pain [*Smerte*]. And yet, if he had not known it, the guilt [*Skylden*] would be less. The movement here is continually relative. If Antigone had not known the factual state of affairs with certainty, she would have been trivial, she would in that case have had nothing but a suspicion to struggle with, and that is too little to engage us tragically. But she knows everything; yet within this knowledge there is still an ignorance that can always keep the sorrow in motion, always transform it into pain. (161; translation modified/159)

Both the modern and ancient Antigone are fully aware of Oedipus's secret, namely that he has married his mother and murdered his father. But for the ancient version, the combination of individual responsibility ("Skyld") and the externally imposed substantial determination ("Lidelse") that generated this "factual state of affairs" is a given to which Antigone simply relates as a positive fact. The modern Antigone, instead, is caught in an infinite unrest. Not because she is unaware as to the facts of the case, without which knowledge, Kierkegaard tells us, there would be no tragedy at all, but because she is unable to determine whether Oedipus himself knew the nature of his situation. If he did *not,* then the element of individual responsibility and pain ("Skyld" and "Smerte") would be less, since we cannot fault him for having committed a crime of which he could not be aware. And if he *did,* then the element of substantial determination and sorrow ("Lidelse" and "Sorg") would be less, since he deliberately transgressed the law and must be held fully responsible. What Antigone cannot know, and what will continually perpetuate her pain, that is, is the question *whether* the situation is primarily a product of Oedipus's individual decision or *whether* it is primarily an outcome of the family's fate, and it is in this undecidability that modern tragedy finds its definition.

At the heart of Kierkegaard's historical distinction, in short, is the claim that for modern tragedy the issue is no longer *that* an individual subjectivity is opposed by a substantive necessity, but rather the question *whether* such a collision has occurred in the first place. That such a reflexivity on the relation of substantive determinations and particular individuality is central to Strindberg's work as well is suggested by a play such as *The Father* (*Fadren,* 1887), where the conflict rests precisely on the impossibility of determining whether Bertha is related to the Captain by biological necessity or whether they are distinct and separate particulars. But in *Miss Julie,* too, there is a structure akin to Kierkegaard's distinction between a "state of affairs" constituted of two contradictory principles and an explicit reflection on that state. At stake is something like what Roman Jakobson in a famous essay termed the "metalingual" function of language, that is, those uses of discourse that are not about the world itself but about our modes of describing the world, and as such focus on the code:

> A distinction has been made in modern logic between two levels of language: "object language" speaking of objects and "metalanguage" speaking of language. But metalanguage is not only a necessary scientific tool utilized by logicians and linguists; it plays also an important role in

> our everyday language. . . . Imagine such an exasperating dialogue: "The sophomore was plucked." "But what is *plucked?*" "*Plucked* means the same as *flunked.*" "And *flunked?*" "*To be flunked* is *to fail an exam.*" . . . All these equational sentences convey information merely about the lexical code of English; their function is strictly metalingual. (69)

In Strindberg's play we have a number of such instances. When Julie refers to Jean as a "gentleman" at the beginning of the play, the latter replies,

> JEAN: Oh you're flattering me.
> MISS JULIE [*offended*]: Flattering you?
> JEAN: My natural modesty forbids me to believe that you would pay someone like me a true compliment, and therefore I permitted myself to suppose that you were exaggerating, or as it is called, "flattering." (76–77/129)

The exchange strongly echoes Jakobson's example, and similar instances can easily be found, such as Jean's definitions of "*mésalliance*" (96/166) and "running away" ("rymma") (106/182). Beyond such strictly code-oriented moments of discursive reflexivity, however, the play also repeatedly operates with similar thematizations of the characters' relation to their fictional world more generally, and in two ways. First, we find a remarkable amount of instances in which the characters' interpretation or assessment of the state of affairs is explicitly questioned, phrases such as, "you don't doubt that, do you Miss Julie?" ("kann ni tvivla på det?"; 87/150), "What's so strange?" ("Vad är det som är så underligt?"; 99/171), "You're not mad at me for going off like that, are you?" ("Du är väl inte ond på mig att jag mankerade . . ."; 75/127), or the numerous statements involving the question "do you think?" ("tror ni"; e.g., 81/138, 89/153, 90/154, 103/178). On the other hand, we have a number of cases in which hypothetical implications of events of the world are considered from the perspective of a specific character's subjective assessment or interpretation, such as when Julie asks Jean after they return from his room, "But what can we do?" ("Men vad skola vi så göra!"; 86/148), or later on, "Do you see any other way out than that we leave . . .?" ("Ser ni någon annan utväg än att vi resa . . . ?"; 96, translation modified/166), and again toward the end: "Do you see any way out of this? Any end to it all?" ("Ser ni någon utväg ur detta, något slut på detta?"; 107/185). All three of these modes of discourse concern themselves not with the referential aspect of language, with describing or establishing what is in fact the case, but with reflections upon that sphere of references, with what different characters mean or think about it or what alternatives they might envision. As such they introduce a markedly reflexive dimension to the text: of the first, more strictly metalingual type we find no less than 7 instances;[14] the second, concerned with subjective states in a narrow sense, occurs at least 48 times;[15] and the third, in which a possible state of affairs seen from a specific interpretative position is at stake, can be found 21 times.[16] A total of 76 times in the course of 71 pages of text and, significantly, a clear increase from the first to the second part: 52 of the total instances take place following the peasants' ballet, strongly emphasizing the rise in reflexivity that occurs after the point of no return.

Like Kierkegaard's modern Antigone, the characters in Strindberg's play are not just caught in a tragic world but constantly discussing it, worrying about it, engaging in the status and conditions of various interpretations about it, querying its possible alternatives. The features that contribute to this aspect could of course easily be increased by including other reflexive elements beyond those narrowly defined here; for example, the large amount of explicitly evaluative statements about the fictional world that do not directly thematize this process of interpretation but clearly contribute to the reflexivity of the play by emphasizing the relation of subject and object at stake.[17] But even in the more conservative terms used above its importance in the play is immediately clear when compared to other texts. Using the same three kinds of reflexive discourse, and choosing a random sample, in Strindberg's own *The Outlaw* (*Den Fredlösa*), published in 1881, the total number of such instances is 21; in his *In Rome* (*I Rom*), from 1870, 19; in *Hermione*, written in the same year, 31; and in *Sir Bengt's Wife* (*Herr Bengts Hustru*), from 1882, and nearly 60 percent longer than *Miss Julie*, 48. Even in *The Freethinker* (*Fritänkeren*), also from 1870, which is exclusively concerned with questions of what people think, we find no more than 41 such occurrences in the text. Going back further still, Adam Oehlenschläger, who provided Strindberg with his earliest model for tragedy (see *Letters* 12), only has 21 such instances in his *Axel and Valborg* (*Axel og Valborg*, 1808), while Friedrich Zacharias Werner's *Wanda* (1809) contains 12, Amandus Gottfried Adolf Müllner's *The Twenty-Ninth of February* (*Der neun und zwanzigste Februar*, 1812) 7, and Bjørnstjerne Bjørnson's *Between the Battles* (*Mellem Slagene*, 1857) 20. The meta-referential aspect of *Miss Julie*'s world stands out clearly against a background such as this and marks its explicit reflexivity as a qualitative difference from its predecessors.

If the content of the play, its two central representational structures, points both forward (the contingency and particularity associated with the moderns) and backward (the necessity and objectivity ascribed to the ancients), then its overarching mode of organization repeats this gesture, in tune with Kierkegaard's dictum: the play looks backward by retaining the dialectical relation that Hegel and Schelling in particular associate with antiquity, and in which each of the conflicting principles is equally justified and thereby necessary and constitutive; and it looks forward by making the freedom and contingency of reflexivity and doubt that characterize modernity the central mode of relation to that relation in the play. As I have argued elsewhere, this same structure can be identified in some of Ibsen's plays as well,[18] which further suggests that it finds particularly fruitful application in the context of nineteenth-century Scandinavia. The condition of modernity here, conceivably, cannot be grasped in terms of neat distinctions, and the three greatest representatives of the theory and praxis of dramatic form in Scandinavia all look elsewhere for its proper articulation. On the margins of European culture the past and present coexist, in uneasy tension and with devastating consequences, which only a new form and genre can organize and represent.

Notes

1. Strindberg's adherence to naturalist principles has also been stressed by Harrison (89–90), Valency (271–278), Josephson (17ff.), and Lamm.

2. All references indicated by two numbers separated by a slash refer to the English translation in the first instance and to the corresponding page of the foreign-language original in the second. When applicable, in cases of a single page reference translations are my own, unless otherwise indicated.

3. The importance of sex as a means for Julie to move across the social structure has also been emphasized by Templeton (472).

4. An insightful theorization of the concept of liminality for the study of literature has been provided by Giuseppe Mazzotta in "Liminalità e utopia della letteratura."

5. This similarity is further strengthened by the fact that Turner associates liminality with a kind of relation between individuals based on a non-social equality, akin to the one identified in the play in the preceding discussion: "It is as though there are here two major 'models' for human interrelatedness, juxtaposed and alternating. The first is of society as a structured, differentiated, and often hierarchical system of politico-legal-economic positions with many types of evaluation, separating men in terms of 'more' or 'less.' The second, which emerges recognizably in the liminal period, is of society as an unstructured or rudimentarily structured and relatively undifferentiated *comitatus*, community, or even communion of equal individuals, who submit together to the general authority of the ritual elders" (96).

6. The references on page 73/121 are lost in the English translation, where the Swedish original uses "infernaliskt" and "fanstyg."

7. The presence of these motives has been emphasized by, amongst others, Aganciski (135), Ward (69), Steene (56), Lamm (107), and Sprinchorn (38).

8. The repeated use of situational echoes or prefigurations in the play has also been noted by Törnqvist (56–58), although from a different interpretative perspective.

9. A further aspect of such stabilizing strategies at the level of discourse might be found in Strindberg's use of inter-textual allusions, several of which have been traced by Bellquist, Carlson (65–68, 71–76), and Dodd (145–47). None of these critics, however, considers the structural functions of these allusions.

10. The contradiction between the preface and the play has been emphasized, amongst others, by Templeton (470), Stockenström ("Dilemma" 50), Shideler (62), Ward (57–58), and Josephson (15).

11. It should be noted that Zola himself dismisses such fatalism as irreconcilable with naturalism (29–30/336). His very objection, however, makes it clear that it is a staple of the standard understanding of the movement.

12. The centrality of the contradiction of stabilizing and destabilizing strategies in the preface is also visible in the fact that Strindberg's discussions of the stage scenery and acting are organized around the same combination (Strindberg, *Miss Julie* 65–66/*Fröken Julie* 110–11).

13. Jauss points to Saint-Évremond and his 1692 essay "De la tragédie ancienne et moderne" as the earliest and most consistent formulation of the qualitative difference between modern and ancients that settles the *Querelle* and gives birth to a new conception of history (34–35, 62–63). In that essay, Saint-Évremond significantly defines ancient drama in terms of its reliance on divine forces, while the moderns ought to opt for the unique human as their proper theme (see especially 175–76).

14. Pages are followed by the number of instances that the given kind of reflexive discourse occurs on it; due to the linguistic specificity of these instances, only references to the Swedish edition are provided. 124: 1; 129: 1; 137: 1; 149: 1; 153: 1; 166: 1; 182: 1.

15. 119: 2; 124: 1; 127: 1; 128: 1; 130: 1; 132: 3; 134: 4; 135: 2; 138: 1; 141: 1; 143: 2; 144: 1; 148: 1; 150: 1; 151: 3; 153: 3; 154: 1; 155: 1; 157: 2; 159: 1; 163: 1; 164: 1; 165: 1; 167: 1; 168: 1; 169: 1; 171: 1; 172: 1; 173: 1; 178: 2; 182: 2; 184: 1; 187: 1.

16. 148: 2; 149: 1; 156: 3; 164: 2; 165: 1; 166: 1; 167: 4; 168: 1; 173: 1; 174: 1; 178: 1; 183: 1; 185: 1; 186: 1.

17. The interpretative instability of *Miss Julie*'s fictional world has also been emphasized from a different perspective by Rokem (115–16).

18. See my "Periphery and Tragedy: Ibsen and the Emergence of a Literary Form."

Works Cited

Agacinski, Sylviane. *Drame des Sexes*. Paris: Seuil, 2008.

Bakhtin, Mikhail. *Problems of Dostoevsky's Poetics*. Ed. and trans. Caryl Emerson. Minneapolis: University of Minnesota Press, 1984.

Bellquist, John Eric. "Rereading *Fröken Julie:* Undercurrents in Strindberg's Naturalistic Intent." *Scandinavian Studies* 60, no. 1 (1988): 1–11.

Benjamin, Walter. "*Trauerspiel* and Tragedy." Trans. Rodney Livingstone. In *Selected Writings,* vol. 1, ed. Marcus Bullock and Michael W. Jennings. Cambridge, Mass.: Harvard University Press, 1996. 55–58.

———. *Ursprung des deutschen Trauerspiels.* Frankfurt am Main: Suhrkamp, 1978.

Bjørnson, Bjørnstjerne. *Mellem Slagene.* In *Samlede Værker,* vol. 7. Copenhagen: Gyldendal, 1901. 1–51.

Bushnell, Rebecca, ed. *A Companion to Tragedy.* Oxford: Blackwell, 2005.

Carlson, Harry G. *Strindberg and the Poetry of Myth.* Berkeley: University of California Press, 1982.

Cooper, Barbara T. "French Romantic Tragedy." In *A Companion to Tragedy,* ed. Rebecca Bushnell. Malden, Mass.: Blackwell, 2005. 452–68.

Cox, Jeffrey N. "Romantic Tragic Drama and Its Eighteenth-Century Precursors: Remaking British Tragedy." In *A Companion to Tragedy,* ed. Rebecca Bushnell. Malden, Mass.: Blackwell, 2005. 411–34.

Dahlström, Carl E. W. L. "Strindberg and Naturalistic Tragedy." *Scandinavian Studies* 30 (1958): 1–18.

Delblanc, Sven. "Strindberg and Humanism." In *Strindberg's Dramaturgy,* ed. Göran Stockenström. Minneapolis: University of Minnesota Press, 1988. 3–13.

Dodd, Philip. "Fairy Tales, the Unconscious and Strindberg's *Miss Julie.*" *Literature and Psychology* 28, nos. 3–4 (1978): 145–50.

Greenway, John L. "Strindberg and Suggestion in *Miss Julie.*" *South Atlantic Review* 51, no. 2 (1986): 21–34.

Harrison, A. Cleveland. "*Miss Julie:* Essence and Anomaly of Naturalism." *Communication Studies* 21, no. 2 (1970): 87–92.

Hegel, G. W. F. *Aesthetics.* In *Lectures on Fine Art,* vol. 2, trans. T. M. Knox. Oxford: Clarendon, 1975.

———. *Vorlesungen über die Ästhetik III.* In *Werke,* vol. 15, ed. Eva Moldenhauer and Karl Markus Michel. Frankfurt am Main: Suhrkamp, 1986.

Hugo, Victor. "Preface de Cromwell." In *Preface de Cromwell and Hernani,* ed. John R. Effinger Jr. Chicago: Scott, Foresman, 1900. 43–104.

Jakobson, Roman. "Linguistics and Poetics." In *Language in Literature.* Cambridge, Mass.: Belknap, 1987. 62–94.

Jauss, Hans Robert. *Ästhetische Normen und Geschichtliche Reflexion in der "Querelle des Anciens et des Modernes."* Munich: Eidos, 1973.

Josephson, Lennart. *Strindbergs drama Fröken Julie.* Stockholm: Almqvist & Wiksell, 1965.

Kant, Immanuel. *Critique of Judgment.* Trans. Werner S. Puhar. Indianapolis: Hackett, 1987.

———. *Kritik der Urtheilskraft.* In *Kants Werke,* vol. 5. Berlin: Walter de Gruyter, 1968. 165–485.

Kierkegaard, Søren. *Either/Or, Part I.* Ed. and trans. Howard V. Hong and Edna H. Hong. Princeton, N.J.: Princeton University Press, 1987.

———. *Enten-Eller, Første Del*. In *Søren Kierkegaards Skrifter*, vol. 2, ed. Niels Jørgen Cappelørn et al. Copenhagen: Gads, 1997.

Lamm, Martin. "*Miss Julie*." Trans. Otto Reinert. In *Strindberg: A Collection of Critical Essays*, ed. Otto Reinert. Englewood Cliffs, N.J.: Prentice-Hall, 1971. 105–16.

Lisi, Leonardo. "Periphery and Tragedy: Ibsen and the Emergence of a Literary Form." *Forum for World Literature Studies*. 2, no. 1 (2010): 28–34.

Madsen, Børge Gedsø. *Strindberg's Naturalistic Theatre: Its Relation to French Naturalism*. New York: Russell and Russell, 1962.

Marcuse, Ludwig. *Die Welt der Tragödie*. Berlin: Franz Schneider Verlag, 1923.

Mazzotta, Giuseppe. "Liminalità e utopia della letteratura." *Intersezioni: Rivista di storia delle idée*. 19, no. 3 (1999): 363–78.

Müllner, Amandus Gottfried Adolf. *Der neun und zwanzigste Februar*. In *Dramatische Werke*, vol. 1. Braunschweig: Friedrich Vieweg, 1828. 1–72.

Oehlenschläger, Adam. *Axel og Valborg*. In *Tragødier i et Bind*. Copenhagen: Bianco Luno, 1852. 344–71.

Rokem, Freddie. "The Camera and the Aesthetics of Repetition: Strindberg's Use of Space and Scenography in *Miss Julie, A Dream Play*, and *The Ghost Sonata*." In *Strindberg's Dramaturgy*, ed. Göran Stockenström. Minneapolis: University of Minnesota Press, 1988. 107–28.

Saint-Évremond, Charles de Marguetel de Saint Denis, seigneur de. "De la tragédie ancienne et moderne." In *Oeuvres en prose*, vol. 4, ed. René Ternois. Paris: Libraire Marcel Didier, 1969. 170–84.

Schelling, W. J. F. *Philosophie der Kunst*. In *Ausgewählte Schriften*, vol. 2, ed. Manfred Frank. Frankfurt, am Main: Suhrkamp, 1985. 181–565.

Schlegel, August Wilhelm. *Vorlesungen über dramatische Kunst und Literatur*. 2 vols. Ed. Edgar Lohner. Stuttgart: W. Kohlhammer, 1966–67.

Schlegel, Friedrich. *Über das Studium der griechischen Poesie*. In *Kritische Friedrich-Schlegel-Ausgabe*. Vol. 1, *Studien des klassischen Altertums*, Ed. Ernst Behler. Badeborn: Verlag Ferdinand Schöning, 1979. 217–367.

Shideler, Ross. "*Miss Julie:* Naturalism, 'The Battle of the Brains' and Sexual Desire." In *The Cambridge Companion to August Strindberg*, ed. Michael Robinson. Cambridge, Eng.: Cambridge University Press, 2009. 58–69.

Sprinchorn, Evert. *Strindberg as Dramatist*. New Haven, Conn.: Yale University Press, 1982.

Staël, Madame de. *De l'Allemagne*. Paris: Charpentier, 1844.

Steene, Brigitta. *The Greatest Fire: A Study of August Strindberg*. Carbondale: Southern Illinois University Press, 1973.

Stockenström, Göran. "The Dilemma of Naturalist Tragedy: Strindberg's *Miss Julie*." *Comparative Drama* 38, no. 1 (2004): 39–57.

———, ed. *Strindberg's Dramaturgy*. Minneapolis: University of Minnesota Press, 1988.

Strindberg, August. "Césarine: On Alexandre Dumas *fils*' Drama *La Femme de Claude*." In *Selected Essays*, ed. and trans. Michael Robinson. Cambridge, Eng.: Cambridge University Press, 1996. 118–21.

———. *Den Fredlösa: Sorgespel.* In *Samlade Verk,* vol. 3, ed. Birger Liljestrand. Stockholm: Norstedts, 1991. 95–150.

———. *Fritänkaren.* In *Samlade Verk,* vol. 1, ed. Birger Liljestrand. Stockholm: Norstedts, 1989. 7–60.

———. *Fröken Julie.* In *Samlade Verk,* vol. 27, ed. Gunnar Ollén. Stockholm: Almqvist & Wiskell Förlag, 1984. 99–190.

———. *Hermione: Sorgspel.* In *Samlade Verk,* vol. 1, ed. Birger Liljestrand. Stockholm: Norstedts, 1989. 133–233.

———. *Herr Bengts Hustru: Skådspel i fem akter.* In *Samlade Verk,* vol. 11, ed. Torbjörn Nilsson. Stockholm: Norstedts, 2001. 267–386.

———. *I Rom: Dramatisk situation i en akt.* In *Samlade Verk,* vol. 3, *Ungdomsdramer,* ed. Birger Liljestrand. Stockholm: Norstedts, 1991. 7–42.

———. *Letters.* Vol. 1. Ed. and trans. Michael Robinson. London: Athlone, 1992.

———. *Miss Julie.* In *Miss Julie and Other Plays,* trans. Michael Robinson. Oxford: Oxford University Press, 1998. 55–110.

———. "On Modern Drama and Modern Theatre." In *Selected Essays,* ed. and trans. Michael Robinson. Cambridge, Eng.: Cambridge University Press, 1996. 73–86.

Templeton, Alice. "*Miss Julie* as 'Naturalist Tragedy.'" *Theatre Journal* 42, no. 4 (1990): 468–80.

Törnqvist, Egil. *Strindbergian Drama: Themes and Structure.* Stockholm: Almqvist & Wiksell, 1982.

Turner, Victor. *The Ritual Process. Structure and Anti-Structure.* Chicago: Aldine, 1969.

Valency, Maurice. *The Flower and the Castle: An Introduction to Modern Drama.* New York: Macmillan, 1963.

Ward, John. *The Social and Religious Plays of Strindberg.* London: Athlone, 1980.

Werner, Friedrich Zacharias. *Wanda, Königen der Sarmanten: Eine romantische Tragödie.* In *Werke,* vol. 4. Vienna: Leopold Grund, 1818. 257–370.

Zola, Émile. "The Experimental Novel." In *The Experimental Novel and Other Essays,* trans. Belle M. Sherman. New York: Haskell House, 1964. 1–56.

———. "Le roman expérimental." In *Oeuvres completes,* vol. 9, ed. Henri Mitterand. Montréal: Nouveau Monde, 2004. 323–48.

NOTES ON CONTRIBUTORS

Maxime Abolgassemi holds a Ph.D. in French and comparative literature from the Université Paris IV Sorbonne. He is a professor at the Lycée Chateaubriand, Rennes (France). He introduced the theoretical concept of *contrefiction,* which he developed through three publications in the French reference journal *Poétique* (2003, 2006, 2009). His first book was *L'écriture d'invention: Écrire pour lire, lire pour écrire* (2001).

Sylvain Briens is a professor of Nordic literatures at the Université Paris-Sorbonne. He holds a Ph.D. in Nordic literature from the Université Paris-Sorbonne, as well as a master's degree in electrical engineering from the Institut National Polytechnique de Grenoble. In 2009 Briens received the Research Prize Guy Ourisson (Cercle Gutenberg). He is the author of *Paris, laboratoire de la littérature scandinave moderne, 1880–1905* (2010), *Lyriska ingenjörer: Tåg och telefon i svensk litteratur* (2009), and *Technique et literature: Train, téléphone et génie littéraire suédois* (2004).

Mads Bunch holds a Mag. Art. in Nordic literature from the University of Copenhagen, Denmark. A former lecturer in Danish and Scandinavian studies at the University of British Columbia, Vancouver, Canada, he is now affiliated with the University of Copenhagen as a Ph.D. fellow and external lecturer. He has published articles on August Strindberg, Henrik Ibsen, Lars von Trier, and contemporary Scandinavian literature. In 2009 he authored the book *Samtidsbilleder—realismen i yngre dansk litteratur 1994–2008,* describing the new wave of realism in Danish and Scandinavian literature around the millennium.

Massimo Ciaravolo studied Scandinavian languages and literature at Milan University, where he became a research assistant in 1996. Since 2005 he has been an associate professor of Scandinavian languages and literature at Florence University. He has published books in Swedish on Hjalmar Söderberg as a literary critic and on the reception of the Söderbergian flaneur among the Finland-Swedish writers at the beginning of the twentieth century. He has written articles in Italian, English, and Swedish on Södergran, Obstfelder, Hamsun, Bang, Ibsen, and Strindberg. He has also translated Scandinavian writers into Italian (Strindberg, Söderberg, Lagerkvist, Dagerman, Solstad, Forsström, Frostenson, Hallberg).

Tobias Dahlkvist is an associate professor in the Department of Comparative Literature and History of Ideas at the University of Stockholm. He studied philosophy, comparative literature, and history of ideas at the universities of Uppsala (Sweden), Heidelberg (Germany), and Pisa (Italy). Dahlkvist's main research interest is the history of pessimism. His publications include *Nietzsche and the Philosophy of Pessimism: A Study of Nietzsche's Relation to the Pessimistic Tradition* (2007); *Förtvivlans filosofi: Vilhelm Ekelund och mottagandet av Giacomo Leopardi i Skandinavien* (2010); and numerous articles on Strindberg, Nietzsche, and fin-de-siècle literature and philosophy.

Anne-Charlotte Hanes Harvey was educated in Sweden and the United States. She is professor emerita of theater at San Diego State University and is now active as a translator and dramaturg. She is interested in the intersection of translation theory and performance theory based on practice, and she has translation credits on Broadway, in other professional theater, and in academe. Her research interests include Strindberg, Ibsen, and translation theory, as well as Scandinavian-American culture, assimilation, and ethnicization.

Leonardo F. Lisi is an assistant professor in the Humanities Center at Johns Hopkins University and holds a Ph.D. from Yale University. His work centers on the literature and philosophy of the nineteenth century, with publications on figures such as Søren Kierkegaard, Henrik Ibsen, Rainer Maria Rilke, Joseph Conrad, W. H. Auden, J. L. Heiberg, and European modernism more generally.

Freddie Rokem is the Emanuel Herzikowitz Professor for Nineteenth and Twentieth Century Art and teaches in the Department of Theatre Studies at Tel Aviv University, where he served as the Dean of the Yolanda and David Katz Faculty of the Arts (2002–2006). He is also a permanent guest professor at Helsinki University, Finland, and has been a visiting professor at Stanford University, the Free University in Berlin, the University of Munich, the University of Stockholm, and UC Berkeley. He was the editor of *Theatre Research International* (2006–2009). Rokem's books include *Performing History: Theatrical Representations of the Past in Contemporary Theatre* (2000), *Strindberg's Secret Codes* (2004), and *Philosophers and Thespians: Thinking Performance* (2010). He has published widely on European and Israeli theater and is also a translator and a dramaturg.

Linda Haverty Rugg is an associate professor in the Scandinavian Department at the University of California, Berkeley. Her first book, *Picturing Ourselves: Photography and Autobiography,* appeared in 1997 and was awarded the MLA's prize for best book in comparative literature that year. She has published articles on Strindberg, Ingmar Bergman, Mark Twain, Kerstin Ekman, and Rainer Rilke; her research interests include ecocriticism, whiteness studies, and autobiography and visual culture.

Anna Westerståhl Stenport is an associate professor and director of Scandinavian studies in the Department of Germanic Languages and Literatures at the University of Illinois at Urbana-Champaign and holds a Ph.D. from the University of California, Berkeley. She is an affiliate associate professor of literature at the University of Gothenburg, Sweden. Her book *Locating August Strindberg's Prose: Modernism, Transnationalism, Setting* was published in 2010, and she coedited a volume of scholarship on Strindberg and gender theory, *Det gäckande könet: Strindberg och genusteori* (2006). She has also written extensively on European modernism, contemporary popular culture and media, and Swedish film, including a book about filmmaker Lukas Moodysson (2012).

Eszter Szalczer is an associate professor of dramatic literature and theater history at the State University of New York at Albany; she holds a Ph.D. from CUNY Graduate College and advanced degrees from Budapest University. Her publications include the books *August Strindberg* (2011) and *Writing Daughters: August Strindberg's Other Voices* (2008). Other recent contributions include a chapter on Strindberg's modernist dramaturgy in *The Cambridge Companion to August Strindberg* (2009) and "Performing Theatre History: The Case of Strindberg's Modernity" in *Changing the Subject: Marvin Carlson and Theater Studies 1959–2009* (2009).